Integration Development in the China Yangtze River Delta

This book systematically investigates the strategic significance and dynamic mechanisms present in the development of the Yangtze River Delta cluster, one of the major drivers of economic growth in China.

The Yangtze River Delta is the most densely populated region in China, with the highest level of economic development. Against the background of China's national strategy that aims to bolster and augment integrated development on the regional level, this study reviews the development process of the region and possible hindrances to further growth. From a wide array of dimensions, it assesses the key influencing factors, including institutional construction, governance mechanisms, spatial layout, government and corporate competition, the market environment, industrial linkages and synergies, collaborative innovation, public service, and social networks. Based on theoretical analysis and empirical studies, the book advances policy suggestions that help to solve the challenges for integrated development in the region.

The volume will benefit scholars and students, as well as investors, business observers, and policy makers interested in the Chinese economy, regional economics, industrial economics, and economic geography.

Zhibiao Liu is Professor at Yangtze Industrial Economic Institute, Nanjing University, China. He specializes in global value chain analysis and regional economic development issues in the Yangtze River Delta.

Ning Xu is Researcher at Yangtze Industrial Economic Institute, Nanjing University, China. He specializes in global value chain analysis and industry innovation research.

Lingchi Kong is Assistant Professor at Yangtze Industrial Economic Institute, Nanjing University, China. He specializes in regional integration analysis and manufacturing spatial distribution analysis.

China Perspectives

The *China Perspectives* series focuses on translating and publishing works by leading Chinese scholars, writing about both global topics and China-related themes. It covers Humanities & Social Sciences, Education, Media and Psychology, as well as many interdisciplinary themes.

This is the first time any of these books have been published in English for international readers. The series aims to put forward a Chinese perspective, give insights into cutting-edge academic thinking in China, and inspire researchers globally.

To submit a book proposal, please contact the Taylor & Francis Publisher for the China Publishing Programme, Lian Sun (Lian.Sun@informa.com)

Titles in economics include:

China's Economic Development
Implications for the World
Cai Fang

State-Owned Enterprise's Ownership Reform
A Chinese Modernization Approach
Zhigang Zheng

Comprehensive Land Consolidation in China
Yan Jinming, Xia Fangzhou

Economic Development in Modern China Before 1949
Guan Quan

Economic Development in Modern China Since 1949
Guan Quan

Integration Development in the China Yangtze River Delta
Edited by Zhibiao Liu, Ning Xu, and Lingchi Kong

For more information, please visit www.routledge.com/China-Perspectives/book-series/CPH

Integration Development in the China Yangtze River Delta

Edited by Zhibiao Liu, Ning Xu
and Lingchi Kong

Routledge
Taylor & Francis Group
LONDON AND NEW YORK

First published in English 2024
by Routledge
4 Park Square, Milton Park, Abingdon, Oxon OX14 4RN

and by Routledge
605 Third Avenue, New York, NY 10158

Routledge is an imprint of the Taylor & Francis Group, an informa business

British Library Cataloguing-in-Publication Data
A catalogue record for this book is available from the British Library

ISBN: 978-1-032-59560-3 (hbk)
ISBN: 978-1-032-59717-1 (pbk)
ISBN: 978-1-003-45594-3 (ebk)

DOI: 10.4324/9781003455943

Typeset in Times New Roman
by Apex CoVantage, LLC

Contents

Figures

Tables

Contributors

Bu Maoliang is Professor at School of Business, Nanjing University, China. He specializes in environmental economics.

Liu Chen is Professor at Yangtze Industrial Economic Institute, Nanjing University, China. He specializes in industrial organization and business management.

Yuwei Du is Researcher at Regional Modernization Institute, Jiangsu Province Academy of Social Sciences, China. He specializes in regional economics.

Yanyan Gao is Associate Professor at School of Economics and Management, Southeast University, China. He specializes in innovation and environmental rules.

Dongmei He is Lecturer at School of Business, Jiangsu Open University, China. She specializes in regional economics.

Yunhui Hou is Associate Professor at School of Economics and Management, Southeast University, China. He specializes in economic development issues.

Jing Jiang is Professor at School of Business, Nanjing University, China. She specializes in economic development issues.

Lingchi Kong is Assistant Professor at Yangtze Industrial Economic Institute, Nanjing University, China. He specializes in regional integration analysis and manufacturing spatial distribution analysis.

Zhi Lian is Graduate Students at School of Business, Nanjing University, China. He specializes in environmental rules.

Zhibiao Liu is Professor at Yangtze Industrial Economic Institute, Nanjing University, China. He specializes in global value chain analysis and regional economic development issues in the Yangtze River Delta.

Jianbing Luo is a post-doctoral student at School of Business, Nanjing University, China. He specializes in regional economic development issues.

Shouhua Wei is Professor at School of Business, Nanjing University, China. He specializes in regional economics.

Fuxiang Wu is Professor at School of Business, Nanjing University, China. He specializes in regional economics.

Jingwei Wu is a PhD student at School of Business, Nanjing University, China. He specializes in regional economics.

Fan Xie is Assistant Professor at Yangtze Industrial Economic Institute, Nanjing University, China. She specializes in regional integration analysis.

Ning Xu is Researcher at Yangtze Industrial Economic Institute, Nanjing University, China. He specializes in global value chain analysis and industry innovation research.

Mingchao Yu is Associate Professor at School of Business, Nanjing Normal University, China. He specializes in international trade issues.

Zhonggang Yue is Professor at School of Economics, Nanjing Post and Communications University, China. He specializes in Global Value Chain Research.

Jianzhong Zhang is a graduate student at School of Business, Nanjing University, China. He specializes in innovation and environmental rules.

1 Implementing the national strategy of higher-quality integrated development of the Yangtze River Delta

Zhibiao Liu

The higher-quality integrated development of the Yangtze River Delta becoming a national strategy in 2018 means the sound affirmation of its endeavor and exploration over the past two decades and means, in the background of the China-US trade war, the advantage of exploring the new driving force of the Chinese economy and utilizing its resilience by means of a regional coordination mechanism has been strategically applied and promoted. It also means that China will build a uniform but open, orderly, and competitive powerful domestic market that is based on regional integration.

The central government requires a higher quality of integrated development in the Yangtze River Delta and sets a high standard of regarding it as a pioneer region, an example and pathfinder. The high standard seeks an integrative development of "integration" and "high-quality" rather than emphasizing certain aspects one-sidedly. Considering the implication of "integration" and "high-quality", this is a grand practical topic worth thorough research.

Section 1 Higher-quality integrated development of the Yangtze River Delta should facilitate the formation of a strong Chinese domestic market

It can be explained from many aspects why the regional economic problem of integrated development of the Yangtze River Delta should be made the national strategy. For example, from the perspective of economic strength and its potential, the development of the Yangtze River Delta plays a leading role in Chinese modernization strategy; from the perspective of forming and completing the regional layout of reform and opening up, this national strategy is helpful for the high-quality development of the east region and the Yangtze River Economic Belt, while the previous national strategies were focused on prospering the less developed areas; and, of course, from the perspective of changing from a decentralized governance to a coordinated one, the national strategy of the modernization of governance system and capacity can also be analyzed. Unlike before, the perspective of this chapter is wider in globalization strategic transformation and culturing and utilizing the powerful Chinese domestic market, trying to discuss the strategic significance of

DOI: 10.4324/9781003455943-1

higher-quality integrated development of the Yangtze River Delta to the formation of a nationally unified market and the development of a high-level open economy.

It is public knowledge that promoting the regional economic integration is one of the basic propositions and strategic measures of the long-term governing concepts of General Secretary Xi Jinping. For example, early in Fujian, General Secretary Xi facilitated the development of a cross-strait economic zone; in Zhejiang and Shanghai, he focused on boosting the integration of the Yangtze River Delta; and in central government, he not only promoted the integration of the Beijing-Tianjin-Hebei Region but made the Higher-quality Integrated Development of the Yangtze River Delta a national strategy. Such practices have proven that the regional economic integration is a unique problem in the process of major economic transition, as well as a vital component of Xi Jinping's theory of the economic development featuring socialism with Chinese characteristics in the new era.

There is a clear theoretical basis for General Secretary Xi Jinping to support the regional economic integration. China, a superscale country with a vast territory and enormous population, has made tremendous economic achievement since the reform and opening up. Yet it has never become a superscale economic entity or market. One of the main reasons is that although the per capita disposable income in China has grown rapidly, it is still far behind that of developed countries, so the real affordable market demand is much smaller than the potential demand, i.e., the real market volume is not big enough. Another reason is market segmentation. The accumulated market size is usually not small; but the actual available economies of scale are insufficient. Therefore China, though a superscale country, has not yet formed a major market system that is uniform but open, orderly, and competitive, which has greatly affected the optimization of industrial division and the capacity of Chinese enterprises utilizing economies of scale, therefore, the efficiency of resource allocation.

This problem is directly related to a significant systematic formed during the economic transition, which is the segmentation of the whole market caused by the market competition of local governments. Decentralized competition has greatly spurred the Chinese economy on the one hand; yet on the other hand, it has caused the "fragmentation", making it difficult to take advantage of a superscale market. For example, the efficiency of resource allocation is severely lowered, as the enterprises can only obtain economies of scale in a regional market rather than a unified huge one. Therefore, regional integration is the prelude of building a nationally unified market; the former will smooth the path to the latter and its blend in the global market. As a result, promoting regional integration is one of the vital methods of expanding the economies of scale in a superscale market. On the one hand, regional integration can only be achieved gradually by dismantling the tangible and intangible administrative barriers and encouraging competition between enterprises; on the other hand, only based on regional integration, a uniform but open, orderly, and competitive powerful domestic market can be built.

The export-oriented Chinese economic globalization strategy Version 1.0 has been implemented over the past decades due to the narrow domestic market scale featured with segmentation. This strategy has produced tremendous profits by producing and exporting primary products relying on the Western developed countries, good price performance ratio, and Western technologies. However, since the global financial crisis in 2008, its precondition has been fundamentally changed. First, with the rampant anti-globalization trend in the current world, the strategic partnership between China and the US may change into a strategic competitive relation, which means curbing China becomes a fundamental strategy in America. Second, the cheap production factors in China have been increasingly weakened, because the competitors with low-cost production factors in the international market are emerging, and the innovation-driven and productivity-enhancing strategy has been required in the domestic market. Third, on the one hand, the Western countries will no longer bear providing a market for Chinese economic growth; on the other hand, China has become a superscale market. In order to optimize its powerful domestic market in the new period of strategic opportunity, China should update its export-oriented economic globalization strategy version 1.0 to version 2.0, i.e., the one based on their domestic demands.

The basic characteristics of this brand-new version are: (1) evolving from a super-country to a superscale economy or superscale market for the constantly rising per capita disposable income; (2) other countries' export-orientation toward China attracted by the internationalization trend of RMB and other non-economic advantages; (3) the numerous opportunities in the strong domestic market, for which the advanced technologies and talents swarm into the globalized cities. Only in this way can an innovation-driven country based on talents and technologies be established.

The implementation of economic globalization strategy version 2.0 is based on the formation of robust domestic demand or a superscale market that can provide more development opportunities for global resources and factors. Therefore, we need to develop a new view on strategic resources: changing the low-price and high-quality production factors into a strong domestic market. In this way, China can promote the formation of a strong domestic market as the mediator between the integrated development of the Yangtze River Delta and the transition of economic globalization strategy and higher-quality opening up: for one thing, the integrated development of the Yangtze River Delta can promote the formation of a strong domestic market; for another, a strong domestic market is based on the Chinese economic globalization strategy and higher-quality opening up. Accordingly, breaking market segmentation and achieving integrated development are essential to establish a uniform but open, orderly, and competitive grand market, and to shift into the economic globalization strategy version 2.0.

Section 2 The order and key fields of higher-quality integrated development of the Yangtze River Delta

The integrated development of the Yangtze River Delta is to eliminate the barriers against the flow of resources and factors in each administrative region's government, opening to the outside and achieving a fully competitive market. Generally speaking, there are two types of barriers against the flow of resources and factors:

resources and technologies related to natural conditions; for example, insufficient infrastructure, which would directly raise the operating costs of integration; and system and mechanisms; for example, the laws, policies, regulations, and monopoly against integration, which would directly increase the institutional transaction costs of integration. Therefore, there are two dimensions that can be used to promote the integrated development of the Yangtze River Delta: strengthening the infrastructure construction, especially transportation and communication to realize interconnection between areas; and emancipating the mind for institutional reform and innovation, to clear away the institutional barriers against integration.

In fact, the main obstacle to the opening up of each area lies in the governments' power above the economy. System precedes technology. Some conditions like infrastructure can be rapidly improved through investment; resource allocation affected by monopoly can be changed by antimonopoly laws; yet there is no initiative to stop the market segmentation set by each government for their benefits of administrative boundaries. These obstacles against the flow of resources and factors were gradually formed by market competition of local governments during economic transition, some of which have become (unspoken) local rules. It is up to the doer to undo the knot. Therefore, with the coordination of central government, the local administrators should contrast their previous laws, regulations, policies, and measures with the competition policy and remove the institutional barriers against the unified market proactively. The investigation of competition policy should be conducted before introducing any new economic policy. These are urgently required for the integration of the Yangtze River Delta as a national policy.

It is necessary to conduct classified reforms and institutional innovations in increasing levels of difficulty based on the possible and potential obstacles in the integrated development of the Yangtze River Delta. An order and key field is required, for which the specific problems should be analyzed and settled one by one to avoid abstract discussion in the extensive areas of the integration and the lack of implementation of the written and oral discussions.

First, the competitive industry sector. The key to promoting the higher-quality integrated development in this field is not about a detailed plan made by the government for regions, industries, products, and services, but to weaken government regulation for an open and full competition to achieve synergy effects and optimal resource allocation. The competitive industry sector cannot go off the beaten track if it follows unified planning and coordinated development. There used to be a popular belief that the industrial distribution in the Yangtze River Delta area is fragmented with severely overlapping layout and increasingly convergent industrial structure, based on the highly similar structure of the three main industries and the similar goals of different cities' industrial planning. Statistics show that 12 out of 16 cities in the Yangtze River Delta region chose electronic information in their "13th Five-Year Plan"; 12 cities chose electronic and information industry; 11 chose automobile as their key industry; 8 chose petrochemical industry. The development of new technology industries was concentrated on IT, biomedicine, advanced material, etc. In fact, the statistical result of industrial convergence is only achieved when there were less than one hundred types of industry. If they are subdivided into thousands or tens of thousands of sub-industries, the phenomenon of "industry convergence" will not exist, according to our observation. In addition, it is inevitable in the market competition for enterprises in different cities to invest in the same areas, which is a rational phenomenon of decentralized decision-making required by market competition. It is not competition or overlapping investment that harms a market; but monopoly without competition, the lack of merger and acquisition mechanisms, and inability to drop out will harm it. These are the essential problems.

Second is the field of public goods production, in which a high-quality integrated development is relatively easier. The key tasks are mainly the forward planning of infrastructure, unified command of construction, interconnection of junctions, and consistency of administration and coordination. It is generally easier to achieve a higher-quality integration development because first, it relies not on market competition, but on the function of government (it has to be the effective coordination between governments for the public interest); second, there will not be any major obstacles or friction with the coordination of superior government in the current Chinese governance system; third, the infrastructure can be improved through mechanisms of sharing construction cost and benefit. Because of the uniformity and indivisibility of infrastructure, local governments initially have to yield their power of planning, construction, and management to a certain organization according to the agreement of integrated development, which is the only way to effectively coordinate the public interests. For example, if the infrastructure construction of the demonstration areas, Qingpu, Wujiang and Jiashan of the Yangtze River Delta integration, was not planned, constructed, and administrated based on the principle, there would be severe problems with coordination and efficiency in these areas.

Third is the expenditure for people's livelihoods. The high-quality integrated development in this field will virtually narrow the gaps of public welfare between different regions or between urban and rural areas. It involves the most extensive groups of vested interests with the hardest goals to achieve, so it requires great prudence. There is basically no ready social condition for integration of the welfare of local residents related to census registers and local financial investment, especially in education, health care, elderly care, subsistence residence, etc., which directly affect the personal interests of local residents. In areas with a relatively abundant supply of resources, the so-called integration of people's livelihoods will make the public resources excessive and dilute the interests of people in metropolises, leading to intense resistance and rejection by local residents. Therefore, the current stage of the integration strategy should not be divorced from reality or be blind to the idea and requirement of narrowing the rich/poor gap, or pursue "equalization", even "synchronization", of people's livelihoods in regions with huge development gaps. The stability of the development gap should be gradually narrowed through the decreasing productivity gap and allocation regulation.

Fourth, the field of investment. Investment can be regarded as an effective tool for integration, because it can lead to the joint shareholding of incremental capital or capital stock. In terms of incremental capital, government-oriented investments or officially guided private investments can substantially integrate regions for a certain cause at the enterprise level, laying the micro-foundation for high-quality integration through the internal governance mechanism of enterprises. For example, the government of Shanghai, leading Jiangsu, Zhejiang, and Anhui provinces, can initiate a co-investment with enterprises in a scientific and technological innovation business in the demonstration area of Yangtze River Delta integration; the governments can guide and help the private enterprises investing in the economic and technological development zone in the process of "going global along the Belt and Road" for the purpose of cooperation with other countries on industrial capacity. In regard to capital stock, encouraging the merger and acquisition in the Yangtze River Delta area can not only solve the longstanding problem of overcapacity, but also integrate the industrial development and market operation materially.

Fifth, scientific and technological innovation. One of the vital goals of the integration of the Yangtze River Delta is to achieve innovation-driven development through the functions of the unified grand market and resource complementarity. Therefore, scientific and technological innovation is not only a vital part of the integration of the Yangtze River Delta, but also a fundamental requirement for the transition from high-speed development to high-quality development. Shanghai has shouldered the great responsibility of building a scientific and technological innovation center with worldwide influence, but it is not easy to succeed based on its current scientific and technological resources and talents. If it can take full advantage of the science and education resources of human capital and industrial bases of Jiangsu, Zhejiang, and Anhui provinces in the integration of the Yangtze River Delta, it will reach the objective within a much shorter time. But we should note that the most important is the cooperation of scientific and technological innovations. Any negligence in the system design may lead to free-riding, hindering the cooperation. In terms of scientific and technological innovation cooperation between enterprises in Western developed countries, we barely see any successful cases or draw enough experiences to find a pattern. This warns us to prepare a rigorous and comprehensive mechanism design, and a clear anticipation about the practical effects of the joint research and development intervened by the government.

Sixth, institutional innovation of the local government. Fundamentally, the vital factor for joint development is establishing a new organization with the function of carrying out competition policies by the local government of the four provinces/cities under the guidance of a central government. From the perspective of efficient and streamlined administration, this organization can be formed by the cooperation of local courts as the executing agency. Competition policy is the most basic principle that guarantees a smooth operation of the united market and the fundamental system of market integration, above all the other economic policies. Under the guidance of competition policy, on the one hand, the market competition in the integrated region is effectively regulated, protecting the competition itself rather than the competitors to raise the competitiveness of the Yangtze River Delta region; on the other hand, certain semi-competitive enterprises under the local governmental jurisdiction are integrated, utilizing the economies of scale and economies of scope; for example, the ports, piers, and airports in the Yangtze River Delta region can be integrated by the relative entity in Shanghai in accordance with the principle joint-stock company. In 2002, Port of Shanghai "rented" Yangshan Port and built Shanghai Yangshan Deepwater Port (Phase 1) with the investment from Shanghai government in 2005; and in 2006, Ningbo Port and Zhoushan Port merged, both presented a $1+1>2$ effect. The two attempts at port integration have broken through the constraints of administrative regions on port service and economic affairs. If the Shanghai Port, of Ningbo-Zhoushan Port, Nanjing Port, Lianyungang, etc. are further integrated, a higher-quality integration will be achieved.

Section 3 Constructing Shanghai-Nanjing-Hefei innovation belt: spatial arrangement of higher-quality integrated development of the Yangtze River Delta

To achieve higher-quality integrated development of the Yangtze River Delta, it is necessary to optimize its industrial spatial arrangement. The land-use intensity in the core areas of the Yangtze River Delta, like the north part of Jiangsu, has currently reached the global warning line, i.e., 30%. In comparison, in Hong Kong, a more developed city, the number is only about 20%. In order to improve people's living condition in the process of integrated development, the optimization of industrial distribution must be closely combined with the adjustment of industrial policies.

Putting aside the problems of demarcating ecological function areas and strict execution, there are two major tasks to optimize the industrial layout in the Yangtze River Delta: building emerging sectors of strategic importance with more technology and additional value according to the input standard of investment per acre and output standard of additional value per acre in areas of high land-use intensity, removing the manufacturing industries that cannot meet the two standards; and equipping the extensive surrounding regions with the ability to absorb the industrial relocation and establish manufacturing industrial clusters through the ramified network of infrastructure, in order to raise the land-use intensity of these areas. Therefore, the construction of a "scientific and technological innovation belt" in the Yangtze River Delta will be on the agenda.

The layout of a scientific and technological innovation belt can concentrate and radiate the high-quality integrated development. On the one hand, the integrated development of scientific and technological innovation can improve the region's ability to gather the science and technology from all over the world, attract funds, technologies and talents from a wider ranger in the world, and raise the regional energy intensity and core competitiveness; on the other hand, as the center of economic development, it can enhance its radiating and driving forces to the adjacent areas. The adjacent areas of the Yangtze River Delta can better utilize the domestic and foreign resources through the platforms and channels brought about by the innovation belt for a higher-quality development and more balanced regional relationship and participate in international cooperation and competition as a representative of China. The integration of both concentration and radiation will be of the highest quality.

Generally speaking, in the current resource allocation in the Yangtze River Delta, the planning for the G60 scientific and technological innovation belt is mainly a benchmark and demonstrative zone of ecological environment within the area, which is neither concentrated nor collective in terms of industrial allocation. From the perspective of space, what the Yangtze River Delta region really needs is reforming the "overcrowded" industrial layout and further enhancing Shanghai-Nanjing-Hefei industrial innovation and science and technology innovation. In this area, especially the three node cities of Shanghai, Nanjing, and Hefei, there are clustered the major and most important research and development institutions and universities, while the cities of Suzhou, Wuxi, and Changzhou have become one of the most industrial innovative areas in the coastal region. In other areas of this belt, especially Anhui and north of Jiangsu, there is a large number of land resources, human resources, and other resources that can be scientifically and industrially integrated. Therefore, the construction of the G60 science and technology belt of prominent economic activities and innovation potential also requires a sufficient utilization of the Shanghai-Nanjing-Hefei industry and scientific and technological innovation. Only through this can it become the vital engine of the high-quality integrated development of the Yangtze River Delta, and the supporting region for Shanghai as the science and technology innovation center with global influence. It is publicly acknowledged that the current G60 belt is not competent for the mission.

In the meantime, the demonstration zone for Yangtze River Delta integration constructed in Qingpu, Wujiang, and Jiashan shoulders the significant mission of setting an example for "building a science and technology innovation center with global influence in Shanghai". It has to be built as a new platform for the innovative origin, demonstrative application, systematic supply, and talent gathering for emerging sectors of strategic importance, to explore policy measures for the cross-regional flow of talent, capital, information, technology, etc., and to realize complementarity, resource sharing, and win-win cooperation between high-tech enterprises in the demonstration zone through assembling the resources of science and technology, innovations and human resources. Without the effective utilization of the innovation resources and capacity of Shanghai-Nanjing-Hefei industry and the scientific and technological innovation belt, it would be impossible to complete the mission.

The Shanghai-Nanjing-Hefei innovation belt is a vital part of the high-quality integrated development of the Yangtze River Delta as well as a model for Chinese regional development. There are some constructive suggestions for turning the concept of spatial arrangement of integrated development into a concept of high-quality development:

First, the Shanghai-Nanjing-Hefei industry and the scientific and technological innovation belt should be planned and developed based on the mindset of the industrial cluster in regions of high-quality development, following the path and goals of integrated development. Scientific and technological innovation is different from industrial innovation: the former is spending money on creating knowledge, while the latter is turning knowledge into wealth; the former requires works of scientists, while the latter requires entrepreneurs. Practice has proved that the combination of the two is the toughest task, and it is also difficult to combine them for innovation-driven development. The combination of the scientific and technological innovation with industrial innovation has existed for a long time in the Shanghai-Nanjing-Hefei region, especially in Nanjing. Although these regions have been investing greatly in scientific and technological innovation, their goals and actions have been divorced from the basic requirement of industrial innovation; and the technologies are mostly imported. Generally speaking, the scientific and technological innovation in this region is closer to the world standard than the industrial innovation. To form a coordinated scientific and technological innovation belt and industrial innovation belt in the future requires that, first, scientists concentrate on innovation and entrepreneurs on resource allocation, and their functions should not be mixed; second, government must create an environment for cluster development, set rules for market operation, and play the role of intermediary agent between the two clusters; third, there must be focus on developing market-oriented and popularized intermediary organizations and market between science and technology and industry; fourth, the utilization of risk capital in capital market: the Shanghai Stock Exchange Science and Technology Innovation Board is currently shouldering the responsibility of supporting the development of high-tech industry.

Second, the interconnection of infrastructure should be given priority, to further optimize and improve the comprehensive transport network in Yangtze River Delta. Specifically, it is necessary to build a world-class port cluster and airport cluster, integrated rail network, dense arterial highway network, and modern high-grade waterway network. This is the "integrated backbone" of the Yangtze River Delta as a world-class city cluster to open to the world in the future: every port, airport, financing institution, storage and base station in is a significant joint. With the deepening of the reform and opening up, people, capital, information, and cargo can be mobilized freely between the joints crossing the administrative border. For this purpose, local governments in the Yangtze River Delta region should yield some power to the organization or delegate some affairs to an experienced institution, for comprehensive planning, design, construction, and management. Without these institutional innovations, it is difficult to achieve a high-quality integration.

Third, the entrance of the scientific and technological innovation belt and industrial innovation belt shall be subject to the negative list management mode, while the enterprise and market conducts in the area are ruled by competition policy to implement a neutral oriented basic economic policy in competition. Governments have been used to planning and regulating the entrance of enterprise with a positive list, but it is too risky to be regulated by either government or entrepreneur. History has proven that the development of industrial clusters never follows the plan; its formation and specific content are spontaneous and random. The industries you wanted may not come as you wish; while the entered enterprise may not be in the positive list, but a high-tech industry. The management mode of a positive list actually overestimates government's rationality and ability to estimate industrial development and limits its conduct of development. In contrast, the negative list management mode not only is easier, but also avoids this series of drawbacks: any high-tech industry can enter freely as long as they meet the green standard, regardless of their ownership, scale, or quality. This mode will provide a feasible condition for markets to select real high-tech industries and manage the enterprise and market conduct by competition policy.

Fourth, local government should be redefined as a provider of institutional innovation and provide the Shanghai-Nanjing-Hefei scientific and technological innovation belt with a universal and integrated business environment and public goods supply. The quality of industrial cluster construction seems to depend on the relationship between enterprises and the quality of the leading company, but the most important factor is actually the government's capacity of institutional innovation and institutional supply. Local government should input innovation ideas into their daily work system, policy system and administration and evaluation system, in order to motivate enterprise innovation. The Shanghai-Nanjing-Hefei scientific and technological innovation belt needs to meet the three requirements of the national strategy, i.e., integration, high quality, and big-picture thinking, to provide scientists and enterprises with world-class innovative service so they can conduct their research and development and innovation freely and use scientific and technological resources more conveniently at a lower cost. In recent years, Suzhou and Shanghai introduced a policy that allows their "scientific and technological innovation vouchers" to be applied in both cities, so their local scientific research subsidies can be used in another city. The three provinces and one city in Yangtze River Delta region have also jointly build a "network for large scientific instrument and equipment sharing", with over 26 thousand large-scale scientific instrument worth over 300 thousand yuan and 23 large-scale scientific device and facilities. In September 2018, the nine cities of the G60 scientific and technological innovation belt have launched "one-stop online services": all the affairs in the nine cities can be settled "through one window, on one website and at one time".

Fifth, the construction of the Shanghai-Nanjing-Hefei scientific and technological innovation belt requires the spirit of a "Sunday engineer[1]" in the new era. The scientific and technological innovation belt is only a geographic concept, rather than an enterprise innovation concept. In order to convert the geographic field into a field of the capacity and development of scientific and technological innovation, the scientists, engineers, and entrepreneurs in this region need to exert their initiative and creativity. Therefore, the spirit of the "Sunday engineer" phenomenon popular in Shanghai, Jiangsu, and Zhejiang in the 1970s and 1980s can still be a good example to learn from in current times. The scientists and R&D designers in the scientific and technological innovation belt should have more communication and cooperation with the entrepreneurs and engineers in the industrial innovation belt, so they can closely exchange their information, knowledge, and skills, guide the direction of scientific research, and develop and improve the connection mechanism between science and technology and industry.

Section 4 The demonstration zone of the Yangtze River Delta: opening to the domestic market and functional orientation

The construction of the demonstration zone of the high-quality integrated development of the Yangtze River Delta is one of the most significant measures for the integration. The goals of the demonstration area, according to Shanghai municipal part secretary Li Qiang in the "Two Sessions" (the National People's Congress and the Chinese Political Consultative Conference) in 2019, are first to establish a new benchmark for implementing the new idea of development; second, set a test field for integrated mechanism and system; third, lead the higher-quality integrated development of the Yangtze River Delta. Secretary Li explained the motivation of the demonstration area as follows:

There are two points of significance of building the "demonstration zone of the integrated development of the Yangtze River Delta"; first, it further supports internal opening up – the measurement of comprehensively deepening reform specified by CPC Central Committee since the Third Plenary Session of the 18th CPC Central Committee can be implemented intensively, broken through and integrated systematically; second, the internal opening up of Shanghai to the Yangtze River Delta and the Yangtze River basin lacks a supporting zone. The construction of the demonstration zone makes it up. Along with the new Pilot Free Trade Zone, it will be one of the two wings in the west and east part of Shanghai, driving its development, playing a pivotal role for external and internal opening up, making Shanghai a better platform for the whole country.

The fundamental motivation for setting a demonstration zone is for Shanghai to build and enlarge a core supporting zone for internal opening up, to better balance the relation between internal and external opening up, and to better play its leading role for the integration of the Yangtze River Delta. It also proves that the leading role of Shanghai was mainly in terms of the export-oriented economy in the past, especially since the beginning of the 1990s; while it is not enough for the internal opening up: there is neither a supporting zone for the Yangtze River Delta and the Yangtze River basin nor a well-organized system of internal opening up. Some national strategic advantages and preferential policies that favor Shanghai are mostly designed to strengthen its central position in regard to international economy, trading, finance, and shipping, which not only cannot be copied or enjoyed by other regions of Yangtze River Delta, but also draws their production factors and caused a polarization effect. There are mainly three reasons for this phenomenon:

The first is related to the trend of export-oriented national strategy. Since the Pudong development and opening in 1992, especially in 2001 when China acceded to the WTO, the opening up of the Chinese development strategy started in the east – to join the global value chain oriented by developed countries, especially America, by crossing the ocean and driving the development through export processing and overseas markets. Therefore, the opening up in this period is development. The importance of utilizing the external market is higher than domestic market; and the urgency of external opening up is higher than the internal one. This is why Shanghai did not take internal opening up as their work priority, think about the cooperation mechanism with other regions in the Yangtze River Delta, or consider building a core supporting zone to connect to Suzhou, Zhejiang, and Anhui.

The second is related to the development phase of the relation between the central and surrounding regions. Shanghai is the publicly acknowledged core of the integrated development of the Yangtze River Delta, differing from other regions like Beijing-Tianjin-Hebei Region and Pearl River Delta region, which are either decentralized (the "non-capital" functions of Beijing have been transferred to other regions) or without a center. Shanghai contains a long-term stable "center-periphery" relation between Jiangsu, Zhejiang, and Anhui, which is at a development phase of resource polarization. Despite transferring some traditional industries to its surrounding regions, Shanghai has presented a higher polarizing force than driving force, absorbing production factors and resources from the whole country and the world, especially neighboring cities of the Yangtze River Delta region. Therefore, under this situation, the peripheral regions on the one hand would like to connect with Shanghai for its overflow effect, but on the other hand they worry about losing their resources to Shanghai. This is why the regions have remained ambivalent and adopted prudent measures in the regional integration.

The third is related to the transition economic system of decentralized competition. The Chinese reform characterized by decentralization of power and transfer of profit since 1978 has made local governments relatively independent with clear boundaries of interests, which have deeply participated in economic operations. They can use administrative power to interfere with the mobility of production factors, leading to anti-integrative market tendencies. In terms of the integrated development of the Yangtze River Delta, although they accept Shanghai as their leader, local governments have been planning for their own benefits and complaining that Shanghai "failed a leading role". Especially for adjacent Jiangsu, the existing problems of the "dead-end path" make it extremely prudent when talking about integration, like the airport construction in the Yangtze River Delta region. Since the global IT industry is centered in the south part of Jiangsu, particularly Suzhou Industrial Park, the Jiangsu government would like the Hongqiao Airport in Shanghai to expand on a more international route. However, Shanghai decided to construct Pudong International Airport, which is far away from the south part of Jiangsu. After Jiangsu had to build their own Shuofang International Airport, Shanghai came around to constructing Hongqiao Transportation Hub.

The strategic significance of building a demonstration zone for opening up to the domestic market at state level are:

First, it is an important signal of the national development strategy transforming into opening up to the domestic market. The China-US trade friction and the trending of the world economy have indicated that one of the vital problems for a long-term and steady development of Chinese economy is how to rapidly change to internal opening up. China is currently at a critical period where opening up to the domestic market is more urgent than opening up to the outside world; the former is the foundation and precondition for the latter. Opening up to the domestic market is mainly opening to local enterprises, especially private ones. Without opening up, their capability as the major creator of wealth in China will be critically restricted, so they cannot compete effectively with foreign companies in the fully opened Chinese market or participate in international competition representing China. Therefore, Shanghai, as the most developed area in the modern economic system in China, the leading role of the integrated development of the Yangtze River Delta, is changing from driving the external opening up in the Yangtze River Delta, the Yangtze River basin and the whole country, to the opening up to the domestic market through the demonstration area.

Second, it is a signal of transforming from overuse markets in developed countries to a vast domestic market. China is in urgent need of correcting the imbalance between opening up to the world and to the domestic market, and between opening to the East and to the West. The core to settle the problem is developing and expanding the domestic market, which requires improving income distribution and redistribution and the increase of productivity. Therefore, the incentive policies for private economy, the motivating power of economic growth, will directly influence and constrain the domestic income level and the expansion of potential markets, and limit the possibility of using domestic demand to absorb advanced factors overseas. The demonstration area of integration will provide domestic enterprises with development opportunities and be important for using the vast domestic demand to build new economic forms and enhancing motivation for development.

Third, it is also a vital signal of the increasing reform of market orientation and a significant decision of local governments transforming the competing system to coordinating system. The competition between local governments in regard to economic growth and revenues used to be one of the impetuses for Chinese economic development, but it also caused severe imbalance in the economic structure. Regional economic integration, an important part of President Xi's thoughts on economic development, plays a significant role in the modernization construction of state governance. Therefore, the demonstration zone of the integrated development of the Yangtze River Delta needs to explore two aspects: one is the market integration, eliminating interference by local governments and the administrative barrier for a fully opened market for complete competition between enterprises; another is government integration. Governments in the region should yield part of their rights to the public institution formed by contract, and accelerate the integration of intercity transportation, medical security, elderly care, and system duplication. In terms of enterprise, the most important is to gradually cancel the administrative measures for ownership and the administrative ranking and identity label, and to build a uniform but open, orderly, and competitive market system.

What about the location of this "demonstration zone of the integrated development of the Yangtze River Delta"? As indicated on a map, the junction of Shanghai-Jiangsu-Zhejiang includes Qingpu District, Songjiang District, and Jinshan District in Shanghai; Wujiang District in Suzhou City, Kunshan City, and

Taicang City in Jiangsu Province; Jiashan County and Pinghu City in Zhejiang Province. Among them, Qingpu District, Wujiang District, and Jiashan County are the closest to the junction. Since it is a demonstration zone, its scale should be limited; otherwise, it would overlap the whole Yangtze River Delta region. Therefore, its scale should equal a county or city: an area containing Qingpu District, Wujiang District, and Jiashan County would be proper.

If this is the future demonstration area for integration, then we have to ask a question: what is its function? Some people suggest that its function should be defined as a demonstration zone for eco-environment protection, but this is a basic problem that every region has to tackle, so it is not necessary to do it in such an important region. In addition, should it be a demonstration area for eco-environment protection? Then the region of the Shanghai-Nanjing-Hangzhou expressway would be more appropriate. Moreover, the junction of administrative regions has been an "administrative vacuum" in the past, and always a cluster of polluting industries. Therefore, the demonstration zone of Yangtze River Delta should strictly carry out environmental protection, but it is not suitable to be built as a demonstration zone for eco-environment protection.

Some people say that it should be a demonstration zone for institutional innovation of integration. To form an integrated system and mechanism is the means of realizing the function of this area, rather than its purpose. Besides, the demonstration of systematic reform does not need to be implemented in a specific and narrow area; it should be conducted in a specific project or big area in the Yangtze River Delta, so it can be extended and duplicated.

The exact positioning of the function of the demonstration zone is quite important, without which it may become a common economic and technological development zone, or a large version of high-tech park, as opposed to the original intention of setting the demonstration zone. All aspects considered, defining the area as a world-influential scientific and technological innovation center would be a strategic option with both global vision and Chinese perspective. There is more logical analysis based on the following facts.

First, the positioning is determined by the fundamental situation that China has to adapt to global competition. China is currently facing a complicated and severe external environment and situation: the result of the China-US trade friction indicates that the capability of independent scientific and technological innovation is directly related to the competitive advantages and rise of a nation.

Second, the positioning is determined by the transition from high-speed growth to high-quality growth. The vital engine of high-quality economy and energy for changing from old to new lies in scientific and technological innovation. General Secretary Xi pointed out that innovation is the primary driving force for development, seeking scientific and technological innovation is seeking development, and seeking development requires seeking scientific and technological innovation. Therefore, scientific and technological innovation is the high-quality development that requires a test field from the economically developed Yangtze River Delta.

Third, the positioning is implementing the significant strategic decision made by the Party Central Committee with Comrade Xi Jinping at its core. The essential discussion on scientific and technological innovation made by General Secretary Xi is the significant guiding thought for the high-quality integrated development of the Yangtze River Delta. Accelerating the pace of marching to an influential scientific and technological innovation center is central party's unwavering target since the 18th National Congress and has been gradually implemented since the 19th National Congress of the Communist Party of China. The positioning of the function of the demonstration area of the integrated development of the Yangtze River Delta should never omit such an important task.

The central party has specifically defined the function of Beijing and Shanghai, two world-class cities, as leading the whole country and world to the promotion of scientific and technological innovation and the implementation of the innovation-driven development strategy and accelerating the process of developing a world-influential scientific and technological innovation center since the 18th National Congress. President Xi emphasized in his speech on the first China International Import Expo on November 5th, 2018: that Shanghai, the biggest economic center in China and the leading role in reform and opening up, should continue expanding with three missions: first, to create a China Pilot Free-Trade Zone in Shanghai; second, to set a Science and Technology Innovation Board in Shanghai Stock Exchange and pilot registration system to support the construction of a Shanghai international finance center and scientific and technological innovation center; third, to support the integrated development of the Yangtze River Delta and make it a national strategy. At this critical time for the negotiation of the China-US trade friction, the three missions for Shanghai indicate great significance.

First, it means that the new target and task for Shanghai is not only building the international center of economy, trading, finance and shipping, but also a "world scientific and technological innovation center," which should be the foundation and priority. At a time when science and technology determine national power, the political and economic status of a scientific and technological innovation center is far higher than other four targets and requires more effort to achieve.

Second, the three missions are the strategic supporting means of the target of a "world scientific and technological innovation center" with an internal logical connection: creating a China Pilot Free-Trade Zone looks like only an expansion of open economy, but it is also helpful for the Yangtze River Delta region to absorb advanced production factors abroad, so they can achieve independent innovation; meanwhile, it is in favor of spreading the power of opening up to other regions; setting the Science and Technology Innovation Board with a registration system not only supports the construction of Shanghai as an international finance center, but more importantly it directly supports the development of scientific and technological innovation using the capital market mechanism under the background of China-US trade friction. In the future, the traditional method of government directly subsidizing strategic emerging industries will not be appropriate. The practices of developed countries have proven that for high-technology industries in their beginning stage, the best way is utilizing the support of risk capital and capital markets. Making the integration of the Yangtze River Delta a national strategy is not only for a unified market and improving its international competitiveness by utilizing economies of scale, but also creates a connection between the external opening up in eastern Shanghai and the internal opening up in western Shanghai, which will realize the coordinated utilization and development of the scientific and technological resources, talents, and educational achievement in the region, accelerate the construction of a leading demonstration area of scientific and technological innovation, and build a new engine for economic development.

Third, the demonstration zone of integrated development of the Yangtze River Delta being positioned as a scientific and technological innovation relies on its basic condition of excellent culture and science education resource and industry. The geography, people, and cultural closeness in the Yangtze River Delta region is the historical basis for the construction of the demonstration area. And the industrial strength, infrastructure, and wide economic social bond established over the 40 years since the reform and opening up are the material basis for it. The most abundant and dense science and education resources, like universities and scientific research institutions, are distributed over the two corridors from east to west in the Yangtze River Delta region, i.e., the G60 scientific and technological innovation belt and the riverside area in Shanghai-Nanjing-Hefei. The demonstration zone of the Yangtze River Delta integration can rely on universities and scientific research institutions, especially the numerous double first-class universities for innovation and entrepreneurship. It can also rely on its advantages of talents, enterprise as an innovation subject, open economy, cluster of science parks, cluster of high-tech industry, etc., to industrialize the achievement of science and technological innovation. In Shanghai and Nanjing, the industrialization is restricted by the high cost of land, labor, and other factors; while in Anhui, Jiangsu, and other riverside regions, there is sufficient development space, numerous science parks, solid development foundations for high-tech industry, and strong capacity of industrialization to make it highly possible to become a demonstration of the coordination of "scientific and technological innovation-industrial innovation".

Fourth, as a demonstration area positioned for scientific and technological innovation, it is consistent to its mission of internal opening up. The export-oriented globalization in the past mainly aimed at attracting foreign investment for export processing. The international enterprises usually regard China as a manufacturing base or sales platform, without being an important research and development center. Under this export-oriented economic pattern, local enterprises are limited to the functions of processing, manufacturing, assembling, and production, following the orders of the foreign companies. However, opening up to private enterprises and utilizing domestic demand requires the enterprises to research, develop. and design products independently. Therefore, more independent brands and technologies will be gradually bred, setting a prominent example of an innovation-driven county.

Note

1 "Sunday engineer" is a group of professionals and technicians who helped township enterprises that lack techniques with their specialties on Sundays and holidays with or without payment. – Translator's notes

References

Quan Heng. The High-quality Integrated Development of the Yangtze River Delta: Exerting the Leading Role of Shanghai. Shanghai Urban Management, 2018 (4).

Fan Jiangyong. Higher-quality Integration: How Should the Yangtze River Delta Be Arranged?. Environmental Economy, 2019 (6).

Zhang Xueliang, Lin Yongran, Meng Meixia. Mechanism Evolution of the High-quality Integrated Development of the Yangtze River Delta: Summary of Experience and Development Tendency. Journal of Anhui University (Philosophy and Social Sciences Edition), 2019 (1).

Liu Zhibiao. Rethink on Regional Integrated Development: Policies and Methods of Promoting the Integrated Development of the Yangtze River Delta. Journal of Nanjing Normal University (Social Science Edition), 2014 (6).

Liu Zhibiao. The Institutional Foundation of the Higher-quality Integrated Development of the Yangtze River Delta. Frontiers, 2019 (4).

2 The driving mechanism for higher-quality integrated development in the Yangtze River Delta

Zhibiao Liu and Liu Chen

President Xi, in his keynote speech at the opening ceremony of the first China International Import Expo on November 5th, 2018, emphasized the importance of supporting the integrated development of the Yangtze River Delta and making it a national strategy, implementing new concepts for development, constructing a modernized economic system, promoting further reform with higher starting points and opening up at higher levels, perfecting the spatial arrangement of Chinese reform along with the development of the Belt and Road, the Yangtze River Economic Belt, and the Guangdong – Hong Kong – Macao Greater Bay Area.

Regional integrated development means that in an extensive economic region, all the regions divided by clear administrative boundaries constantly eliminate the institution, system, mechanism, policies, and other artificial obstacles that obstruct the mobility of resources in the process of regional development, to achieve full opening up and competition of markets. Empirically, the phenomenon and tendency of non-integrated development in China, a major developing country, between and within regions are extremely severe; and it is no easier to reduce them than it is to reduce those between countries. It is especially true of the Chinese economy at the system's transitional period. The main reasons are as follows: first, in the past, the administrative programs, orders, and regulations have segmented the national economy into pieces which still play a role in resource allocation in the process of economic transition; for example, local industrial policies are important for resource allocation. Therefore, before the substituted mechanism, i.e., the market intermediate organization and institution matures, the "pieces" of administrative mechanisms will hinder market integration. Second, it is restricted by the developmental stage. Local government can widely and directly interfere with market activities through state-owned enterprises which are kept and even developed in the process of economic transition. Such behavior would surely cause administrative boundaries, leading to a segmented market, difficulties with integration, the prevalence of localized industrial policies, and the segmentation of the economic system.

Looking back into the past, the Yangtze River Delta region has been constantly exploring the path of coordinated development under the system of the time: the Shanghai economic zone was first set in 1982; a joint conference of 15-city collaborative offices in the Yangtze River Delta was formed spontaneously in 1992

DOI: 10.4324/9781003455943-2

and upgraded to a major summit in 1997; and a regular meeting of major leaders in the Yangtze River Delta was developed in 2005. Since the current administrative system gives governments too much power to intervene in market activities and local governments have been planning for their own benefits, the administrative barriers have hindered the effect of regional integration. In April 2018, General Secretary Xi commanded that Shanghai should further play a leading role, while Jiangsu, Zhejiang, and Anhui should make full use of their advantages in pursuing the higher-quality integrated development of the Yangtze River Delta. At this point, the integrated development of the Yangtze River Delta has become a consensus and will become an example of the exploration of regional integration in China.

This chapter studies the strategic significance of the integrated development of the Yangtze River Delta and the impact of system and mechanism, focusing on the research and design of motivational mechanisms of the higher-quality integrated development of the Yangtze River Delta, and providing policy suggestions for it.

Section 1 The demonstrative significance of the integrated development of the Yangtze River Delta as a national strategy

Promoting overall development through regional integration has become an important part of the economic development policy in China in recent years. Boosting the regional economic development is one of the significant methods and distinct characteristics of President Xi through his long-term practice, a vital means to implement regional coordinated development, an important part of Xi Jinping's socialist economic thought with Chinese characteristics for a new era, and a significant role of theoretical and practical governance of a state.

As the Secretary of Zhejiang Provincial Committee of the CPC, Comrade Xi went to Shanghai and inspected its development many times, strongly advocating for the economic integration of the Yangtze River Delta. In 2003, a Zhejiang party and government delegation led by Comrade Xi signed the *Agreement on Further Promoting Shanghai-Zhejiang Economic Cooperation and Development* with Shanghai and the *Agreement on Further Strengthening Economic and Technological Exchange and Cooperation* with Jiangsu. He required an integration of Zhejiang with Shanghai in terms of infrastructure construction, industrial division, exploitation and market expansion of tourism resources, environmental protection, as well as science and technology, information, education, talents, etc. In March 2007, Comrade Xi assumed his new post in Shanghai, which provided him with a better stage to facilitate the close cooperation between Shanghai and Zhejiang. He pointed out that the construction of Shanghai as "four centers" cannot rely solely on Shanghai but also needs the whole Yangtze River Delta and Yangtze River basin. On February 28th, 2014, General Secretary Xi applied his experience of promoting the economic integration of the Yangtze River Delta to the Beijing-Tianjin-Hebei Region coordinated development strategy, put forward "seven endeavors", and required a breakup of the conservative mindset to complete the top design objective of Beijing-Tianjin-Hebei Region integration. Three months later, he went to Shanghai for an inspection and asked local leaders to accelerate the integrated development of the Yangtze River Delta. In April 2018, General Secretary Xi made a vital announcement on promoting the integration of the Yangtze River Delta again, clarifying the goal of "higher-quality integrated development", the path of "Shanghai playing its leading role, while Jiangsu, Zhejiang and Anhui mak[e] full use of their advantages", the key insurance of "united together for implementation", and the direction for cooperation and development in the Yangtze River Delta in the new era.

The report of the 19th National Congress stated that "the implementation of the regional coordinated development strategy" requires "the support of the eastern region in taking the lead in pursuing optimal development through innovation". Supporting the integrated development of the Yangtze River Delta as a national strategy is the concrete action to implement the report. According to the instructions of General Secretary Xi in April 2018, the general goal of "higher-quality integration" and the path of "Shanghai playing its leading role, while Jiangsu, Zhejiang and Anhui making full use of their advantages The integrated development of the Yangtze River Delta becoming a national strategy will make the experience in the region duplicable and expandable, so it can play a leading role in the new round of reform and opening up in China, participate in global competition, and accelerate the construction of a world-class city cluster in the Yangtze River Delta.

1. The Yangtze River Delta region will become a standard and example of implementing new thoughts on development and promoting high-quality development

The implementation of new thoughts on development and promotion of high-quality development can be achieved through setting a standard and example. For instance, as one of the most dynamic and innovative areas in Chinese economic society, the Yangtze River Delta can exploit an innovation-driven path to high-quality development by integrating the abundant science and education with robust modern industries. Another example: since the Yangtze River Delta region has adopted the method of industrialization of pushing urbanization early and has achieved a relatively high developmental level, it has a fairly high agricultural modernization and small urban-rural gap. Its experience is gradually forming a path and pattern of the synchronous development of industrialization, informatization, urbanization, and agricultural modernization which can be duplicated and promoted across the whole country. In addition, the resource, environmental, and ecological problems in the region are severe due to its earlier extensive industrialization, so the sustainable development of the new round of industrialization remains a significant issue to be explored. Finally, the problems of how to transform the export-oriented economy into a high-level two-way open economy, and how to raise the percentage of public sharing for a shared development, also need the relatively developed regions to take the lead in exploring the methods and providing experiences and lessons for other regions' attempts at implementing new development.

2. The Yangtze River Delta will become the pioneer and main force to establish the modern economic system

Establishing a modern economic system is the guiding principle of the economic construction in future China. The developed regions should lead by example. Under the national strategy of the high-quality integrated development of the Yangtze River Delta, first, a second "Greater Bay Area" next to the Guangdong – Hong Kong – Macao Greater Bay Area, i.e., the Yangtze River Delta Greater Bay Area can be constructed in order to drive the industrial upgrading, scientific, technological, and financial innovation in the world-class city cluster in the area and provide new energy for Chinese developments. Second, by setting up an institutional platform for regional cooperation, for example, the G60 scientific and technological innovation belt, a world-class manufacturing industrial cluster and a demonstration area for the coordinated development of strategic emerging industries can be built. Third, Shanghai can better play its leading role, focusing on the construction of "five centers", i.e., engaging mainly in producer service and lowering the transaction cost of the economic operations in the area; the surrounding area should engage in the advanced manufacturing industry, high-tech industry, and strategic emerging industries to reduce the manufacturing costs in the Yangtze River Delta region and comprehensively increase the competitiveness of the modern economic system.

3. The Yangtze River Delta will become the forerunner and model for the promotion of deepening reform at a higher starting point

The deepening reform at a higher starting point requires a large-scale opening up to the domestic market and further external opening up. In the past, China has adhered to external opening up without sufficient opening up to the domestic market, which leads to relatively severe ossification of internal development mechanisms, like insufficient transformation of government functions and lack of private enterprises. Large-scale opening up to the domestic market first requires the eradication of administrative barriers, regions racing for opening up, and all the market entities being treated equally without discrimination, before the regional high-quality integrated development can be accelerated. The function, range, and extent of governmental interference in the market should be restricted in the first place, so that private enterprises can participate in the market competition. If the Yangtze River Delta region can break the administrative barrier, then it can duplicate and promote the policies in Shanghai Free-Trade Zone and Port, and the policy of financial reform in Zhejiang can amplify the effect of reform.

4. The Yangtze River Delta will become a demonstration area and standard of promoting a higher-level opening up

Higher-level opening up should deal with the problem of how to improve the quality and connections between inside and outside. The Yangtze River Delta region was a typical export-oriented economy; but the new round of high-level economic globalization requires it to change from eastward opening up to an all-dimensional opening up; its priority from exporting commodities to exporting capital that drives commodity sales; from attracting forging capital to attracting advanced technologies and talents; from utilizing others' markets to its own in order to expand domestic demand; and from attracting foreign capital through building science parks and preferential policies to the provision of advanced institutional platforms and hardware to science and technology personnel.

5. The Yangtze River Delta will become the main energy source for perfecting the spatial arrangement of reform and opening up in China

If we say that the east region is to China what China is to the world in terms of economy, then the leading city of the east region is the Yangtze River Delta. The city cluster in Yangtze River Delta is undoubtedly an important platform for the Chinese economy to participate in the global market. It, along with the Beijing – Tianjin – Hebei Region and the Guangdong – Hong Kong – Macao Greater Bay Area, will become the new driving force of the Chinese economy.

Section 2 The intrinsic dynamic mechanism of the higher-quality integrated development of the Yangtze River Delta

There are two factors that influence the regional development in economic transition: the first are the natural and technological ones, such as landform, transportation, infrastructure, etc.; the other is artificial barriers, such as institutions, systems, mechanisms, policies, etc. The former influences and determines the cost and efficiency of the regional integrated development: the differences of developmental cost and levels exist as long as there are different locations and technologies. The latter generally refers to the costs brought about by systems and mechanisms and need to be eliminated with great effort, because only the differences of institutions and policies can systematically and widely influence the rational allocation of factors and resources, leading to artificial developmental differences. In other words, regional integrated development depends mainly on whether each region can open sufficiently and whether there are artificial system and policy obstacles; while natural conditions and technological factors are not the necessary and sufficient conditions for regional integration but are an influence on its efficiency and therefore on the economic development level. Of course, the two factors are interactional. For example, the improvement of transportation and infrastructure is the basis of regional integration and helps to remedy the institutional segmentation and accelerate the market integration, while the elimination of systematic barriers and segmentation in turn can facilitate the cross-regional cooperation in infrastructure and efficient utilization of technologies in larger markets on a large scale.

The core of an economic system and mechanism is to correctly handle the relationship between the government and the market. Therefore, to improve the high-quality integration in the Yangtze River Delta and construct a drive-mechanism for it means a coordinated effort between government and market so they can fully perform their functions. The strong impulse of government will create an environment where the market can play a decisive role. It is important to satisfy the interest demands of both sides in competition and negotiation and develop an engine for driving the integration.

The cooperative development of the three provinces and one city has entered a brand-new phase after the integrated development of the Yangtze River Delta became a national strategy. Based on their early achievement on interconnectivity, ecological protection, industrial innovation, market reform, public service, etc., the key to implementing the national strategy lies in the question of how to pursue a higher-quality integration and design an interest-sharing mechanism at the executive level based on the consensus on the decision-making level, because only when all the participants are making a profit can it be an executable and sustainable integration.

The non-integration of Yangtze River Delta in the past, whether it was the obstructed transportation or infrastructure or market obstruction caused by the system and mechanism, is the result of regional protectionism. It is understandable that local governments administrate for their own short-term interests in the past and present, so the key is to design a driving mechanism for them to race to opening up. There might be some obstacles to the establishment of this mechanism:

1. Diffusing effect and siphon effect

Whether a region decides to participate in integration depends on the diffusing effect and siphon effect of the place and its surroundings. If the neighboring city siphons more local resources, or the local resources diffuse more to other cities, then it means the regional competition prevails over cooperation. In the past when export-oriented was the significant strategy, Shanghai and its surrounding areas in Jiangsu and Zhejiang both needed to attract FDI of processing trades. Therefore, the motivation for Shanghai to lower the trade cost of the manufacturing industry through interconnection with its neighbors was weakened. Currently, Shanghai clings to its "four centers" core function, devoting itself to a new function of representing a worldwide high-level. Such a staggered developmental strategy has laid the foundation for integration.

2. Industrial coordination and industrial isomorphism

The development of high-tech industries nowadays mainly involves the IT industry, biomedicine, equipment and instruments, new energy and material, etc., upon which the substantial economic development of a region and country also rely. Therefore, regions are inevitably competitive over these industrial fields, adopting all kinds of favorable policies to support their localization, which has been the developmental practice in all the regions since the financial crisis in 2008. It has become a pattern for regions to centralize resources for a few hot industries in order to drive regional transformation and upgrading, so it is quite difficult to ask regions to abandon their policy-favored industries because of industrial policy coordination.

3. Market protection and local development

One of the government's means to support local enterprises is the entry restriction and favorable policies in terms of government procurement; for example, the taxi market can only use locally produced automobiles, the restrictions on non-local beer brands entering the local market, and forbidding the entrance of enterprises from other places on the grounds of limits on special industry. Although protecting and supporting a few enterprises in local markets may eventually damage their own interests, some short-sighted regions still believe that market protection can be an effective method and refuse to join the unified big market.

4. Radiation and competition of public goods

There are competitions among the regions in regard to the location and construction of airports, ports, significant scientific and technological instruments and laboratories, and other infrastructures of public goods. The market competition of local governments under the institutional structures with clear interest boundaries is bound to be the maximum of monopolistic benefits within their administrative boundaries and the minimum costs, the embodiment of which are the "overflow" of public goods and construction costs shouldered by central governments or others. It has caused not only unbridled competition and overlapping construction of public goods but also site selection and construction methods for the purpose of regional interest maximization, rather than for the integration of the Yangtze River Delta.

In terms of establishing a driving mechanism for the integration of the Yangtze River Delta, the functions of both a "strong government" and "strong market" are required, but in a particular order. The purpose of better exerting the governmental function is to build an environment for exerting market function, which is manifested in the following two aspects.

First, the strong push of government needs to be first exerted before the market can function. This is because:

(1) Local protectionism is formed by governments and can only be broken by governments. It means that among almost all the factors influencing the structure and efficiency of market operations, whether tangible barriers against interconnection or system and mechanism barriers, only governments can effectively and drastically warp, segment, and restrict markets in the long run. Therefore, in regard to the purpose of forming a unified market, eliminating market barriers, building a development environment of fair competition, and raising the efficiency of resource allocation, governments themselves need to be reformed to reach a balance between industrial policies and competition policies.

(2) The independent policies of local governments to pursue their own benefits will inevitably cause social cost, so limited intervention by the central government and the administration of the Yangtze River Delta region is necessary. To achieve the integration of the Yangtze River Delta, the local regulations and policies need to be gradually amended and unified under the nationally uniform system of laws and regulations, and those in conflict with integration need to be abolished. In the current stage, it means reducing the interference of negative externality between regions and coordinating the existing economic and social development strategy in order to cater to the regional economic integration intentionally.

Second, the market should be playing a more important role after the preliminary competition rules are established by the government. When governments have reached a consensus on the publicly accepted integrative fields like infrastructure, their tasks of providing an external environment for improving integrated development are primarily completed. In the process of a deeper level of interest adjustment, only market mechanisms can cause the endogeny effect of economic integration. The current functions of market mechanisms in the integration manifest in the following aspects:

(1) Guarantee the interest appeal of micro-entities in the integration of the Yangtze River Delta. The construction of all kinds of platforms and environments will ensure that basic-level government, enterprises, and other stakeholders can fully express their interests, so they can guarantee that the ideas and blueprints of integration will conform to the market's intrinsic rules and can be carried out smoothly.
(2) Settle the conflict over regional interests in the integration based on the principle of marketization. The problems of in-depth integrative cooperation, for example, like the location and differentiated positioning of airports, ports, and other infrastructures, ways of constructing significant scientific research platforms, cooperative modes of innovative platforms, etc. are all related to the vital interest adjustments of each area and conflicts between them. Even though they can be settled through administrative orders, the temporary balance cannot continue on the micro-level. The scheme would only work when it is formed by the relevant subjects through sufficient bargain and dynamic regulations following the market principles and adopting the price mechanism as the main regulating measure.
(3) Utilize the functions of enterprise in the integration of the Yangtze River Delta. In the process of local governments reducing their restrictions on enterprises' cross-regional activities, the natural barriers caused by the administrative division can be overcome by enterprise integration. As the barriers that influence the cross-regional free-flowing production factors being broken by the reform of systems and mechanisms, enterprises are the most sensitive ones to notice the business opportunities in the region of the Yangtze River Delta and to integrate resources within the region. When all the enterprises are conducting

resource allocation at the enterprise level based on the comparative advantages of each place in the Yangtze River Delta region, the integrated structure is naturally formed.

Section 3 The developing path of the higher-quality integrated development of the Yangtze River Delta

In order to locate the most suitable engine for the higher-quality integrated development of the Yangtze River Delta, there are several aspects we need to consider:

1. The influence of Shanghai as the leading role of the economy in the Yangtze River Delta region

The basic regional cooperative pattern is that Shanghai should fully play a leading role, while Jiangsu, Zhejiang, and Anhui should make full use of their advantages. Currently, the leading role of Shanghai is mainly manifested in its advanced producer services and coordination of manufacturing development in other regions. Economists believe that a reasonable distribution within a region requires relatively low manufacturing and trade costs. In the Yangtze River Delta, Shanghai can lower the trade cost while Jiangsu, Zhejiang, and Anhui can control the manufacturing cost to reach a regional coordination. Therefore, the standard of a world-class city or city cluster should be the proportion of producer services; for example, the development level of finance, shipping, commerce, etc. In Shanghai, the percentage of producer services of GDP and service industry are 50% and 70% respectively, which should be high enough to support high-quality development in the region. The path for Jiangsu, Zhejiang, and Anhui utilizing their advantages means they are further integrated in the global value chain; and their control over the high-end and high-value-added links is enhanced. In the past, they were integrated into the global value chain passively through traditional manufacturing industries and export processing with low added value; but now, centered on the Belt and Road Initiative, the regions should actively build a global industrial division and value chain system based on themselves. According to the office of regional collaboration of the Yangtze River Delta, in a survey about regional integration, 90% hope that the involved region should be better stimulated by Shanghai through infrastructures and system design. Based on the current regional structure of the development of the Yangtze River Delta, if Shanghai cannot play a leading role, then other places will not be able to benefit from its transitional development, leading to a slow formation of the integrated structure of the Yangtze River Delta. Shanghai's leading role includes at least the following aspects: first, set the stage for driving the surrounding area. For example, the neighboring regions are actively connecting the "dead ends" to accept the Shanghai influence; while Shanghai may not benefit from them, it needs to consider the long-term and general interests. Second, aiming at constructing a globally outstanding city, Shanghai needs to focus on its functional advantages and "four centers" positioning and gradually reduce the general labor-intensive manufacturing industries with high energy consumption and preferential policies that attract OEM FDI. Transferring these industries and FDI to regions with more carrying capacity in the Yangtze River Delta is helpful for dealing with its problems with imbalance and insufficiency. Third, the scientific and technological platform, financial platform, and human resource platform in Shanghai should open to the whole Yangtze River Delta to prepare for the global resource introduction and allocation.

2. The major mission and content of the integrated development of the Yangtze River Delta needs to be further clarified

The high-quality development of the Yangtze River Delta requires the collaboration of major reform measures. The regional integrated development is essentially the high-level opening up of each place within the region, the core of which is to eliminate administrative barriers set by the government, and the high quality requires the transformation of governmental functions, especially its block on the local commodities and factor market. The integrated development of the Yangtze River Delta should not be discussed at an abstract level; it requires some progressive reform and cooperation first in some key fields (for example, infrastructure, tourism industry, etc.), in order to rapidly accelerate the overall innovation. The integration of Zhejiang and Jiangsu, the key point of the integrated development of the Yangtze River Delta, need to construct "one circle, two belts and one corridor": "one circle" is the areas around Taihu Lake, focusing on the development of optimization of industrial structure and collaborative governance of ecological environment to deal with the negative externality of environmental problems like pollution in Taihu Lake. "Two belts" are the Nanjing-Hangzhou ecological and economic belt, to explore the coordinated development of ecological protection and high-tech parks, and the canal cultural and economic belt. "One corridor" is the science and technology corridor. In terms of how to utilize the productive service of Shanghai and achieve high-level opening up and innovation, the government can set a high-tech industry fund and invest in promising projects. The key to the integration of Zhejiang and Anhui is the ecological and environmental problems in Xin'an River and the collaborative development of tourism resources. The focus of the integration of Jiangsu and Anhui is the transformation of manufacturing capacity, i.e., how to transfer the overcapacity in Jiangsu to Wanjiang region, and how to build a city and business area centered on Nanjing, which will also influence Hefei, Bengbu, and Xuzhou.

3. Duplicate and promote the national pilot policy in the Yangtze River Delta region

The significant policies piloted in the Yangtze River Delta have covered commerce, finance, scientific and technological innovation, and many other vital aspects. Many other regions have expressed their strong intention to learn, introduce, and implement these policies, especially the policy of Shanghai's free-trade zone and free port, the policy of demonstration area of modernization construction in south Jiangsu, and the policy of financial reform in Zhejiang. The Yangtze River Delta region as a whole can apply to the central government for a certain administrative authorization, so that the local governments can duplicate and promote the national pilot policies orderly under certain condition in a certain range. Or the policy-making organization of the Yangtze River Delta region can apply to the relevant government department and promote universal pilot policies in some parts of the area. The duplication and promotion of the achievements of those pilot reforms and measures in the Yangtze River Delta will definitely amplify the effect of reform.

4. Integrate the regional resources by constructing a tangible "enclave economy" and an intangible "Internet platform"

The effective mode and experience of the previous "enclave economy" can be applied in a wider range and to more entities to benefit more regions and enterprises. With the strictest environmental protection policies carried out in the whole region of the Yangtze River Delta, the current "enclave economy" cannot just follow the regional industrial transfer passively; it should become the pilot site of a division of labor in the industrial value chain and innovation chain. Other than the tangible "enclave economy", an intangible Internet platform also needs to be established to integrate resources of education, health care, industry supply chain, etc. to benefit all the participants. For example, the medical treatment and trans-provincial settlement of the high-level hospitals in the Yangtze River Delta region should be further improved; an overall platform for large-scale research equipment sharing in the region and a platform for inspection equipment in key industries such as automobile and medicine can be established.

5. Encourage mergers and acquisitions in the Yangtze River Delta

When all the places have focused on the development of strategic emerging industries, it is impossible to avoid industrial isomorphism and overlapping, let alone within the market economy where investors are making decisions based on incomplete and unpredictable information. The coordination in the Yangtze River Delta to form a specialized and differentiated industry position for each place does not mean telling each region what they should or should not do: the coordination would not work without the agreement of each city. The excess and convergence of an industry is not the problem; the problem is the lack of an auto-clearance mechanism in the market, i.e., without the mechanism of merger and acquisition or break and closedown in the market, there will inevitably be severe overcapacity and structural conflict. Generally speaking, a mechanism of merger and acquisition in the unified big market would automatically break the artificial market barriers and confine the excess and overcapacity in a certain range, leading to the formation of differentiated industry positions through sufficient mergers, acquisitions, and cooperation in the region.

6. The coordination function of large-scale enterprise in the region

There are multiple domestic and international large-scale enterprise groups in the Yangtze River Delta, covering advanced manufacturing, Internet economy, and many other fields. These enterprises are the "chain leader" of global and domestic value chains. When they conduct cross-regional investment and resource allocation according to the market principles in the Yangtze River Delta region, the work division of regional integration becomes the division within their industry chain, value chain, and innovation chain. The difficulty of coordination within an enterprise is much lower than that between governments. It is possible that enterprise groups, in terms of industry allocation, can position their service link mainly in Shanghai and manufacturing link in Jiangsu, Zhejiang, and Anhui; the former would reduce the trade cost of commodities and service production, while the latter would lower its manufacturing costs. In terms of regional opening up, the provinces and cities in the Yangtze River Delta region can organize the local enterprises to cooperate with countries along the Belt and Road routes to invest and construct manufacturing base, consolidating their "chain leader" status in the value chain.

7. Establishing the competition rules gradually in the Yangtze River Delta region

The mid- and long-term objective of the integration of the Yangtze River Delta is to form a uniform rule of market competition. By building a competition system free of government interference based on market competition, the region can facilitate the transition from "developmental competition" to "equal competition", constrain the governmental participation in the market operation, and establish a competition policy to replace industrial policy as the predominant option. When all the members have benefited from the integration, they will voluntarily follow the competition rules. Currently, some specific protocols in transportation, environmental protection, public service, and other fields of strong externalities can gradually be reached to coordinate the competitive rules in each region. The legally established regional competition rules will be the best example the integration of the Yangtze River Delta can set for the whole country.

8. The high-quality integrated development of the Yangtze River Delta needs to be fully combined with the Yangtze River Economic Belt and the Belt and Road initiatives

For a long time, China and the Yangtze River Delta is mainly opened to the east, so the Yangtze River Delta as the front zone has developed rapidly. But now China needs to build a new structure of opening to both east and west, especially west, which requires China and the Yangtze River Delta to build a value chain division system based on facing the whole world, with countries and regions along the Belt and Road. In this process, on the one hand, Shanghai and other central cities may become the cluster of corporate headquarters and transfer the traditional manufacturing function to regions along the Belt and Road. Through the Belt and Road construction, the Yangtze River Delta region can help entrepreneurs to jointly invest in industrial parks in countries and regions along the Belt and Road. On the other hand, the high-quality integrated development of the Yangtze River Delta should also be fully combined with the construction of the Yangtze River Economic Belt, transferring the local enterprises to the regions in the middle and upper reaches of the Yangtze River to avoid the excessive moving to Southeast Asia and achieve an actual industrial "overflow effect" rather than "offshoring effect".

References

Gao Changchun. Thoughts and Countermeasures of Cooperative Governance of Innovation Network in the Yangtze River Delta Region. Science Development, 2018 (9).

Quan Heng. The High-quality Integrated Development of the Yangtze River Delta: Exerting the Leading Role of Shanghai. Shanghai Urban Management, 2018 (7).

Jiang Nan. G60 Science and Technology Belt: Significant Engine of the Higher-quality Integrated Development of the Yangtze River Delta. Jiangnan Forum, 2018 (6).

Xu Qin. The Integrated Development of the Yangtze River Delta under the Multi-center Structure. Modern Economic Research, 2018 (9).

Hong Yinxing, Wang Zhen et al. New Trend in the Integration of the Yangtze River Delta. Shanghai Economy, 2018 (5).

Liu Zhibiao. Regional Cooperation to Foster an International Manufacturing Center in Yangtze River Delta. Journal of Nanjing University (Philosophy, Humanities and Social Sciences), 2005 (1).

Liu Zhibiao. Rethink on Regional Integrated Development: Policies and Methods of Promoting the Integrated Development of the Yangtze River Delta. Journal of Nanjing Normal University (Social Science Edition), 2014 (6).

3 The process of the high-quality integrated development of the Yangtze River Delta

Lingchi Kong, Zhibiao Liu and Ning Xu

Section 1 Introduction

Regional economic integration is not only the trend of global development, but also an endogenous necessity in China. From the perspective of the development trend of the global economy, the world is increasingly multi-polarized, the connection and interaction between major economic entities are getting closer, and the mutually open dependent and cooperative community of shared futures between countries has become a primary trend. From the perspective of the domestic microscopic situation and national strategy, it has become a urgent endogenous requirement for the transformation and upgrading of the regional economy to perfect the regional cooperation mechanism for resource integration, complementary to each other; collaboration and sharing, to cope with developmental challenges cooperatively; to develop new impetus for growth and competitive advantages; and to achieve regional coordinated, orderly and sustainable development. Since the reform and opening up, the Yangtze River Delta region has experienced a rapid process of integration. However, because of the widening surrounding areas and the dominant internal problem of developmental imbalance, there are still some underlying problems that need to be settled urgently to achieve high-quality integrated development. It shows a vital realistic value to scientifically assess the process of the integrated development of the Yangtze River Delta, clarify its main characteristics and weak links, and then propose countermeasures and suggestions accordingly.

The current literature has focused on the development path and policies of the integrated development of the Yangtze River Delta. Some scholars evaluated its development level by measuring single indicators from different aspects. Hou Binhui et al. (2009) analyzed the economic structure of the Yangtze River Delta city cluster through social network analysis. Zhang Xueliang et al. (2018) sorted the industrial policies and adopted standard location quotients to analyze and measure the process of the industrial integrated development in the Yangtze River Delta. Li Peixin et al. (2019) conducted measurement and analysis on the spatial structure of the Yangtze River Delta region from the perspective of urban size distribution, spatial distribution, and network distribution. It is noticeable that the measurements of

DOI: 10.4324/9781003455943-3

single indicators have their advantages but are inevitably biased. They only reflect one significant aspect or factor in the process of integration (Liu Zhibiao, 2019). Regional integrated development is a complicated system including multiple aspects and factors, so it needs to be examined through an overall perspective of economic and social development.

Some scholars have established an indicator system for integration assessment. For example, Estrada and Arturo (2011) built a system to comprehensively measure the regional development and integration level through a GDRI model of four dimensions (i.e. regional politics, society, economy, and technology) and 98 variables. Zhou Liqun and Liangke (2010) measured and compared the economic integration of the Beijing-Tianjin-Hebei Region, the Yangtze River Delta region, and the Pearl River Delta from 1989 to 2007 from the perspective of market integration and policy integration using an analytic hierarchy process and standard deviation. Gu Haibing and Min (2017) built an evaluation index system of internal and external incentives for regional economic integration from the perspective of market, industry, infrastructure, public service, policy, and system integration. Li Shiqi and Pingfang (2017) carried out a brand-new exploration on the evaluation of the integration of the Yangtze River Delta from the aspects of market unification, factor homogeneity, developmental cooperativity, and system uniformity. Zeng Gang and Fenglong (2018) founded an assessment indicator system for the integrated development of the Yangtze River Delta by weighted average, standardization, spatial analysis, etc. from the perspectives of economic development, scientific and technological innovation, communication and service, and ecological protection. In conclusion, the current comprehensive measurements, although covering different aspects of regional integration, lack the theoretical basis for their selection of evaluation indicators. Their indicator systems failed to highlight the properties of the integration of the Yangtze River Delta. Some index weights are influenced by the subjectivity of scholars without considering the changes in statistics.

Given all that, based on the systematic induction of the integrated development of the Yangtze River Delta, this chapter will quantify and measure its process from 2000 to 2018, analyze its characteristics and problems, and provide some specific policy suggestions to accelerate the process. The innovative aspects of this chapter are:

(1) a comprehensive indicator system containing ten dimensions, i.e., space, market, industry, innovation, transportation, information, trade, public service, ecological environment, and system; and an objective evaluation of the Yangtze River Delta for future research.
(2) a systematic induction of the guidelines of regional integration, which reveal the carrier, basis, supporter, requirement, security, etc. of regional integrated development, provides a theoretical basis for selecting evaluation indexes, and supplements the current literature.

Section 2 The measuring principle, system, and method of the level of the high-quality integrated development of the Yangtze River Delta

1. Measuring principle

Regional integrated development means in a relatively wide economic range, the administrative unites with clear boundaries to gradually eliminate artificial institutional barriers that obstruct the mobility of resources and factors through reform and opening up, and achieve regional high-quality development through cooperation, opening up, and competition (Liu Zhibiao and Chen Liu, 2018). Facilitating the high-quality integrated development of the Yangtze River Delta means effectively utilizing the developmental function of the regional community and its "accumulative effect" and "diffusing effect", to construct a developmental system of close interconnection, regionally unified markets, reasonable work distribution, innovation and collaboration, convenient transportation, shared information and resources, trade openness, adequate public services, high-quality ecological environment, and coordinating systems (Kong Linngchi and Liu Zhibiao, 2019). The specific conceptions are described here:

(1) Spatial integration

Spatial integration is the significant carrier of regional integrated development. According to theories of new economic geography, the spatial economic process in the regional integrated development is non-monotonous. The economic activity follows the distribution law of "scatter-concentration-diffusion", followed by the "inverted U curve" change of regional gaps. From the perspective of economic development, it is helpful to narrow the economic gap by actively adjusting the spatial structure of regional development, balancing the spatial interaction force between regions, and enhancing the driving effect of the developed regions on the developing regions.

(2) Market integration

Market integration is the micro-foundation of regional integrated development. Market integration is the basic mechanism for eliminating regional economic and non-economic barriers, fair competition conditions, mutual entrance permit, free mobility of production factors, and cross-regional management of enterprise. To promote market integration, it is necessary to build a dynamic and ordered market environment, and to form a united market for all commodities and factors; for example, an integrated market for consumer goods, capital and labor, etc.

(3) Industrial integration

Industrial integration is the strong support for regional integrated development. Industrial integration is done to form a reasonable industrial work division system between regions, which requires maximizing the economies of scale and scope and arranging a rational industrial distribution, avoiding blind industrial expansion and repetition.

(4) Innovation integration

Innovation integration is the endogenous power of regional integrated development. Innovation integration is organizing and integrating resources through the collaborative interaction between enterprises, universities, scientific research institutions, and governments within the innovation system to promote the exchange and sharing of innovative achievements between places within the region and gradually becoming a source of key generic technology, cutting-edge technology, modern engineering technology, and revolutionary innovation.

(5) Transportation integration

Transportation integration is the basic hardware of regional integrated development. The current mission for transportation integration in the Yangtze River Delta is to build a modern comprehensive transportation system, to achieve joint construction and sharing of transportation infrastructure, to form interconnectivity between regions, and to greatly enhance transportation service and management.

(6) Information integration

Information integration is the technological base of regional integrated development. It is helpful to weaken the effect of geographic segmentation on production and consumption by breaking the information blockade, constructing a regional information interactive net, and completing information transmission mechanisms, which will also help to realize cross-regional cooperation, resource integration, value chain construction, etc., and effectively reduce the material and capital input for development and the trade cost for market operations.

(7) Trade integration

Trade integration is the intrinsic requirement of regional integrated development. Reducing or eliminating the international (inter-provincial) trade obstacles is conducive to taking advantage of economic effect and overflow effect, building direct and indirect technological economic relations, and gradually forming a unified international (domestic) market.

(8) Public service integration

Public service integration is the essential requirement of regional integrated development. Public service integration means enhancing administrative coordination so that people are endowed with equal rights of education, health care, cultural service, social security, etc. It also optimizes public service supply, completes the joint construction and sharing mechanism of public service, and promotes the sharing of education resources, cross-regional health care service, interactive development of cultural industry, and interconnection of social security to provide the masses with more sense of acquirement.

(9) Ecological environment integration

Ecological environment integration is the inevitable requirement of regional integrated development. Green growth and ecological civilization help to continuously develop economic and social productive forces and improve production and living quality. The key to promoting ecological environment integration in the Yangtze River Delta is to strengthen the regional environmental protection coordination and strive to promote the implementation of the joint action plan and practical measures.

(10) System integration

System integration is the basic guarantee of regional integrated development. There are huge differences between policies and institutions in different regions. Without a coordinated system and mechanism, scattered administrative power will inevitably lead to various conflicts and contradictions. Fundamentally, integrated regional development requires coordinating regional policies and systems to break down the barriers caused by administrative division and to fundamentally support regional integrated development.

2. Measuring system

Based on this logic and the indicator-selecting principle of being scientific, feasible, comparable, and targeted, an indicator system of the level of regional integrated development containing these ten sub-systems and 40 measurement indexes are established and shown in Table 3.1.

3. Measurements and data source

These indicators of spatial, market, industry, innovation, and trade can reflect the progress of regional integrated development. However, there is a lack of better indicators for transportation, information, public service, and ecological environment. Although "integration" does not equal assimilation or synchronization, regional integrated development is also manifested in the facilitation of regional transportation and information infrastructure, information application, education, health care, culture, social security, expenditure on environmental protection, and the narrowing gap of environmental quality to some extent. Therefore, the chapter adopts the Coefficient of Variation (CV) to analyze the internal diversity of some indexes, i.e., the dispersion degree of the statistics of an indicator. The formula is:

$$CV = \frac{S}{EQ}$$

Therein, standard deviation $S = \sqrt{\frac{\sum_{i=1}^{n}\left(x_{ij} - \overline{x}_j\right)^2}{n}}$, mean value $EQ = \frac{\sum_{i=1}^{n} x_{ij}}{n}$.

Table 3.1 Indicator system of the level of regional integrated development

Sub-system	*Criterion*	*Specific measurement index*
Spatial integration	Regional economic gap	Gini coefficient
	Economic influence	Economic connection
		Accessibility
Market integration	Commodity market integration	Relative price variance of consumer goods
	Factor market integration	Relative price variance of fixed-asset investment
		Relative price variance of staff real average income
Industrial integration	Industrial division	Krugman Specialization Index
	Industrial isomorphism	Structural similarity coefficient
	Industrial cluster	Location quotient
Innovation integration	Innovation input	Percentage of R&D to GDP in industrial enterprises above designated size
		Percentage of R&D staff to the total staff in industrial enterprises above designated size
	Innovation output	Authorized and accepted three domestic patents per capita
		Percentage of volume of transaction in technology market to GDP
	Industry-university-research collaborative innovation	Percentage of funds from enterprise to the expenditure for R&D of institutions and universities
	Cooperation and exchange of innovation achievement	Export technique
		Import technique
Transportation integration	Thickness of transportation network	Thickness of railway network
		Thickness of highway network
Information integration	Informationalized infrastructure	Toll optical cable length per square kilometer
		Number of Internet broadband ports per hundred people
	Information application	Mobile phone penetration rate
		Internet penetration rate
		Numbers of telecom service per capita
Trade integration	Inter-provincial trade	Inter-provincial trade degree of dependence
		Cargo exchange between national railway administrative regions
	International trade	Foreign trade degree of dependence
		Foreign capital degree of dependence
Public service integration	Education	Student/teacher ratio in primary school, middle school, and high school
	Health care	Number of health workers per 10,000 people
		Number of hospital beds per 10,000 people
	Culture	Number of books in public library per capita

Sub-system	*Criterion*	*Specific measurement index*
	Social security	Coverage rate of basic endowment insurance of city and town de jure population
		Coverage rate of basic medical insurance of city and town de jure population
Ecological environment integration	Energy conservation and emission reduction	Electricity consumption per unit of GDP
		Emission of wastewater and solid waste per unit of GDP
	Environmental quality	PM2.5 and PM10
		Frequency of acid rain
Institutional integration	Policy and system coordination	Publishing of plan or agreement
		Discussion and settlement of dispute
		Establishment of decision-making agency

The statistics of the selected indicators are mainly from the State Statistics Bureau, Chinese railway official website, Wind database, Chinese economic and social development statistical database, *China Statistical Yearbook (2018), China Industrial Economic Statistical Yearbook (2017), China Statistical Yearbook on Science and Technology (2017), China Transport Yearbook (2017)*, Statistical Communiqué of the People's Republic of China on the 2018 National Economic and Social Development (Shanghai, Jiangsu, Zhejiang and Anhui), and the annual report on the 2018 national technology market statistics.

Section 3 The process of the high-quality integrated development of the Yangtze River Delta

1. The progress of spatial integrated development in the Yangtze River Delta

The Yangtze River Delta is one of the regions with the top comprehensive economic strength. For example, in 2018, the three provinces and one city in the Yangtze River Delta produced 23.5% of economic aggregate with less than 4% of national land area and 16% of the de jure population. From the perspective of GDP per capita, there are distinct gaps between provinces in the Yangtze River Delta region. In 2018, the GDP per capita in Shanghai reached 120 thousand yuan, in Jiangsu 110 thousand, and in Zhejiang 100 thousand, which all exceeded the national average. However, the number in Anhui is less than 50 thousand yuan, lower than the national average.

As shown in Figure 3.1, based on the Gini coefficient from 2000 to 2018, the differences in the economy of scale within the Yangtze River Delta were narrowed. Further observation indicated that from 2000 to 2012, the Gini coefficient in the region was dropping year by year and the economic gap was gradually shrinking. However, since 2013, the Gini coefficient has risen slightly, and the regional gap has expanded slowly.

As shown in Table 3.2, from the perspective of economic correlation, the economic correlation and economic dependency of Anhui on Jiangsu are much higher

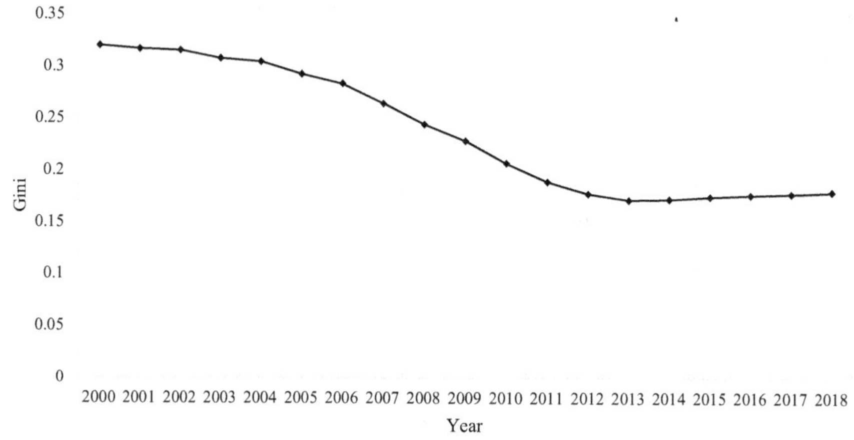

Figure 3.1 The trending of the Gini coefficient in the Yangtze River Delta

Table 3.2 The economic correlation within the Yangtze River Delta in 2018

		Shanghai	*Jiangsu*	*Zhejiang*	*Anhui*
Shanghai	Economic correlation	–	6.9811	4.7506	0.7723
	Dependency	–	55.83%	38.00%	6.18%
Jiangsu	Economic correlation	6.3218	–	12.7537	13.9097
	Dependency	19.17%	–	38.66%	42.17%
Zhejiang	Economic correlation	7.8919	12.7537	–	1.2988
	Dependency	35.96%	58.12%	–	5.92%
Anhui	Economic correlation	0.7723	13.9097	1.3178	–
	Dependency	4.83%	86.94%	8.24%	–

than those of Shanghai and Zhejiang, which means Anhui has not yet deeply integrated into the Yangtze River Delta region. In addition, the economic correlation of Jiangsu, Zhejiang, and Anhui to Shanghai is relatively low, meaning that Shanghai as a leading role is not influential enough.

As shown in Figure 3.2, in terms of accessibility index, the spatial pattern of accessibility in the Yangtze River Delta region is relatively balanced. In 2018, the weighted average travel time in Jiangsu is the shortest, indicating the closest connection with other places in the region. In contrast, Anhui has the longest weighted average travel time, indicating the worst accessibility, but the gap between Jiangsu and Anhui is only 32 minutes.

2. The process of market integrated development in the Yangtze River Delta region

The mobility of commodities and factors mainly depends on the price variance and rate of return. Therefore, the measurement of market integration would usually

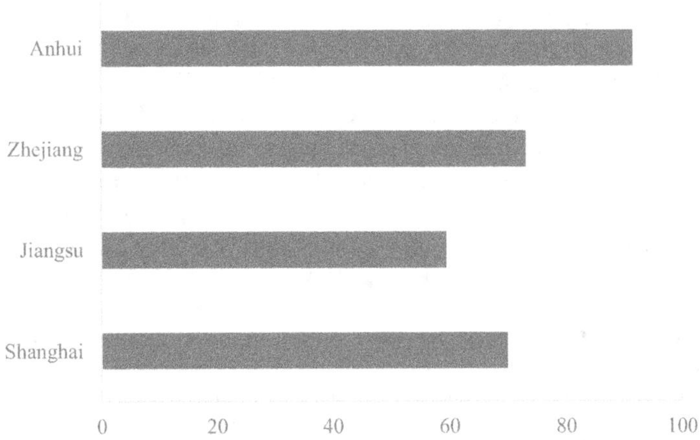

Figure 3.2 The accessibility of the three provinces and one city in the Yangtze River Delta region

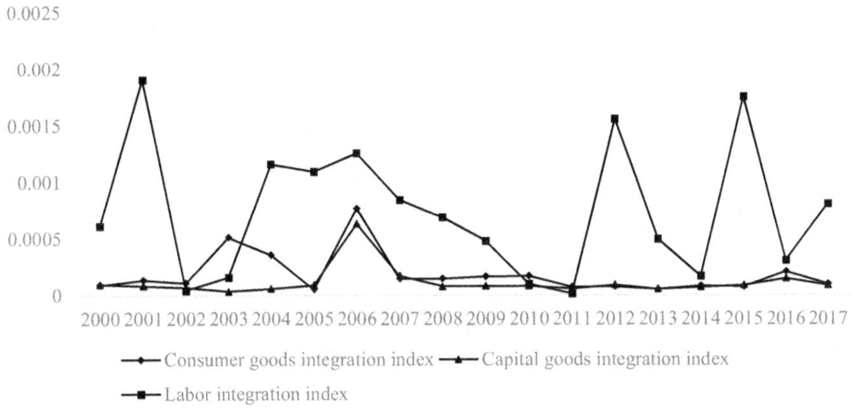

Figure 3.3 The changing trend of market integration index in the Yangtze River Delta region

be relative price variance based on the "law of one price", to see whether the price or (the trend of) rate of return is consistent. This chapter studies the progress of market integration in the Yangtze River Delta from the perspective of the consumer goods market, capital goods market, and labor market.

Figure 3.3 indicates that the market segmentation index of consumer goods and capital goods presents a convergent tendency with a continuously declining fluctuation and has no distinctive difference in its trend. In other words, the market segmentation of consumer goods and capital goods has been gradually reduced, i.e., their market integration tends to be strengthened. Further observation shows a relatively violent fluctuation of relative price variance in the labor market, indicating a less obvious tendency of integration of the labor market in the Yangtze River Delta region. Generally speaking, the segmentation index of the consumer goods market is lower than those of the capital goods market and labor market, i.e., the integration level of the commodity market is better than that of the factor market. It can be seen that, in the high-quality integrated development of the Yangtze River Delta, promoting market integration should pay more attention to market-oriented reform in factor markets; specifically, the reform of market access, household registration system, financial system, fiscal system, investment and financing system, price, listing system, etc., significantly reduce the governmental direct allocation of resources and let the market play a decisive role.

3. The process of industrial integrated development in the Yangtze River Delta region

The industrial structure statistics in 2018 showed that there has been a distinct gradient difference in industrial structure between places in the Yangtze River Delta. In Shanghai, the percentage of the tertiary industry is 40 percentage points higher than the secondary industry, presenting a "tertiary-secondary-primary" industrial structure led by the service sector of the economy. In Jiangsu and Zhejiang, the percentage of tertiary industry is slightly higher than that of the secondary industry, indicating a "tertiary-secondary-primary" industrial structure characterized by an equally important service and secondary sector. In Anhui, the percentage of tertiary industry is slightly lower than that of the secondary industry, forming a "secondary-tertiary-primary" industrial structure, i.e., the secondary industry remains as fuel to economic growth (see Table 3.3). Thus, it can be seen that the industrial development in the Yangtze River Delta regions shows a gradient difference and chronological consistency, which is in favor of industrial integrated development.

As shown in Figure 3.4, the Krugman specialization indexes of the Yangtze River Delta have been slowly rising since 2010, indicating a gradually manifested difference and rationalized division of labor of the industrial structure. Although it is a certain achievement of industrial integrated development, the index remains

Table 3.3 The structural overview and added value gross of the three main industries in the Yangtze River Delta in 2018

Region	*Absolute value (100 million yuan)*				*Industrial structure (%)*			
	Shanghai	*Jiangsu*	*Zhejiang*	*Anhui*	*Shanghai*	*Jiangsu*	*Zhejiang*	*Anhui*
The primary industry	104	4,142	1,967	2,638	0.3	4.5	3.5	8.8
The secondary industry	9,733	41,249	23,506	13,842	29.8	44.5	41.8	46.1
The tertiary industry	22,843	47,205	30,724	13,527	69.9	51.0	54.7	45.1

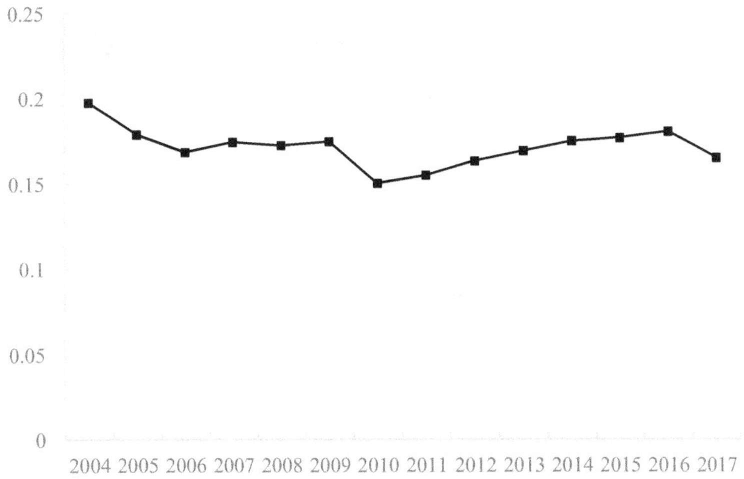

Figure 3.4 The changing trend of the Krugman Specialization Index in the Yangtze River Delta region

Table 3.4 The similarity coefficient of industrial structure in the Yangtze River Delta region in 2017

	Shanghai	*Jiangsu*	*Zhejiang*	*Anhui*
Shanghai		0.9306	0.9405	0.8837
Jiangsu	0.9306		0.9971	0.9902
Zhejiang	0.9405	0.9971		0.9812
Anhui	0.8837	0.9902	0.9812	

around 0.2, indicating a relatively low level of the specialized regional labor division.

From the perspective of the structural similarity coefficient, the similarities between Shanghai and other provinces of the Yangtze River region are relatively low, while those between other provinces such as Jiangsu, Zhejiang, and Anhui are relatively high, causing severe industrial isomorphism and low-level competition (see Table 3.4). Consequently, Yangtze River Delta region has not yet been given full play to the coupling effect. There is still severe blindness in productivity distribution and convergence of industrial structure.

From the location quotient of manufacturing in Table 3.5, it can be seen that the industry with the location quotient above 1 is mainly the high-end manufacturing industries in Shanghai, Jiangsu, and Zhejiang and mid- and low-end manufacturing industries in Anhui. Therefore, the industrial distribution of the Yangtze River region has its advantages and complementarity. Further observation reveals that the competitive industries in the region still present a high overlap ratio. For example, the manufacturing industries with a location quotient above 1 in Zhejiang

Table 3.5 The manufacturing industries with the location quotient above 1 in the Yangtze River Delta regions in 2016

Region	*Industry*
Shanghai	Food manufacturing industry, metal production industry, general equipment manufacturing industry, special equipment manufacturing industry, transportation equipment manufacturing industry, electrical machinery and equipment manufacturing industry, communication device, computer and other electronic equipment manufacturing industry, manufacturing industry of measuring instruments and machinery for cultural activity and office work.
Jiangsu	Textile industry, raw chemical materials and chemical product manufacturing industry, chemical fiber manufacturing industry, metal production industry, general equipment manufacturing industry, special equipment manufacturing industry, electrical machinery and equipment manufacturing industry, communication device, computer and other electronic equipment manufacturing industry, and manufacturing industry of measuring instruments and machinery for cultural activity and office work.
Zhejiang	Textile industry, paper making and paper products industry, chemical fiber manufacturing industry, metal production industry, general equipment manufacturing industry, transportation equipment manufacturing industry, electrical machinery and equipment manufacturing industry, and manufacturing industry of measuring instruments and machinery for cultural activity and office work.
Anhui	Agricultural and sideline food processing industry, beverage processing industry, tobacco processing industry, pharmaceutical industry, non-metallic mineral industry, general equipment manufacturing industry, special equipment manufacturing industry, transportation equipment manufacturing industry, electrical machinery and equipment manufacturing industry.

are almost the same as those in Jiangsu, and those in Jiangsu are the same as those in Shanghai.

From the perspective of the manufacturing industry, promoting integrated development in the Yangtze River Delta requires strengthening the comparative advantages of Shanghai in the food manufacturing industry, special equipment manufacturing industry, transportation equipment manufacturing industry, etc.; those of Jiangsu in the raw chemical materials and chemical product manufacturing industry, communication device, computer and other electronic equipment manufacturing industry, and manufacturing industry of measuring instruments and machinery for cultural activity and office work; those of Zhejiang in the textile industry, paper making and paper products industry, chemical fiber manufacturing industry, general equipment manufacturing industry, and electrical machinery and equipment manufacturing industry; and those of Anhui in the agricultural and sideline food processing industry, beverage processing industry, tobacco processing industry, pharmaceutical industry, and non-metallic mineral industry.

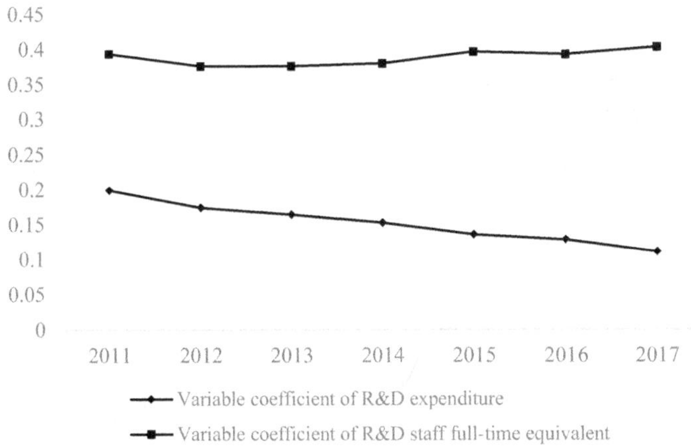

Figure 3.5 The variable coefficient of the innovation input in the Yangtze River Delta region

4. The process of innovation integrated development in the Yangtze River Delta region

In recent years, the investment in R&D of industrial enterprises above the designated size in the Yangtze River Delta region has been increasing rapidly, and its proportion to the GDP has been expanding continuously. From Figure 3.5, we can see that the variable coefficient of the proportion has declined to about 0.1, indicating a shrinking gap in investment between those industrial enterprises. In comparison, the variable coefficient of the proportion of R&D staff full-time equivalent to the overall employees is increasing gradually, indicating a relatively big gap between those enterprises in terms of their investment in R&D staff full-time equivalent with a slowly expanding trend.

The Yangtze River Delta is one of the most innovative regions in China. In 2017, the number of accepted three domestic patents per capita reached 1.2 million in the Yangtze River Delta, and the number of licensed three domestic patents per capita exceeded 570 thousand. The volumes of transactions in the technology market in 2017 exceeded 2 trillion yuan. Figure 3.6 shows that the number of accepted and licensed patents per capita and the variable coefficient of the percentage of volumes of transaction in the technology market to GDP all dramatically decreased, i.e., the regional gap of innovation output in the Yangtze River Delta is shrinking.

The industry-university-research cooperative innovation can be indirectly measured by cash flow. As shown in Figure 3.7, the proportion of enterprise-funded R&D expenditure of institutions and universities in Shanghai, Jiangsu, and Zhejiang before 2007 was far more than that in Anhui. Since 2007, the proportion of enterprise funds in Shanghai has been shrinking, while that of government funds has been rising. In general, the proportion of enterprise-funded R&D expenditure

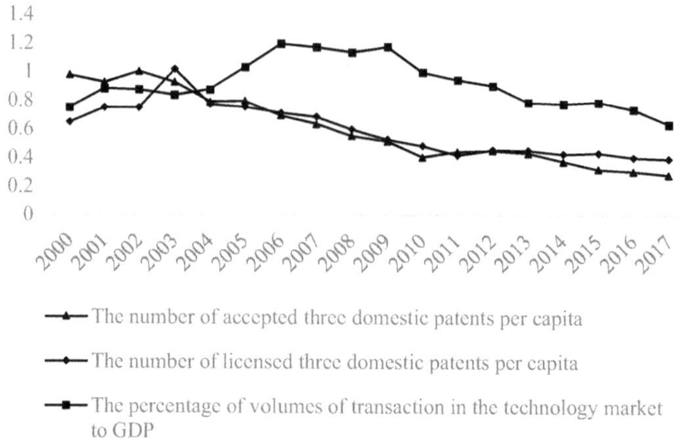

Figure 3.6 The variable coefficient of the innovation output in the Yangtze River Delta region

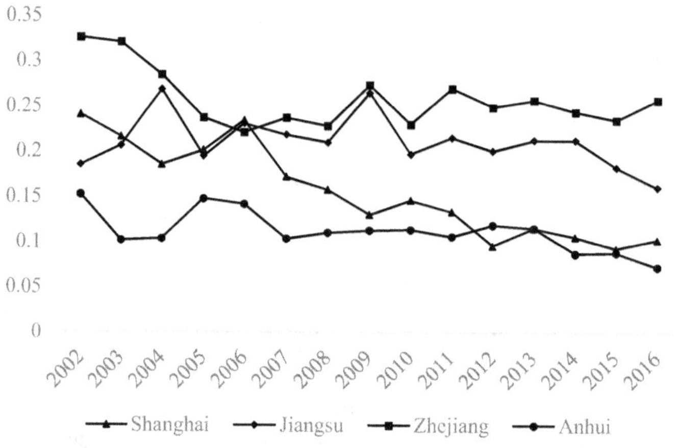

Figure 3.7 The changing trend of the proportion of enterprise-funded R&D expenditure of the institutions and universities in the Yangtze River Delta region

of institutions and universities still has some room for growth, indicating the huge potential of industry-university-research cooperative innovation.

The transaction of scientific and technological achievements is one of the important methods for the cooperation and exchange of innovation achievement, and a significant part of innovation integration. Technology export and absorption can to some extent reflect the polarity and diffusing effect of regional innovation. As shown in Table 3.6, Shanghai and Jiangsu are innovation centers in the Yangtze River Delta region and even the whole country; and their contracts and transactions related to exporting and absorbing techniques are much higher than those in

Table 3.6 The transaction in technology in the Yangtze River Delta in 2017

Region	*Export technique*			*Import technique*		
	Contract number	*Volume of transaction (100 million yuan)*	*Growth rate (%)*	*Contract number*	*Volume of transaction (100 million yuan)*	*Growth rate (%)*
Shanghai	21,223	810.62	3.79	22,661	712.14	64.85
Jiangsu	37,258	773.99	21.77	38,911	919.55	1.54
Zhejiang	13,704	324.73	63.70	18,444	469.87	62.97
Anhui	18,211	249.57	14.81	17,953	270.68	34.22

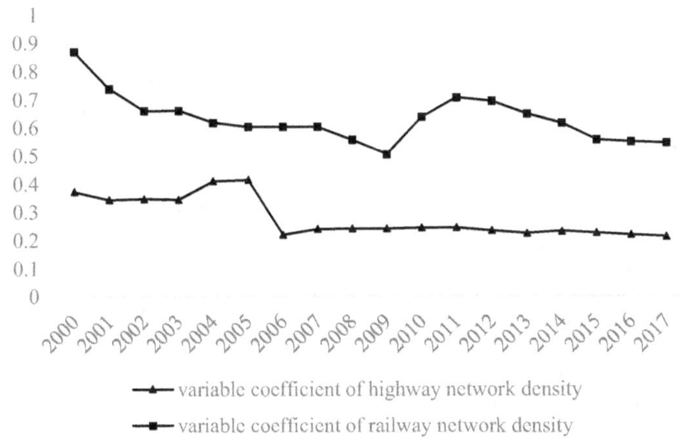

Figure 3.8 The variable coefficient of the transportation network in the Yangtze River Delta region

Zhejiang and Anhui, indicating a strong capacity of innovation cooperation. Zhejiang shows a high growth rate of technology export and absorption, indicating a prominent vitality of innovation cooperation.

5. The process of transportation integrated development in the Yangtze River Delta region

The transportation integration in the Yangtze River Delta region has achieved certain results since 2000. Hub airports, hub ports, railway networks, highway networks, and other regional fast-traffic backbone networks have been established. From Figure 3.8 we can see that the variable coefficient of railway network density presents a declining tendency, while that of highway network density maintains a relatively low level, which means that the networked transport system in the Yangtze River Delta region is continuously improving to better serve the transportation of people and cargo and facilitate further development of the integration of the Yangtze River Delta region. Further observation shows that the variable coefficient of railway network density is much higher than that of highway network density, indicating a huge difference in railway density between the Yangtze River Delta regions. Therefore, it is important to vigorously promote the construction of a national railway channel and accelerate the construction of a crisscross and convenient interurban railway network. The variable coefficient of highway network density remains around 0.2, which means that further improving the transportation capacity of inter-provincial highways in the Yangtze River Delta region requires further penetration for the blocked communication between provinces to raise their accessibility.

6. The process of information integrated development in the Yangtze River Delta region

Facilitating the coordinated development of information infrastructure and information resource sharing is significant for higher-quality integrated development in the Yangtze River Delta region. Figure 3.9 demonstrates that the internal difference between information infrastructure and information application in the Yangtze River Delta region keeps narrowing, providing technical support and leading to the improvement of information integration. It is worth noticing that the upgrade and coordinated arrangement of information infrastructure can set the stage for information integration, but the more important thing is to seize the industrial opportunity brought about by the Internet of things, cloud computing, mobile communication, and other emerging information technologies, innovatively build an industrial internet platform, clarify the focus, complement each other with their advantages, cooperate with a due division of labor, pool the wisdom and efforts of everyone, and promote the cross-regional distributed production and operation based on data. It is also necessary to push the sharing of administrative data, vigorously promote the development of social information synergy and integration, and

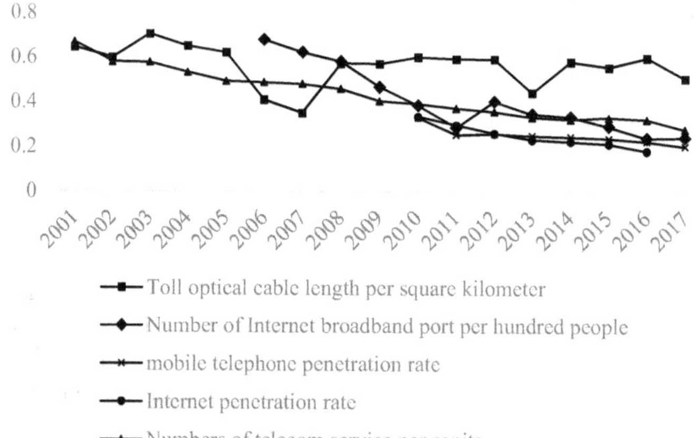

Figure 3.9 The variable coefficient of the informationalized development in the Yangtze River Delta region

form an overall connected information application in terms of people's livelihoods, shipping and transportation, urban safety, etc.; for example, strengthening the information integration of health care and social insurance, the information sharing of environmental governance, and transportation service intellectualization.

7. The process of trade integrated development in the Yangtze River Delta region

The provincial trade degree of dependence of Shanghai and Zhejiang is much higher than those of Jiangsu and Anhui, indicating a higher level of inter-provincial trade openness in Shanghai and Jiangsu (see Figure 3.10). Therefore, it is understandable for Jiangsu and Anhui to encourage the development of similar local industries, but they should be cautious about protective measures that limit the entrance of products from other provinces or preempt local products, which would cause severe regional protectionism and market blocks and sabotage trade contacts and integration in the Yangtze River Delta region.

From Table 3.7 we can see that Jiangsu, Zhejiang, and Anhui all have a high proportion of internal delivery numbers, indicating an autarchy in a relatively closed situation by the government, which weakened inter-provincial trade.

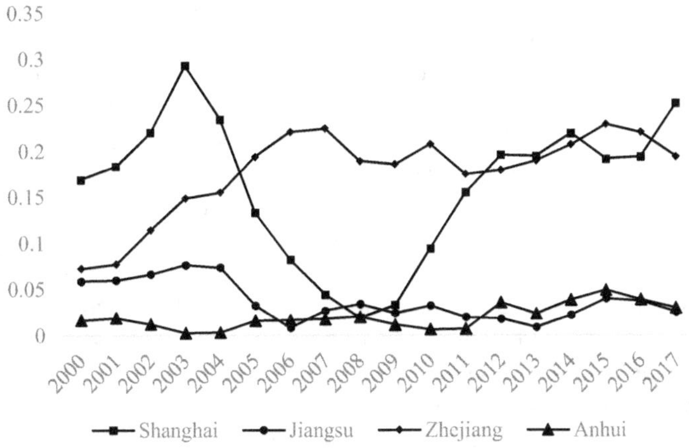

Figure 3.10 The changing trend of provincial trade degree of dependence in the Yangtze River Delta

Table 3.7 Cargo exchange between administrative regions of national railway in 2016

To From	*Shanghai*	*Jiangsu*	*Zhejiang*	*Anhui*	*National total*
Total	737	7,354	3,836	8,624	
Shanghai	3	15	14	12	444
Jiangsu	49	816	34	448	5,335
Zhejiang	50	26	1,822	20	3,219
Anhui	36	1,686	317	5,221	9,263

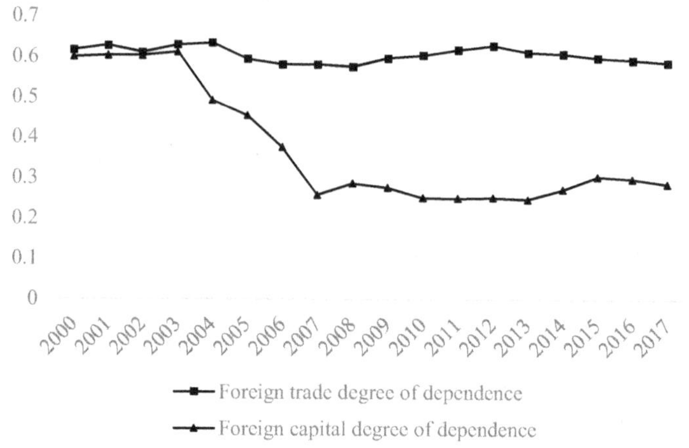

Figure 3.11 The variable coefficient of the international trade in the Yangtze River Delta region

International trade integration is a vital means of relieving regional economic competition and sharing global markets. Figure 3.11 shows that there is a huge gap between the cities within the Yangtze River Delta regarding foreign trade degree of dependence; i.e., their developmental levels of foreign trade show big differences. The main reasons lie in the explosive growth of the foreign trade in Suzhou, Zhejiang, and Shanghai since the reform and opening up, leading to an aggregation of highly exteriorized industries and acceleration of these places changing into a "world factory" and "international manufacturing base", and an objectively enlarged gap between them and Anhui. In the current stage, the focus of promoting trade integration in the Yangtze River Delta is to build a value chain division system centered on itself, allocating Suzhou, Zhejiang, and Shanghai to different links of the value chain so they can jointly participate in global competition.

Further observation of Figure 3.11 reveals a relatively low difference in foreign trade degrees of dependence within the Yangtze River Delta region; i.e., the regional distribution of foreign direct investment is relatively balanced. It means that on the one hand, the differences in investment environment are shrinking; on the other hand, governments have tended to be in agreement in terms of adopting policy means like tax preference, land, or industrial subsidy for investment promotion. The promotion of the economic integrated development in the Yangtze River Delta region is conducive to avoiding the herd behavior of rushing to short-period projects and the vicious competition for limited market and resources.

8. The process of public service integrated development in the Yangtze River Delta region

As shown in Figure 3.12, the internal differences in education and health care within the Yangtze River Delta region are slowly shrinking. The variable

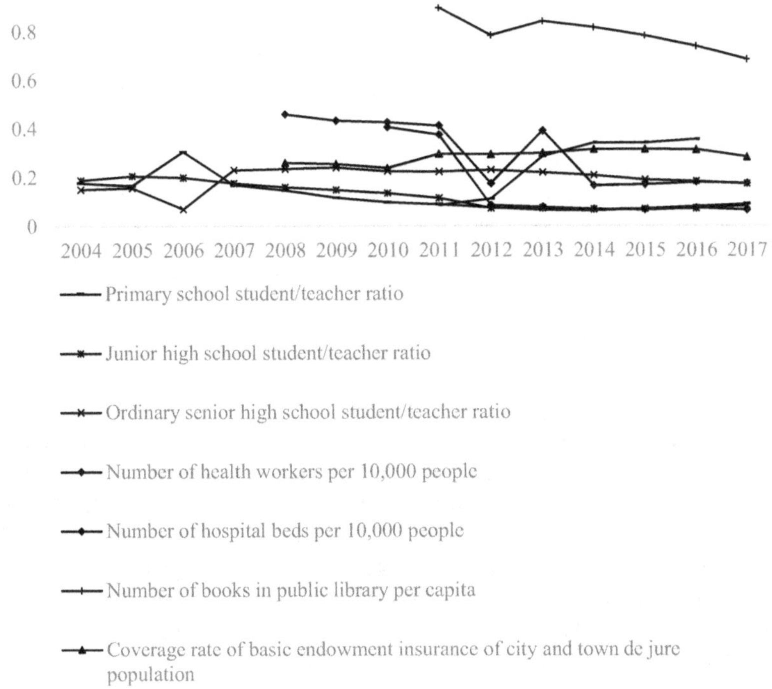

Figure 3.12 The variable coefficient of the public service in the Yangtze River Delta region

coefficients of the coverage rate of endowment insurance and basic medical insurance of the urban de jure population show a distinct increase, indicating an expansion of internal gaps in social insurance. In the future, the interconnection of social insurance within the Yangtze River Delta region should be strengthened, and the convenience of cross-regional social insurance services should be raised. In addition, the variable coefficient of the number of books in public libraries per capita is distinctly higher than other indexes, indicating a relatively large but narrowing internal gap of cultural infrastructure.

9. The process of ecological environment integrated development in the Yangtze River Delta region

With its thriving industries and delicate ecological environment, this aspect becomes the weak link of high-quality integrated development in the Yangtze River Delta region. As Table 3.7 indicates, in 2017, the emission of wastewater per unit of GDP in Shanghai, the electricity consumption and emission of solid waste per unit of GDP in Jiangsu, the electricity consumption and emission of wastewater per unit of GDP in Zhejiang, and the electricity consumption, emission of wastewater, and solid waste per unit of GDP in Anhui were all relatively high. Further

Table 3.8 The echo-environmental indexes in the Yangtze River Delta region

Item	*Shanghai*	*Jiangsu*	*Zhejiang*	*Anhui*
Electricity consumption per unit of GDP (KWh/10 thousand yuan)	498.48	676.37	809.96	711.01
Emission of wastewater per unit of GDP (ten thousand ton/100 million yuan)	6.92	6.70	8.77	8.65
Emission of solid waste per unit of GDP (ten thousand ton/100 million yuan)	0.05	0.14	0.09	0.44
Annual average density of PM2.5 (microgram/cubic meter)	39	49	35	56
Annual average density of PM10 (microgram/cubic meter)	55	81	57	88
Frequency of acid rain (%)	47.6	15.6	62.6	7.4

observation has found that in 2007, the annual average density of PM2.5 and PM10 in both Jiangsu and Anhui were higher than the second level in the Ambient Air Quality Standards (National Standard GB 3095–2012), indicating relatively severe atmospheric pollution.[1] The air quality in Shanghai and Zhejiang is better than Jiangsu and Anhui, but their annual average densities of PM2.5 were also slightly higher than the second level in the Ambient Air Quality Standards (National Standard GB 3095–2012). The frequency of acid rain in Shanghai and Zhejiang were also much higher than those in Jiangsu and Anhui. Therefore, the air quality levels in Shanghai and Zhejiang were not promising, either.

10. The process of system integrated development in the Yangtze River Delta region

The appeal and action of the masses for integrated development has a long history because of the developed economy, geographical and consanguineous closeness, and cultural connection in the Yangtze River Delta region. In 1982, the Shanghai Economic Zone founded by the State Council became the first concept of the Yangtze River Delta economic area. In 1992, the local governments in the region established a joint conference on urban economic cooperation; and in June the same year, the State Council held a forum for planning for the Yangtze River Delta region and areas along the Yangtze River, clarifying the range of the Yangtze River Delta. In 1997, the Forum for the Coordination of Urban Economy in the Yangtze River Delta Region was founded, which changed from biennial to once a year in 2004. Since the 21st century, the construction of the integrated development mechanism in the Yangtze River Delta has upgraded from inter-city fellowship activities to an all-around practical cooperation and strategic collaboration in Shanghai, Suzhou, and Zhejiang, with rising levels of regional coordination and improving systems of the Forum for the Coordination of Urban Economy. In 2001, Shanghai, Suzhou, and Zhejiang launched the "forum for Shanghai-Suzhou-Zhejiang economic cooperation and development", created by the executive vice governors and mayor. In 2004, the Shanghai-Jiangsu-Zhejiang Major Leader's Forum marked the integration of the Yangtze River Delta region rising to provincial level. In 2008, the participation of Anhui marked the expansion of Yangtze River Delta integration to Anhui Province. After years of efforts, the Yangtze River Delta cooperation at the governmental level has formed a provincial governmental cooperation mechanism with communications of senior leaders, missions clarified at forums, coordination through liaison teams, and pushes for implementation by task forces. Since 2011, the Yangtze River Delta region has successively signed *Agreement on Launching Arbitration of Personnel Dispute and Work Communication, Emergent Joint Work Program of the Environmental Pollution Dispute Settlement in the Yangtze River Delta, General Framework of Compensation for Water Ecology in the Yangtze River Delta, Framework of Judicial Cooperation in the Yangtze River Delta, Framework Agreement on Political and Legal Collaborative Communication in the Yangtze River Delta, Cooperation Agreement on the Labor Security Supervision in the Pan-Yangtze River Delta*, etc. to continuously complete the mechanism of collaboration and dispute settlement.

In order to further perfect the normal and long-acting system and mechanism, the Regional Cooperation Office of the Yangtze River Delta was officially established in February 2018. It researched and formulated the *Action Plan for Integrated Development in the Yangtze River Delta (2018–2020)* and has been expanding the regional cooperation. In April 2018, General Secretary Xi made a significant instruction on promoting integrated development in the Yangtze River Delta, which clarified the goal of "higher-quality integrated development", the path of "Shanghai playing its leading role, while Jiangsu, Zhejiang and Anhui making full use of their advantages", the key guarantee of "being cohered for implementation", and pointed out the direction for cooperation and development in the Yangtze River Delta in the new era. In December 2018, at the opening ceremony of the first China International Import Expo, General Secretary Xi announced in his speech that:

> we will support integrated development of the Yangtze River Delta region. We will make it a national strategy and implement our new development philosophy in real earnest. We will build a modern economic system, and adopt higher standards for reform and opening up. The region will develop in tandem with the Belt and Road Initiative, the Beijing-Tianjin-Hebei coordinated development area, the Yangtze River Economic Belt and the Guangdong-Hong Kong-Macao Greater Bay Area, and will help improve the overall layout of China's reform and opening up.

In March 2019, Prime Minister Li Keqiang brought up in a government work report that integrated development of the Yangtze River Delta region should be made a national strategy by formulating and implementing an overall plan. The integrated development in the region has met the historic opportunity to enter a brand-new stage.

The power that may really distort integration in the long run comes down to the institutional obstacles. The construction of a cross-regional coordination mechanism still faces the empirical challenges of policy matching, legislation, capital, and other safeguard mechanisms. In the process of economic transition in China, the "non-balanced strategies" conventionally adopted by either central or local government are in essence creating policy differences, i.e., a policy discrimination that currently hinders integrated development between regions in China (Zhibiao and Liu, 2018).

Section 4 The characteristics and problems of the high-quality integrated development of the Yangtze River Delta

These analyses indicate a narrowing gap between regions in the Yangtze River Delta, more dynamic economic relations, a raised level of industrial division and cooperation and market integration, a distinctively strengthened scientific and technological innovation capacity, improved infrastructure and public service, and facilitating system and mechanism. However, there are still some in-depth problems in the process of further integration left to be solved (Linngchi and Zhibiao, 2018).

First, Shanghai as the leader is not strong enough to fully integrate Anhui into the Yangtze River Delta region. Theoretically, Shanghai plays the leading role in driving the economic development of the less developed places. However, in practice, the "polarization effect" of Shanghai's economy is far greater than its "spillover effect". In terms of the intensity index of economic relation, the value of Jiangsu, Zhejiang, and Anhui to Shanghai are all relatively low, and in terms of the accessibility index, Jiangsu is better than Shanghai. Therefore, Shanghai has not yet presented enough diffusion effect in the leading role. Moreover, Anhui is not yet fully integrated into the Yangtze River Delta region because it has a weak economic connection to Shanghai and Zhejiang, the worst traffic accessibility, and backward values of most indexes of high-quality integrated development.

Second, the integrated development of the factor market falls behind the commodity market. From the perspective of the market segmentation index, the value of the consumer market in the Yangtze River Delta region is lower than that of the capital goods and labor market, which means the integration of the commodity market is better than the factor market. The severe fluctuation of the relative price variance in the labor market especially indicates unstable development with constant adjustment. Labor market integration can promote the optimization and reorganization of labor factors through aggregation and diffusion of the regional labor force, which is significant for regional integrated development. The key to accelerating the labor market integration in the Yangtze River Delta is to innovate the operational mechanism of the labor market, especially to abolish the household registration system that restricts labor mobility and the unequal public welfare systems, to deepen the trans-regional service of education, health care, elderly care, and other public service institutions for cross-regional free mobility of the labor force, and to achieve coordination of the labor force and spatial distribution of production.

Third, without an overall coupling effect, there is still a high overlap ratio of competitive industries. Based on the Krugman Specialization index, the differences in industrial structure in the Yangtze River Delta region has gradually emerged; the specialized division of labor in industrial structure between regions has become rationalized, and the industrial integration has made some progress. However, the indexes are on the low side, indicating a relatively low level of specialized division of labor. Based on the index of structural similarity coefficient, there is still a prominent convergence of industrial structure in the Yangtze River Delta region, especially between Jiangsu, Zhejiang, and Anhui, indicating an intense low-level homogeneous competition. From the perspective of the location quotient, the industrial distributions in the Yangtze River Delta region, although highly overlapped in terms of competitive industries, are complementary with their respective advantages. The manufacturing industries with the location quotient above 1 in Zhejiang are almost the same as those in Jiangsu, and those in Jiangsu are the same as those in Shanghai.

Fourth, there is an expanding gap between regions in terms of investment in innovative talent and huge potential for industry-university-research cooperative innovation. Based on the variable coefficient of the ratio of R&D staff in the industrial enterprises above the designated size, we can see a gradually expanding gap between regions regarding the investment in innovative talents. From the perspective of capital transactions, the ratio of enterprise funded R&D expenditure in institutions and universities is not high, indicating a huge potential of industry-university-research cooperative innovation. In the future, the Yangtze River Delta region, based on the thread of deepening innovation-driven development and the means of establishing a regional technology transfer system and joint constructing and sharing of innovation resource, accelerates the network construction of regional collaborative innovation and makes the Yangtze River Delta a globally influential scientific and technological innovation power and industrial power.

Fifth, the density of railway network varies in different regions, so the trans-provincial "dead ends" need to be connected urgently. The variable coefficient of the railway network density is much higher than that of the highway network, indicating a huge difference of railway density between regions in the Yangtze River Delta. Although the variable coefficient of highway network density remains at a relatively low level, it is noticeable that the transportation integration of the Yangtze River Delta requires not only the quantitative change at the surface, but also the connection between provinces to promote the inter-provincial accessibility and the construction of infrastructures, such as railway, highway, port and shipping, and airport, etc., to optimize the regional resource allocation and build an interconnected, cooperative, and service sharing modern comprehensive transportation system.

Sixth, the development of social information collaboration and integration is relatively low. Based on the variable coefficient, the internal differences of the construction of information infrastructure and the information application in the Yangtze River Delta region are constantly reducing, technically supporting and guiding the improvement of the level of information integration. However, further facilitation is required concerning opening and sharing of administrative data, fully connected information application in the areas of people's livelihoods, shipping and transportation, urban security, etc.; for example, strengthening the information integration of health care and social insurance, information sharing of environmental protection, and intelligentized transportation service.

Seventh, low inter-provincial trade intensity and big differences between regions. Based on the inter-provincial trade degree of dependence, Jiangsu and Anhui should pay more attention to avoiding regional protectionism and market blockade and promote trade contacts and integration. From the perspective of cargo exchange between national railway administrative regions, the local governments of Suzhou, Zhejiang, and Shanghai pursued self-sufficiency and lowered inter-provincial trade intensity under relatively closed conditions. From the perspective of foreign trade degree of dependence, the relatively big gap within the region means that a value chain division system centered on itself should be established, in order to rationally allocate Suzhou, Zhejiang, and Anhui to different links of the global value chain and jointly participate in the international industry competition. From the perspective of the foreign capital degree of dependence, the distribution of places with foreign direct investment is relatively balanced. Local governments should avoid vicious competition for limited markets and resources.

Eighth, the internal gap of social insurance is expanding, and that of cultural infrastructure is enormous. From the increasing variable coefficient of the coverage rate of endowment insurance and basic medical insurance of the urban de jure population, we can see an increasing internal gap in social insurance between regions in the Yangtze River Delta. In the future, the interconnection of social insurance should be guaranteed to facilitate the cross-regional service of social insurance. In addition, the variable coefficient of the number of books in public libraries per capita is distinctly higher than other indexes, indicating a relatively big but narrowing internal gap of cultural infrastructure.

Ninth, the ecological environment is relatively delicate, which is a weak link in high-quality integrated development. The indexes of electricity consumption per unit of GDP, emission of wastewater and solid waste per unit of GDP, PM2.5 and PM10, and frequency of acid rain indicate that the environmental situation in the Yangtze River Delta is not optimistic. In the future, the integrated development in the Yangtze River Delta should pay more attention to ecology, strengthen protection of the ecosystem and eco-space, form a virtuous cycle of protection and exploitation, facilitate collaborative prevention and control of atmospheric pollution, enhance the synergetic supervision and management of environment, perfect the cooperative mechanism of environmental protection, research and set up a pluralist mechanism for ecological compensation, raise the supply capacity of high-quality ecological products, and build a natural ecology, human settlement, and regional landscape that matches the world-class city cluster.

Tenth, with the deepening regional cooperation, the system and mechanism are defective. The main force that may constantly twist the process of integration is the systematic obstacle. Over the years of endeavor, the construction of cross-regional collaborative mechanisms in the Yangtze River Delta has achieved remarkable results but still faces practical challenges in imperfect safeguard mechanisms, such as matching policies, legislation and funding, and interest coordination mechanisms. The regional differentiation caused by the regional policies led by central government and local developmental policies is the main factor of non-integrated structure formed by the Chinese system.

Section 5 Basic strategies of facilitating the high-quality integrated development of the Yangtze River Delta

In the process of promoting higher-quality integrated development, the urgent endogenous demands for achieving coordinated, orderly, and sustainable development are to reduce the regional segmentation caused by administrative barriers to the utmost extent, decrease the vicious competition caused by regional benefit protection, the problem of inefficient development and environmental deterioration, objectively coordinate the economic policies of each member, and reach a relatively fair state of regional interest allocation through reasonable mechanisms of interest sharing and compensation.

1. Shanghai plays its leading role, while Jiangsu, Zhejiang, and Anhui make full use of their advantages

Under the condition of promoting the higher-quality integrated development, Shanghai and other places no longer have a simple center-periphery relation where others integrate into Shanghai or Shanghai influences them. It becomes a cooperative, equal, and synergetic relationship, focusing on engagement, resource integration, constantly promoting function layout interaction, and forming a spatial pattern with rational labor division, complementary advantages, and characteristics of each part. Shanghai should voluntarily reduce general labor-intensive high-energy-consumptive manufacturing industries and focus on the development of a modern service economy. By accelerating the construction of a modern industrial system focused on a service industry and investing in a modern service industry and strategic emerging industries, Shanghai can keep strengthening its urban functions like service, management, gathering, and distribution and innovation. Along with the advantage of a developed economy, encouraging enterprises transfer their production chains to Suzhou, Zhejiang, and Anhui, and then form a reasonable spatial arrangement and industrial chain, making the Yangtze River Delta a region of comprehensively low transaction costs and manufacturing costs. On this basis, the coordinated development of the manufacturing cluster and service cluster will obscure administrative boundaries and promote the main mechanism of integrated development in the Yangtze River Delta in a wider spatial range. Moreover, Shanghai's science and technology platform, financial platform, and human resource platform are gradually open to other regions, setting the stage for their acceptance and allocation of global resources.

2. Transition of local governmental function and construction of regional common market

The construction of the regional common market requires the region to unify policies, reduce trade cost for factor mobility, expand configuration space for enterprise, and achieve mutual product admittance, free mobility of production factors, and cross-regional operation of enterprises. There is a saying that "the only one who can fix the problem is the one who created the problem". The non-integrated development of the market is largely related to the government, so the construction of a regional common market also depends on the government. Three measures are used to construct the regional common market. First, the construction of the regional common market requires breaking regional blockage and market segmentation, which means implementing government reform; for instance, abolishing the administrative powers that hinder the construction of the common market so the economic-oriented government will change to public service-oriented, transforming governmental functions into providing public service, social administration, maintenance of social order, etc., eliminating the obstacles to the system and mechanism that lead to market non-integration, and giving the market a decisive role for reasonable resource allocation (Kong Lingchi, 2019). Second, the construction of the regional common market requires reducing interference in the operating activities of economic entities, giving "national treatment" to all the economic entities, and striving to form a policy-undifferentiated favorable external environment. Moreover, it demands promoting the reform of the diversified ownership at a deeper level and urges local governments to reduce or even cancel their restrictions on the ownership of enterprises. As a result, the actions of enterprises (for example, where they should go, where their products should go, and where their production factors are from) are mainly led by the market rather than the administration. Third, releasing some administrative power through agreements achieves the coordination for integration. For example, in the basic public factor market like talent, technology, credit investigation, transportation, communication, ecological protection, etc., unifies system, standards, and ports constructed through regional coordination can accelerate the connection and integration of economic policies.

3. Build a regional open market and opening up on all fronts

Under the backdrop of higher-quality integrated development in the Yangtze River Delta, the construction of regional open market means opening up on all fronts and cooperating at a higher level and wider range. First, the focus of opening to foreign capital should be changed from the manufacturing industry to service industry, introduce the regional headquarter, R&D institution, and marketing center of multinational corporations, and construct a modern industrial system centered on the service industry. The cooperation between Shanghai and Suzhou/Zhejiang/Anhui should be strengthened by making Shanghai a taker or transfer station of the outsourcing business of high-end services, while Suzhou/Zhejiang/Anhui voluntarily carries on some procedures or links; for example, the software industry and software outsourcing in Nanjing, Jiangsu. Second, the transition from the introduction of foreign capital and encouragement of exportation to a two-way opening up requires the construction of a value chain division system based on itself by the Yangtze River Delta, facing the whole world and countries along the "Belt and Road". In the process, Shanghai and other center cities will probably become the cluster of enterprise headquarters. By establishing industrial parks along the "Belt and Road", the traditional manufacturing functions of the Yangtze River Delta will be transferred to other countries. In addition, encouraging the external foreign direct investment of the enterprises in the Yangtze River Delta region by means of mergers and acquisitions or building R&D centers abroad will take full advantage of the international scientific and technological resources and enhance the capability of independent innovation. Third, the focus changes from opening to other countries to opening to the domestic market. The high-quality integrated development in the Yangtze River Delta should be fully combined with the construction of Yangtze River Economic belt so the enterprises in the region will be transferred to upper-middle reaches, avoiding the excessive transfer of related industries to Southeast Asia and achieving the spillover effect.

4. Cooperate and support the construction of free trade area; duplicate and promote the reform and innovation experience

The purpose of China (Shanghai) Pilot Free Trade Zone is to explore new approaches and accumulate experiences for the overall reform and expansion of opening up. With the development of institutional innovation in the Shanghai free trade zone and the accumulation of duplicate experiences, other cities will be cooperating, sharing opportunities, and supporting the construction of free trade zones, so that the function of the Yangtze River Delta national strategic platform will be raised. The recent pilot reform of the regional customers' clearance integration, launched by the General Administration of Customs, and the innovation achievements of customs supervision will be first promoted and applied in the Yangtze River Economic Belt and other regions. In the meantime, the duplication and promotion of Shanghai's free trade zone can be explored through different approaches, which means that other cities do not have to become a "free trade zone" before they can adopt its policies; they can practice first to lay a solid foundation. For example, the Singapore-China Cooperation financial innovation pilot zone in Suzhou Industrial Park allows the enterprises in the park to seek finances and loans and issue bonds in RMB in Singapore; the Kunshan Pilot Zone will make a breakthrough in terms of deepening cross-strait industrial cooperation and innovating mechanisms through in-depth cooperation in the service industry and financial industry. Similar innovative platforms in all the cities in the future should bear the function of regional coordinated development, especially in terms of negative list management and opening up the service industry. They should draw on the experience of free trade zones: tear down policy barriers and promote in-depth integration.

5. Give weight to the enterprises and set unified competition rules

The full market competition is the micro-foundation for the high-quality integrated development in the Yangtze River Delta. First, enterprises are the main actor in the market economy, so their cross-regional development will automatically cause the endogenous growth of economic integration. With the basis of a growing domestic demand, the enterprises in the Yangtze River Delta should be supported and encouraged to conduct mergers and acquisitions, achieve industrial cooperation and coordination, and take advantage of the market structure effect and competition synergetic effect. Second, the implementation of industrial policies should be adjusted to promote the economic transaction from "developmental competition" to "fair competition", i.e., lateral, functional, and competitive industrial policies will gradually replace the preferential ones, so that all economic entities will receive the "national treatment" and equal policies in terms of industrial entry barrier, tax, fiscal subsidy, administrative supervision, government procurement, etc. A good external environment without policy differentiation will be formed through information openness and transparency. In addition, it is also important to set up unified competition rules, gradually revise or abolish local policies or regulations that contradict integration, coordinate industrial policies and economic development strategies, duplicate and promote the successful pilot national policies, such as those on free trade areas and scientific and technological innovation centers, and proactively adapt to the needs for the regional economic integration.

6. Build a regional linkage mechanism and broaden cooperation field

A linkage mechanism of innovation, transportation, information, and pollution prevention and control should be established in the Yangtze River Delta region. First, we need to actively promote the innovative cooperation of institutions that research advanced technologies, the joint construction and sharing of large-scale scientific instrument and equipment, and the interconnection of innovative public service platforms. Relying on the leading enterprises, which would play a coordinating role in the link of government, industry, universities, research institutions and consumers, and in the construction of innovative centers of manufacturing industry in each region, a batch of cross-regional and cross-industry research institutions will be founded. For example, enterprises in Zhejiang and Anhui cooperate with scientific research institutions in Shanghai and Jiangsu to transform their research into productivity. Second, the linkage mechanism requires constructing an efficient and convenient comprehensive three-dimensional transportation network to drive and support the integrated development of the Yangtze River Delta region, and to further improve the capacity of the multi-modal system of collecting and distributing. It also needs to strengthen the connection between each port, producing place and consumer markets, the linkage between transportation infrastructure and major ports, and joining with air transportation. To form a modern system of collecting and distributing with short-haul distance, low cost and high efficiency, intelligent transportation should be significantly developed in the linkage mechanism. Third, to build an intangible internet platform in the tangible enclaves. With the advanced experience of Jiangyin-Jingjiang Industrial Park and the substantial economy in enclaves, internet platforms can be built to develop the "Jiangsu manufacturing industry + Internet" and "Zhejiang Internet + manufacturing industry". Fourth, the cooperation of ecological environmental protection and resource-saving between regions should be strengthened; for example, establishing a joint prevention and control mechanism for pollution and setting up a hierarchical layout based on regional economic development levels and environmental pollution situation. A fund for an ecological environment in the Yangtze River Delta should be set up as a compensation mechanism for the construction of regional ecological function areas.

7. Put specific projects into effect and promote cooperative coordination

By learning from the pragmatic spirit of the Europeans, we need to start cooperative coordination from the specific projects and avoid abstract discussions for a long time in a wide range. The scheme of reintegrating Europe, brought up by then-French Foreign Minister Schuman, stood out among numerous schemes because it did not extensively discuss the problem of a unified European market in the future, but focused on explicit fields like coal, steel, and atomic energy. It formulated a feasible plan to unify the European market to establish a common market in France, Germany, Italy, Belgium, Holland, and Luxembourg without any tariff, quota, or barriers to entry so their products could be produced and freely mobile. Similarly, the Yangtze River Delta region also needs to achieve their joint cooperation through certain specific projects, gradually break regional administrative barriers in market-oriented activities, and develop the mechanisms of self-union, self-coordination, and self-development of business entities. The specific joint strategic ideas and measures can be infrastructures; for example, the connection of airports and ports; or a significant scientific and technological cooperative research, like new-energy automobiles and the integration of charging facilities.

It is also necessary to strengthen the top-level design and explore a better decision-making mechanism for cross-regional collaboration. The cross-governmental cooperation in the Yangtze River Delta remains at a negotiation level without an overall top-level design or plan to push it forward, so it has been hindered in terms of implementation and specific actions, leaving no room for close cross-regional cooperation. Therefore, first, aiming at serving the big picture of national development and based on the overall development and long-term interests of the Yangtze River Delta, it is important to form a common code of conduct, deepen the full connection of all kinds of projects, and make full use of their planning and leading roles in regional integration. Second, it should be considered to build a vertical functional management mode at the national level with ministers and commissions and agencies as the main body, to formulate a strategy for regional development as its macro-environment and policy orientation, to set up effective incentive mechanisms for the cooperation between local governments, and to solve the problem of local administrative barriers and segmentation in the process of the integrated development in the Yangtze River Delta from a higher level. In addition, a joint handling mechanism is required to coordinate the conflict and dispute in the process of cooperation between local governments, ensure the normal operation of economic orders, promote the extension of room for benefits, ease the conflict of interests between regions, and maintain a balance of interests.

Note

1 The second level in the Ambient Air Quality Standards (National Standard GB 3095–2012): 35 microgram/cubic meter for PM2.5, 70 microgram/cubic meter for PM10.

References

Hou Binhui, Liu Zhibiao, Yue Zhonggang. Social Network Analysis on the Process of Economic Integration in the Yangtze River Delta. China Soft Science, 2009 (12).

R. Estrada, M. Arturo. The Global Dimension of the Regional Integration Model (GDRI-Model). Modern Economy, 2011 (3).

Zeng Gang, Wang Fenglong. Evaluation and Promotion Strategies of Urban Integration Development Capability in the Yangtze River Delta Region. Reform, 2018 (12).

Gu Haibing, Zhang Min. An Analysis of Regional Economic Integration Index Based on the Yangtze River Delta City Cluster. Journal of Renmin University of China, 2017 (5).

Kong Lingchi. Promoting the Higher-quality Integrated Development in the Yangtze River Delta Based on the Modern Market System (2019). Economic Daily, 2019–02–15. http://views.ce.cn/view/ent/201902/15/t20190215_31480520.shtml

Kong Lingchi. Boosting the Integration in the Yangtze River Delta through Multi-linkage. Economic Daily, 2019–05–10 (12).

Kong Linngchi, Liu Zhibiao. Report on the Development Level of the Higher-quality Integrated Development in the Yangtze River Delta (2018). Guangming Daily, 2019–04–08 (16).

Zhou Liqun, Xia Liangke. Measurement and Comparison of the Regional Economic Integration: Evidence from Beijing-Tianjin-Hebei Region, the Yangtze River Delta Region and the Pearl River Delta Region. Jianghai Academic Journal, 2010 (7).

Li Peixin, Zhang Xueliang. Research on the Spatial Structure Characteristics and Spatial Integrated Development. Journal of Anhui University (Philosophy and Social Sciences Edition), 2019 (3).

Li Shiqi, Zhu Pingfang. Findings and Suggestions from the New Exploration in the Evaluation of Yangtze River Delta Integration. Nanjing Journal of Social Sciences, 2017 (7).

Zhang Xueliang, Li Lixia. Solving the Dilemma in the Industrial Integrated Development in the Yangtze River Delta. Reform, 2018 (12).

Liu Zhibiao. The Institutional Foundation of the High-quality Integrated Development of the Yangtze River Delta. Frontiers, 2019 (3).

Liu Zhibiao, Kong Lingchi. Characteristics, Problems and Basic Strategies of the Integrated Development in the Yangtze River Delta Region. Journal of Anhui University (Philosophy and Social Sciences Edition), 2019 (5).

Liu Zhibiao, Chen Liu. The Demonstrative Mechanism and Driving Mechanism of the Integrated Development in the Yangtze River Delta Region. Reform, 2018 (12).

4 The high-quality integrated development of the Yangtze River Delta and the innovation of governance mechanism

Zhibiao Liu

The national strategy of the higher-quality integrated development in the Yangtze River Delta region focuses on the two developmental problems: "high-quality" and "integration". Its purpose is, through the transformation of the development mode and remodeling of economic and geographic patterns, to make the Yangtze River Delta a dynamic growth pole of national development, a model for national high-quality development, a demonstrative area of basic realization of modernization and regional integrated development, and a new height of reform and opening up in the new era.

Having been made from national strategic planning after over 30 years, its core problem is no longer "how to look at it" but "what to do" and "how to do it". In other words, the focus of the integrated development in the Yangtze River Delta is the leftover operational problems: with relatively independent boundaries of interests, rounded administrative power, and diversified development level and structure, how should the four provinces and cities break through their restricted mindset and traditional regional protectionism, raise their regional efficiency of resource allocation and capacity of absorbing global resource through regional governance mechanism for a synergetic, coordinated, and negotiatory development?

The previous practices have proved that the content of high-quality integrated development in the Yangtze River Delta has been quite abundant, including "overall planning, transportation network, unified environmental protection standard, simplified administration, all-pass card for people's livelihood and amity of residents". The starting point of the high-quality integrated development is a significant problem of sequence which directly determines the result of integration. Doubtless, during the transition of the economic system, market integration is the key to the high-quality integrated development in the Yangtze River Delta, because only with market-oriented development and the basis of market integration can the enterprises be active, can we define the boundary, function, and mission of government and market, can the transition of resource allocation mechanism be driven, and can the grand goals and daunting mission of this national strategy be achieved.

For this purpose, based on the significant proposition of analyzing the integrated development in the Yangtze River Delta with the core of market integration, we point out that the high-quality integration in the Yangtze River Delta requires the construction, completion, and innovation of a regional governance mechanism that

DOI: 10.4324/9781003455943-4

matches market integration. In the future, we should take competitive policies as the means of promoting the high-quality integrated development of the market in the Yangtze River Delta according to the requirement of deepening the socialist market economy system. Finally, using the regional equity trading market as an example, we conduct a case study on the financial market integration in the Yangtze River Delta, pointing out that in the process of financial market-oriented reform, China has to coordinate other economic policies based on the competitive policies and build a synergy environment of policy for market integration.

Section 1 The high-quality integrated development of the Yangtze River Delta centering on market integration

The practices of the regional integration in the Yangtze River Delta over the past 30 years have demonstrated that during the transition of economic systems where central government delegated power and interest to local governments and dispersed competitive entities, although the marketization degree of the Chinese economy has enormously increased both the cross-provincial market integration with the ease of regional protectionism as well as the problem of the "economy of administrative region", i.e., the administrative segmentation and fragmented competition in the economic operation, has not been solved completely: in fact, new forms of market segmentation appeared in some aspects, as many researchers have noticed.

The fragmented competition in the "economy of administrative region" is the most detrimental to the economic efficiency of resource allocation, which leads to the incapacity of absorbing resources through a powerful market and promoting enterprise to achieve economies of scale in a unified market to enhance international competitiveness. In the Third Plenary Session of the 18th Central Committee of the CPC, it was pointed out that "building a market system that is uniform but open, orderly and competitive is the basis of enabling the market to play a decisive role in resources allocation". The report delivered at the 19th National Congress further emphasized the importance of abolishing the rules and practices that jeopardized the unified market and fair competition. It also pointed out that the reform of the economic system should be focused on improving the ownership system and market-oriented allocation of factors to realize effective motivation of property rights, free mobility of factors, flexible prices, fair and orderly competition, and the survival-of-the-fittest enterprise mobility. Where shall we start the construction of a unified market and the allocation of a factor market? The answer in a major economy lies in the regional market's integrated development, which equals eliminating region segmentation and barriers to factor mobility and implementing mutual opening up for products and factors to be efficiently allocated following the rules of market. This is the core and basis of constructing a national unified market. In addition, from the perspective of development stages, the situation in China, a developing economic giant, is complicated with huge regional gaps. Therefore, the mission cannot be accomplished overnight but needs to be done region by region, step by step. For example, it should start from the Yangtze River Delta region with shared culture, geographic proximity, and a developed economy. Based on the regional market integration, mutual opening up of each integrated economic zone will be encouraged to form a nationally unified market, which would be the optimal order and procedure of reform.

Since the Yangtze River Delta is the most developed region in China, the Party Central Committee decided to make its high-quality integrated development a national strategy, which is an affirmation of its endeavor and exploration of integration over the past twenty years and a specific movement in completing the overall planning of reform and opening up in China, exploring new driving forces for economic development and utilizing the resilience of the economy under the background of the China-US trade friction. It also means that China is ready to construct a uniform but open, orderly, and competitive domestic market based on the regional market integration.

If regional market integration is the starting point of constructing a unified market and market-oriented allocation of factors, then what is the beginning of the high-quality integrated development in the Yangtze River Delta region? The answer is the encouragement and support of market integration. The reasons are:

First, only with the core of market integration can the segmented "economy of administrative region" be bound together to form an open regional economy, and the regional small-scale market to a large-scale one. The total economic scale in the Yangtze River Delta, although ranking tops in China with relatively good purchasing power determined by the per-capita income in the region, is not large enough for enterprises to realize economies of scale. This is because the market in the Yangtze River Delta, similar to that in any region in China, is not unified for the provincial administrative segmentation. There are numerous non-integrated phenomena even within a province, let alone in the three provinces and one city. For example, there are a large number of manufacturing enterprises and ports whose actual outputs are much lower than their designed capacities. If the market were integrated, these enterprises with severe overcapacity would be merged so that the surviving enterprises would reach an optimal scale with a reasonable industrial division.[1] But in reality, enterprises are separated and they compete without market regulation, so their merger and acquisition face multiple obstacles. If the market segmentation was broken down to achieve mutual openness between regions and freedom of highly efficient enterprises to merge with the less efficient ones, making enterprises the subject of decision-making, it would be possible to form an integrated and unified market and achieve regional integrated development with the core of market integration.

Second, the transition to the development mode and mechanism of economic globalization for the integrated development in the Yangtze River Delta should be based on the core of market integration. In the previous export-oriented economic globalization, the Yangtze River Delta region has actively and sufficiently made use of world markets, but not enough of regional or domestic markets. The manufacturing industry in Jiangsu and Zhejiang is a typical example: by means of the full implementation of the strategy of export-oriented economic development, it sold a large amount of excess capacity to the overseas market. Under the current anti-globalization trend, the international market cannot provide the driving force for the economic development in the Yangtze River Delta anymore. Therefore, it is increasingly urgent to develop a strong domestic market. Only a strong regional market formed by means of regional market integration, and a domestic super market scale gradually formed based on it, can help build economic globalization based on the strong domestic demand of a major economy, like the American one. With the support of super-scale domestic demand and the industrial division and enterprise scale formed through competition, the driving mechanism for constant economic growth can be provided for preliminary modernization.

Third, only with the core of market integration can the Yangtze River Delta attract global advanced innovative factors, develop an innovative economy in China, rise along the industrial chain, and achieve high-quality development. The previous comparative advantage of the Yangtze River Delta was production factors, acquiring long-term low-value-added income through its processing and manufacturing exports. Since the OEM products are developed and designed in advance, the OEM enterprises only need to follow the blueprint without the techniques of innovation. The advantage of the low-price factor in the Yangtze River Delta is gradually weakened because of the rise in manufacturing costs and the entrance of foreign companies. A new comparative advantage is rising, which is the increasingly powerful domestic market scale along with the regional market integration. This strong regional unified market or domestic market is conducive to achieving scale economies' effect and international industrial competitiveness for the Chinese enterprise, to their investment in opening businesses around the world, and to outsourcing the knowledge-intensive links like R&D and design to foreign enterprises and learning from them in the process. In conclusion, it helps Chinese enterprises absorb intellectual capital, technological capital, and human capital from the host countries, form a brand-new global division of work or intra-production specialization, and rise from the bottom of GVC to become an organic part of the global innovation chain.

Fourth, only with the core of market integration can the Yangtze River Delta break through the conventional mode of segmented governance and enter the new phase of economic integrated collaborative governance. The market-oriented allocation of production factors, i.e., free mobility and combination in a wider range, especially the free mobility and competitive allocation of the labor force, is the core and significant content of market integration. Only when the production factors centered on labor force achieve market-oriented allocation can the regional economic integration be achieved; otherwise, any so-called integration is not completed without getting rid of the basic characteristics of "segmented governance" completely. The so-called "segmented governance" is mainly administrative restrictions on the market-oriented allocation of production factors. The regional developmental competition based on it is mainly reflected in the high-speed, high-input, and low-quality economic development without sufficient factor mobility. The inter-regional cooperative governance based on the market integration requires regions to construct a unified and open market, break the mindset of sectionalism, and jointly explore the governance structure and mechanism in favor of the integration in the Yangtze River Delta region in terms of unified planning management, overall land management, mechanism of factor-free mobility, mechanism of finance and taxation sharing, joint construction and sharing of infrastructure, planning and coordination of public service, joint protection of ecological environment, etc.

According to the obstructive factors of market integration, the most significant problems in promoting high-quality development in the Yangtze River Delta lie in the following aspects:

Competitive development between local governments was encouraged in the past, but now the cooperative and coordinated development since the national strategy of integration is preferred. The competition between local governments used to be an important driving force for Chinese economic development, as well as the key factor in market administrative segmentation and fragmentation. The heart of the "administrative region economy" problem lies in: first, the performance evaluation system of local government should be changed from valuing their GDP and fiscal revenue to achieving integrated development in order to change their code of conduct and external pressure. Second, government participation and interference in market should be bound. Their powers need to be restricted to the regulation of public interest in the market, rather than a pursuer of profitable activities. Third, the governments can release certain public powers to relevant integrative organizations through some specific agreements or negotiations, in order to transform competition into cooperation.

Second, promoting market integration should start from a detailed project in the region. We need to learn from the pragmatic spirit of the Europeans when they built the European Community and avoid abstract discussion in a wider range without a decision. The European Community started from the coordination function of committees of coal, steel, and atomic energy, and gradually developed into the euro-system. For the numerous fields that need to be coordinated in the Yangtze River Delta, we can start from the easier ones, i.e., eliminating the obstacles to governmental cooperation on public projects; for example, connecting the "dead ends", construction of regional light rail, mandatory administration or shareholding integration of ports, etc. And then we gradually can tackle the difficult ones, like obstacles to household registration, education, and other aspects of people's livelihoods. When the people start to benefit from the market integration, they will naturally support this national strategy, which means a stronger driving force and a higher possibility of success.

Third, in the process of advancing market integration, it is important to give weight to the initiatives of enterprises or enterprise groups. First, the merger and acquisition of enterprises in the region should be encouraged. The micro-level merger and acquisition changes the market regulation of enterprise between regions into internal coordination within an enterprise, which would be an effective tool of market integration because it leads to intense integration effect. Second, large enterprises or enterprise groups play an integrative role in the construction of industrial clusters, which blurs the boundary of administrative regions and is the spatial carrier of market integration. Industrial clusters can also adopt the configuration of modern productivity developed by the "polarization-diffusion" mode in economic areas. For example, if we construct a scientific and technological innovation industrial cluster based on the ecological corridor along the Nanjing-Hangzhou line, then the integrated high-tech industries will cover the three provinces of Suzhou, Zhejiang, and Anhui. Third, a value chain that connects the integration in each region should be constructed based on the intra-production specialization of domestic enterprises. For example, the value chain is based on market fair trade, the captured semi-tight-coupling value chain, and the tight-coupling vertically integrated value chain. Based on these value chains, the developmental strategy of the Yangtze River Economic Belt and the Belt and Road Initiative can be combined in order to jointly invest in the countries along with the project and transfer the abundant and competitive capacity in China in the process of the enterprises' "going out" together.

Section 2 Taking competition as the major governance mechanism of the high-quality integrated development of the Yangtze River Delta

The difficulty of promoting market integration in the Yangtze River Delta lies in the innovation and construction of its governance mechanism. There are even some opposing views about it. For example, in terms of market integration of the "administrative region economy" in the Yangtze River Delta with independent interest boundaries, a popular view is to strengthen the holistic view of the national strategy, set up a higher-level administrative institution, or merge institutions to reinforce the governmental coordinative function, in order to further promote market integration. There is also a belief that only when the tangible and intangible barriers set by the administrative entities are eliminated through competitive policies can the market entities be activated, and can the competitive relations be perfected to achieve the integration coordinated by competition in the process of opening up. In the meantime, more people propose that the construction, completion, and innovation of the governance mechanism in the region is the optimal method of achieving market high-quality integrated development in the current administrative system.

What exactly is the governance mechanism? Does it mean establishing all kinds of coordinating administrative mechanisms based on the integration of the Yangtze River Delta? Born out of the planned economic system, the Chinese economy is likely to fall back into the mindset and habit of planned economy when it meets problems caused by insufficient market mechanisms. Facing the market confusion and disorder in the previous decentralized government, some people refused to open market competition and improving market order but blamed the deficiencies of the transition of the economic system and proposed the idea of "take back the decentralized affairs and manage them uniformly". With such an idea, the first proposed solutions to any obstacle or conflict of interest in market integration would be merging the administrative regions or asking for a higher-level coordinative administrative institution above the three provinces and one city in the Yangtze River Delta. However, administrative means cannot solve the problem caused by the system of "administrative area economy". If they were effective and invincible, then why would the previous planned economic system collapse? If the merger of administrative areas were successful, why would the central government spend great effort on the integrated development strategy instead of merging Shanghai, Suzhou, Zhejiang, and Anhui and restoring the concept of East China? Therefore, the key lies in a regional administrative mechanism adapted to market integration, rather than going back to the old systems.

One of the results of market integration is certainly the "overall" development pattern of the economy in the Yangtze River Delta region. However, the means of market integration should not be a unified administrative mechanism, but competition policy generated within the economic system of the developed market, according to the requirements of the socialist market economy system.

First, competition policy is the legalized mandatory governance mechanism that protects competition itself, rather than competitors, so it is conducive to market integration coordinated by market competition. Under the unified competition policy, all the discriminated restrictions against market entities are canceled; race conditions are fairer; enterprises of different ownership, technological levels, and scales are treated equally. Therefore, the only competition left in the market is about efficiency: the ones with low efficiency will be ruthlessly sifted out; the ones with high efficiency can remain in the market. By this means, the surviving enterprises are those that can create value and wealth for society and contribute to high-quality development.

Second, competition policy is the legalized mandatory governance mechanism that defines the function of government in the market. It not only helps with eliminating all the administrative powers against market integration by objecting to administrative monopoly, but also advocates abolishing all the regulations and practices that obstruct unified market and fair competition and restricts the space and fields of government intervention on the market, in order to define the function and power boundary of government in the market. One of the important forces of governmental intervention against market integration is the administrative monopoly of enterprises in markets endowed by government. Administrative monopoly excludes other enterprises from entering the market, charges a high price, and assigns their services and products to clients. Such monopolistic behaviors are detrimental to social welfare and market efficiency, so the opposition to administrative monopoly means encouraging market integration. In the international market, China is transforming from following the global rules to making and implementing them. When the process is complete, the government will have very limited administrative power to intervene in the space and fields of markets. Besides, since any economic policy will be rectified and reviewed based on competitive policies, those against competition law will be rejected for review and re-formulation. Therefore, all the governmental powers stronger than economic forces will be restricted by competition law.

Third, competition policy is the legalized mandatory governance mechanism that restricts enterprises from monopolizing the market. It objects to the enterprises' monopoly position achieved through aggressive and predatory means, and thereby is conducive to breaking all market forces against integration. Enterprises can form market forces through innovation, management, advertising, and merger and acquisition in market competition. Although market force was manifested as a monopoly, the capacity of monopoly does not necessarily mean it has to be charged. Only the enterprises which attacked their competitors with force and harmed them or their clients will be accused based on competition law. Allowing enterprises to form market power encourages them to compete based on efficiency; while not allowing them to harm competitors is protecting fair competition in the market. The synergy effect of competition policy indicates that it is the institutional foundation of market integration.

Fourth, competition policy is the legalized mandatory governance mechanism that encourages the merger and acquisition of enterprises in order to achieve market integration. It can be regarded as a micro-basis means and method of macroeconomic integration. Many non-integrated affairs caused by governmental intervention and low efficiency can be changed through the market-oriented operation of enterprises. For example, consider severe overcapacity: governmental interference would cause high risks of bursting financial bubbles and economic fluctuation with high costs and uncertain actual effects. In contrast, encouraging the merger and acquisition of the enterprises with better performance would not only solve the overcapacity, but also develop some super-scale corporations which may become Chinese multinational corporations through competition. Sometimes the overcapacity in an industry can be solved only by some board meetings about layout adjustment after mergers and acquisitions. Because of the strong function of M&A to achieve market integration, it is proposed that the M&A should be vigorously promoted for market integration in the Yangtze River Delta; and the national competition policies should leave some space for flexible operations when the integration strategy is applied across the country.

To achieve the high-quality market integrated development, apart from construction, completion, and innovation of governance mechanism, inter-governmental coordination and cooperation can also be encouraged and advocated. Especially in terms of planning, transportation, environmental protection, governance, and people's livelihoods, market mechanisms cannot deal with all the problems through competition while governments have to shoulder their natural responsibilities. Therefore, cross-governmental cooperative and coordinative governance need to be strengthened. This is especially significant for the externality of markets and market efficiency. Such coordination and cooperation would be based on the principle of "sharing the cost and benefit". All the parties need to reach an agreement or make some rules and regulations through negotiations and delegate some relevant governmental power to a certain department under the collective supervision of all participants. The delegation of governance rights should be regarded as a vital method of governmental coordination and cooperation for market integration in the Yangtze River Delta region.

Section 3 Case study of the integrated development of the equity market in the Yangtze River Delta region[2]

The main obstacles to market integration in the Yangtze River Delta region, besides the system of administrative segmentation, are also related to the administrative pattern and system of the national competent department, which has been ignored in previous research on the "administrative region economy". It is previously acknowledged that the difficulty of breaking down the "administrative area economy" lies in the governmental interference in market activities in power-decentralized places. Currently, breaking down an "administrative area" lies in the conduct of a central government and its competent department. The present policy restriction on the trans-regional operating of the equity market in the Yangtze River Delta region is an interesting story about the formation of "administrative area economy" in China under the administrative pattern of a national competent department. From this case, we can see the crux of the integration of financial markets in the Yangtze River Delta and understand the necessity of the coordination of other economic policies based on the competition policy.

Currently, the cross-regional operation of the equity exchange market is strictly restrained through the whole country: each province/city can only have one equity market that only accepts local enterprises. This is a severe obstruction of the business expansion and service function of local markets, especially the ones with high operation levels. The obstructive factor is not local government or financial enterprises, but the policies that limit the cross-regional operation of the financial enterprises made by the financial department. The original purpose of such policies was to prevent financial risks and mass disturbance of investors caused by the out-of-control growth of regional equity markets and lack of effective supervision and control. The two documents, *Circular on Regulating the Development of Regional Equity Markets* (issued by the General Office of the State Council [2017] No. 11) and *Interim Measures of the China Securities Regulatory Commission for the Supervision and Administration of Regional Equity Markets* (Order No. 132 of the China Securities Regulatory Commission), specifically include the restriction on cross-regional operation of regional equity markets, in order to solve the "illegal issuance of shares and fundraising" caused by the "undefined subject of regulatory responsibility" on enterprises listed in other regions.

Our front-line research discovered that these rules not only fail to strengthen the regulation of capital market but also cause regulation omission. If, following the path of regional market integration, the eligible equity markets are allowed to conduct cross-regional operations, for example, the Shanghai equity market and the stock exchanges in Jiangsu, Zhejiang, and Anhui are allowed to conduct integrated listing transactions in the Yangtze River Delta, then it would be easier to solve the problem of financing for small, medium, and micro businesses and the imbalanced development between regions through promoting the capital market allocation in the process of financial market integration.

The research discovered that the competent department constrains the cross-regional operation of equity market by the aforementioned documents, which is a non-integrative regulation path and cannot solve the problem of relative financial risks:

First, the cases of illegal fundraising are increasing. According to the data from the Supreme People's Procuratorate, the trial number of illegally taking public deposits and fundraising fraud from 2016 to 2018 rose year by year, reaching 15,302 accused of illegally taking public deposits and 1,962 for fundraising fraud in 2018. The objective data indicated that the restrictive policies did not stem the rising trend of such cases: thus, illegal fundraising is not related to where the enterprise is listed.

Second, the mass disturbance of investors is not effectively prevented. In 2017, the "Qiaoxing Bond issue" in Guangdong Stock Exchange caused tens of thousands of people to be trapped in a crisis of cashing in; in 2018, P2P lending platforms collectively collapsed, causing a large amount of rights protection of investors. Since the investors are not restricted by the rules, the regional equity markets would face investors from the whole country whether or not they operate cross-regionally. Therefore, they would have to take the risks of investors' impairment of rights and interests and the challenge of mass disturbance. As a result, it is groundless to worry about the mass disturbance of investors caused by the cross-regional operation of local markets.

Third, the concepts of "market supervision" and "administrative supervision" are mixed, leading to supervision omission. Restricting the enterprises in the regional stock market to its provincial administrative area is confusing the concepts of market supervision and administrative supervision. In fact, the main part of "market supervision" is the information disclosure of the listed enterprises and the trading behavior of investors, so the supervision is targeted at market entities including listed enterprises, not their registered places or management. For those listed enterprises of other administrative areas, the regional equity market can still play a supervisory role in terms of information disclosure to protect investors. And for the public security, industry and commerce, tax and other "administrative supervision", China adopts a localized management, which means the location of judicial or other decisions depend on the agreement of both parties. The content and perspective of "market supervision" and "administrative supervision" are different: the Shanghai and Shenzhen Stock Exchange and National Equities Exchange and Quotations never stress that "market coverage area should match the supervision coverage", which does not mean that stock exchange can play an administrative supervision role of local government, or that local government cannot supervise those listed enterprises.

The problems caused by limiting the cross-regional operation of equity market are:

First, it makes some regional equity markets harder to survive, and causes waste of resources for the poor performance of the well-operated markets. According to the industrial statistics, since the restriction on cross-regional markets and enterprises, the net profit decrease of the regional equity market in 2018 is

28.49%; more than one-third of all regional equity markets saw a loss; most of them survived on government support. The reasons are on the one hand, the lack of a sustainable profit model for the low-level management of most regional equity market, and on the other hand, some regional equity markets survived on the commission of the issuance of privately raised bonds and local government bonds before Order No. 132 of the China Securities Regulatory Commission, so they have been in the plight since the Order only allows the issuance and transfer of corporate stock and convertible bonds.

Second, the industrial structure cannot be optimized to promote the development of an equity market without unified market competition. The restriction on the cross-regional operation of equity market, i.e., forcing enterprises to choose local equity market through administrative power, not only ignores enterprises' will against their legitimate right of making operative decisions voluntarily, but also constrains the healthy competition between markets, making it impossible to improve service for sustainable industrial development. Practices have improved so that only through sufficient competition in a unified market can the service in trading markets be improved to promote the survival of the fittest and the reasonable allocation of social resources.

Third, it is impossible to support the development of a substantial economy and new driving forces through direct financing. Although each province has a regional equity market, its financial environment is diversified. Those less advanced regions, without enough resources of professionals, operative experience and means, market credibility, geographic advantages, or number of investors, perform badly in terms of their financing function. Under the circumstances of difficulty financing local and forbidden financing outside, the development of a substantial economy and new driving forces are hard to improve. In addition, the restriction on the service of markets with good resource endowment blocks the cross-regional free mobility of capital and regional coordinated development.

In fact, the development effect of constructing an integrated regional equity market would be prominent: it can immensely improve the rapid growth of medium- and small-sized enterprises and promote the economic development of the location of listed enterprises. Currently, the equity market in the Yangtze River Delta is completely capable of conducting cross-regional operations, especially the Shanghai Equity Exchange with its advantages in terms of professionals, operative experience and means, market credibility, geographic advantages, and numbers of investors. In 2017, when the restrictive policies were published, there were around 1,500 cross-regional listed enterprises in the whole country, mainly in the Shanghai, Tianjin, and Chongqing equity markets. Their listing was permitted and supported by the local governments and they successfully received their development fund. Many medium- and small-sized science and technology enterprises presented a rapid increase in their business performance with direct financing after being listed. They have made prominent contributions to local employment, finance and tax, technological innovations, etc., and become the local top enterprise. Therefore, according to the requirement of the national strategy of the high-quality integrated development in the Yangtze River Delta region, there are some suggestions for the non-integrated equity market:

(1) Cancel the restriction on regional operations and raise the efficiency of resource allocation in the process of regional integrated development. All the regulations and practices that hinder a unified market and fair competition should be abolished to optimize the configuration and resources, encourage healthy competition, break administrative monopolies, and let the market decide the value of its equity market and its fate. The markets sifted through competition are more standardized and easier to supervise. More importantly, enterprises will receive financial support from markets with abundant financial factors through resource allocation, realizing the purpose of promoting the local economic development by attracting foreign capital. This measure can be started from the national strategy of the integrated development in the Yangtze River Delta region as a demonstration. The trial must be based on competition policy to coordinate other economic policies. All the economic policies introduced by a national department should be rectified and adjusted by the competition policy, creating a good environment of synergetic policies for market integration.
(2) Implement the "three unifications". To standardize the development of regional equity markets, a "unified platform" should be set up based on the existing "unified supervision" by China's Securities Regulatory Commission: the new back-end system includes the registration of custody of securities, trade matching, acting trading system, security fund settlement, etc. The "unified basic system" is to formulate unified market self-supervision rules, which focuses on setting up a unified standard to protect the interests of investors and the principles of verification and information disclosure for an equal, fair, and open market. The "three unifications" are conducive to the listing of enterprises in multiple places for their diversified financing demands and fundamental to the interconnection of capital markets of different levels.
(3) Encourage exploration and institutional innovation. The report delivered at the 19th National Congress advocated financial innovation and the capacity of serving a real economy. The trial and exploration on equity markets are conducive to raising the market function of regional integration, enhancing the growth of more innovative businesses, and reserving resources for incubating more scientific and technological enterprises for the Shanghai Stock Exchange STAR Market. Therefore, it is advised to allow the innovation of eligible equity markets in the Yangtze River Delta on the basis of unified supervision; for example, breaking the operational restriction of administrative area; the trial of a joint-listing system in the Yangtze River Delta Stock Exchange.

Notes

1 Over the past decades, too many enterprises survived even during the severe overcapacity because of the export orientation to take advantage of foreign markets and the government subsidies.

2 The research in this case study was supported by the general managers of Shanghai Equity Exchange, Zhang Yunfeng and Han Meimei, who provided the author with valuable information and materials. We hereby express our appreciation to them.

References

Liu Chaoming. Regional Development and Policy Model in the Process of Economic Integration. The Journal of Quantitative & Technical Economics, 2002 (11).

Deng Huihui, Yang Luxin. Efficiency Loss and Optimization Path of Market Segmentation under High Quality Development. Zhejiang Social Sciences, 2019 (6).

Lin Lihua, Zhang Juntao, Li Xiaofeng. Literature Review and Prospects of Market Segmentation. Productivity Research, 2018 (9).

Liang Qi. Inspirations from the Process of EU Integration. Academic Research, 2009 (8).

Hong Tao, Ma Tao. Has There Been a Market Foundation for Coordinated Development of Regions? A Research Based on the Perspective of Chinese Market Integration. Journal of Nanjing University (Philosophy Humanities and Social Sciences), 2017 (1).

Wang Xiaoye, Tao Zhenghua. The Competitive Policy of WTO and its Influence on China and the Significance of Antimonopoly Law. Social Sciences in China, 2003 (9).

Liu Zhibiao. On Key Points and Breakthroughs in Building Unified Market in China – Plus Analysis of Equalization of Environment for Market Competition of "OTC" Trading. The Journal of Jiangsu Administration Institute, 2015 (7).

Liu Zhibiao. The Institutional Foundation of the High-quality Integrated Development of the Yangtze River Delta. Frontiers, 2019 (3).

Zhang Zhidong, Wu Di, Zhou Shudou. Mobility of Production Factors, Regional Coordinated Integration and Economic Growth. Journal of Industrial Technological Economics, 2018 (11).

5 Growth spillover and market integration in the Yangtze River Delta region

Bu Maoliang, Gao Yanyan, and Lian Zhi

Section 1 Introduction

Since the reform and opening up, the non-integration of the regional market has been a major problem ailing the transition of economic development in China. The problems of local protectionism, overlapping construction and vicious competition, etc. have reflected the severity of market non-integration from different aspects. Under this background, recent years have witnessed a wave of market integrated development in the Yangtze River Delta region (YRD): provinces and cities have gradually abandoned the narrow view of fighting for themselves, broken inter-provincial borders, established the Changjiang Delta Cities Economic Coordination Committee aiming at cooperation and joint development, and removed the market segmentation barriers step by step.[1] This is a significant example of the national market integration and a case to study. In 2018, President Xi proposed in his keynote speech at the opening ceremony of the first China International Import Expo to support the integrated development in the YRD and make it a national strategy, to implement new development philosophy in earnest, to build a modern economic system and adopt higher standards for reform and opening up, to develop in tandem with the Belt and Road Initiative, the Beijing-Tianjin-Hebei coordinated development area, the Yangtze River Economic Belt, and the Guangdong-Hong Kong-Macao Greater Bay Area, and to help improve the overall layout of reform and opening up. Facing the new conditions and environments, further research and discussion on the vital engine for Chinese economic development, namely the integration of the YRD, have been more theoretically and empirically significant.

This formation mechanism of the market integration in the YRD has presented the following phenomena. First, the process from non-integration to integration is a progressive change. Second, the YDR does not welcome the joining of relatively less developed regions[2]: its market integration targets only its internal market. Third, differing from the market integration of the countries and regions in the European Union, government plays an important role in China's market integration.

This chapter attempts to elaborate on the mechanism of market integration from the perspective of its "asymmetric spillover effect" on the regional economy under the background of inter-governmental competition. The following contents include: a review of the existing literature; a theoretical model to prove the influence

DOI: 10.4324/9781003455943-5

of "asymmetric spillover effect" on the promotion of local government and thus the effect on their different market policy choices; the empirical analysis to verify the different spillover effect under different economic development level by two methods based on 16 cities in the YRD in 2001–2007; and finally, the conclusion and inadequacy of this research.

Section 2 Literature review

The existing literature mainly studies the reasons for formation of Chinese market integration from the perspective of government conduct. Among the early research, the "fragmented economy" proposed by Shen Liren and Dai Yuanchen (1990) and the "cellular economy" by Lyons (1985) reflected the situation of market non-integration. In recent years, the empirical research of Young (2000) and Poncet (2002) further revealed the degree of non-integration of the Chinese market: Young (2000) described the market segmentation in China as "fragmented internal market and fief controlled by local government"; while Poncet (2005) believed that the inter-provincial market segmentation in China was similar to the segmentation between countries in the European Union or between the US and Canada. The result of the two studies aroused intense backlash in both China and the whole world. Some scholars questioned their theories. For example, Naughton (2000) and Bai Chong'en et al. (2004) both concluded that the level of Chinese market integration has increased through the input-output data and regional specialized data respectively. Li Shantong et al. (2004) discovered that the market segmentation, although largely reduced, still exists by conducting a questionnaire survey. Zou Weixing and Liqun (2010) believed that with the enhanced economic foundation and transition of development methods in recent years, the regional economic integration degree in the Beijing-Tianjin-Hebei region, the Yangtze River Delta region, and the Pearl River Delta all distinctly rose with a narrowing gap and clear converging trend. Fan Jianyong and Yun (2011), by using the trading data of the manufacturing industry from the Multi-regional Input-output Model for China based on the gravity model, took the boundary effect of cross-regional transaction as the measuring indicator of market non-integration and concluded that the product market in China was not severely segmented, the integration of which could be further improved by eliminating the exogenous trade barriers.

The aforementioned research is focused on the definitive and quantitative judgment on the degree of market integration or non-integration, which is conducive to deepening the understanding of market (non-)integration in China, while this chapter pays more attention to the formative mechanism of market (non-)integration. Most research on this aspect discussed the reasons for market non-integration. Lin Yifu and Liu Peilin (2014) believed that the continuation of the catching-up strategy before reform and opening up drove each region to make their catch-up plans, which caused local protectionism. Lu Ming et al. (2004) proposed that "the less developed regions would lose their revenue of current division when they chose not to participate in the division system, but they would thereby raise their status in the negotiation of the future income of division and distribution", so they would prefer market segmentation. Zhou Li'an (2004, 2007) first explained the market non-integration from the perspective of local government promotion. Since the superior government would review the performance of subordinate local governments and promote the top ones, "it left very narrow room for them to cooperate but huge intension to compete". The empirical research based on provincial panel data by Lu Ming and Zhao (2009) concluded that "raising the degree of market segmentation when it is relatively low is conducive to the local economic growth, but is detrimental when the degree exceeds certain critical value". Ding Congming et al. (2018) believed that the diversity of culture and dialect exerts a potential influence on market segmentation. The highly overlapped dialect distribution and administrative division caused the underestimation of the influence of dialect diversity on market segmentation. Based on this theory, an empirical analysis found that the numerous dialects are a significant factor that hinders the formation of market integration in China. Wang Jiankang (2019) advocated that the proportion of the state-owned economy accelerated the local market segmentation to some extent. These perspectives can explain why the market non-integration happened, but not why the market integration happened. Xu Xianxiang et al. (2007) concluded that market integrated regions have a higher economic growth rate than the non-integrated ones by comparing the YRD and other regions in China. Liu Shenglong and Angang (2011) verified the positive influence of transportation infrastructure on regional trade in China through the census data of inter-provincial volume of freight transportation from the Chinese Ministry of Transport, indicating that the improvement of transportation infrastructure facilitates regional economic integration. Wang Jiankang (2019) believed that urbanization, fiscal expenditure, international trade, technology gap, and infrastructure construction are conducive to eliminating the local market segmentation and facilitating market integration. These conclusions can explain why the market integration happened, but not the continuous existence of non-integrated regions.

By reviewing the existing studies, it is noticed that most of them (1) did not consider the market non-integration and integration as a continuous state: the neglect of the relation between the two leads to the biased explanation for only non-integration or integration, but not the transition between them; (2) did not consider the influence of regional differences (especially the gap in economic development levels) on the process of market integration; (3) failed to combine the model with empirical studies. This chapter is based on this analysis.

Section 3 Theory model

1. Fundamental assumption

The model in this chapter regards the transition from market non-integration to integration as a continuous change that could be effectively interfered with by government. From the perspective of inter-governmental competition, the degree of market integration is in fact the strategic choice of local governments. Based on the real-life situation, the government in the model would always choose the process of raising the degree of market integration (but not the opposite).[3] To simplify the model, two states have been chosen to represent the degree of market integration – exante (the initial state) and expost (the changed state).[4] The model assumes that there are two competing economic areas: the developed area *i*, and the less developed area *j*; their respective economic growth g_i and g_j contains two parts (Xu Xianxiang et al., 2007):

$$g_i = \left(mx - x^2\right) + \theta_i xy \tag{5.1}$$

$$g_j = \left(my - y^2\right) + \theta_j xy \tag{5.2}$$

The first part (the number in brackets) indicates the competition for promotion between local officials: they would promote their regional economic growth as far as possible for the maximum promotion opportunity. In the formula, $m>0$ is a constant; *x* and *y* represent regions ($x\geq0$ and $y\geq0$); and *i* and *j* the officials' effort. Formula (5.1) and (5.2) demonstrate that the regional economic growth would rise along with the official's effort in a certain range.

The second part ($\theta_i xy$ or $\theta_j xy$) represents the spillover effect on regional economic growth caused by the transition from exante to expost.[5] In the formula, $-1<\theta_i<1$, $-1<\theta_j<1$, θ_i and θ_j are not necessarily equal, indicating an asymmetry of spillover effect on developed and less developed regions. θ_i or θ_j above zero means positive spillover effect; below zero means negative.

U_i and U_j represent the possibility of promotion for government officials in region *i* and region *j*, as shown in formulas (5.3) and (5.4). According to the theories from Zhou Li'an (2007), the superior government inspects the economic performance of the subordinate regional governments and promotes the ones with better performance, based on the criteria of regional economic growth. Such relative performance evaluation has caused Political Tournaments,[6] causing inevitable attention to the influence from their competitors, which is represented by α and β. Since the purpose of superior government is to maximize economic growth in the areas of subordinate governments, while the purpose of the latter is maximum promotion possibility, the two goals may contradict. Hypothetically the subordinate governments in the model focus on only economic growth in their competition (i.e., always targeting to maximize their economic growth), which means the superior government can regulate α and β when designing the political tournaments to uniformize their purpose.

$$U_i = g_i + \alpha g_j \tag{5.3}$$

$$U_j = g_j + \beta g_i \tag{5.4}$$

2. Model deduction

Since the maximum promotion opportunity is the goal of local governments, they will prepare the possibility of promotion under market non-integration strategy and market integration strategy and choose the higher one.

(1) Market integration strategy

The condition for maximizing the possibility of promotion U_i in area *i* is:

$$\frac{\partial U_i}{\partial x} = 0 \Rightarrow m - 2x + \theta_i y + \alpha\theta_j y = 0$$

Therefore:

$$x = \frac{m + (\theta_i + \alpha\theta_j)y}{2} \tag{5.5}$$

Similarly, since $\frac{\partial U_j}{\partial y} = 0$,

$$y = \frac{m + (\theta_i + \beta\theta_j)x}{2} \tag{5.6}$$

Based on formulas (5.5) and (5.6), the functions of the optimal degree of effort in areas *i* and *j* are respectively:

$$x^* = \frac{m\left[(\theta_i + \alpha\theta_j) + 2\right]}{4 - (\theta_i + \alpha\theta_j)(\theta_j + \beta\theta_i)} \tag{5.7}$$

$$y^* = \frac{m\left[(\theta_j + \beta\theta_i) + 2\right]}{4 - (\theta_i + \alpha\theta_j)(\theta_j + \beta\theta_i)} \tag{5.8}$$

Plug x^* and y^* into g_i and g_j, and based on $\frac{\partial g_i}{\partial \alpha} = 0$ and $\frac{\partial g_j}{\partial \beta} = 0$, we will have the value of α and β.

$$\alpha = \frac{\theta_i(1 + \theta_i)}{2 + \theta_i - \theta_i\theta_j} \tag{5.9}$$

$$\beta = \frac{\theta_j(1 + \theta_j)}{2 + \theta_j - \theta_i\theta_j} \tag{5.10}$$

Plug α and β into formulas (5.7) and (5.8), and we will have the optimal degree of effort of officials in areas *i* and *j*:

$$x^* = \frac{m}{4}\left(1 + \frac{1+\theta_i}{1-\theta_i\theta_j}\right) \tag{5.11}$$

$$y^* = \frac{m}{4}\left(1 + \frac{1+\theta_j}{1-\theta_i\theta_j}\right) \tag{5.12}$$

Plug x^* and y^* into formula (5.1) and (5.2), we will have the optimal economic growth in areas *i* and *j*:

$$g_i^* = \frac{m^2}{16} \cdot \frac{\left(2+\theta_i-\theta_i\theta_j\right)\left(2+\theta_i\right)}{1-\theta_i\theta_j} \tag{5.13}$$

$$g_j^* = \frac{m^2}{16} \cdot \frac{\left(2+\theta_j-\theta_i\theta_j\right)\left(2+\theta_j\right)}{1-\theta_i\theta_j} \tag{5.14}$$

Based on formulas (5.9), (5.10), (5.13) and (5.14), we will have the promotion possibility of officials in areas *i* and *j* based on the following market integration strategy:

$$U_i^* = \frac{m^2}{16} \cdot \frac{1}{1-\theta_i\theta_j}\left[3\left(\theta_i+1\right)^2 + \left(1-\theta_i\theta_j\right)\right] \tag{5.15}$$

$$U_j^* = \frac{m^2}{16} \cdot \frac{1}{1-\theta_i\theta_j}\left[3\left(\theta_j+1\right)^2 + \left(1-\theta_i\theta_j\right)\right] \tag{5.16}$$

(2) Market non-integration strategy

Under this strategy, θ_i and θ_j equal zero, and the deductions of other variables are the same as those under the market integration strategy. Therefore, based on formulas (5.15) and (5.16), we will have the promotion possibility of officials in areas *i* and *j*:

$$U_i^{10} = U_j^{10} = \frac{m^2}{4} \tag{5.17}$$

(3) Strategy comparison

ΔU_i and ΔU_j represent the promotion possibility under market integration minus that under market non-integration in areas *i* and *j* respectively. Based on formulas (5.15), (5.16) and (5.17), we have:

$$\Delta U_i = \frac{m^2}{16} \cdot \frac{3\theta_i}{1-\theta_i\theta_j}\left(2+\theta_i+\theta_j\right) \tag{5.18}$$

$$\Delta U_i = \frac{m^2}{16} \cdot \frac{3\theta_j}{1-\theta_i\theta_j}\left(2+\theta_i+\theta_j\right) \tag{5.19}$$

Since-1<θ_i<1 and -1<θ_j<1, 2+θ_i+θ_j>0, 1-$\theta_i\theta_j$>0. Based on that, we have the following propositions: (1) if θ_i>0, ΔU_i>0; if θ_i<0, ΔU_i<0. (2) if θ_j>0, ΔU_j>0; if θ_j<0, ΔU_j<0. (3) if θ_i=θ_j=0, ΔU_i=ΔU_j=0.

These propositions reflect that the positivity or negativity of ΔU_i and ΔU_j depend on that of θ_i and θ_j. When θ_i and θ_j are both positive or negative, deduction one stands: driven by the competition for promotion, if the spillover effects are positive, then the promotion possibility of local governments should be raised for market integration; if those are negative, then the possibility should be reduced for market non-integration. It explains the reasons for market integration and continuous market non-integration.

Deduction one considers the situation when the spillover effects of two regions are both positive and negative. It is also possible that there is one positive and one negative in the two regions. Similarly, deduction two also stands based on these propositions: if the spillover effect of market integration in the less-developed region is positive and that in the developed region is negative, then the former would be eager to achieve market integration, while the latter would refuse. Therefore, the market integration between them would be difficult to realize. Deduction two reveals the root of regional conflict in the process of market integration in the YRD.

Section 4 Empirical analysis

Our theoretical model is based on two crucial hypotheses: first, the direct relation between economic growth and promotion, which has been supported by numerous empirical studies and will not be repeated here; second, the asymmetry of the spillover effect, which has not been studied or proven and will be the main content of this section. We will first establish an index to measure the degree of market integration in the YRD, i.e., the market integration index in the YRD, and then conduct relative variable inspections.

1. The market integration index in the YRD

The index must include information on time series to reflect the change in the degree. However, if YRD is observed as a whole, the empirical analysis will be unreliable for the limited periods in the time series. Considering the advantages of panel data, we chose 16 cities in the YRD as the cross-sectional data of the market integration index.[7]

The common methods of constructing the market integration index include the production approach, trade approach, business cycle approach, and price approach (Yu Donghua and Liu Yun, 2009; Chen Min et al., 2007). This chapter adopts the price approach for the following two reasons: first, other approaches, although they can reflect the changing in market integration, are often influenced by some non-market interference factors[8] which are hard to control; second, other approaches cannot provide a panel data at the city level for the limited statistics.

The price approach measures the degree of market integration by the differences in commodity prices between regions: a narrowing gap indicates the rise in market integration. One of the advantages of this approach is that it directly reflects the situation of market integration, because "market integration refers to the smooth transmission of price signals and information across spatially separated markets" (Goletti Francesco et al., 2007). Samuelson's "iceberg" cost model laid a solid foundation for the price approach. It manifested that it is impossible to equalize p_i and p_j, the prices in two regions, because of transaction cost: they may rise or drop at the same time or separately; but as long as their relative prices are within a range, the markets in the two regions are regarded as integrated. Based on the theory, Parsley and Wei (1996, 2001) exploited a new method of measuring the market integration by the variance of relative price $\mathrm{Var}\left(P_i / P_j\right)$. If $\mathrm{Var}\left(P_i / P_j\right)$ narrows with time, then the fluctuation range of relative price is decreasing, the "iceberg" cost *(c)* decreases and the degree of market integration increases. Goletti Francesco et al. (2007), Yu Wen and Huang Jikun (1998) and Poncet (2005) conducted research on the integration degree of the specified market like rice, agricultural products, etc. by this approach. And Parsley and Wei (2001), Fan Aijun et al. (2007), and Gui Qihan et al. (2006) measured the integration degree of comprehensive markets containing varieties of products. The research on the comprehensive markets manifested another advantage of the price approach, i.e., it can collect more information to inspect the degree of market integration comprehensively.

Using the price approach to calculate the market integration index requires first the consumer price of all kinds of commodities in the 16 cities which are provided by the *Yangtze River Delta and Pearl River Delta Statistical Yearbook*.[9] The earliest data from the Yearbook in 2000 is incomplete, so we choose 2001–2007 as the sample range. There are eight classes of commodities: food, tobacco and alcohol; clothing; household facilities and articles and services; healthcare and personal articles; transportation and communication; recreation; education and cultural articles, and residence. Because of the insufficient data on tobacco and alcohol, only the other seven catalogs are chosen as original data.

With the reference of Parsley and Wei (2001), Fan Aijun et al. (2007) and Gui Qihan et al. (2006), the specific procedures of the establishment of the index are described as follows: first, we pair the 16 cities into 8 groups with 2 cities each, and choose the price index of the same catalog to get the difference of relative price ΔQ_{ijt}^{k}, and its absolute value $\left|\Delta Q_{ijt}^{k}\right|$. The calculation of price difference is based on the following formula, which utilizes the link index of commodities provided by the statistical yearbook and solves the heteroscedasticity and skewness by logarithm.

$$\Delta Q_{ijt}^{k} = \ln\left(\frac{P_{it}^{k}}{P_{it-1}^{k}}\right) - \ln\left(\frac{P_{jt}^{k}}{P_{jt-1}^{k}}\right) = \ln\left(\frac{P_{it}^{k}}{P_{jt}^{k}}\right) - \ln\left(\frac{P_{it-1}^{k}}{P_{jt-1}^{k}}\right) \tag{5.20}$$

In this formula, k represents the commodity catalog. The absolute value can erase the influence of the order of two cities in a group. After the first step, we will have the relative price difference data of a total of 5 880 ($7 \times 120 \times 7$) sets, i.e., seven catalogs of commodity, 120 city pairs ((C_{16}^2) in seven years. Second, we de-mean the $\left|\Delta Q_{ijt}^k\right|$ to eliminate the heterogeneity of each category of commodities (Parsley and Wei, 1996), and get q_{ijt}^k. Third, by calculating the variance of q_{ijt}^k, we will have 840 (120×7) observations $\mathrm{Var}\left(q_{ijt}\right)$, which measures the fluctuation range of price: the larger the range, the less the integration degree. Fourth, we merge the variance based on cities by calculating the mean of variance of one city and others, to find the market integration index inte e_{it} of each city with 112 (16×7) observations.

The market integration index of 16 cities in the YRD from 2001 to 2007 is shown in Table 5.1. Since the index indicates price variance, the high value means the lower the integration degree, and the lower value means the higher the integration degree. The dots in Figure 5.1 are the average values of the market integration index in the YRD based on the data over the years, the fitted curve of which reflects a dropping trend, indicating the increase of market integration degree in the YRD.

2. Empirical analysis

Based on these indexes, this chapter conducts further exploration of the "asymmetric spillover effect", which originates from regional differences. Since the regions in the YRD are similar in terms of geographic position, the biggest difference is probably economic development level. The purpose of this empirical research is whether the differences in development level between regions can lead to the regional difference in the spillover effect (i.e., the asymmetry of the spillover effect), which will be verified by introducing interaction terms and dummy variables.

Table 5.1 The market integration index of 16 cities in YRD (2001 to 2007)

City	*Year*						
	2001	*2002*	*2003*	*2004*	*2005*	*2006*	*2007*
Shanghai	4.759	4.740	2.573	3.721	6.239	5.116	1.495
Nanjing	4.327	9.047	3.295	5.019	3.430	4.466	3.213
Suzhou	3.540	6.918	3.295	5.002	2.809	2.572	1.278
Wuxi	5.123	6.441	2.591	3.006	2.385	3.388	1.482
Changzhou	3.168	6.855	2.977	3.147	1.933	2.700	1.529
Zhenjiang	4.778	5.592	1.272	4.067	2.648	2.140	2.138
Nantong	3.989	2.738	1.706	3.668	4.029	2.704	1.120
Yangzhou	3.499	5.476	2.253	3.161	3.622	2.047	2.050
Taizhou	15.868	18.314	2.855	6.499	3.688	1.925	1.472
Hangzhou	5.114	21.155	2.927	1.989	3.127	2.145	1.555
Ningbo	4.595	7.333	2.181	2.502	5.268	3.894	2.172
Jiaxing	6.254	6.007	3.704	4.716	2.547	6.452	1.115
Huzhou	5.769	6.788	1.781	3.195	2.299	2.967	2.044
Shaoxing	3.557	6.460	5.683	3.579	2.349	2.609	1.328
Zhoushan	2.253	7.120	1.882	2.976	3.313	3.271	1.151
Taizhou	4.020	6.390	2.687	6.176	4.309	3.121	1.480

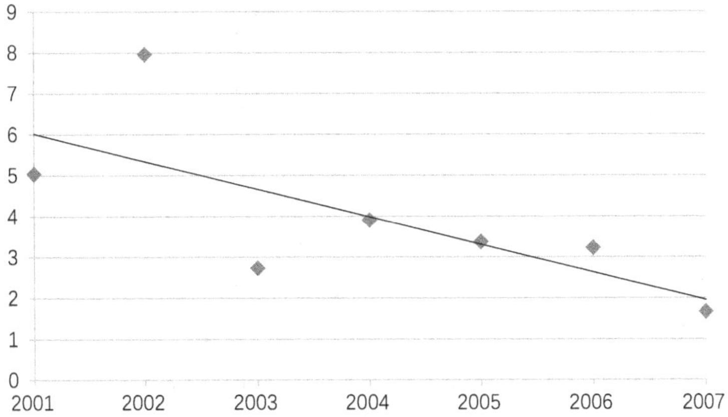

Figure 5.1 Market integration index in YRD (2001–2007)

(1) The empirical inspection is based on the interaction term

The measurement model of economic growth we adopted is from Barro (2000), with the additional market integration index and the interaction term of the market integration index (hereinafter referred to as MII) and economic development level as the explanatory variable. Measurement model 1 is shown here:

$$\text{growth}_{it} = \beta_0 + \beta_1 \cdot \text{inte}\, e_{it} + \beta_2 \cdot \text{inte}\, e_{it} \cdot \ln pg_{it} + \gamma \cdot X_{it} + \alpha_i + \varepsilon_{it} \tag{5.21}$$

$growth_{it}$ represents the growth rate of GDP per capita in city i and year t; the right part of the equation is a series of explanatory variables, the most significant ones among which are the coefficients of market integration degree (inte) and the interaction term of inte and economic development level (ln*pg*, representing the logarithm of GDP per capita). X includes a series of control variables: economic development level and its quadratic term ($\ln pg^2$, representing the square of ln*pg*), degree of opening (tra, representing a total volume of foreign trade divided by GDP), the share of government consumption in GDP (gov),[10] and fertility rate (fer).[11] β is the constant term; α represents unobserved factors related to the specific cities; ε indicates random disturbance. The main source of the original data of these variables is the *Yangtze River Delta & Pearl River Delta and Hong Kong & Macao SAR and Taiwan Statistical Yearbook (2003–2008)*; some missing data are from the *China City Statistical Yearbook* of the corresponding years. Table 5.2 provides the statistical description of the variables.

The estimated result of Model 1 is shown in Table 5.3. The most concerning interaction term of the marketed integration index and economic development level is negative and passed the significance test, which means the difference in economic development level indeed causes the variance of the influence of market integration

Table 5.2 The statistical description of variables

Variable	*Number of observations*	*Average value*	*Standard deviation*	*Minimum value*	*Maximum value*
growth	112	0.139496	0.018811	0.079456	0.180697
Inte	112	3.984	2.960477	1.115185	21.15522
inte*ln*pg*	112	40.3825	28.695 38	11.51674	216.7416
Ln*pg*	112	10.25453	0.494591	9.100414	11.23836
$\ln pg^2$	112	105.3978	10.10431	82.81754	126.3007
Tra	112	0.306283	0.16676	−0.18732	0.8044
Gov	112	0.060374	0.0261499	0.032229	0.1539961
Fer	112	2.01056	0.219249	1.211941	2.618125

Table 5.3 The influence of market integration considering the interaction term on economic growth

Variable	*re*	*fe*	*rebs*	*Febs*
Inte	0.016 5**	0.015 1**	0.016 5*	0.015 1*
inte*ln*pg*	−0.001 7**	−0.001 5**	−0.001 7*	−0.001 5*
Ln*pg*	0.355 1***	0.360 2***	0.355 1***	0.360 2***
$\ln pg^2$	−0.016 0***	−0.016 1***	−0.016 0***	−0.016 1***
Tra	0.049 1***	0.048 3***	0.049 1***	0.048 3***
Gov	0.015 2	0.077 5	0.015 2	0.077 5
Fer	0.022 9***	0.030 0***	0.022 9***	0.030 0***
Constant term	−1.875 8***	−1.934 2***	−1.875 8***	−1.934 2***
R-sq	0.780 5	0.786 7	0.780 5	0.786 7

Note: re represents the regression of random effect; fe represents the regression of fixed effect; rebs represents Bootstrap regression of random effect; febs represents Bootstrap regression of fixed effect. * means $p<0.1$, ** means $p<0.05$, *** means $p<0.01$.

on economic growth. The coefficient of MII in both the fixed effect model and random effect model is positive and also passed the significance test. The result of the Breusch-Pagan test indicates no distinct heteroscedasticity of models. With the possible measuring errors considered, we further sample 200 times by the method of Bootstrap, and the result of which is shown in the last two columns of the table. In the result of the Bootstrap test, the positive/negative sign of β_2 remained unchanged; the significance level varies slightly but is still distinct. The result of the Hausman test indicates a prominent difference between the estimated result of fixed effect and random effect. Therefore, only the fixed effect model can reach a consistent result.

To further illustrate the effect of the regional economic development level, we have the following equation based on the regression equation of evaluating the partial derivatives of MII through economic growth:

$$\frac{\text{dgrowth}}{\text{dinte}} = \beta_1 + \beta_2 \ln pg_{it} \tag{5.22}$$

Since β_2<0, the value of the right part of the equation lowers along with the increase in economic development level. The value of the partial derivative can be calculated through the values of β_1, β_2 and lnpg_{it}. The results show that there are 73 negative partial derivatives out of the total 112 observations. Therefore, unlike the conclusion of Lu Ming and Zhao (2009), the increase of MII leads to a decrease in economic growth for most of the regions in the YRD, which means that market non-integration brings about a decline in economic growth, while the market integration promotes economic growth.

(2) The empirical test is based on the dummy variable

We further test the hypothesis of the "asymmetric spillover effect" through the dummy variable of economic development level D_{it}. We apply the median to construct the dummy variable; i.e., by ranking the GDP per capita in the 16 cities in the 7 years, we will find the median is 29,346 yuan. If the GDP per capita in the city i and year t is lower than the median, then the D_{it}=0; if it is higher, then D_{it}=1. The control variable here is the same as measurement model 1. This approach divides the total sample into two groups: low economic development level and high economic development level. The advantage of dummy variable regression is that we can compare the groups of the different levels without losing the degree of freedom.[12]

The equation of measurement model 2 takes out the interaction term and adds the dummy variable. The equation is as follows:

$$\begin{aligned}\text{growth}_{it} &= \beta_0 + \sigma_0 \cdot D_{it} + \beta_1 \cdot \text{inte}_{it} + \partial_1 \cdot D_{it} \cdot \text{inte}_{it} \\ &+ \gamma \cdot X_{it} + \lambda \cdot D_{it} \cdot X_{it} + \alpha_i + \varepsilon_{it}\end{aligned} \qquad (5.23)$$

The key factor here is the coefficient of $D_{it}\cdot\text{inte}_{it}$, δ_1 and its significance, because δ_1 reflects the different influences of market integration in sample groups of high development level and low development level.

Table 5.4 presents the estimated result of Model 2. Coefficient δ_1<0 and passes the significance test. It means that compared with the sample group of low development level, in the sample group of high development level, the higher the MII, the more harmful to economic growth; i.e., market segmentation is more disadvantageous to regions of higher economic development level than to those of lower economic development level. The regression of the prior approach leads to the same result. With the model robustness considered, a further Bootstrap test is conducted with 200 samplings, the result of which is shown in the last two columns of the table. In the conclusion of the Bootstrap test, δ_1 remains the same sign and passed the significance test. The result of the Hausman test indicates that there is a distinct difference between the estimated result of fixed effect and random effect. Therefore, only the fixed effect model can reach the consistent estimated result.

In conclusion, the influence of market integration on economic growth differs for the level of economic development, which means that the same degree of

Table 5.4 The influence of market integration considering dummy variables on economic growth

Variable	*re*	*Fe*	*rebs*	*febs*
inte	−0.0002	0.0004	−0.0002	0.0004
*D**inte	−0.0021*	−0.0025**	−0.0021*	−0.0025*
ln*pg*	0.1251	0.3763	0.1251	0.3763
lnpg^2	−0.0046	−0.017	−0.0046	−0.017
tra	0.0460***	0.0460***	0.0460***	0.0460***
gov	0.1398	−0.064	0.1398	−0.064
fer	0.0107	0.0258***	0.0107	0.0258**
D	0.3466	1.2816	0.3466	1.2816
*D**ln*pg*	−0.0595	−0.2502	−0.0595	−0.2502
*D**lnpg^2	0.0021	0.0119	0.0021	0.0119
*D**gov	0.0161	0.0116	0.0161	0.0116
*D**fis	−0.1709	−0.1179	−0.1709	−0.1179
*D**fer	0.0246*	0.0199	0.0246	0.0199
Constant term	−0.6949	−1.9885	−0.6949	−1.9885
R-sq	0.7851	0.8097	0.7851	0.8097

Note: re represents the regression of random effect; fe represents the regression of fixed effect; rebs represents Bootstrap regression of random effect; febs represents Bootstrap regression of fixed effect. * means $p<0.1$, ** means $p<0.05$, *** means $p<0.01$.

market integration under different economic development levels will bring diversified effects. Therefore, the hypothesis of the asymmetric spillover effect in the theoretical model is in line with the real situation.

Section 5 Conclusion

The comprehensive research on the market integration in the YRD should be focused on not only the market integration itself, but also on market non-integration and the conflicts in the process. The three are closely related internally, so neglecting any of them will cause one-sidedness in the research. The existing research on market integration in the YRD partially explained the reasons for market integration or non-integration, but not their transformation or the conflict in the process. From the perspective of the "asymmetric spillover effect" and under the framework of regional government competition, this chapter identifies the transforming mechanism from market non-integration to integration. By the deduction with the help models, it is concluded that the rising possibility of promotion caused by the positive spillover effect will drive local governments to choose market integration, while the dropping possibility caused by the negative will drive them to market non-integration. This conclusion explains not only the transformation from market non-integration to integration, but also why some regions did not transfer. The models in this chapter illustrate that the "asymmetric spillover effect" is also a root of the conflict between regions over market integration: the two regions with positive and negative spillover effects will make the totally opposite decision.

In the empirical part of this research, 16 cities in the YRD from 2001 to 2007 are chosen as the sample for panel data. Both approaches provide the direct empirical basis for the existence of the "asymmetric spillover effect". Another significant finding of the empirical analysis is that market non-integration obstructs economic growth for most samples, which means that the YRD has passed the stage of "beggar-thy-neighbor" and entered the stage of promoting economic growth through market integration. Since the 18th National Congress of the Communist Party of China, promoting the overall economy for rapid leaps and development through regional integration has become the mainstream of economic development strategy in China. To integrate the YRD into the whole region requires not only top-level design and support from the superior government to reduce governmental interference in the economy and form a diversified incentive and promotion mechanism, but also the abandonment of the narrow idea of minding their own business by local governments and the deepened understanding of their roles in regional work division to promote development in the YRD. Currently, the "performance racing" of regional governments is common in the short term. The key is effective system design and policy demand, to realize a positive cycle of competition and support the integration of the YRD constantly.

In addition, the expansion of the YRD itself is also an opportunity and challenge for its integration process. The joining of Anhui, on the one hand, completes the existing regional work division in the YRD, and reduces the cost of labor force exports in Anhui and the industrial migration in Suzhou, Zhejiang, and Shanghai. On the other hand, the gap in economic development levels between Anhui and other regions brings up stricter requirements for integration. Under the new conditions, the interaction and cooperation between provinces and cities should be closer than before to release the integration advantages of complementing each other and add stronger energy to the economic development in China.

The models and empirical research in this chapter prove the complexity of market integration and non-integration, help us understand the behavior motives of governments at different developmental levels for market integration, and thus provide some reference for the promotion of national market integration and coordinated regional development by the central government. There are inevitably some limitations of this research. First, the model is based on static analysis rather than dynamic. Second, the conclusion of empirical research is preliminary, requiring further evidence to support the theoretical model. The following research will continue improving the model and enriching the conclusion.

Notes

1 See *Decennial Chronicle of Changjiang Delta Cities' Economic Coordination Committee* (Yangtze River Delta Urban Economic Coordination Committee, 2007)

2 In 2014, the State Council issued the Guiding Opinions on Relying on the Golden Waterway to Promote the Development of the Yangtze River Economic Belt. It clarified for the first time that Anhui, as a part of the YRD city cluster, should participate in the integrated development of the YRD. However, since Anhui is new to the group and its overall economic development level is far behind Suzhou, Zhejiang, and Shanghai, the

analysis of this chapter will focus on the traditional "small Yangtze River Delta", i.e., Suzhou, Zhejiang, and Shanghai.

3 The model also applies to the analysis of transition from market integration to non-integration.

4 Complete market integration and non-integration are both extreme conditions. For the convenience of model processing, this chapter regards the condition before the improvement as market non-integration; and that after the improvement as market integration.

5 Pi Jiancai (2008) elaborated the revenue and cost of market integration: revenue is from the geographic agglomeration effect and the rising efficiency of resource allocation caused by market expansion; while cost is from the increasing income gap between regions – the bigger the gap, the higher the cost. The spillover effect here is similar to the net income in Pi Jiancai's research.

6 See Zhou Li'an (2007) for more information about the political tournament mode.

7 The 16 cities are Shanghai, Nanjing, Suzhou, Wuxi, Changzhou, Zhenjiang, Nantong, Yangzhou, Taizhou, Hangzhou, Ningbo, Jiaxing, Huzhou, Shaoxing, Zhoushan, and Taizhou.

8 The basis of production approach is whether the structure converges. The changes of Chinese regional production structure may signify that China is gradually getting rid of the unreasonable pattern under planned economy, rather than being influenced by regional protectionism or market non-integration (Naughton, 1999). The basis of trade approach is the change of trade flows, which might be caused by the change of elasticity of product substitution (Parsley and Wei, 2001), factor endowment, economic scale, etc. (Engel and Rogers, 1998). Business cycle approach is based on the synchronism of business cycle (Xu, 2002). However, market non-integration is only part of the multiple reasons for economic cycle asynchronism (Lu Ming and Chen Zhao, 2009).

9 The statistical yearbook of Shanghai, Jiangsu, and other cities also contains the data of consumer price indexes, but their statistical calibers are different, which leaves *Yangtze River Delta and Pearl River Delta Statistical Yearbook* the only source of the CPI data of the 16 cities.

10 The government consumption does not contain the expenditures of education, science, culture and health as generally accepted in research.

11 Here uses the logarithm of fertility rate as Barro (2000) did.

12 There is also a cost to this approach: the GDP per capita being simply divided into two classes will cause much information loss but lead to some more intuitive conclusions.

References

Fai Aijun, Li Zhen, Liu Xiaoyong. The Empirical Study on Market Segmentation of China and Its Influence Factors Based on Commodity Market. Nankai Economic Studies, 2007 (10).

Robert J. Barro. Inequality and Growth in a Panel of Countries. Journal of Economic Growth, 2000 (3).

Y. Chen, H.B. Li, L.A. Zhou. Relative Performance Evaluation and the Turnover of Provincial Leaders in China. Economics Letters, 2005 (6).

Bai Chong'en, Du Yingjuan, Tao Zhigang, Tong Yueting. Local Protectionism and Industrial Concentration in China: Overall Trend and Important Factors. Economic Research Journal, 2004 (4).

Ding Congming, Ji Zhenlin, Lei Yu, Liang Zhenqiao. Diversity of Dialect and Market Integration: A Perspective of Synthetic Metropolitan Area. Economic Research Journal, 2018 (11).

Yu Donghua, Liu Yun. The Measurement and Identification of Local Protection and Market Segmentation – A Literature Review Based on the Methodology. World Economic Papers, 2009 (2).

Goletti Francesco, Ahmed Raisuddin, Farid Naser. Structural Determinants of Market Integration: The Case of Rice Markets in Bangladesh. The Developing Economies, 2007 (3).
Pi Jiancai. Regional Integration under the Local Governmental Competition. Economic Research Journal, 2008 (3).
Wang Jiankang. Spatial-temporal Patterns and Influencing Factors of Market Segmentation in China. Scientia Geographica Sinica, 2019 (1).
Fan Jianyong, Lin Yun. Product Homogeneity, Local Protectionism of Investment and Measurement of Product Market Integration in China. Economic Research Journal, 2011 (11).
H.B. Li, L.A Zhou. Political Turnover and Economic Performance: The Incentive Role of Personnel Control in China. Journal of Public Economics, 2005 (9).
Zhou Li'an. Governing China's Local Officials: An Analysis of Promotion Tournament Model. Economic Research Journal, 2007 (7).
Zhou Li'an. The Incentive and Cooperation of Government Officials in the Political Tournaments: An Interpretation of the Prolonged Local Protectionism and Duplicative Investments in China. Economic Research Journal, 2004 (6).
Zhou Li'an, Li Hongbin, Chen ye. Relative Performance Evaluation: An Empirical Analysis of Turnover of the Chinese Local Officials. China Journal of Economics, 2005 (1).
Shen Liren, Dai Yuanchen. The Formation, Drawback and Root of Fragmented Economy in China. Economic Research Journal, 1990 (4).
T.P. Lyons. China's Cellular Economy: A Test of the Fragmentation Hypothesis. Journal of Comparative Economics, 1985 (2).
Chen Min, Gui Qihan, Lu Ming, Chen Zhao. How to Maintain China's High Growth Rate via Scale Economy – An Empirical Study of Economic Opening and Domestic Market Segmentation. China Economic Quarterly, 2007 (10).
Lu Ming, Chen Zhao. Fragmented Growth: Why May Economic Opening Worsen Domestic Market Segmentation?. Economic Research Journal, 2009 (3).
Lu Ming, Chen Zhao, Yan Ji. Increasing Return, Development Strategy and Regional Economic Segmentation. Economic Research Journal, 2004 (1).
B. Naughton. How Much Can Regional Integration Do to Unify China's Market. How Far Across the River, 2000 (1).
D.C. Parsley, S.J Wei. Convergence to the Law of One Price without Trade Barriers or Currency Fluctuations. New York: Social Science Electronic Publishing, 1996.
D.C.,Parsley, S.J. Wei. Limiting Currency Volatility to Stimulate Goods Market Integration: A Price Based Approach. New York: Social Science Electronic Publishing, 2001.
S. Poncet. A Fragmented China: Measure and Determinants of Chinese Domestic Market Disintegration. Review of International Economics, 2005 (3).
S. Poncet. The "Non-integration" Trend of Chinese Market? Comparative Analysis on the Market Integration in China and the World. World Economic Papers, 2002 (1).
Gui Qihan, Chen Min, Lu Ming, Chen Zhao. Does the Commodity Market in China Tend to Segmentation or Integration: An Analysis Based on Relative Price. The Journal of World Economy, 2006 (2).
P. Samuelson. Theoretical Note on Trade Problems. The View of Economics and Statistics, 1964 (2).
Li Shantong, Hou Yongzhi, Liu YunZhong, Chen Bo. The Analysis on Survey of Local Protection in China Domestic Market. Economic Research Journal, 2004 (11).
Liu Shenglong, Hu Angang. Transportation Infrastructure and Regional Economic Integration in China. Economic Research Journal, 2011 (3).
Zou Weixing, Zhou Liqun. Analysis of Regional Economic Integration: Yangtze River Delta, Pearl River Delta and Bohai Rim Region. Reform, 2010 (10).

Yu Wen, Huang Jikun. Grain Market Reforms of China: A Study in the Perspective of Rice Market Integration. Economic Research Journal, 1998 (3).
Xu Xianxiang, Li Xun, Wang Meijin. Regional Integration, Economic Growth and Political Promotion. China Economic Quarterly, 2007 (7).
X.P. Xu. Have the Chinese Provinces Become Integrated under Reform. China Economic Review, 2002 (13).
Yangtze River Delta Urban Economic Coordination Committee. Decennial Chronicle of Yangtze River Delta Urban Economic Coordination Committee (Two volumes). Shanghai: Wenhui Press, 2007.
Lin Yifu, Liu Peilin. Local Protectionism and Market Integration: An Inspection from the Perspective of Development Strategy. China Center for Economic Research (Working Paper Series), 2014.
A. Young. The Razor's Edge: Distortions and Incremental Reform in the People's Republic of China. The Quarterly Journal of Economics, 2000 (4).

6 Competition among local governments and industrial structure convergence

Wu Fuxiang

Section 1 Introduction

For more than 30 years, since the reform and opening up, the Chinese economy has been growing rapidly. A vital economic logic behind it is that the tournament of bringing in business and investments between local governments within the framework of financial decentralization and an official promotion system has increased regional economic development (Zhou Li'an, 2007). However, the Chinese economy has entered a period of a new normal, featuring a shift from high-speed growth to medium-high growth, a shift from quantity and speed to quality and efficiency, a shift to an innovation-driven growth model, and a shift to multiple challenges. A long-term extensive investment leads to the industrial structure convergence between regions and the severe overcapacity in heavy-asset industries.[1] As a result, the tournament model of local governments is hard to sustain. Fundamentally speaking, the benefits of attracting investments for competition by local government is from the opening pattern under the framework of the WTO, where the southeastern coast was inserted into GVC through OEM. Chinese industrialization is driven by foreign direct investment, which makes attracting foreign capital the main method of driving local economic growth. However, the advantages of geographic location have caused severe centralization in capacity distribution and the one-way flow trend of all kinds of production factors toward major coastal cities, leading the transformation of the economic geography of China. Currently, with the enormous economic volume in China and sluggish growth of foreign investments, external forces can no longer lead the transformation of economic geography. In the meantime, the extremely imbalanced benefit level between regions urgently requires a two-way flow of factors to drive cross-regional industrial cooperation.

For this purpose, the central government has explicitly put forward strategic measures for optimizing the spatial pattern of economic development, including the Belt and Road Initiative, Asian Infrastructure Investment Bank, Internet Plus, supply-side structural reform, expansion of the pilot free trade zone, coordinated development of Beijing-Tianjin-Hebei region, Yangtze River Economic Belt, etc. Among them, the supply-side structural reform is based on the framework of the new political economy. It emphasizes the major principle of socialist political economics with Chinese characteristics in the economic reform. From an industrial

DOI: 10.4324/9781003455943-6

perspective, the supply-side structural reform should be focused on solving overcapacity and promoting industry transformation and upgrading, the key to which is guiding the industrial development by remodeling the logic of the political economy for regional economic development.

For example, under the general background of the Belt and Road Initiative, the mobility of industrial capital and foreign investment attraction coexist. From this perspective, China needs to not only upgrade its function in GVC but also establish a reasonable domestic value chain and remodel economic geography through reallocation and adjustment of production capacity. The Yangtze River Delta region, as the most dynamic part of China's economy, based on a series of significant strategic plans like *Regional Planning for the Yangtze River Delta Regional, Guiding Opinions on Promoting the Development of the Yangtze River Economic Belt by Relying on the Golden Waterway, Yangtze River Delta City Cluster Development Plan*, etc. should play a demonstrative role for other places in China. However, local governments followed the logic of competing in attracting capital when being led by the central government to industrial transformation, which leads to the current surging tide of investment and industrial isomorphism (Lin Yifu et al., 2010). Theoretically speaking, the regions with similar resource endowments can more easily form similar or basically identical industrial structure. For example, in the highly externalized YRD, regions have similar structures in terms of the foundation of industrial development and the position in GVC. In the process of the regional industrial upgrade, the late-developed state-owned enterprises tend to achieve a consensus on the next promising industry (Li Yifu, 2007). The irrational investment in the same or similar industries by regional governments and enterprises will inevitably cause the problem of regional industrial isomorphism.

Since the division of labor was proposed by Adam Smith, industrial isomorphism has always been criticized; people tend to relate it to repetitive construction and industrial inefficiency. Under the overall background of supply-side structural reform, the development goals of solving overcapacity and raising supply quality require lower industrial isomorphism, so that the industrial structural adjustment can follow the change in demand structure. Under the current price system led by local governments, their objective functions are mutually independent, which is why investment convergence may lead to an industrial structure convergence between regions. Therefore, the question we need to clarify is to what extent is the isomorphism in the industrial structure in the export-oriented regions exemplified by the YRD? What are the reasons for industrial isomorphism? Does the modest industrial isomorphism promote regional economic integration and coordinated development? Especially under the framework of the new political economy, the problems of regional equality and efficiency have become national strategic problems. In order to answer these questions, this chapter, from the perspective of the match between industrial structure and factor structure, reveals the logic of industrial isomorphism in the political economy and explores the possible path of local governments coordinating the industrial division and cooperation between regions.

This chapter contains the following contents: Section two reviews the research context of cross-regional industrial cooperation and the contribution margin of this chapter; Section three deduces the cause of industrial isomorphism and its influence on regional development based on the matching model of heterogeneous industries and enterprises; Section four conducts statistical analysis and inspects the problem of industrial isomorphism and overcapacity of subdivided industries, taking the YRD as an example; Section five is the variable inspection, verifying the relative propositions by the data of subdivided industries in the YRD; and Section six is the conclusion and policy suggestions.

Section 2 Literature review

Generally speaking, China, as a major economic entity successfully transformed from planned economy to market economy, still needs to explore and improve its mechanism and system. Wu Jinglian (2014) pointed out that the systematic obstacles ultimately are caused by excessive government interference in resource allocation and economy, which lead to market fragmentation, local protectionism, administrative monopoly, industry protection, and market segmentation. Tian Guoqiang and Chen Xudong (2015) believed that in the GDP growth tournament, local governments tend to neglect the comparative advantage of local factors and compatibility of industrial structure, and prefer industries with quick returns, low barriers to entry, and mature techniques. The soft constraint on resource allocation and immature accountability mechanism of local governments and leaders of state-owned enterprises also fostered the problem of industrial isomorphism and overcapacity.

In the research on the micro mechanisms of the cause of regional industrial isomorphism, Hu Xiangting and Zhang Lu (2005) conducted empirical research on the samples from the whole nation, and discovered that the increase in trade cost would lead to a similar industrial structure, while the influence of governmental direct investment is uncertain. The changing trend of the regional industrial structure in China is not convergence, but a diversified development based on comparative advantage. Liu Zaiqi and Xu Yanfei (2014) proposed that the influence of local governmental behaviors on industrial isomorphism is different before and after the reform of the tax distribution system. Before the reform, government behaviors characterized by market segmentation intensified the regional industrial isomorphism; after the reform, the government behavior is primarily "land management", which weakens regional factor mobility and trade barriers, helps leverage comparative advantages of each region, and promotes specialized regional industry development. Yu Donghua and Lv Yinan (2015) studied the photovoltaic industry in China and concluded that local governments would support enterprises to clump together to develop strategic emerging industries for short-term profit. Therefore, the government subsidies on land price, finance support, and other kinds of government interference would cause over-investment, industrial structural convergence, and overcapacity. Besides government intervention, the internal limitation and drawbacks of the market mechanism is also an important reason for convergence. Lin Yifu et al. (2010) believed that in the process of industrial upgrading of the late-developing countries at the lower end of the GVC, their enterprises tend to invest in well-developed industries with relatively mature techniques and saturated markets in developed countries. Under the environment of seriously incomplete information, their investment would flock to the same industries, leading to severe industrial isomorphism and overcapacity. In fact, the blindness of market entities is not the only reason for overcapacity; the lagging market regulation is also an important factor. The research of Hong Yinxing (2016) proposed that the consumption demand of residents upgraded when they entered the phase of middle income. They would pay more attention to health, security, and quality. However, the production and service remained in the phase of low income. The sluggish development of product heterogeneity and industry transformation and upgrading would inevitably cause insufficient effective supply and the co-existence of lower-end supply and inefficient supply, leading to the problem of accumulating stock and overcapacity.

How to deal with the market drawbacks caused by regional industrial isomorphism? Liu Wei (2016) indicated that the key to system reform is to improve the market system and maintain market order. In the theoretical system of the new political economy, the market's decisive role in resource allocation can only be played when the contradiction of too much government interference and insufficient government function was solved, i.e., leaving the plight of market failure and government failure. From the perspective of supply-side structural reform, the reform and transformation of the Chinese economy are boosting the transition of the socialist market economy with Chinese characteristics under the ownership reform, with public ownership playing the dominant role and the unified framework of cultivation market mechanism. Regarding the plight of market reform, Tian Guoqiang (2013) believed that achieving the goals of market reform requires a suitable incentive and evaluation mechanism of government performance, and the implementation of reform policies. Wei Xinghua (2015) proposed that we should secure the order of the market economy, eliminate market fragmenting, and legally regulate the intervention of government in market and enterprises. Li Yining (2015) also pointed out that law-based governance is consistent with deepening economic reform. Only a robust law system and strict practice can guarantee the success of economic reform.

In regard to industrial isomorphism specifically in the YRD, the early researchers studied it through calculating the structural similarity coefficient based on the three main categories or industrial sectors. For example, Fan Jianyong (2004) concluded that under the framework of new economic geography, integration would certainly cause the spatial transition of the manufacturing industry and increasing structural diversity between regions. The research found that Zhejiang and Shanghai participated more significantly in the internal labor division in the YRD than Jiangsu, leading to intense spatial adjustment. Although it was believed that the integration in the YRD would cause spatial transition of the manufacturing industry and differentiation of regional structures, it did not reveal the internal reasons for the change, quantitatively measure or evaluate the industrial isomorphism, or analyze the formative mechanism of regional professionalization. Jin Xiangrong and Zhu Xiwei (2002) also did not conduct quantitative analysis, but studied the formation of regional professionalization and explained it as the spatial competition between industry-specific factors and common factors. Bai Chong'en et al. (2004) researched the determining factors and changing trends of the industry concentration quantitatively. The target of this research is the whole country. It focused on local protectionism when considering the determinant of regional concentration of industries. It also took economies of scale and cluster effect of industry into account, but it missed the inter-regional industrial isomorphism and its formative mechanism.

This research on regional industrial isomorphism is mainly based on a macro-structure of the classification of the three main industries, without observation of the structure of subdivided industries. The degree of structural similarity of the regional manufacturing industry is much lower than that of the tertiary industry. Although there is isomorphism to some extent from the perspective of the similarity coefficient, if looking from the aspect of product structure inside the manufacturing industry, the phenomenon of regional industrial isomorphism is not severe at all. In addition, only through quantitative measurement can we objectively evaluate whether there is an industrial isomorphism, overlapping construction, or vicious competition. The research between Wang Yeqiang and Wei Houkai (2007) and Yu Liangchun and Fu Qiang (2008) has provided some inspiring theories from this perspective. The former inspected the data of 28 manufacturing industries in China under the theoretical framework of spatial competition, concluding that the regional comparative advantages suppressed the geographical cluster of industries; the latter studied the interaction between regional administrative monopoly and industrial isomorphism based on the provincial panel data.

In fact, industrial isomorphism is related to regional competition and regional factor matching, as well as the regional trade barrier and the relevance of intermediates, which is not emphasized in these research findings. As pointed out in the research of Krugman and Venables (1996), when there were trade barriers and intermediates, regional economic integration and professionalization are the result of both aggregation and dispersion. These forces originated from the integration of the capital market and free mobility of factors (Anwar, 2006). Even in regions with similar technical competence and factor endowment, competition and human resource accumulation are still the essential driving power of regional professionalization and inter-regional trade (Rotemberg and Saloner, 2000). The regional industrial objectives and long-term professionalization trend are related to the government's industrial choice and policies to maximize their comparative advantages (Kalemli-Ozcan et al., 2001). The marginal contribution of this chapter is focusing on the role of local government in the competition of moving factors and trade of intermediates. Based on the perspective of supply-side structural reform in the new political economy, we built a regional competition model matching the heterogeneous industry and labor force to analyze the cross-regional production capacity cooperation, the degree of industrial isomorphism in the YRD based on the data of subdivided industries and provide microscope testimonies to the development strategy of cross-regional production capacity cooperation.

Section 3 The model of industrial heterogeneity-manpower matching

1. The fundamental model

The key to both industrial isomorphism and cross-regional production capacity cooperation lies in the allocation of production factors in regions and industries. Generally speaking, the regional industrial system originates from first the allocation of industrial capital in regions, then leads the allocation of the labor force in industries, thus forming a stable matching relation between industry and labor force. Therefore, by referencing the matching theory of Costinot and Vogel (2010), this chapter conducts a model analysis of the relevance of labor skills and technical complexity in regional competition and factor matching. Unlike the modeling logic of Costinot and Vogel, we focused on the influence of local government intervention in the balance of matching, the classification of ownership, and the analysis of the vital mechanism of the conflict and harmony of industrial spatial allocation.

Presumably there is a certain volume of the labor force and industry in each region in the economic system. The labor force is consistent with different skill level s of continuous skill distribution, so its density function is $V(s)$, and the distribution interval $s \in [\underline{S}, \overline{s}]$.

There is only one ultimate consumer good in the economic system, on which laborers spend all their income: the utility function of the monotonic increasing function of the ultimate product. The production of it requires a series of continuous intermediate products, the function of which is in D-S form:

$$Y = \left\{ \int_{i \in I} B(i)[Y(i)]^{(\sigma-1)/\sigma} d\sigma \right\}^{\sigma/(\sigma-1)} \tag{6.1}$$

In formula (6.1), Y(i)>0 means the input of intermediate product with technical complexity i, $i \in [\underline{i}, \overline{i}]$; $1 < \sigma < \infty$ represents the substitution elasticity of the intermediate product. The $B(i) \geq 0$ means exogenous technical parameter. If $B'(i) \geq 0$, then the industry with higher technical complexity can produce more ultimate product with a unit of input. In other words, i is also the index that describes the industrial level: the higher it is, the higher-end the industry.

The production of the intermediate product also requires the input of the labor force, which is substitutable. The production function of intermediate products is:

$$Y(i) = \int_{\underline{s}}^{\overline{s}} A(s,i) L(s,i) ds \tag{6.2}$$

In formula (6.2), $L(s,i) \geq 0$ means the input of labor force with skill level s in the industry of level. $A(s,i)$ represents the matching degree of the labor force and industry. If $A(s,i)$ is logarithmic supermodular, i.e., for any $i' > i, S' > S$, the inequation $A(i', S')A(i,S) > A(i', S)A(i, S')$ stands. This quality means that the production efficiency of a heterogeneous labor force will present more differences in industries of higher levels. Since the labor force can freely move through sectors, the payment is only related to skill levels.

The profit function of the sector of ultimate product is: $\Pi = \left\{ \int_{i \in I} B(i)[Y(i)]^{(\sigma-1)/\sigma} d\sigma \right\}^{\sigma/(\sigma-1)} - \int_{\underline{i}}^{\overline{i}} p(i)Y(i)di$. p(i) represents the price of the intermediate product at level i. The profit function of the manufacturer of intermediate goods is: $\prod(i) = \int_{\underline{S}}^{\overline{S}} [p(i)A(s,i) - w(s)]L(s,i)ds$. w($s$)>0 represents the payment of labor force with skill level s.

In the competitive balance with maximized consumer (labor force) utility, profit of enterprises, free entrance and exit of enterprises, and zero profit, there is a corresponding functional relationship between the labor force and industry: $i = M(s), M(\cdot)$ is the strictly increasing function, with boundary value $\underline{i} = M(\underline{s}), \overline{i} = M(\overline{s})$.[2] Function $M(\cdot)$ is the basic matching function of labor force and industry.

2. Short-run equilibrium

There is region 1 and region 2 in the economic system. In the short term, production factors, i.e., industrial capital and labor force, cannot flow across regions while resources are allocated among industries. Products can be transported freely between regions without cost. The original endowment conditions are different: the technical complexity of industry in region 1 is higher than in region 2, i.e., $\overline{i_1} > \overline{i_2}$, indicating a comparative advantage of developing high-end industry in region 1. The different industrial structure leads to a diversified labor force structure, i.e., $\overline{s}_1 > \overline{s}_2$, $\underline{s_1} = \underline{s_2}$.

When products flow freely without trade cost, the price of intermediates is equal. Under the condition of zero profit, $i \in \left[i_2, \overline{i_2} \right]$ for any industry. The labor force skill level in region j is S_j^i, and $w\left(s_j^i\right) = p(i)A\left(s_j^i, i\right)$. If the salary of the labor force with the same skill in the two regions are different, for example, $w_1(s) > w_2(s)$, then $M_1(s) > M_2(s)$, so the labor force in region 2 with skill level s can raise their salary to $w_1(s)$. when they move to sectors of skill complexity $M_1(s)$. Therefore, free trade of product makes the two regions match the same labor force in the same industry, i.e., when $s \in [\underline{s_2}, \overline{s}_2], \cdot M_1(s) = M_2(s)$. It indicates that the surplus labor force with high skill in region 1 would generally match with the high-end industries.

From the perspective of the global industry division, China is generally at the lower link of GVC. In the process of dynamic industrial upgrading, the top-level design inevitably requires local government to learn from the experience of industry development in developed countries. Therefore, the local governments tend to be influenced by the effect of "opportunity convergence" in terms of industry selection: enterprise investment would surge into certain strategic emerging industries. Driven by the GDP tournament and the urge to expand the tax base, local governments would provide subsidies in regard to land, loans, and other aspects to enterprises who choose to enter these industries. Improper government interference lowers the entry barrier and intensifies repeated construction and industrial convergence, which would inevitably lead to overcapacity during the downturn of market demand. Based on the current research, governmental behavior, local resources, transportations and historical factors of industrial structure all influence the converging or diverging trend to some extent. Especially after the decentralization of authority and tax reform, the transition of power structure strengthened the convergence of local industrial structures. Compared to before the reform, the current financial power and tax regulations in China are gradually centralized, while the power of investment and financing and the administration of enterprises are decentralized to local governments. There are two effects: on the one hand, the fiscal revenue of the local government was reduced; on the other hand, local governments are endowed with more freedom of economic decision-making. The former causes the long-term imbalance of financial revenue and expenditure between regions, while the latter enlarges the local governments' desire of expanding investment to improve growth. The centralization and decentralization of the power of finance and tax, investment, and financing make local governments strongly wish to solidify their tax base to secure fiscal revenue. Under such a financial and taxation system, local enterprises that significantly contribute to local taxation would naturally be protected.

Therefore, presumably, local governments would make some industrial policies, for example, "optimizing industrial structure" and developing "strategic emerging industry", and intentionally bring in some highly sophisticated industries without sift of market competition for their performance and tax base. If the industrial structure of region 2 is the same as that of region 1 after introducing industries, the matching pattern of the labor force and industry has changed; the function of the new one is $\hat{M}_2(s)$. Since the labor force structure in region 2 remained the same while higher-level industries have been brought in, the higher-level labor force would rapidly be matched to high-level industries, while the industrial-level other labor force matched to would also be raised correspondingly. According to trade theory, the factor price of the two regions is the same, but the salary of the labor force with the same skills is not, because of the different industrial structures. The new matching function is:

$$M_1(\mathrm{s}) < \hat{M}_2(s), \forall s \in \left[\underline{s}_2, \overline{s}_2\right] \tag{6.3}$$

From the perspective of industry, then:

$$M_1^{-1}(\mathrm{i}) > \hat{M}_2^{-1}(i), \forall i \in \left[i_1, \hat{i}\right] \tag{6.4}$$

Formula (6.3) indicates that the labor force in region 2 after the introduction of higher-level industries would be matched to higher industries, leading to an increase in overall output in region 2. Correspondingly, the tax base in region 2 would be expanded to meet the development demand of local government. However, formula (6.4) illustrates that in the industries of the same skill complexity, the labor force in region 1 has a higher skill level than that in region 2, which means a differentiated output efficiency, especially in the high-level industries: some high-end industries in region 2 showed some properties of low-end industries. Therefore, we have the following propositions:

Proposition 1: in the matching model of skill and capacity in the two regions, the local government's preference for industrial development orientation and their GDP tournament and urge to expand tax base enlarge the effect of the growing power of finance and taxation, local investment and financing, and administration of enterprise, strengthen the driving power of subsidies in regard to land and loan etc. entering the "strategic emerging industries", leading to the mismatching of laborers' skill level and industry's technical complexity, and the plight of "high-end industry becomes low-end" in regions with poorer endowment.

Proposition 1 indicates that market failure and improper interference by local government have disturbed regional industrial distribution. Excessive government support and entry limitation are the main types of government interference. Supportive policies are simply the differentiated treatment of the investment project and policy measures for different enterprises, causing the convergence of industrial structure and regional overcapacity.

In fact, higher-level industries should have a higher entry barrier, i.e., a high demand for investment quality and quantity in talents, techniques, and capital. However, some investment is blinded by administrative means, dragging the high-end industries into low-level repetitive competition and lowering their levels. The large number of low-quality products generated through excessive investment cannot be absorbed by the market, leading to low-end overcapacity and hindering the smooth operation of the economy.

3. Long-run equilibrium

In the long run, the mobility of the labor force factor is hypothetically weaker than that of industrial capital, because of the convenience of capital investment brought about by the household registration system and advanced financial system. Labor force cannot flow between regions, while industrial capitals can with certain replacement costs of the enterprise migration. Under the current price system, the investment of state-owned and state-holding enterprises, representing the investment willingness of local governments, are less market-oriented, while the investment decisions of private and foreign-invested enterprises, made based on the Tiebout model,[3] are relatively highly market-oriented. Therefore, local protectionism would usually generate negative effects on industrial structures. Although it can guarantee the fiscal revenue of local government to some extent, local government, when protecting the local economy, would neglect its function of the Tiebout model when enterprises vote with tier feet in the economic decision making, causing potential conflicts in terms of solving repetitive construction and industrial isomorphism.

Furthermore, the replacement cost of the migration of private enterprise is C_p, while that of state-owned and state-holding enterprises is C_S, and $C_S > C_P$. Based on the logarithmic supermodel of intermediate production function (2), it is known that the higher-level industries will have a higher elasticity of labor force skill level. Therefore, there is a critical value in industry level i^*: when $i > i_P^*$, $\Pi_1(i) - \Pi_2(i) \geq C_P$. It means that the private enterprises whose level is higher than i^* will migrate to region 1. However, the replacement cost of state-owned and state-holding enterprises is relatively high, i.e., $i_S^* > i_P^*$. When C_S is relatively high, the inequation $\Pi_1(i) - \Pi_2(i) \geq C_S$ is impossible, so the state-owned and state-holding enterprises would not migrate. Therefore, we have the next proposition:

Proposition 2: in the matching model of skill and capacity in the two regions, the convergence and divergence of long-term investment sources and qualities are the main factors that determine industrial isomorphism. Evaluating regional industrial isomorphism requires the inspection of the property right of all kinds of investment, which is the key to the conflict and harmony of industrial spatial distribution. The investment of state-owned and state-holding enterprises leads to a rise in industrial isomorphism. The industrial choices and policies made by local governments under the mechanism of the Tiebout model to maximize their comparative advantages can effectively reduce industrial isomorphism.

Based on proposition 2, we could know that $\partial i^* / \partial \overline{S}_2 > 0$, indicating that the local government has fully considered the Tiebout model when making decisions about direct investment, i.e., when the fiscal expenditures are mainly spent on local infrastructure and human resources under the combined multiplier effect and spillover and feedback effect, the policies will increase the spatial differentiation of inter-regional industrial structure through the connection between local market effect and price index effect.

Proposition 2 only stands when the government investment in state-owned and state-holding enterprises, compared to the investment on local infrastructure and reformation of enterprises, breaks away from the local economic cycle for lack of external economic effect. For example, after years of processing trade, the YRD has formed a relatively complete division system in the international manufacturing system predominated by multinational cooperation. Therefore, generally speaking, the current industrial structure of subdivided industries in the YRD is harmonious without the so-called structural conflict. First, for a long time, the organizational structure of the enterprises in the YRD, influenced by both foreign capital and private companies, has completely broken the pattern of government capital monopolizing industrial development, which means a sufficient degree of market competition between enterprises. Second, enterprises are relatively proactive in terms of organizational management and industrial spatial distribution. Although the enterprises' development in another place may be interfered with by the government, such interference is quite limited. In addition, the work division within enterprises in the YRD and the industrial labor division system under the market-oriented conditions are mainly based on the efficiency-increasing profit principles brought about by specialized labor division. Especially under the mechanism of the Tiebout model, the spatial distribution of the productivity of local enterprises, including foreign-invested enterprises, has reflected the comparative advantages of industrial division between regions, with a low possibility of repetitive construction and vicious competition.

Section 4 Statistical description of the variances between regions and industrial structure

1. Research samples and variable definition

Since agriculture, service industry, and industries of mining, electricity, steaming, thermal water, gas, and tap water are highly dependent on specific resources and population distribution, this chapter takes the manufacturing industry as the analysis object. In terms of the time, the reform of decentralization in China was from 1980 to 1994; the transition of the administration pattern of central and local power is after the tax reform in 1994, while the rapid improvement of regional economic integration is at the beginning of the 21st century. With the consideration of the adjustment of statistical caliber, this chapter chooses 27 industries in manufacturing in the YRD from 2000 to 2014 as the research samples.[4]

(1) Dissimilarity of industrial structure (called *Distruct*)

Theoretically, the indexes of dissimilarity of industrial structure include industrial structure conversion value, Moore structure conversion value, structure entropy index, and industrial structure similarity coefficient.[①5] The measurement and calculation in this chapter adopt the index measurement methods of Krugman (1991). For the dissimilarity of industry i, the measuring formula is: $\text{Distruct}^{i}_{nm,t} = \sum_{n}^{N} \left| \frac{Y_{in,t}}{Y_{n,t}} - \frac{Y_{im,t}}{Y_{m,t}} \right|, n, m = 1,2,3$ representing Jiangsu, Shanghai, and Zhejiang respectively, and $n \neq m$. represents time; while i represents industry; $Distruct^{i}_{nm,t}$ reflects the industrial isomorphism of industry i represented by the value of industrial output in area n and m, and time t. The smaller value means the more severe isomorphism; the bigger means the more severe dissimilarity.

(2) Degree of industry market competition (called *Dmar*)

This variable is used to reflect the degree of market competition in the subdivided manufacturing industry in the YRD. Although there are numerous indicators that measure marketization, few of which are based on the industry level. According to the theory of optimal resource allocation efficiency in the market, factors always flow into the industries with the highest rate of return, stabilizing the inter-regional industrial structure on their competitive advantages. Based on the data of the industrial output of private and foreign-invested enterprises in subdivided manufacturing industries, this chapter designs a vital index of product market competition in subdivided industries from the aspects of absolute and relative quantity. From the perspective of relative quantity, we first calculate the dissimilarity of non-state-owned economy proportion through the method we used for *Distruct* and then calculate its reciprocal. The closer the proportions, the bigger the variable.[6] From the perspective of absolute quantity, we calculate the average value of the non-state-owned economy proportion in three regions to reflect the volume of the product market of the industry. According to the index measurement method, the closer the proportion, the bigger the market scale and the degree of marketization. See formula (6.5) for the specific measurement, in which y represents the output value of non-state-owned enterprises.

$$\text{Dmar}_{nm,t}^{i} = \frac{1}{3}\sum_{n}^{N}\frac{y_{in,t}}{y_{n,t}} / \sum_{n}^{N}\left|\frac{y_{in,t}}{y_{n,t}} - \frac{y_{im,t}}{y_{m,t}}\right| \tag{6.5}$$

(3) Dissimilarity of government intervention (called *Dinter*)

This variable is used to reflect the dissimilarity of government intervention in industrial development. Under the current mechanism of finançe, taxation, and official evaluation, industrial taxation is one of the significant motivations for government intervention. By adopting the measurement method of *Distruct, Dinter* is measured through the dissimilarity of taxation in subdivided manufacturing industries. If regional governments are all optimistic about certain industries and willing to support them for economic growth, then they are strongly motivated to support the industries with short-term returns in a flock.

(4) Dissimilarity of state-owned industrial investment (called *Dgov*)

This variable describes the degree of the government's direct participation in market economic activities. Because of the lack of the investment data of the state-owned enterprise in subdivided manufacturing industries in some provinces, the data source of this chapter is the annual average balance of the net value of fixed assets in state-owned and state-holding enterprises. By means of the measuring method of *Distruct*, this chapter uses the dissimilarity of the data to reflect the different investment willingness of local governments.

(5) Activity level of construction transformation investment (called *Dtiebout*)

This variable is the activity level of construction and transformation in the subdivided manufacturing industries under the current price system. The measuring method is the same as *Dmar*, with the statistical yearbook as the data source. It describes not only the local government's public expenditure, but also the investment willingness in the construction and transformation of all kinds of economic entities including private and foreign-invested enterprises. The local government's investment in industrial infrastructure objectively influences the industrial convergence or divergence, representing the investment willingness of enterprises under the mechanism of the Tiebout model.

The data is from the yearbook of each province and city from 2001 to 2015. Some missing data is supplemented by the method of interpolation. The "*Dgov*" is a stock concept, while "*Dtiebout*" is an incremental concept, expressed in "renovation and transformation investment in subdivided industries".

Figure 6.1 Distruct of some manufacturing industries in YRD

2. Analysis of structural differences between regions and industries

First, *Distruct* of manufacturing subdivided industries in the YRD from 2000 to 2014 is measured and calculated. Representative industries are pharmaceutical manufacturing, non-metallic minerals, chemical fiber, ferrous metal, transportation, textile, communication device, etc.[7]

As Figure 6.1 shows, the regional isomorphism problem is severe in some industries, such as pharmaceutical manufacturing, non-metallic minerals, chemical fiber, and ferrous metal; and not in transportation, textile, or communication devices. The reasons are that first, the regions in the YRD are close to each other with similar resource endowment, industry and commerce, and development conditions, which leads to not only similar industrial structure, but also a wider range of industrial clusters. Second, from the perspective of industry, the heavy-asset industries, typically the chemical fiber, petrochemical, and ferrous metal industries, make a significant contribution to local taxation and GDP growth. Therefore, under the current taxation and official evaluation system, they are heavily protected and supported by the government. Third, from the perspective of dynamic industry upgrading, the governments' consensus on prospective industries, such as new material, new energy, and biological medicine, leads to the investment in a flock.

Figure 6.1 also indicates that transportation, textile, and communication devices present not only a severe dissimilarity, but an expanding trend, which means they are developing toward the coordination of regional labor division and deepened industries. In the open international production system, the industrial spatial distribution in China is directly driven by the international capital led by multinational corporations to a large extent. Although the resource endowment is similar in the YRD (electronics, automobile, machinery, chemical engineering, medicine, etc. have become the major industries in most cities), there are differences of leading industries. For example, from 2007 to 2014, the top three industries in Jiangsu are communication device, chemical product, and electric machinery in sequence, accounting for about 34% of the local manufacturing industry; those in Shanghai are communication device, transportation, and generic equipment, accounting for 43%; those in Zhejiang are textile, electric machinery, and chemical products, accounting for 30% (see Table 6.1).

According to the gross output distribution of industrial enterprises above the designated size, this chapter also calculates the structural entropy index and industrial structure similarity coefficient of the mainstay manufacturing industries in 16 core cities of the YRD and classifies the competitive industries into four basic types based on development phase: (1) electric + automobile + heavy chemical industry, represented by Shanghai; (2) electric + heavy chemical industry, including Suzhou and Nanjing; (3) light textile industry, represented by Shaoxing, Nantong, Jiaxing and Huzhou; (4) balanced development, including Hangzhou, Wuxi, Ningbo, Changzhou, Taizhou, Zhenjiang, Yangzhou, and Taizhou. Although the leading

Table 6.1 The proportion of top eight industries to the total industrial output value in YRD (%)

Ranking	*Jiangsu (66.14)*		*Shanghai (72.67)*		*Zhejiang (58.21)*	
	Industry	*Proportion*	*Industry*	*Proportion*	*Industry*	*Proportion*
1	Communication device	14.37	Communication device	19.63	Textile	11.53
2	Chemical products	11.20	Transportation	15.29	Electric machinery	9.99
3	Electric machinery	8.62	Generic equipment	8.29	Chemical products	8.37
4	Ferrous metal	7.82	Chemical products	7.90	Generic equipment	7.72
5	Transportation	7.10	Electric machinery	6.87	Transportation	7.29
6	Textile	6.41	Ferrous metal	5.69	Communication device	4.46
7	Generic equipment	6.10	Petroleum refinery	4.96	Chemical fiber	4.45
8	Instruments and apparatus	4.53	Special equipment	4.05	Metal products	4.41

Data source: the statistical yearbook of Jiangsu, Shanghai, and Zhejiang from 2008 to 2015 and the yearbook of foreign trade.

industries of these cities are repetitive to some extent, they also present distinct differentiation and complementarity. Textile, chemical, and pharmaceutical manufacturing industries have formed relatively complete industrial chains with closely related upstream and downstream industries; each of them contains one or more links in the chain. Therefore, the industrial structure similarity coefficient is higher than reality.[8] In fact, according to the result of the location quotient, the more categories of industries and smaller the regions, the higher the *Distruct*.

Based on the theory of industrial cluster, the partial convergence of industrial structure is inevitable when economic development reaches a certain stage. It is utilizing the comparative advantage and competitive advantage, and the necessary condition of market division. The convergence of industrial structure to some degree is the foundation of the industrial cluster; and some modest isomorphism will also lead to industrial cluster and division through effective competition. For example, the cities along the Shanghai-Nanjing rail line have initially presented a rational industrial spatial division within the YRD. It needs to be mentioned that there are still some problems, like low utilization of cost, diseconomies of scale, overlapping construction, excessive competition over foreign capital, resource, and market, within the YRD manufacturing industry. Although they have not yet hindered the industrial development of the YRD, the regional economic growth, relying on the cheap production factors of the Midwest, is facing the challenge of new trade protectionism, raising the cost of labor and raw materials, overall overcapacity, appreciation of RMB exchange rate, etc.

Section 5 Quantitative inspection of the industrial structure differences of the Yangtze River Delta

1. The measurement models

Based on theoretical analysis and statistical description, the measurement model of influence factors of industrial structure factors is established to inspect propositions 1 and 2. Considering the path dependency of the industrial structure, the lag phase is introduced in the model. The measurement equation is:

$$\begin{aligned} Distruct_{i,t} &= \alpha_0 + \alpha_1\ Distruct_{i,t-1} + \alpha_2\ Dmark_{i,t} \\ &+ \alpha_3\ Dinter_{i,t} + \alpha_4\ Dgov_{i,t} \\ &+ \Sigma\varphi_j \cdot Dtiebout_{i,t-j} \\ &+ \varepsilon_i + \gamma_t + \mu_{it} \end{aligned} \tag{6.6}$$

In formula (6.6), $Distruct, Dmark, Dinter, Dgov, Dtiebout$ represent dissimilarity of industrial structure, degree of industry market competition, dissimilarity of government intervention, dissimilarity of state-owned industrial investment and activity level of construction transformation investment in this statistical analysis respectively. Considering the lagging effect of the Tiebout model, this model adds construction transformation investment first-order and second-order lagged terms in the equation. Since the investment of a state-owned enterprise is a stock index, it is directly brought into the model based on the processing principles of the stock index in the Cobb – Douglas production function. ε_i represents unobservable industrial fixed effect; γ_t the time effect; μ_{it} random error term.

In regression, there is a lagged term of explained variable in the model. Additionally, there might be an endogenous problem of simultaneous causality between industrial structure and investment. Therefore, the estimated results reached through ordinary least squares (OLS), fixed effect (FE), and random effect (RE) are not consistent. To solve the problem, this chapter adopts the Generalized Method of Moments (GMM). Because of the discrepancy between differential GMM and system GMM and the influence of weak instrumental variables and small sample size on differential GMM, this chapter chooses the system generalized method of moments (SYS-GMM), which can not only integrate the estimated information of difference equation and advection equation but also raises the estimating efficiency. Therefore, the estimated panel data model of SYS-GMM is our final option.

This chapter selects the indexes for 14 years (from 2000 to 2013). Tobacco and petroleum refinery are removed from the inspection because of their particularity. Therefore, the research contains 364 samples from 26 industries. Taking *Distruct* as the explained variable, we introduce its first-order lagged term, *Dmark, Dinter, Dgov, Dtiebout* first-order and second-order lagged term in the model in sequence.

2. Interpretation of measurement result

Table 6.2 reports the result of regression equation (6.6). It indicated that the *Distruct* is positive correlated to its first-order lagged term, *Dinter, Dgov, Dtiebout* first-order lagged term with a distinct regression effect; while negatively correlated to *Dmark*. For example, in the model (1) and (2), one-phase lagged Distruct and the current Distruct represent a positive correlation, which is consistent with the fact that regional industrial structure is influenced by historical factors. Therefore, the adjustment of the regional industrial structure requires a process of gradual transformation.

Considering the robustness of measuring results, this chapter also lists the regression result of differential GMM. Columns (5) and (6) in Table 6.2 show that the results of the two methods are similar, indicating the validity of the measuring result by the model. The inspection basically verifies our propositions.

Specifically speaking, the *Distruct* in YRD is influenced by the following factors:

(1) *Dmar*

Dmar and *Distruct* present a negative correlation. As propositions 1 and 2 revealed, local government interference and property rights reflect the degree of product marketization of an industry. Therefore, the measuring result and the propositions are logically consistent internally. The highest efficiency of resource allocation is in the perfect competition market environment where regional industrial

Table 6.2 The GMM inspection of the influence factors of *Distruct*

Variable	*SYS-GMM*			*DIF-GMM*		
	(1)	*(2)*	*(3)*	*(4)*	*(5)*	*(6)*
Constant	0.0585***	0.0355***	0.0153***	0.0190**	0.0168*	0.0144***
	0.00631	−0.0012	0.00205	0.0083	0.0096	0.0107
	0.0024*	0.0289*	0.0309	0.0648	0.0978	0.0736
	0.0591	0.0493	0.0533	0.0655	0.0826	0.0993
Dmark	−0.0008***	−0.0006**	−0.0005**	−0.0005***	−0.0008***	0.0005**
	0.0002	0.0003	0.0002	0.0001	0.0002	0.0002
Dinter		0.249***	0.238***	0.254***	0.227***	0.242***
		0.0620	0.0542	0.0546	0.0537	0.052
Dgov			0.0861***	0.0819**	0.0692*	0.0759***
			0.0312	0.0394	0.0367	0.0286
				0.0042***	0.0053***	0.0057***
				0.0011	0.0015	0.0013
					0.000 8	0.0012
					0.0014	0.0013
Wald	18.87	25.78	39.84	59.57	68.04	115.38
	0.0118	0.0000	0.0000	0.0000	0.0000	0.0000
AR (2)	0.4754	−1.1424	0.354	0.3168	−0.3303	0.3430
	0.6345	0.2533	0.7233	0.7514	0.7412	0.7315
Saragan	23.5954	24.3480	23.124	19.2177	23.8924	17.755
	0.9950	0.9929	0.9960	0.9996	0.9920	0.9726

Note: data source is the same as Table 6.1; all empirical results are processed by stata12. ***, **, and * represent 1%, 5%, 10% significance level respectively. The null hypothesis of the Wald test is that the variable is exogenous (H:/athrho=0). AR (2) is mainly used to test whether the difference of disturbing terms shows second-order self-correlation. Saragan test is used to observe the over-identification of instrumental variables.

structure matches local comparative advantage, and regional industrial isomorphism is avoided. Under the condition of incomplete information, market entities inevitably flock to the same certain industries, which causes regional industrial isomorphism. The incompleteness of the current system further enlarges market failure. To pursue short-term economic profits, local governments, without considering their real situation, introduce inordinate preferential policies to support the development of some emerging industries. For example, the local government, taking advantage of the systematic flaws in terms of land property rights, soft budget constraints, and environmental protection, provides enterprises entering the region with substantial subsidies. The industrial cost and externalized risks cause twisted enterprises, overlapping construction, and overcapacity.

(2) *Dinter*

Dinter has a significant positive correlation with *Distruct*, indicating that if local governments prefer the same industries, then they will have similar *Distruct*. Consistent with the severe industry isomorphism of chemical fiber and ferrous metal that statistics showed, this verifies proposition 1. The reason is that these heavy-asset industries have a strong capacity for tax and profit, which provides the government with strong motivation to intervene. For example, local government supported the industries that make a great contribution to taxation through preferential credit and trade barriers, causing factor mismatch and regional overcapacity at the provincial level.

(3) *Dgov*

Dgov and *Distruct* have a significant positive correlation, which verifies the conclusion of proposition 2: the smaller the *Dgov*, the smaller the *Distruct*. The investment of state-owned enterprises in manufacturing industries represents governmental interest appeal. Therefore, local government, in order to adjust industrial distribution and upgrade industries, will make their choice through the investment of state-owned enterprises. If the enterprises in different regions tend to invest in the same industry, then repetitive construction and industrial isomorphism will be inevitable.

(4) *Dtiebout* of enterprise

The higher *Dtiebout* of the enterprise, the better the chance it has to achieve a differentiated regional industrial distribution. This index, although it reflects the government's distributional difference in public expenditure on industries, mainly illustrates the attitude and choice of private enterprise, foreign-invested enterprises, and all kinds of economic entities on industrial construction and transformation. Government-led industrial infrastructure investment can effectively raise the industrial matching capacity and public service capacity, while the spatial "spillover effect" of infrastructure and the Tiebout model mechanism can form a rational regional work division and specialized production and solve the factor mismatch through the mobility of talent and industry. This variable can well explain the matching problem between factor and industry, reflecting the willingness of "voting with one's feet". It is because of the dynamic change of investment source and direction that regional industrial structure presents a complicated periodical change in terms of industry, space, time, and other aspects.

Section 6 Conclusion and illumination

From the perspective of supply-side structural reform in the new political economy, this chapter conducts research on the problems of regional competition, the matching problem between labor skill and technical complexity, and cross-regional production cooperation. The research indicates that industrial isomorphism should not be decided indistinctly. For example, similar development conditions, mismatch of factors and industry, and market failure in the YRD lead to the industrial isomorphism of pharmaceutical manufacturing, non-metallic mineral and ferrous metal, etc., while communication manufacturing and transportation do not have isomorphism but have differentiation and cooperation through work division. From the perspective of more subdivided industries and lower-level administration, the regional *Distruct* is more distinct, indicating that the core cities of the cluster play a cohesive role in industrial labor division. The empirical result further illustrates that the region's industrial structure and current industrial work division mode are driven jointly by all the investments. Industrial isomorphism is caused by the irrational behavior of market entities and improper interference of local government, including the differences of all kinds of investment sources led by government and investment qualities, and the differentiated location in international work division voluntarily chosen by enterprises to improve their export competitiveness under the open condition. Among them, the investment of state-owned and state-holding enterprises tends to converge, leading to a rising rate of industrial isomorphism, while the industry construction and enterprise renovation and transformation investment under the mechanism of the Tiebout model can lower the industrial isomorphism distinctly.

This research is illuminating in terms of how to deal with the industrial work division within a region and regional overall planning and development strategy at the national level. It requires the government to not only pay more attention to the inspection of industrial investment orientation, but also to strengthen the coordination of industrial work division between regions, especially regional overall planning, to reduce regional administrative barriers and the mismatch of market and resource caused by competitive industrial investment, and improve the congregate industrial structure and coordinated work division through institutional improvement. For example, in terms of the industries in the YRD, Shanghai can continue transferring labor-intensive industries outward and focus on capital- and technology-intensive industries, port industries, urban information industries, and the R&D of communication and transportation devices; Zhejiang can keep absorbing the labor-intensive industries transferred from Shanghai and Jiangsu, focusing on the textile industry and electrical equipment manufacturing; Jiangsu can maximize its technical advantages of advanced manufacturing industry and deploy resources for establishing a complete industrial chain of equipment manufacturing and biological medicine through the dynamic adjustment of absorbing and releasing production capacity.

In order to implement the national strategy of regional coordinated development, it is necessary to accelerate the supply-side structural reform that can keep the regional economic development vigorous. The highly efficient institution and up-to-date open innovation can optimize the environment for the production and operation of market entities and realize the potential of "mass entrepreneurship and innovation initiative". When the market plays its decisive role in allocating resources, the government performs the role of "night watch" by building a new economic development model of "effective market and government". By transforming government function and reducing improper government intervention in the market, the government can finally play its role of serving and guiding the adjustment of industrial structure, especially by providing timely information on industrial investments and market demand based on the theories of the new political economy.

Comparative advantages like labor force are becoming one of the main factors in restraining the geographical concentration of the manufacturing industry in China. Combined with the factors of technical preference, market scale, and industrial relationships, it has caused a distinct technical spillover effect. The closer regions are, the more strongly they will be affected by their mutual spillover and feedback effects. Therefore, in order to coordinate the mid-west revitalization and support the national development strategy of establishing the mid-west growth pole, it is necessary to narrow the economic gaps between regions and strengthen the industrial coordination between the east, middle, and west areas. The east part shoulders more obligation. First, its industrial structure needs a transformation and upgrading as soon as possible to raise its position in GVC, follow the path of joint development and independent innovation with the comparative advantage of enterprises, and achieve coordinated development of basic industry, joint development of emerging development, and complementary development of mainstay industry. Second, the east part needs to transfer the traditional manufacturing industry to fringe areas through cross-regional industrial cooperation and focus on the high-end productive service industry. In addition, the first developed regions should provide more subsidies to peripheries so that they can also benefit from the industrial development of core areas. In this regard, the government needs to consider the overall planning for the regional development by guiding or directly arranging some industries in the middle and west parts. By expanding investment channels and strengthening the regional investment management for cross-regional industrial transfer, the deficiency of improving regional equality and welfare simply by means of central fiscal transfer can be offset.

Notes

1 *The Operation of Raw Material Industry Economy in 2014 and its Prospect in 2015*, published by The Ministry of Industry and Information Technology of the Chinese government.
2 See Costinot and Vogel (2010) for more detail.
3 The so-called "Tiebout model", i.e., "voting with one's feet", means enterprise or resident acquires their preferred public goods by moving.
4 The tobacco industry was eliminated because of its special function of regional taxation.
5 ① The formula of industrial structure conversion value is: $K = \sum^{N} |S_{it+1} - S_{it}|$; the formula of structure entropy index is: $SEI = \sum^{N} S_i \log(1/S_i)$; the formula of Moore structure conversion value is: $M_1^+ = \sum_{i=1}^{N} W_{i,t} W_{i,t+1} / \left(\sum_{i=1}^{N} W_{i,t}^2 \right)^{1/2} ; \left(\sum_{i=1}^{N} W_{i,t+1}^2 \right)^{1/2}$; the formula of industrial structure similarity coefficient is: $S_{ij} = \sum_{k=1}^{n} \left(x_{ik} / x_{jk} \right) / \sqrt{\sum_{k=1}^{n} x_{ik}^2 \sum_{k=1}^{n} x_j^2 k}$. N represents number of industries; S_{it+1} the industrial constituent ratio in the report period; S_{it} the constituent ratio of base period; S_i the ratio of value added of industry i; $W_{i,t}$ the proportion of industry i in phase t; $W_{i,t+1}$ the proportion of industry i in phase $t+1$.

6 It is a perfect competition market when the market power of sub-industries in each region are close.
7 Contact the author for the complete statistical data and charts.
8 The result of industrial structure similarity coefficient indicates that the value between Jiangsu and Zhejiang is the highest: always above 0.9; that between Jiangsu and Shanghai is the second, around 0.8; and 0.7 for Shanghai and Zhejiang. In addition, the coefficient showed a periodical change at different development stages, consistent to the periodical change of all kinds of new investment dissimilarity.

References

Sajid Anwar. Factor Mobility and Wage Inequality in the Presence of Specialization-based External Economies. Economics Letters, 2006.

Bai Chong'en, et al. Local Protectionism and Industrial Concentration in China: Overall Trend and Important Factors. Journal of International Economics, 2004 (8).

Amaud Costinot, Jonathan Vogel. Matching and Inequality in the World Economy. Journal of Political Economy, 2010 (8).

E. Cutrini. Using Entropy Measures to Disentangle Regional from National Localization Patterns. Regional Science and Urban Economics, 2009, 39 (2).

Yu Donghua, Lv Yinan. Government Improper Intervention and Overcapacity of Strategic Emerging Industries – A Case Study of Chinese Photovoltaic Industry. China Industrial Economics, 2015 (10).

Tian Guoqiang. The 18th National Congress and the Future of China's Reform. Journal of International Economics, 2013 (3).

Tian Guoqiang, Chen Xudong. The Transformation of the Developmental Drive and Institutional Management and Construction of Chinese Economy New Phase. Journal of the Party School of the Central Committee of the CPC, 2015 (10).

Fan Jianyong. Integration of the Yangtze River Delta, Regional Specialization and Change of Manufacturing Spaces. Management World, 2004 (11).

K. Kalemli-Ozcan, et al. Economic Integration, Industrial Specialization, and the Asymmetry of Macroeconomic Fluctuations. Journal of International Economics, 2001, 55 (1).

M. Klimenko Mikhail. Industrial Targeting, Experimentation and Long-run Specialization. Journal of Development Economics, 1998 (12).

P. Krugman, Geography Trade. Leuven, Belgium and Cambridge: Leuven University Press; MIT Press, 1991.

P. Krugman, J. Venables Anthony. Integration, Specialization, and Adjustment. European Economic Review, 1996 (2).

Zhou Li'an. Governing China's Local Officials: An Analysis of Promotion Tournament Model. Journal of International Economics, 2007 (7).

Yu Liangchun, Fu Qiang. Study on Interaction Between Local Administrative Monopoly and Industrial Structure – Based on Panel Data Between Provinces. China Industrial Economics, 2008 (6).

Julio J. Rotemberg, Garth Saloner. Competition and Human Capital Accumulation: A Theory of Interregional Specialization and Trade. Regional Science and Urban Economics, 2000, 30 (4).

C. Tuan, et al. The Place of FDI in China's Regional Economic Development: Emergence of the Globalized Delta Economies. Journal of Asian Economics, 2007 (2).

Liu Wei. Developing Socialist Political Economy with Chinese Characteristics in the Combination of Marxism and China's Practice. Journal of International Economics, 2016 (5).

Jin Xiangrong, Zhu Xiwei. The Origin and Evolution of Specialized Industrial Districts: A historical and theoretical Approach. Journal of International Economics, 2002 (8).
Hu Xiangting, Zhang Lu. Local Protectionism and Regional Specialization: A Model and Econometric Evidences. Journal of International Economics, 2005 (2).
Wei Xinghua. Socialist Market Economy and Law-based Governance. Journal of International Economics, 2015 (1).
Wang Yeqiang, Wei Houkai. Characteristics of Industries, Competition for Space and the Geographic Concentration in Manufacture. Management World, 2007 (4).
Lin Yifu. Wave Phenomenon and the Reconstruction of Macroeconomic Theories for Developing Countries. Journal of International Economics, 2007 (1).
Lin Yifu, Wu Hemao, Xing Yiqing. "Wave Phenomena" and Formation of Excess Capacity. Journal of International Economics, 2010 (10).
Li Yining. Law-based Governance and Deepening Economic Reform. Journal of International Economics, 2015 (1).
Hong Yinxing. Accurate Understanding of the Goal and Task of Structural Reform of the Supply Front. China Industrial Economics, 2016 (6).
Liu Zaiqi, Xu Yanfei. The Economic Behavior Pattern of Government and Evolution of Industrial Structure in the Process of Marketization. Business and Management Journal, 2014 (9).

7 The evolution of economic spatial pattern in the Yangtze River Delta region

Dongmei He and Yuwei Du

Section 1 Introduction

Under the background of economic globalization and marketization, the increasing mobility of resources makes the regional administration of economic activities hard to sustain. Therefore, the regional integrated development is gradually becoming an important part of the economic development strategy in China (Wu Bojun et al., 2006). The Yangtze River Delta region (YRD), as one of the significant economic growth poles in China, first started regional integration in China with the best foundations and highest degree, regarded as a "test field" and "pacesetter" of Chinese integration and coordinated development. Early in 1961, the government set up the East China Bureau to coordinate the cooperative development in the YRD. Since the reform and opening up, the YRD regional cooperation has been further strengthened to meet the requirement of a developing market economy; the integrated development in the YRD has gradually become a significant issue of regional coordinated development. In 1983, the State Council set up the Shanghai Economic Zone to coordinate the cooperation among Jiangsu, Zhejiang, Anhui, Jiangxi, and Fujian, and organized a forum on the regional planning of the YRD and riverside areas in 1992. Thereafter, some relevant government sectors have been promoting YRD's integrated development by setting up Changjiang Delta City's Economic Coordination Committee (1996), Joint Conference of Mayors in YRD (1997), and Summit of Mayors in YRD (2003). At the symposium on economic and social development in the YRD held by the State Council in 2007, the strategy of "YRD integrated development" was first brought up at the state level, followed by some vital documents: *Guiding Opinions of the State Council on Further Promoting Reform, Opening and Economic and Social Development in the Yangtze River Delta Region* (2008), *The Regional Planning of Yangtze River Delta (2011–2020)*, and *Yangtze River Delta City Cluster Development Plan* (2016). The YRD integrated development moved into the fast lane with the expansion of its strategic connotation, cooperation fields, and system and institutions. Since the 18th CPC National Congress, China has entered a new era of high-quality economic development, providing new strategic opportunities for integrated development in the YRD. In 2018, the Party Central Committee led by Comrade Xi Jinping required that the leading and driving role of Shanghai shall be underscored; while Jiangsu,

DOI: 10.4324/9781003455943-7

Zhejiang, and Anhui shall lend their respective strengths to the higher-quality integrated development in the YRD. The Government Work Report of 2019 officially brought up the idea of making YRD integrated development a national strategy, endowing it with more connotation of the new age and the significance of a historical mission. The high-quality integrated development in the YRD has become the strategic support for serving the Chinese big picture in the new era and a vital practice of regional integrated development in China.

In terms of regional integrated development, economic integration is in first place and geographically manifested as inter-regional balance and coordination of the economic development level. Therefore, theoretically, the practice and promotion of regional integration is inevitably accompanied by the reduction of the internal economic gap. In other words, the narrowing regional economic gap and coordinated development are the result of regional economic integrated development, which means that regional economic spatial pattern can be used to objectively evaluate the effect of integration. Has the economic gap in the YRD shrunk, or has the level of economic development converged after years of integrated development? How can we narrow the inter-regional economic gap and improve the high-quality integration in YRD more effectively? This chapter attempts to provide a scientific theoretical elaboration and policy enlightenment from the perspective of spatial economics by inspecting the evolution trend, agglomeration characteristics, and driving factors of economic patterns in the YRD.

This study is related to two types of research: one on regional economic gap and one on economic integration in the YRD. Regional economic gap, a generally accepted problem by researchers of economics and geography, is one of the core issues of regional economics in a developing country (Li, 2008). A long-term regional developmental gap would obstruct effective resource allocation, weaken the efficiency of regional work division and cooperation, and severely hinder economic growth with a series of social problems (Zhao Wenliang et al., 2011; Eriksson et al., 2017). In terms of theoretical research, the inverted U-shaped hypothesis by Williamson, the Circular cumulative causation by Myrdal, and the convergence hypothesis by neo-classical economists all acknowledged the existence of a regional development gap but held different opinions on its evolving trend (Williamson, 1965; Myrdal, 1957; Chen Hongquan and Zhang Yunfeng, 2016). There are three types of relevant empirical research: the first one adopts static analysis (Gini coefficient, variable coefficient, standard deviation, comprehensive entropy, etc.) and spatial analysis (Theil index, regional segregation index, inconsistency index, exploratory spatial analysis). It conducts in-depth studies on the spatial and temporal evolution of different developmental gaps based on indexes including GDP per capita, disposable income per capita, national income per capita, etc., and reaches differentiated results. Although there are some controversies about the changing trend in China, most researchers agree that the Chinese regional developmental gap is still significant compared with developed countries (Guan Xingliang et al., 2012; Feng Changchun et al., 2015; Yan Dongsheng et al., 2017). The second type inspects the convergence of a regional economy by an econometric model based on economic growth differences. For example, Pan Wenqin introduced geographic space factor into the classic research framework of σ-convergence, β-convergence, and club convergence, and discussed the spatial effect of inter-provincial growth convergence in China. The third type inspects the influence factors of regional economic growth gap through descriptive analysis or regression analysis. The result shows that the influence factors include natural environment, historical foundation, geographic differentiation, labor force quality, macro policy, ownership structure, degree of marketization, industrial structure, investment scale, urbanization process, foreign trade, globalization, etc. (He Canfei and Liang Jinshe, 2004; Jin Yu et al., 2006; Song Weixuan et al., 2013).

The economic integration in the YRD is also one of the hot topics of Chinese academic research. For a long time, the deficient law and regulation, government performance examination and reform of state-owned enterprise led to "administrative region economy", i.e., rigid constraints of administrative division on regional economy, which hinders the progress of economic integration in the YRD (Liu Junde and Shu Qing, 1993; Sandra, 2002; Bai Chong'en et al., 2004). Some scholars measured and evaluated the level of economic integration in the YRD with different indexes. Qian Huixiong (2010) measured the integration in YRD through the gap of actual and theoretical output distribution in the region. Guo Xiaohe and Wang Laiquan (2012) conducted an empirical analysis by convergence model of economic growth, Barro regression equation combined with gravity model, and revised boundary effect model, and discovered a distinct economic integration trend in the YRD with a decreasing boundary effect and increasing convergence. Chen Kun and Wu Li (2013) measured the market integration in 20 cities in the YRD through relative price and discovered a general integration trend. Li Shiqi and Zhu Pingfang established a comprehensive evaluation index system by referencing the research framework of the EU integration index and concluded that the integration degree in the YRD is increasing, while its pace is slowing down.

Some scholars studied the paths and policies of economic integration in the YRD. Hong Yinxing and Wu Jun (2012) pointed out that in order to achieve multicenter economic integration in the YRD, the effective link of service industries between cities of different levels must be strengthened, with Shanghai considered a global city. Liu Zhibiao (2014) believed that limiting government participation in market competition and breaking administrative barriers are the main measures of achieving an inter-regional competitive opening up and promoting regional economic integration. He also emphasized the importance of starting from specific project cooperation, selecting a suitable industrial organizational form with enterprises as the main body, updating industrial clusters, transforming the focus from industrial policy to competition policy, encouraging the merger and acquisition of enterprises in the region, and maximizing the function of the Shanghai free trade zone. Zhang Xueliang and Li Lixia (2018) proposed the path of improving the industrial integrated development in the YRD, i.e., perfecting the mechanism of "Market-oriented and government-guided", establishing networked industrial clusters, advocating the cooperation between development zones, and forming a reasonable industrial work division system based on industrial chain, value chain, and innovation chain.

In conclusion, the existing research on regional economic gaps is generally focused on a single spatial scale rather than city clusters; most of them adopted quantitative analysis or traditional measurement models to research the driving factors of economic pattern evolution, without considering the influence of space (Xiao Zhouyan, 2013). In terms of research on economic integration in the YRD, the current studies have all neglected the spatial connection and spillover effect between regions. In comparison, Zhai Renxiang's research (2016) attempted to bring the spatial spillover effect into the economic integration and convergence of the economic growth gap. This research has inspired our study, but it failed to explore the changing trend of economic development patterns in the YRD since its focus is on the spatial interconnections between factors of regional economic growth, so it did not describe the economic development gap between regions in the YRD. Therefore, this chapter, from a dynamic spatial perspective, first analyzes the characteristics of economic evolving patterns in 2000–2015 through the methods of focus evolvement and Theil index and discusses the spatial aggregation effect by means of exploratory spatial data analysis (ESDA); based on these steps, the driving factors of the regional economic evolvement are further explored through the spatial econometric model.

The empirical research in this chapter discovered that the economic development in the YRD has always been unbalanced: the east and north parts are high-density economic areas, and the east-west gap is bigger than the north-south gap; however, the regional economic gaps all experienced the changing process of "expansion first and then shrink". The economic gap in the YRD is mainly led by the "core-edge" gap: the gap in the core area is gradually narrowed, while that in marginal area presents an "N-shaped" process of "expansion-shrink-expansion". It is also discovered that the economic spatial pattern in the YRD presents a distinct autocorrelation. The spatial agglomeration of inter-city economic development similarity showed an evolution rule of "rapid rise-balance-slow decrease". The economic spatial structure showed a distinct "core-edge" pattern: the core area includes Shanghai, south Jiangsu, and northeast Zhejiang, while the edge area is north Jiangsu, southwest Zhejiang, and Anhui. The formation of the economic spatial pattern in YRD is caused by factors of industrialization, urbanization, human capital, industrial structure, and other new economic geographic factors; the spatial spillover effect caused factor mobility and the influence of economic policies. The economic policy factors always play an important role when spillover effect is strengthened and new economic geographic factors are weakened. The following contents are the sample data and research method in Section two; the evolution of economic spatial pattern in the YRD in Section three; the inspection on spatial economic agglomeration in the Yangtze River Delta region based on ESDA in Section four; the analysis on the driving factors of the evolution of economic spatial pattern in the YRD in Section five; and the conclusion and illumination for policy making in Section six.

Section 2 Sample data and research method

1. Sample and data source

Based on *Yangtze River Delta City Cluster Development Plan*, the YRD region in our research includes 41 prefecture-level cities in three provinces, i.e., Suzhou, Zhejiang, and Anhui, and one municipality, i.e., Shanghai. Among them, Shanghai, Nanjing, Zhenjiang, Changzhou, Wuxi, Suzhou, Yangzhou, Taizhou, Nantong, Hangzhou, Ningbo, Shaoxing, Jiaxing, Huzhou, Zhoushan, and Taizhou are the core area, while the rest of the cities are fringes. According to the stages of the integrated development in the YRD defined by Zhang Zhao'an (2006), the most recent stage is characterized by the dual driving force of cooperation and competition since the start of the 21st century. Therefore, the chapter focuses on the economic pattern in the YRD since 2000: the samples are chosen from 2000 to 2015 with prefecture-level cities as research units. In terms of data sources, the spatial data is from a 1:4 million national fundamental geographic information system; the economic data is from the statistical yearbooks of Shanghai, Jiangsu, Zhejiang, and Anhui, as well as statistical bulletins. Taking the administrative division in 2010 as the baseline, all the data of cities with administrative division adjustment are estimated based on the relevant data and rectified based on their changing trends.

2. Research method

(1) Regional economic center

The evolving path of the economic center generally reflects the change of regional economic developments and spatial differences (Feng Zongxian and Huang Jianshan, 2006). If a region is composed of n secondary area(s) i, then the "economic center" of the region can be calculated through the following formula:

$$\bar{X} = \left(\sum_{i}^{n} M_i X_i\right) / \Sigma_i^n M_i ; \bar{Y} = \left(\sum_{i}^{n} M_i Y_i\right) / \Sigma_i^n M_i \quad (7.1)$$

In the formula, (X_i, Y_i) represents the longitude and latitude of secondary area i; M_i is the economic attribute value of i; spatial mean value $(\bar{X}, \bar{Y})$ means the longitude and latitude of the economic center of the research area. The spatial displacement of the economic center in different years can be calculated through the following formula:

$$D_{l-k} = C\sqrt{\left(\bar{X}_l - \bar{X}_k\right)^2 + \left(\bar{Y}_l - \bar{Y}_k\right)^2} \quad (7.2)$$

l and k represent different years respectively; $(\bar{X}_l, \bar{Y}_l)$ and $(\bar{X}_k, \bar{Y}_k)$ the longitude and latitude of economic center in year l and k; C is 111.111, the coefficient that transforms geographic coordinates (°) into plane distances (Zhou Minliang, 2000).

(2) Theil index

The Theil index decomposes the regional differences at various scales; the most common one (hereinafter referred as T index) is adopted in this research (Feng Changchun, 2015):

$$T = \sum_{i=1}^{N}\left[\left(\frac{Y_i}{Y}\right)\log\left(\frac{Y_i / Y}{P_i / P}\right)\right] \tag{7.3}$$

In formula (7.3), N is the number of regions; $\frac{Y_i}{Y}$ is the proportion of GDP in region i to the overall regions; $\frac{P_i}{P}$ is the proportion of population in region i to the overall regions. The bigger T index represents a bigger regional economic development gap, and vice versa.

This research takes prefecture-level cities (Shanghai as a complete unit) as the basic spatial unit, and decomposes the YRD according to inter- and intra-regional rules:

$$T = T_{BR} + T_{WR} = \sum_{i=1}^{n}\left[\left(\frac{Y_i}{Y}\right)\log\left(\frac{Y_i / Y}{P_i / P}\right)\right] + \sum_{i=1}^{n}\left\{\left(\frac{Y_i}{Y}\right)\Sigma_j\left[\left(\frac{Y_{ij}}{Y_i}\right)\log\left(\frac{Y_{ij} / Y_i}{P_{ij} / P_i}\right)\right]\right\} \tag{7.4}$$

In the formula, T represents the general economic gap in the YRD; T_{BR} and T_{WR}为 are the inter-regional gap and intra-regional gap respectively; i represents regions, dividing the YRD into core area and fringe area (n=2); Y_i and P_i are the GDP and number of permanent residents in region i respectively; Y and P are the overall GDP and permanent residents in YRD respectively; j is a prefecture-level city in region i (Shanghai as a complete unit), 16 in the core area and 26 in the fringe area; Y_{ij} and P_{ij} are the GDP and permanent residents in city j of region i respectively.

(3) Exploratory spatial data analysis

ESDA is the set of a series of the method and technique of spatial data analysis, centered on the measurement of spatial relevancy. By describing the spatial distribution of data and visualizing them, it can identify abnormal values, test the spatial agglomeration of economic phenomenon, and show the spatial structure of data, in order to reveal the spatial interaction mechanism between research objects (Pu Yingxia, 2005). There are mainly two types of tools:

(1) Global spatial autocorrelation. The formula of Global Moran's I, one of the significant statistics for measuring global spatial autocorrelation, is:

$$I = \frac{n}{\sum_{i=1}^{n}\sum_{j=1}^{n} W_{ij}} \frac{\sum_{i=1}^{n}\sum_{j=1}^{n}\left[W_{ij}\left(x_i - \bar{x}\right)\left(x_j - \bar{x}\right)\right]}{\sum_{i=1}^{n}\left(x_i - \bar{x}\right)^2} \tag{7.5}$$

In the formula, n represents the number of regions; x_i is a certain attribute value of region i; $\bar{x}$ is the population mean of the attribute; W_{ij} is the spatial weight matrix. I>0 means positive correlation; I<0, negative correlation; I=0, not correlated.

(2) Local spatial autocorrelation. Local Moran's I_i is further testing the maximum and minimum value of the inter-regional economic development locally. The local spatial autocorrelation of spatial unit i is:

$$\begin{aligned} I_i &= \frac{n^2}{\Sigma_i \Sigma_j W_{ij}} \frac{\left(x_i - \bar{x}\right)\Sigma_j W_{ij}\left(x_j - \bar{x}\right)}{\Sigma_j\left(x_j - \bar{x}\right)^2} \\ &= Z_i \sum_{j=1}^{n} W_{ij} Z_j \end{aligned} \tag{7.6}$$

In formula (7.6), z_i and z_j are the standardized attribute value of region i and j respectively; W_{ij} is the spatial weight matrix. Taking a standardized variable as the horizontal axis and spatial lag as vertical axis, we will have a Moran scatter plot in the rectangular coordinate system to describe the agglomeration of different forms. The four quadrants represent four types of local spatial connection between neighboring regions. The significance of Local Moran's I_i can be tested through standardized statistics $I_i = I_i - E\left(I_i\right) / \sqrt{\mathrm{Var}\left(I_i\right)}$ (Chen Li et al., 2017).

(4) Spatial econometric model

Based on different spatial effects, the spatial econometrics model can be classified as spatial autoregressive model (SAR) and spatial error model (SEM). The forms of the two models are respectively (Chen Li et al., 2017):

$$\text{SAR: } y = \rho\left(I_T \otimes W_N\right) y + X\beta + \varepsilon \tag{7.7}$$

$$\text{SEM: } y = X\beta + \mu, \mu = \lambda\left(I_T \otimes W_N\right)\mu + \varepsilon \tag{7.8}$$

In the formulars, y is the vector of the explained variable in dimension $nT\times l$; X is the explanatory variable matrix in dimension $nT\times k$; β is the parameter vector in dimension $k\times i$; ρ and λ are the SAR coefficient and spatial auto-correlation coefficient respectively; ε is the error vector in dimension $nT\times l$; and $\otimes$ is Kronecker product. The spatial econometric model fitting mainly adopts the maximum likelihood function. In terms of model selection, the spatial correlation is tested by comparing LM statistics (LM-Lag and LM-Error); then the model with relatively significant statistics will be chosen.

Section 3 The evolution of economic spatial pattern in the Yangtze River Delta region

1. Analysis on the evolution of regional economic overall pattern based on its center

Based on the relevant indexes of economic center in the YRD from 2000 to 2015 (see Table 7.1) and its evolution path, we have noticed the following characteristics of the evolution:

First, in terms of location, the economic center of the YRD city cluster moves within 119°58'1.2"E~120°5'29.04"E and 31°13'13.44"N~31°20'7.08"N, mainly in the southeast of Wuxi-Yixing city, northeast of Suzhou, and the Taihu Lake riverside, where Suzhou borders Wuxi. Compared to the geometric center, the economic center is in the southeast, indicating an imbalanced regional economic development: the east and south parts are high economic density areas.

Second, based on the evolution track, the economic center is moving toward northwest: the longitude displacement (13.821km) is bigger than the latitude displacement (12.762km). It shows an expansion of imbalance of economic

Table 7.1 The location, moving direction, and displacement of economic center in YRD in 2000–2015

Year	*Location of economic center*		*Inter-annual movement*	
	Longitude (°)	*Latitude (°)*	*Direction*	*Displacement (km)*
2000	120.0479	431.2556	–	–
2001	120.0602	31.2492	Southeast	1.5520
2002	120.0715	31.2375	Southeast	1.7981
2003	120.0894	31.2210	Southeast	2.7012
2004	120.0914	31.2204	Southeast	0.2360
2005	120.0878	31.2239	Northwest	0.5583
2006	120.0841	31.2278	Northwest	0.5942
2007	120.0859	31.2295	Northeast	0.2788
2008	120.0708	31.2441	Northwest	2.3219
2009	120.0503	31.2626	Northwest	3.0768
2010	120.0362	31.2698	Northwest	1.7527
2011	120.0183	31.2823	Northwest	2.4304
2012	119.9979	31.3011	Northwest	3.0884
2013	119.9855	31.3158	Northwest	2.1340
2014	119.9766	31.3273	Northwest	1.6078
2015	119.9670	31.3353	Northwest	1.3939

Data source: author's measurement and calculation

development in east and west of the YRD from 2000 to 2015, i.e., the east/west gap is bigger than the north/south gap. Based on the inter-annual displacement, the bigger value indicates a bigger gap in the rate of economic growth between cities, in which an average of 1.701 6km of the economic center, the relatively stable displacement from 2000 to 2015 means a stable development environment for the macro economy in the YRD.

Third, from the perspective of evolution phases, the 16-year evolution of the economic center can be divided into two stages: in 2000–2004, it moved 6.22km to the southeast with increasing longitude, decreasing latitude, and expanding distance to the geometric center, indicating an enlarging east/west gap and imbalanced south/north development; in 2004–2015, the economic center went 18.81km back to the northwest with a narrowing distance to the geometric center. The decreasing longitude and increasing latitude indicate a shrinking gap between east and west, imbalance between south and north, and regional economic inequalities.

In conclusion, the economic center moved 15 times from 2000 to 2015: 4 times toward the southeast, 10 times northwest, and one time northeast, with relatively distinct fluctuation. From 2000 to 2004, the economic center moved toward the southeast; since 2014, it has been moving to the northwest with the expanding city cluster to the west and the enhancing economic strength of the west part of the region. However, since Shanghai is still the leading city with a relatively strong driving force, the location of the economic center remains southeast, indicating the existence of a regional economic gap. Its evolving path presented a general regression trend, and the overall regional economic gap in the YRD showed a basic characteristic of "expansion-reduction".

2. Decomposition of regional economic pattern based on Theil Index

Chronologically, from 2000 to 2015, the overall regional economic gap in the YRD presented a narrowing gap (see Figure 7.1). The changing range and trend of the gap varies in different times: from 2000 to 2003, the gap was generally expanding with its T index reaching its maximum value at 0.3617 in 2003; then it started to drop and reached its minimum value at 0.2598, indicating a trend of "modest increase before continuous decrease", the same as the characterization result of the economic center evolving trend.

From the perspective of regional decomposition, the economic gap in different spatial scales shows different evolving patterns over time: first, the inter-regional T index within the YRD dropped from 0.224 in 2000 to 0.171 in 2015; the mild change is consistent with the general changing trend in the YRD. The overall T index in the YRD fluctuated slightly from 0.1311 in 2000 to 0.0888 in 2015, with only a drop of 0.0423. Therefore, it can be concluded that the gaps, no matter whether they were in general, inter-regional, or intra-regional, all slowly narrowed; the inter-regional gap decreases faster than the intra-regional ones. It means that the promotion of YRD integration facilitates economic growth and the expansion of market space

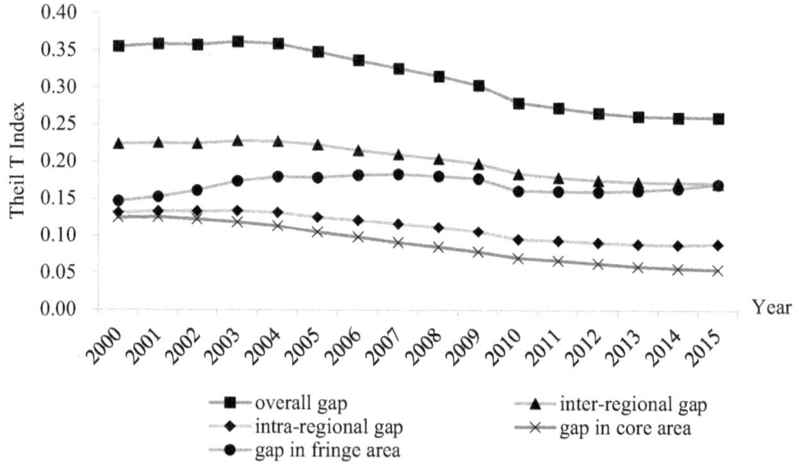

Figure 7.1 The changing trend of T indexes of overall, inter-regional and intra-regional economic gap in YRD in 2000 to 2015

from east to west, from south to north, and bridges the regional economic gap. Second, unlike the changing trend in other spatial scales, the T index of the fringe area presented an N-shaped path within the range of 0.1470 (2000) to 0.1832 (2007): it reached its maximum 0.1832 in 2007 and slightly dropped to 0.1597 in 2012, then started to rebound, presenting an "expansion-reduction-expansion" characteristic. The gap in the core area is the smallest among all the scales. It showed a smooth and mild decreasing trend, only a slight rise in 2000–2001, and its annual average (0.0890) is about half of that in the fringe area (0.1683). Focusing on this phenomenon, our research notices that the economic foundation, speed of development, and industrial structure in the fringe area, including north Jiangsu, southwest Zhejiang, and all of Anhui, present great differences between cities; the cities in the core area, with a solid economic foundation, have formed economic zones in Shanghai, Nanjing, Hangzhou, and around Taihu Lake, the influence of which makes the cities develop shoulder to shoulder, with relatively minor differences.

From the perspective of the source of the regional economic gap (see Table 7.2), from 2000 to 2015, the average contribution of inter-regional gap to total gap (65%) is much higher than that of intra-regional gap (35%) without a distinct changing trend, indicating that the inter-regional gap is the main source of the regional gap in the YRD. In the meantime, the intra-regional gap should not be neglected. It means that decreasing the inter-regional gap is the main task of promoting the coordinated development of the YRD regional economy, i.e., it requires the joint force of both adjustment and transformation of fringe areas and the strong economic influence of core areas.

In general, the YRD regional economic pattern presented a changing trend of "mild rise before continuous drop". From the perspective of local composition, the overall evolving pattern of both inter- and intra-regional gaps are consistent

Table 7.2 The decomposition and contribution rate of the T index of YRD regional development gap in 2000 to 2015

Year	*Total gap (T)*	*Inter-regional gap*		*Intra-regional gap*		*Gap between the two major areas*	
		T_{BR}	*Contribution rate to T (%)*	T_{WR}	*Contribution rate to T (%)*	$T_{core\ area}$	$T_{fringe\ area}$
2000	0.3552	0.2240	63.08	0.1311	36.92	0.1247	0.1470
2001	0.3586	0.2253	62.83	0.1333	37.17	0.1255	0.1527
2002	0.3575	0.2242	62.72	0.1333	37.28	0.1223	0.1612
2003	0.3617	0.2279	63.02	0.1337	36.98	0.1184	0.1739
2004	0.3589	0.2273	63.34	0.1315	36.66	0.1133	0.1798
2005	0.3484	0.2231	64.04	0.1253	35.96	0.1051	0.1788
2006	0.3367	0.2155	64.00	0.1212	36.00	0.0983	0.1821
2007	0.3262	0.2100	64.38	0.1162	35.62	0.0911	0.1832
2008	0.3155	0.2042	64.71	0.1114	35.29	0.0851	0.1806
2009	0.3034	0.1975	65.09	0.1059	34.91	0.0784	0.1771
2010	0.2793	0.1839	65.84	0.0954	34.16	0.0698	0.1607
2011	0.2725	0.1792	65.73	0.0934	34.27	0.0666	0.1603
2012	0.2659	0.1751	65.85	0.0908	34.15	0.0627	0.1597
2013	0.2615	0.1730	66.14	0.0886	33.86	0.0586	0.1613
2014	0.2599	0.1721	66.21	0.0878	33.79	0.0561	0.1643
2015	0.2598	0.1710	65.83	0.0888	34.17	0.0547	0.1699

Data source: author's measurement and calculation

with that of the general one: the former is the leading source, while the latter should not be neglected, either. The gaps in the fringe area presents an N-shaped "expansion-reduction-expansion" characteristic, indicating a relatively distinct variance compared to that of the core area. The phenomena mean that the overall gap is narrowing; the imbalanced pattern in the fringe area still exists and shows an expanding trend because of historical basis, geographical position, and national policy, and the gap between the fringe and core area is shrinking as a result of the high-quality integrated development in the YRD.

Section 4 Effect analysis of the spatial economic agglomeration in the Yangtze River Delta region based on ESDA

This section adopts Exploratory Spatial Data Analysis (ESDA) to study the economic agglomeration in the YRD from 2000 to 2015 to further explore the spatial dependency and heterogeneity of each economic entity (city) in the YRD, and to reveal the spatial correlative characteristics of the regional economy.

1. Global spatial correlation test

Based on formula (7.5), the result of the global autocorrelation of GDP per capita of prefecture-level city in the YRD indicates that both the Global Moran's I index and Z value are positive and have passed the significance test, which means

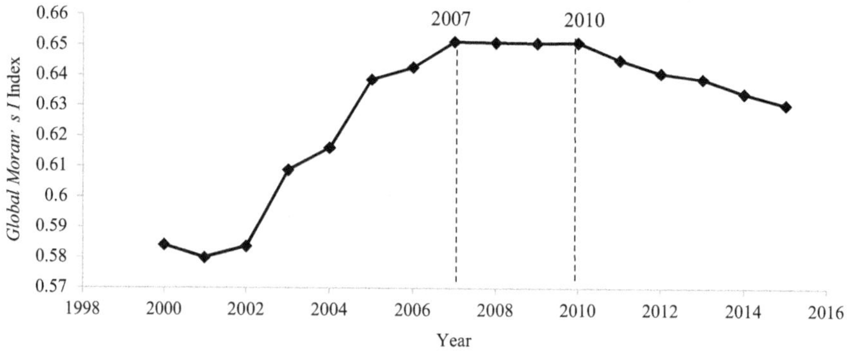

Figure 7.2 The global Moran's I index of GDP per capita of prefecture-level city in YRD in 2000–2015

that the economic development between prefecture-level cities presents a positive spatial autocorrelation with characteristics of spatial agglomeration. Based on the changing trend of Global Moran's I index (see Figure 7.2), in the 2000–2007, 2007–2010, and 2010–2015 time periods, it rose rapidly, kept steady, and then dropped slightly. In 2000–2007, the index generally increased fast, except for a minor decrease in 2001, indicating an enhancing spatial agglomeration effect between prefecture-level cities. It reached a peak in 2007, indicating a concentrated distribution pattern of cities with similar economic development levels. In 2007–2010, the stable index means a minimal fluctuation of the economic spatial pattern. In 2010–2015, the decreasing trend of the index means a weakening economic spatial agglomeration effect in the YRD.

2. Local spatial autocorrelation test

Based on the changing trend of Global Moran's I index in 2000–2015, 2007 is the turning point when the rising trend started to drop. In order to further inspect the characteristics of regional spatial agglomeration, the three points in 2000, 2007, and 2015 were chosen to calculate the Local Moran's I index based on the formula (7.6). The corresponding Moran scatter diagrams are shown in Figure 7.3. The results show that the prefecture-level cities in the first and third quadrants are at absolute predominance: the economic spatial pattern of prefecture-level cities in the YRD presents the HH type (high development level of itself and neighboring regions) and LL type (low development level of itself and neighboring regions) with a distinct economic spatial variation. There is less HL type and LH type: four and two in 2015 respectively. The presentation of cities that passed significance test in a map will form the LISA agglomeration distribution. The results indicate that under the transformation of regional development and patterns, the general economic agglomeration pattern presented a stable "core-fringe" mode: in 2000–2015, the core area of Shanghai, south Suzhou, northeast Zhejiang is

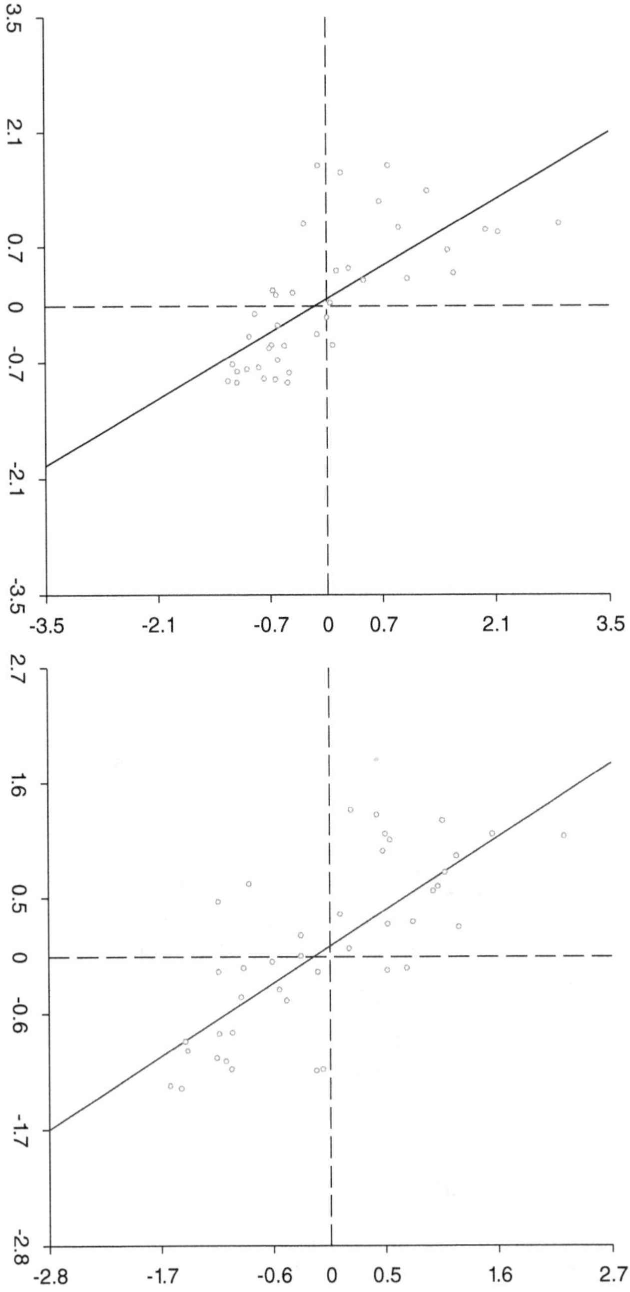

Figure 7.3 The Moran scatter diagrams of economy in prefecture-level cities in YRD in 2000, 2007, and 2015

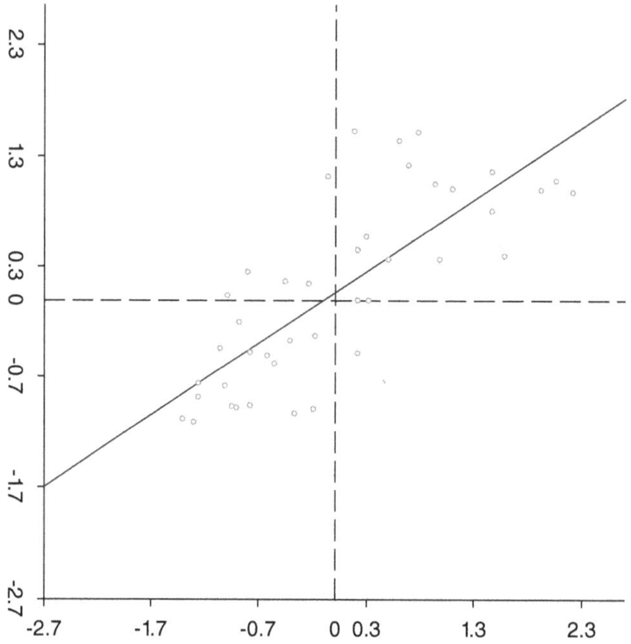

Figure 7.3 Continued

the economic growth pole of the YRD, while its peripheral areas, mainly north Suzhou, southwest Zhejiang, and all of Anhui, are the typical fringe area. The existing "core-fringe" pattern means that the regional development gap still leads the development progress in the YRD.

In terms of the spatial agglomeration of economic development, 2007 and 2010 are two turning points where the spatial pattern in YRD presents a characteristic of "rapid raise-stability-slow decrease". From the perspective of local trend, the prefecture-level cities of similar high-level are in the core area represented by Shanghai, south Suzhou, and northeast Zhejiang; the low-level area in the fringe area is represented by north Suzhou, southwest Zhejiang, and all of Anhui. The economic development level in the YRD showed a distinct difference, i.e., a typical core-fringe pattern.

Section 5 Analysis on the driving factors of the evolution of economic spatial pattern in the Yangtze River Delta region

The research on spatial agglomeration indicates that the GDP per capita of prefecture-level cities in the YRD is positively correlated to geographical position, so it is necessary to take spatial correlation into consideration when choosing the spatial econometric model for studying the driving factors of the evolution of economic spatial pattern in the YRD.

1. The theoretical analysis on driving factors

Traditional economic geography believes that the imbalanced distribution of superior factor endowment and economic geographical environment leads to the uneven spatial distribution of economic activities and therefore regional economic development gaps (Zhou Jialai and Li Gang, 2008). In reality, cases of good economic and geographical conditions and abundant resource endowment leading to relatively high-level economic development are not rare. However, traditional economic geography cannot explain two significant phenomena: first, some regions without geographic or endowment advantages become economically developed; second, two regions with the same or similar initial conditions went through completely different developmental paths. The search for reasons for the economic gap beyond simple economic geographical factors promotes the emergence of new economic geography that further explains how regional natural endowment leads to original economic activities; then the economic activity space is influenced by the increasing returns of new economic geographical factors and accompanied by these factor mobilities. For the YRD region, the core area is the main factor inflow area, while the fringe area is the outflow area. The aggregation of production factors in the core area is because of the better infrastructure, higher education level, and bigger market space. The mobility and aggregation of factors are essentially beneficial to its optimized distribution and promotion of economic efficiency, but are also the main reason for regional economic gaps. In addition, governmental economic policy is equally important to regional economic development. It can indirectly influence the industrial distribution through factors like economy and geography and directly change regional economic development. Therefore, we study the driving factors of the evolution of economic spatial patterns in the YRD from the perspectives of the new economic geography, factor mobility, and economic policy.

2. The selection and statistical description of variables

This chapter adopts the economic development level in prefecture-level cities as the explained variables and their GDP per capita for measurement. By referring to relevant research, the following explaining variables are chosen:

(1) New economic geographic factors

Under the circumstances of free mobility of resource factors and the driving force of local market and external economies of scale, economic activities have been aggregating in advantageous regions, intensifying the economic gap between developed and developing regions. The levels of urbanization and industrialization reflect the regional advantages, while the development of the secondary and tertiary sectors of the economy is the key to the efficiency of resource allocation. The main reasons for external economies of scale lie in the knowledge externality caused by human capital aggregation and capacity of the local market. Therefore, the selected new economic geographic indexes are: the level of industrialization (*Indus*), measured by the industrial product per capita of prefecture-level cities;

level of urbanization (*Urban*), measured by the percentage of urban population to total permanent population in prefecture-level cities; industrial structure, represented by the weight of product of secondary and tertiary section (*Sect*2 and *Sect*3); and human capital (*Human*), represented by the proportion of college, university, high school, and primary school students to the total permanent population.

(2) Factor mobility

The marginal productivity of different production factors varies, and so does their demand and their mobility characteristics. For example, the high-level factors, such as labor force and capital, flow smoothly, while the low-level factors like land rarely flow. Therefore, the factor mobility that caused the economic gap in the YRD is mainly that of high-level factors, the mobility of which is closely related to transportation and other infrastructures. Here we mainly inspect two indexes: capital mobility (*Capital*), the scale of which is estimated by the method of Gao Quansheng (2004), and transportation (*Trans*), measured by the density of expressways in prefecture-level cities.

(3) Economic policy factors

Regional economic policy significantly influences the regional economic pattern. Central government policies aim to narrow the regional economic development gap on the one hand, and adjust and optimize resource structure to raise the distribution efficiency on the other. After comprehensive consideration, the selected explaining variables are: investment policy (*Invest*), measured by the fixed investment per capita in prefecture-level cities; and the degree of market openness (*Open*), measured by foreign trade dependence. The descriptive statistics of all the variables are shown in Table 7.3.

3. Analysis of regression result

The research on the regression results (see Table 7.4) revealed that the spatial autoregressive model (SAR) can better present the influence of spatial dependence

Table 7.3 The descriptive statistics of index variables

Variable	*Sample number*	*Maximum*	*Minimum*	*Average*	*Standard deviation*
PGDP (ten thousand yuan)	656	10.638	0.247	2.6	1.938
Indus (ten thousand yuan)	656	25.047	0.077	5.023	5.103
Urban	656	0.894	0.103	0.498	0.155
*Sect*2	656	0.747	0.216	0.495	0.092
*Sect*3	656	0.678	0.234	0.381	0.064
Human	656	5.961	0.012	0.16	0.233
Capital	656	2.146	0.02	0.417	0.39
Trans (km/km^2)	656	0.132	0	0.027	0.021
Invest (ten thousand yuan)	656	8.323	0.069	1.554	1.367
Open	656	2.882	0.004	0.341	0.438

Data source: author's measurement and calculation

Table 7.4 The regression result of SAR

Variable	*2000–2015*		*2000–2007*		*2007–2015*	
PGDP	*SAR*	*SEM*	*SAR*	*SEM*	*SAR*	*SEM*
Indus	0.1472***	0.1439***	0.1906***	0.203***	0.0925***	0.0721***
	(21.06)	(19.17)	(23.64)	(23.04)	(10.38)	(7.26)
Urban	−2.1636***	−1.9488***	−0.4588**	−0.2389	−0.5564	−0.8705
	(−6.79)	(−5.28)	(−2.3)	(−1.05)	(−1.19)	(−1.63)
Sect2	−2.028 3***	−2.2932***	−0.1826*	−0.153	−9.813***	−7.4138***
	(−7.21)	(−7.91)	(−1.75)	(−1.46)	(−10.2)	(−6.79)
Sect3	0.5062	1.2954***	−0.324	0.1054	8.0532***	−3.4114**
	(1.21)	(2.85)	(−0.16)	(0.47)	(6.78)	(−2.41)
Human	0.0198	0.0152	1.0196***	−1.1057***	0.0229	−0.0094
	(0.46)	(0.35)	(3.62)	(−3.66)	(0.84)	(−0.27)
Capital	0.0466	0.4226***	−0.04	0.2081	0.4491***	0.5553***
	(0.46)	(3.71)	(−0.25)	(1.18)	(3.89)	(4.53)
Trans	8.667 3***	4.6026***	0.748	0.2991	−3.807	−5.0866*
	(6.63)	(3.06)	(0.87)	(0.32)	(−1.48)	(−1.82)
Invest	0.17 8***	0.1876***	0.3162***	0.331***	0.06**	0.1492***
	(7.33)	(6.85)	(11.04)	(10.75)	(2.1)	(4.21)
Open	−0.1146*	−0.2094***	−0.2017***	−0.2663***	−0.509***	−0.4701***
	(−1.74)	(−2.76)	(−4.84)	(−5.86)	(−5.16)	(−4.5)
Spatial rho	0.501*** (15.81)	0.9246*** (65.68)	0.3622*** (11.46)	0.9124*** (35.94)	0.6611*** (15.2)	0.9317*** (58.77)
R^2	0.9591	0.9114	0.9762	0.9556	0.942 9	0.8408
Log-likelihood	−14.474 1	−51.0946	401.4074	375.6726	92.8097	70.0368
LM-lag	31.576**		29.137***		25.359***	
Robust LM-lag	18.235***		27.657***		6.247*	
LM-error	18.368*		6.267*		7.138**	
Robust LM-error	0.1593		0.756		0.627	

Note: the numbers in brackets are *t* value; ***, ** and * represent statistical significance at levels of 1%, 5%, and 10% respectively.

on the economic spatial pattern in the YRD, so the SAR is chosen as the final explanatory model for analyzing the driving factors.

In general, *Indus, Sect3, Human, Capital, Trans,* and *Invest* have promoted urban economic development; while *Urban, Sect2,* and *Open* are negatively correlated with urban economic development. From the perspective of different time periods, in 2000–2007, the urban economic development level was mainly affected by new economic geography factors and economic policy factors. The acceleration of industrialization, the spatial mobility of capital factors, and the spillover of human capital significantly raised the economic development level, while urbanization negatively influenced the urban economy. The rising proportion of the secondary sector, leading to an imbalanced industrial structure, also brought about a negative effect on the economy, as did market openness. At this stage, under the comprehensive effect of these factors, the economy of developed regions rose steadily while that of less developed regions was limited by the backward economic basis, leading to an expanding economic gap. In 2007–2015, the regional economic spatial pattern transformed and the gap narrowed. The completing market mechanism enlarged the scale of capital mobility, facilitated the resource distribution, raised the efficiency of the market economy, and improved the environment for economic development. In the meantime, the expanding fixed investments and proportion of the tertiary sector and improving industrialization in less developed regions have all contributed to the narrowing regional gap. The weakened spatial agglomeration effect has changed the spatial pattern.

From the perspective of the spatial spillover effect, the coefficients of both overall and a period effect passed the significance test, which further proved the mostly positive spatial agglomeration effect of economic development in the YRD; i.e., all the factors that affected the GDP of a city would also affect the neighboring cities through spatial transmission mechanism; for example, the imitation of economic policies and spillover effect of raising human capital. In addition, the spatial spillover effect increases with time, which means that the factor mobility and government cooperation between neighboring cities enters a higher level with the deepening integration of the YRD and has a positive effect on the economic development of peripheral cities. Therefore, at the phase of high-quality development, the promotion of regional integration may become the new power for regional economic growth.

Different variables exert different effects on urban economic development, whether it is the new economic geography, factor flow, or economic policy factors. These all play a certain role in the economic evolution of the Yangtze River Delta region. For the new economic geographic factors, the industrialization level has always been a promoting factor for urban economic development. Human capital is also positively correlated to economic development, but was only significant in 2000–2007. The possible reason lies in the influx of talents into the developed regions for their advantages at the beginning; but as the mobility of human capital slowed down with the improvement of other regions, so did the promotion to economy. Urbanization, seemingly against theories, has a negative influence. However, some regions in the YRD are passively urbanized through administrative policies without enough industries or consumption abilities to support the urbanization. Such urbanization is not the result of industrialization or economic development, but is a possible reason for "urban disease" or "excessive urbanization". The influence of industrial structure varies based on the different types of industries: the proportion of the secondary sector causes significant negative effects via structure imbalance, while the tertiary sector brings positive effects through structural optimizing and upgrading. As for factor mobility, in 2007–2015, cross-regional capital mobility significantly promoted economic development; the accumulating effect of transportation and other infrastructures on economy is significantly beneficial to economic development in the long run. Among the economic policy factors, economic factors have further aggregated in developed regions driven by the market; the increase of fixed investments distinctly promoted economic development, and the openness of the market also significantly affected economic development. Yet the effect turned negative with the deepening of reform and opening up, because excessive foreign trade dependence squeezed out the domestic market demand.

Comprehensively compared, the influence of one variable at different time periods also varies, which is caused by the corresponding characteristic of the YRD economy being in different developmental stages. In 2000–2007, the influence is mainly caused by new economic geographic factors and economic policy factors; in 2007–2015, the same added factor mobility. In general, the factors changed along the regional developmental environment; economic policy has always played an important role, while the spatial spillover effect and factor mobility enhanced and the new economic geographic factor weakened.

Section 6 Conclusion and illumination for policy making

Narrowing regional economic gaps and promoting regional coordinated development are important contents of regional integration. The high-quality integrated development in the YRD means, first, the balanced coordination of economic development in the region, which is why the objective evaluation of the YRD economic spatial pattern and discussion of the driving force of its evolvement are of vital importance. Based on the evaluation and discussion, this chapter compared the spatial evolving rules of YRD development gaps in 2000–2015 and explored the driving force of its changing patterns in different time periods. The main conclusions are:

(1) In 2000–2015, the economic center of the YRD is to the southeast of the geometric center, which means an imbalanced regional economic development, i.e., the economic density is higher in the east and south; and the east/west gap is larger than the north/south gap. It means that despite the general evolving process of "expansion before reduction", the economic gap in the YRD still exists.
(2) The decomposition of regional gap based on the Theil index verified the overall economic pattern in the YRD as "slight raise before continuous drop", and further decomposed the general gap into inter- and intra-regional gaps. The general evolving trend of the two is consistent with that of the overall gap. The inter-regional gap plays a leading role, while the intra-regional gap should not be neglected either. The one in the fringe area presents N-shaped characteristics of "expansion-reduction-expansion", which is more significant compared to the steadily narrowing gap in the core area.
(3) The research on spatial agglomeration revealed the distinct spatial autocorrelation of economic spatial patterns in the YRD. The spatial agglomeration of inter-city economic similarity presented a pattern of "rapid increase, steadiness and slow drop". From the perspective of locality, the agglomeration of distinct regional economic high value appeared in the core areas represented by Shanghai, south Suzhou, and northeast Zhejiang, while that of low value was in fringe areas represented by north Suzhou, southwest Zhejiang, and all of Anhui. The economic spatial structure presented a clear "core-fringe" pattern.

(4) The economic spatial pattern is the result of multiple factors: industrialization, urbanization, human capital, industrial structure, and other new economic geographic factors leading to the flow of production factors from less-attractive areas to more-attractive areas. The guiding role of relevant economic policies also altered the economic pattern. In addition, the effect of factors varies in different time periods: in 2000–2007, the predominant factors are new economic geographic ones and economic policies; in 2007–2015, the factor mobility is more significant while the other two still exist. In general, the economic policy factors always play an important role, while spillover effect and factor mobility are strengthened and new economic geographic factors are weakened.

Based on these conclusions, we have reached the following illuminations for promoting the high-quality integrated development in the YRD:

(1) The overall economic development gap in the YRD is shrinking, which means that the economy of fringe areas, affected by the industrial transfer from the core areas, has increased rapidly. However, in the process of accepting the industrial transfer and narrowing the economic gaps, based on their conditions, the less developed regions need to think thoroughly about how to break loose from the previous extensive and passive economic growth methods, drive growth by innovation, change from gross expansion to structural optimization, and find the high-quality economic development path that suits the region.
(2) In the process of the transformation of economic development patterns, the distinct "core-fringe" regional gap still exists, which means that the effective elimination of inter-regional economic gap requires more attention under the overall transformation of development pattern. In order to solve the problem, we need to grasp the fundamental factors that drive the mobility of economic factors, to remove any barriers against factor (especially capital, labor force, and other high-level factors) mobility through reform, innovation, and coordination of system, institution, and policy, and to optimize configuration for accelerating the high-quality development in the YRD.
(3) The distinct spatial spillover effect of urban economic growth means that neighboring cities need to strengthen the coordinated development with each other in the process of facilitating regional development for an effect of "1+1>2". To achieve this effect, resource sharing is the key. As the leading city, Shanghai should initiate cooperation with other places, including joint research on scientific and technological innovation, data opening and sharing, strategic industrial alliance, etc., to generally raise the economic innovation and competitiveness in the YRD. On the other hand, it should also vigorously promote the joint construction and sharing of infrastructure and public service. The diversified, convenient, and high-level public products and services will bring the people in the YRD better resources.

References

Wu Bojun, et al. Regional Economic Development under Government Handling. Shanghai: East China University of Science and Technology Press, 2006.

He Canfei, Liang Jinshe. Spatial Change of Chinese Regional Economic Gap: Marketization, Globalization and Urbanization. Management World, 2004 (8).

Feng Changchun, Zeng Zanrong, Cui Nana. The Economic Disparities and Their Spatio-temporal Evolution in China since 2000. Geographical Research, 2015 (2).

Bai Chong'en, Du Yingjuan, Tao Zhigang, Tong Yueting. Local Protectionism and Industrial Concentration in China: Overall Trend and Important Factors. Economic Research Journal, 2004 (4).

Yan Dongsheng, He Tian, Chen Wen. Population Agglomeration, Economic Dispersion and Inconsistent Pattern: Evidence from the Yangtze River Delta. Economic Geography, 2017 (9).

R. Eriksson, H.K. Hansen, L. Winther. Employment Growth and Regional Development: Industrial Change and Contextual Differences between Denmark and Sweden. European Planning Studies, 2017 (4).

Chen Hongquan, Zhang Yunfeng. Economic Development Disparities and Spatial Pattern Evolution in Coastal Area of Jiangsu Province. Scientia Geographica Sinica, 2016 (2).

Qian Huixiong. Measurement of Economic Integration in the Yangtze River Delta Region. Finance and Trade Research, 2010 (10).

Zhou Jialai, Li Gang. Distance of Regional Economic Development: New Economic Geography, Element Flow and Economic Policy. Economic Theory and Business Management, 2008 (9).

Liu Junde, Shu Qing. On Administrative Division, Administrative Management System and Regional Economic Development Strategy. Economic Geography, 1993 (4).

Chen Kun, Wu Li. Research on the Economic Integration in the Yangtze River Delta Based on Relative Price. Shanghai Journal of Economics, 2013 (12).

Chen Li, Zhu Xigang, Yang Yang et al. Spatial Pattern Evolution of County Economy in Yunnan Province of China Based on Spatial Econometrics. Economic Geography, 2017 (1).

N. Li. Regional Development Differences and Harmonious Development Policy in China. Journal of Sichuan University of Science & Engineering (Social Sciences Edition), 2008 (1).

Zhou Minliang. Economic Center, Regional Gap and Coordinated Development. Social Sciences in China, 2000 (3).

G. Myrdal. Economic Theory and Underdeveloped Regions. London: Gerald Duckworth and Co., 1957.

Gao Quansheng. Inter-regional Capital Flow in China and its Structural Transformation. Journal of Statistics and Information, 2004 (5).

Zhai Renxiang. Regional Economic Integration and Regional Convergence in Yangtze River Delta: Based on Spatial Durbin model. Mathematics in Practice and Theory, 2016 (4).

P. Sandra. The "Non-integration" Trend of Chinese Market? Comparative Analysis on the Market Integration in China and the World. World Economic Papers, 2002 (2).

Li Shiqi, Zhu Pingfang. Finding and Suggestions from the New Exploration in the Evaluation of Yangtze River Delta Integration. Nanjing Journal of Social Sciences, 2017 (7).

Song Weixuan, Chen Wen, Peng Ying. Spatial Pattern of Urban-rural Income under the Background of Regional Integration in the Yangtze River Delta. Scientia Geographica Sinica, 2013 (9).

Zhao Wenliang, Chen Wenfeng, Meng Deyou. Spatio-temporal Pattern Evolution of the Interaction among the Cities in Central Plains Economic Zone. Economic Geography, 2011 (10).

Pan Wenqing. The Economic Disparity between Different Regions of China and its Reduction. Social Sciences in China, 2010 (1).

J.G. Williamson. Regional Inequality and the Process of National Development: A Description of the Patterns. Economic Development and Cultural Change, 1965 (4).

Guo Xiaohe, Wang Laiquan. Boundary Effect and Economic Integration in the Yangtze River Delta. Journal of Statistics and Information, 2012 (5).

Guxn Xinglinag, Fang Chuanglin, Luo Kui. Regional Economic Development Disparity of China: An Application of Spatial Field. Scientia Geographica Sinica, 2012 (9).

Zhang Xuelinag, Li Lixia. Practical Exploration and Dilemma Elimination of Regional Ecological Integration in the Yangtze River Delta. Reform, 2018 (12).

Pu Yingxia, Ge Ying, Ma Ronghua et al. Analyzing Regional Economic Disparities Based on ESDA: Case study on Jiangsu Province. Geographical Research, 2005 (12).

Hong Yinxing, Wu Jun. The Polycentralization of Yangtze Delta Region and the New Development of Integration. Academic Monthly, 2012 (5).

Jin Yu, Chen Zhao, Lu Ming. Industry Agglomeration in China: Economic Geography, New Economic Geography and Policy. Economic Research Journal, 2006 (4).

Zhang Zhao'an. Metropolitan Area and Regional Economic Integration: The Economic Integration in the Yangtze River Delta. Shanghai: Shanghai University of Finance and Economics Press, 2006.

Liu Zhibiao. A Rethinking of Regional Economic Integration: Policy and Method of Promoting the Integrated development in the Yangtze River Delta. Journal of Nanjing Normal University (Social Science Edition), 2014 (11).

Xiao Zhouyan. Spatial Effect of Population – Economic Distribution Consistency in China. Population Research, 2013 (9).

Feng Zongxian, Huang Jianshan. Dynamic Variation Track and Contrastive Research of Economic Gravity Centre and Industrial Gravity Centre of China from 1978 to 2003. Economic Geography, 2006 (3).

8 Government-industry-academy cooperation and Yangtze River Delta integration

Ning Xu and Fan Xie

Section 1 Introduction

Innovative integration is the core content and vital characteristic of high-quality integrated development in the YRD. The YRD innovative integrated development means, targeting at increasing innovation output, integrating sufficiently all kinds of innovation entities, and forming regional innovation collaborations to finally establish an organic and unified innovation ecosystem in the YRD. It contains two dimensions: cooperation between innovation entities and regional innovation coordination. The former aims at innovation output. It means an innovation organization pattern that contains government, enterprise, and institutions for technological breakthroughs, i.e., government-industry-academy cooperation. It is a community of research and development based on the orientation of both scientific research and markets to promote the effective combination of technology supply and demand, the efficiency of knowledge transmission and the application of technologies, and work as a platform and network. This means the cooperation and sharing of innovation behaviors between regions. It influences innovation outcomes mainly through two approaches: technology spillover and absorption. The innovation outcome in this chapter indicates the industry-end output, represented by the sales revenue of new products which is defined as those adopted new principles, new technologies, new materials, or new breakthroughs in terms of technology, structure, material, etc. with distinctly improved performance or function, or presented inventiveness, advancement, and adaptability within a certain region or field. It can effectively measure the level of regional innovation output. The mechanism of innovative integration in YRD is shown in Figure 8.1.

This chapter on the one hand discusses the three mechanisms of the innovative integrated development in the YRD; on the other hand, by referencing the functional equation of geographic innovation output by Feldman and Florida (1994), Furman et al. (2000), and Furman and Hayes (2004), it quantitatively analyzes government-industry-academy cooperation, technology spillover, absorption ability, scientific and technological innovation input, basis research of universities and institutions, foreign direct investment, etc., and tests their influence on innovation output. The contents of the chapter are: theoretical analysis and research hypothesis in Section 2; measurement of some important indexes in the YRD and quantitative

DOI: 10.4324/9781003455943-8

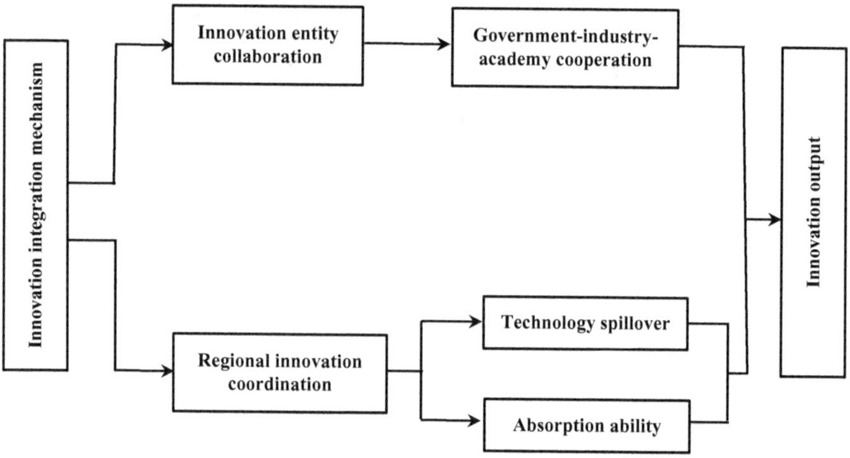

Figure 8.1 The mechanism of innovative integration in YRD

analysis in Section 3; the test of these indexes through measurement models in Section 4; empirical result and discussion in Section 5; and research conclusions and illumination in Section 6.

Section 2 Theoretical analysis and research hypothesis

1. The YRD innovation integration mechanism from the perspective of government-industry-academy cooperation

Government-industry-academy cooperation means the cooperation between government, enterprises, and universities, in which enterprises are the demand side of technology; universities are the supply side; and government plays a resource coordinating and financial supporting role. The gathering of economic resources, knowledge resources, and human resources from different economic entities are of significance in order to promote the optimized configuration of all kinds of production factors for technological innovation. Numerous empirical researchers have proved that the cooperation between regional innovation entities can not only improve the innovation of research and development but also accelerate the technology diffusion. The research of Jorde and Teece (1990) discovered that under the market structure of government-industry-academy cooperation, the scientific and technological incentive policies can widely and rapidly provoke knowledge spillover, which is beneficial to the development of new technologies and commercialization. Schartinger et al. (2001) discovered the main cooperation pattern between enterprise and universities based on their research on the Australian innovative enterprises and universities that the former provides R&D funds to the latter, while the latter transfers knowledge to the former through human capital flow. Such interaction helps to bring about new products and technologies and

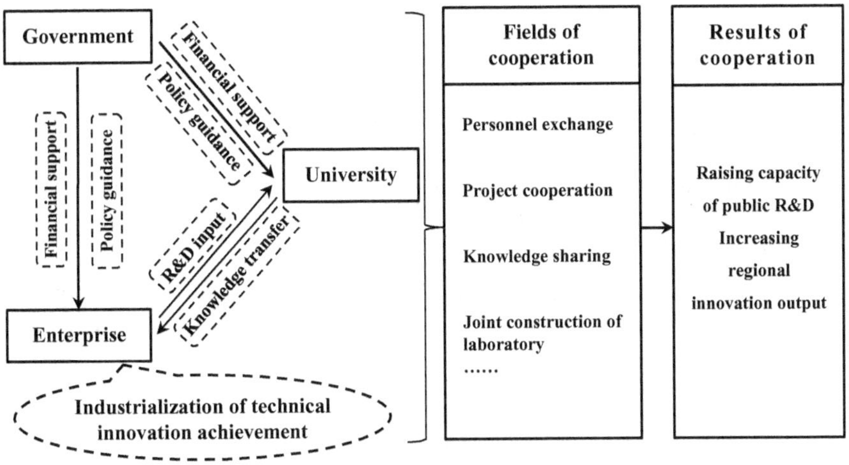

Figure 8.2 The influence and effect of government-industry-academy cooperation and its mechanism

raise innovation efficiency. Wu Yuming (2009) conducted an empirical test on the relationship between government-industry-academy R&D cooperation and innovation output, taking 31 provincial regions as spatial samples, and concluded that the cooperation under governmental guidance is a good mechanism for promoting patent innovation output in China (see Figure 8.2).

From the perspective of enterprise and universities, their cooperation has vital significance:

(1) The cooperation is helpful for the industrialization of technical innovation achievement. Unlike inventions, scientific and technological innovation is an economic behavior and a comprehensive activity that commercializes and marketizes the scientific and technological outcomes for economic benefits. Before cooperation, science is only a general productivity in the form of knowledge; it can only be transformed to actual productivity when applied in production as technologies. The innovation outcomes of universities and research institutions are mainly the scientific and technological periodicals, published books, and patents, which can flow into enterprises as explicit knowledge through this cooperation. It solves the problems of incubation and commercial value of research projects in universities and institutions, and increases the knowledge base of enterprises to improve their independent innovation ability.

(2) The cooperation is complementary. From the perspective of resource integration, the innovation resource allocation is different in universities and enterprises. It is impossible for any innovation entity to have absolute predominance of all types of innovative production factors, yet innovation activities would usually require heterogeneous resources. Only through

cooperation can we break through the limitation of human resources and fund in a single economic entity, achieve complementarity and sharing of innovation factors, and accelerate the free mobility of resources for the development of research projects.

(3) The cooperation can avoid overlapping investments in research. To achieve the same research purpose, participants should be given different tasks through a reasonable assignment system. This can effectively avoid over-investment caused by competition and lead the technological innovation to the optimal level.

In the new pattern of government-industry-academy cooperation for scientific research and innovation, government is an important participant in the role of fund support and policy guidance.

(1) In terms of fund support, the current government support for scientific and technological innovations is mainly the fiscal appropriation for university research expenditures, the proportion of which reflects the importance of innovation for the country. The higher proportion of government subsidies means a more solid foundation of government-industry-academy cooperation and more guaranteed innovation output.
(2) In terms of policy guidance, the government has introduced a series of preferential policies for an improved innovation environment to reduce the risks and costs of innovation and encourage research. The policies include the guiding ones for the beginning stages, such as talent attraction and fiscal subsidies, and for later stages, such as preferential policies for transformations of scientific and technological achievement and intellectual property protection. More participation of government support will lead to stronger willingness for cooperation between enterprises and universities, which is beneficial to technological innovation. Based on this analysis, we propose the following hypothesis:

Hypothesis 1: government-industry-academy cooperation improves regional innovation output.

2. The YRD innovation integration mechanism from the perspective of technology spillover

The influence of technology spillover on innovation output has always been a key issue in academia. Arrow (1964) believed that technologies have the property of public products, so the inventors could not possess the whole innovation achievement. In other words, there might be the phenomenon of "free-riding" caused by externality. The R&D outcome of some specific innovation entities can not only improve their own innovation capability, but also produce positive externality through technology spillover. Later, more scholars have explored the technology spillover effect from three main aspects: first is the influence of external technology spillover on recipients from the perspective of existence and

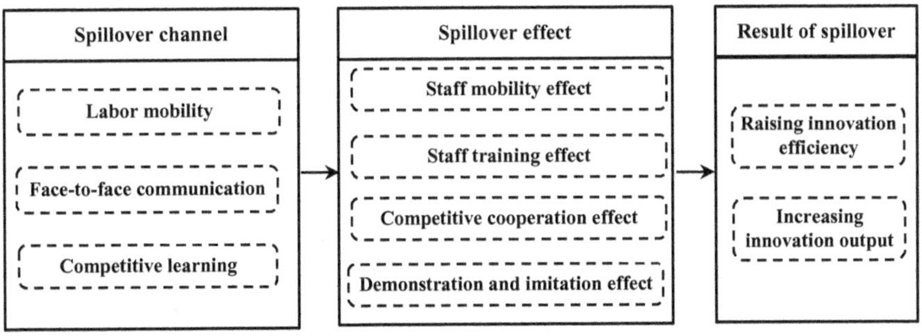

Figure 8.3 The influence and effect of technology spillover

contribution of technical spillover. Chen Liu (2007) and Wang Peng and Zhang Jianbo (2013) have conducted an empirical analysis on the output effect of international technology spillover represented by foreign direct investment. Second is the comparative analysis and measurement of different forms of technology spillover effect. Wei Shouhua et al. (2010) discovered that the local technology spillover effect, compared with the international one, generally presented a positive externality, i.e., the local environment and R&D efforts are key to the competitive advantage and innovation performance. Third is the factors that influence the economic entities' absorption of technology spillover. The research of Liu and Buck (2007), taking Chinese high-tech industry as a sample, discovered that the technology's absorption ability is the precondition of a spillover effect rather than the international technological spillover channels, such as FDI, import and export, and R&D expenditure of international enterprises.

Feldman (1999) pointed out that the external technology spillover effect is beneficial to the spatial agglomeration of economic activities and the convenience of idea exchange for economic entities. The advanced technologies in the spillover can help with the insufficiency of knowledge and supply cost in the region, in order to promote industrial agglomeration and innovation output. However, the achievement of technology spillovers depends on specific mechanisms. This chapter divides the influence mechanism of technology spillover on innovation output into three aspects – labor mobility, face-to-face communication, and competitive learning. The specific analysis is shown as follows (see Figure 8.3):

(1) Technology spillover in labor mobility

Technology is rooted in individuals. Labor mobility can improve the technology spillover and consequently drive independent innovation through the effect of staff turnover and training. First, staff can enrich their knowledge structure and technology skills by job-hopping. From the perspective of the enterprise, they can both acquire staff members' knowledge and techniques and weaken their competitors by recruiting people with similar research experience. Second, the pre-work professional training can bring about the positive externality of labor mobility. In conclusion, labor mobility can promote the technology spillover between enterprises. The acceleration of labor mobility will deepen the degree of technology spillover.

(2) Technology spillover in face-to-face communication

The face-to-face communication in industrial clusters creates a good environment and conditions for technology mobility between enterprises. On the one hand, some technologies cannot be coded. They are rooted in specific actions or situations, so they cannot be transmitted through publications. On the other hand, face-to-face communication not only spreads the current technologies but also helps economic entities to integrate others' resource advantages, master the overall information, and accelerate the production and application of new technologies.

(3) Technology spillover in competitive learning

The specialized industrial agglomeration not only strengthens the sense of competition, but also creates a better learning atmosphere. When they need to raise their innovation capacity for competitive advantages, enterprises tend to learn the advanced technologies by supervising their competitors. They are closely connected by dense relationship networks through both competition and cooperation, improving the stock of existing technologies. Based on this analysis, we have:

> Hypothesis 2: technology spillover positively improves regional innovation output.

3. The YRD innovation integration mechanism from the perspective of absorption ability

Absorption ability is the comprehensive capability of a country or region to effectively use the external technology spillover influenced by the recipient's economic system, financial development condition, market system, and many other factors. In practice, the technology spillover effect does not necessarily exist. It depends on all kinds of factors, as well as the absorption ability of the economic entity. Kedia and Bhagat (1988) first brought up the concept of "absorption ability" in their research on international technology transfer. Based on this, Cohen and Levinthal (1989) pointed out the R&D expenditure is significant for an enterprise in two aspects: first, it can directly promote scientific and technological innovation; second, it is beneficial to strengthen the enterprise's ability to recognize, understand, and apply the external technologies, i.e., the absorption ability effect of R&D expenditure. Zahra and George (2002) further divided the absorption ability into potential and practical abilities: the potential absorption ability means the access and recognition of external technologies without a guarantee of effective usage, while the practical one means the enterprise's ability to absorb and commercialize the external technologies, which reflects the actual degree of utilization of an external technology environment and is the key to enterprise innovation. Technology spillover has a significant influence on regional industrial development and

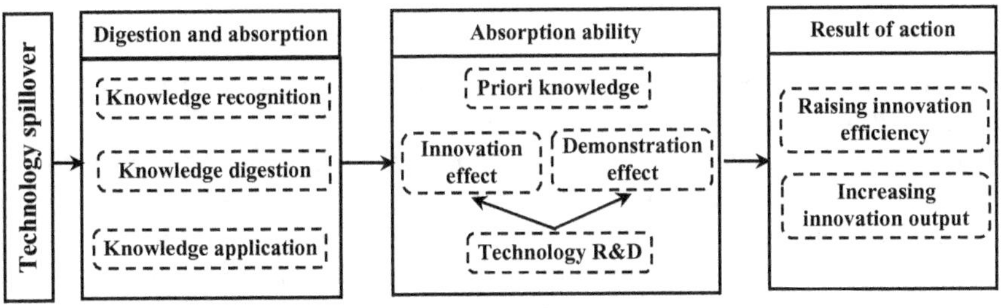

Figure 8.4 The influence and effect of absorption ability

innovation activities, the absorption of which is the determining factor in taking advantage of external technologies and the premise of innovation efficiency. Therefore, the research on technology spillover and absorption ability is of practical significance for the innovative integrated development in the YRD.

After Cohen and Levinthal (1989) brought up the concept of absorption ability, scholars have conducted numerous studies on its definition from different aspects, including knowledge recognition, digestion, and application. However, these discussions have focused on the understanding and application of knowledge itself within a specific academic field. They have certain guiding significances for the absorption ability under the background of technology spillover and industrial agglomeration, but do not completely fit. This chapter, based on the existing research and the specific background of regional technology spillover and innovative integration, divides the absorption ability into two types (see Figure 8.4):

(1) Absorption ability based on priori knowledge

Priori knowledge is the economic entities' technology stock gradually accumulating in their daily learning and practice closely related to the recognition, digestion, and application of external technologies, and is the key factor that determines absorption ability. The more stock of priori knowledge they have, the easier it is to adopt external technology, and the stronger their capability of accessing and assimilating complex technologies.

(2) Absorption ability based on technology R&D

Technology R&D is helpful for enterprises to improve their own scientific and technological innovation and their ability to absorb and assimilate external technologies, i.e., it increases the ability of both independent innovation and imitative innovation through the innovation effect and demonstration effect. The introduction and utilization of new technologies should be based on a certain knowledge stock and absorption ability. When the absorption ability affects the competitive ability, enterprises should strengthen their technological R&D to raise their absorption ability, which means the two are mutually promoted. The economic entities with relatively strong technology R&D capability would also have a strong absorption ability of regional technology spillover. Based on this analysis, we propose:

Hypothesis 3: the higher absorption ability is more helpful for raising the regional innovation output.

Technology spillover and absorption ability are two inter-related concepts, like the two sides of a coin. They reflect the process of technology diffusion from the aspects of the technology supply side and the recipient side, including both the unconscious spontaneous process; for example, the developed regions would drive the less developed regions because of the externality of scientific and technological innovation; and the subjective process; for example, the same spillover source would have different effects on different recipients due to their various economic level, innovation capacities, etc. The innovation effects of technology spillover and absorption ability are usually inequivalent: the former is the whole technology resource that can be utilized externally; the latter is only the parts that the entity actually used. Therefore, the innovation effect of absorption effect is less than or equal to that of technology spillover. Based on this analysis, we propose that:

Hypothesis 4: compared to absorption ability, technology spillover has a more distinct improving effect on regional innovation output.

Section 3 Data measurement

1. Government-industry-academy cooperation

Government-industry-academy cooperation reflects the closeness of the R&D cooperation between innovation entities in YRD areas. Generally speaking, university researchers emphasize academic value and significant scientific discovery, while enterprises pursue profit maximization, market value, and business prospects. Their target will be connected when the two enter the field of technology incubation. The scientists' knowledge innovation achievement requires market orientation to enter the incubation stage for its industrialization; the entrepreneur sees through market demands and requires advanced technology as orientation. Their cooperation is conducive to the integration of technology supply and market demand and the interconnection of academic value and commercial value. The cooperation between enterprise and university has always been led by government, manifested mainly in governmental funding support for academia without a distinct policy orientation regarding enterprise R&D. Therefore, this chapter compares the proportion of YRD university R&D funding from government and enterprise to measure the cooperation between innovative entities in the region.

Figure 8.5 describes the proportion of R&D funds from governments in YRD universities in 1998–2017. In 1998–2005, the proportions from high to low are: Anhui, Jiangsu, Shanghai, and Zhejiang. The ratio in Jiangsu rose slowly since 2006 and was surpassed by Shanghai and Zhejiang. From a regional comparison perspective, Anhui took the leading position except in 2010; its ratio rose slowly with fluctuation. Shanghai and Zhejiang kept steady increases, and the former is slightly higher than the latter. Jiangsu increased slowly and kept a relatively low position in the given period. In general, in the three provinces and one city in the

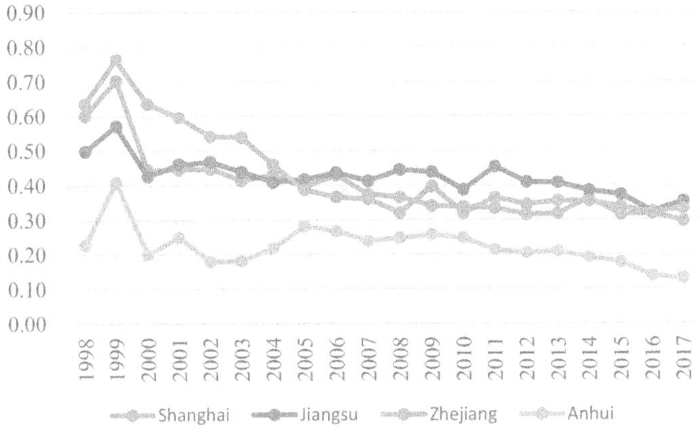

Figure 8.5 The proportion of R&D fund from government in universities in YRD

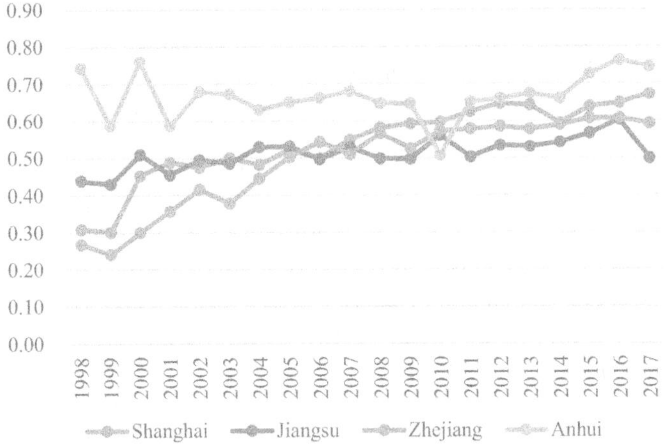

Figure 8.6 The proportion of R&D fund from enterprises in universities in YRD

YRD, the R&D funds from the government have all risen and stayed above 50% since 2005, indicating a increasing degree of emphasis on technology innovation by the government.

Figure 8.6 describes the proportion of R&D funds from enterprises in YRD universities in 1998–2017. In 1998–2004, the proportion from high to low are: Zhejiang, Shanghai, Jiangsu, and Anhui. Jiangsu surpassed the first two in 2015 and maintained its leading role. From the perspective of regional comparison, the proportion in Jiangsu is the highest with the smallest fluctuation; Shanghai and Zhejiang were at similar levels with the same dropping trend; Anhui stayed at a low level all the time. In general, in the three provinces and one city in the YRD, the R&D funds from enterprises was less than 50% with a dropping trend, indicating insufficient cooperation between enterprises and universities and the regional R&D innovation system.

2. Technology spillover

Technology spillover reflects the technology diffusion effect between geographical units in the YRD. The basic theory of technology spatial diffusion is that a technology spreads from its innovation origin to the neighboring areas with a decreasing density, presenting a distinct neighbor effect. Therefore, by referring the research methods of Caniels and Verspagen (2001) and Funke and Niebuhr (2005), the calculation of technology spillover in the YRD is shown here:

$$S_j = \frac{\delta_j}{d_{ij}} e^{-\left(\frac{1}{\delta^{\circ} j} G_{ij} - \mu^{\circ} j\right)^2}, i \neq j \tag{8.1}$$

$$G_{ij} = \ln \frac{K_i}{K_j} \tag{8.2}$$

In the formula, S_j represents the amount of spillover region j received from region i; δ_j represents the learning ability of region j (for example, represented by education expenditure); d_{ij} means the geographical distance between region i and region j; G_{ij} means the knowledge differences between region i and region j (K is represented by the R&D expenditure stock); μ_j is the corrective constant (for example, average knowledge density, measured through the number of schools per square kilometer).

The amount of technology spillover in a geographic unit is relevant to the learning ability of the region and the geographic distance and knowledge difference between regions. Table 8.1 reflects the inter-regional technology spillover effect in YRD in 2010–2017. The results are:

(1) Shanghai, as the leader, did not exert a distinct diffusing effect, because Anhui province has not been fully integrated into the YRD region. Theoretically, Shanghai as the core city in the YRD should drive the economic and social development in less-developed regions. However, the technology spillover effect of Shanghai failed Anhui in practice. On one hand, it is because of the location of Anhui, indicating that the reciprocal effect between "core cities" is stronger than the "periphery cities". On the other hand, Shanghai receives less technology spillover than it spreads, and the gap expands every year. Therefore, Shanghai does not have a strong willingness to seek cooperation voluntarily.

(2) Jiangsu is the province that receives and spreads the most technology spillover on average under the cooperation model, because of both its location in the center and the large scale of education and R&D expenditure, which leads to a distinct increase of learning ability and innovation capability. Therefore, it influenced the surrounding regions.

Table 8.1 The technology spillover effect in YRD in 2010–2017

			2010	*2011*	*2012*	*2013*	*2014*	*2015*	*2016*	*2017*
Shanghai	Receive from	Jiangsu	1.62	1.83	2.33	2.69	2.98	3.25	3.33	3.68
		Zhejiang	2.42	2.74	3.49	4.03	4.46	4.87	4.99	5.53
		Anhui	0.97	1.10	1.40	1.61	1.78	1.95	2.00	2.21
	Spread to	Jiangsu	3.62	4.30	5.20	5.56	6.52	6.83	7.38	7.89
		Zhejiang	4.37	5.22	5.93	6.65	7.13	7.92	8.65	9.31
		Anhui	0.96	1.18	1.61	1.87	2.05	2.06	2.28	2.44
Jiangsu	Receive from	Shanghai	3.62	4.30	5.20	5.56	6.52	6.83	7.38	7.89
		Zhejiang	3.50	4.17	4.74	5.32	5.71	6.34	6.92	7.45
		Anhui	2.66	3.27	4.46	5.20	5.70	5.73	6.34	6.77
	Spread to	Shanghai	1.62	1.83	2.33	2.69	2.98	3.25	3.33	3.68
		Zhejiang	4.34	5.16	6.24	6.68	7.82	8.20	8.85	9.47
		Anhui	6.02	7.17	8.67	9.27	10.86	11.38	12.29	13.15
Zhejiang	Receive from	Shanghai	4.37	5.22	5.93	6.65	7.13	7.92	8.65	9.31
		Jiangsu	4.34	5.16	6.24	6.68	7.82	8.20	8.85	9.47
		Anhui	1.06	1.31	1.79	2.08	2.28	2.29	2.54	2.71
	Spread to	Shanghai	2.42	2.74	3.49	4.03	4.46	4.87	4.99	5.53
		Jiangsu	3.50	4.17	4.74	5.32	5.71	6.34	6.92	7.45
		Anhui	1.94	2.32	2.63	2.96	3.17	3.52	3.85	4.14
Anhui	Receive from	Shanghai	0.96	1.18	1.61	1.87	2.05	2.06	2.28	2.44
		Jiangsu	6.02	7.17	8.67	9.27	10.86	11.38	12.29	13.15
		Zhejiang	1.94	2.32	2.63	2.96	3.17	3.52	3.85	4.14
	Spread to	Shanghai	0.97	1.10	1.40	1.61	1.78	1.95	2.00	2.21
		Jiangsu	2.66	3.27	4.46	5.20	5.70	5.73	6.34	6.77
		Zhejiang	1.06	1.31	1.79	2.08	2.28	2.29	2.54	2.71

(3) Zhejiang province could receive net technology inflow from Shanghai and Jiangsu in the integrated development model of the YRD. Based on the data of spillover levels, the reciprocal effect between Zhejiang and Jiangsu was more distinct because of their relatively small technology gap and knowledge difference, which benefits fully utilizing innovation factors and absorbing technology spillover, as theories on spatial geography indicate. However, Zhejiang also needs to shoulder the net outflow to Anhui.
(4) Anhui is the province that benefits the most under the cooperative model in the YRD. It receives positive technology externally from Shanghai, Jiangsu, and Zhejiang. The received amounts from high to low are Jiangsu, Zhejiang, and Shanghai. It can be understood that the technology level of Anhui is at the low end, so it needs to acquire technology spillover by learning from and imitating the neighboring regions. This also proves the significance of spatial distance to the amount of received technology spillover.

3. Absorption ability

The absorption ability reflects the YRD regions' ability to absorb and assimilate technology spillover. According to Borensztein et al. (1995), pure knowledge inflow is not enough to generate a technology spillover effect; whether the external advanced knowledge can improve the recipient's technology depends on the recipient's absorption ability. Therefore, we adopted the research method of Watanabe et al. (2001) and Tang Qing and Fu Qiang (2010) to measure the regulatory effect of absorption effect between external technology spillover and innovation performance. The approach is shown here:

$$Z_i = \frac{1}{1+\frac{\Delta T_S}{T_S} / \frac{\Delta T_i}{T_i}} \frac{T_i}{T_S} \tag{8.3}$$

$$A_i = Z_i \times \Sigma_{j=1}^{3} RD_j \tag{8.4}$$

In the formula, j represents the neighboring region ($i \neq j$); Z_i represents the coefficient of assimilation ability of technology spillover in region i; T_i represents the technology and knowledge stock from independent R&D in region i; T_s means the sum of knowledge stock in other regions; ΔT_i represents the annual increment of knowledge stock from independent R&D in region i; ΔT_s represents the annual increment of knowledge stock in other regions; A represents the absorbed spillover of technology and knowledge stock.

The absorption ability is not only related to the knowledge stock from independent R&D in region, but also influenced by the spillover of technology and knowledge stock from neighboring regions. Figure 8.7 describes the changing track of absorption ability of the three provinces and one city in the YRD from 1999–2017. In terms of growth rate, they all increased rapidly; Jiangsu, surpassing Shanghai in 2003, stayed at the top; Zhejiang was basically the same as Shanghai with a slightly higher increase rate; Anhui also showed a rising trend year by year. From

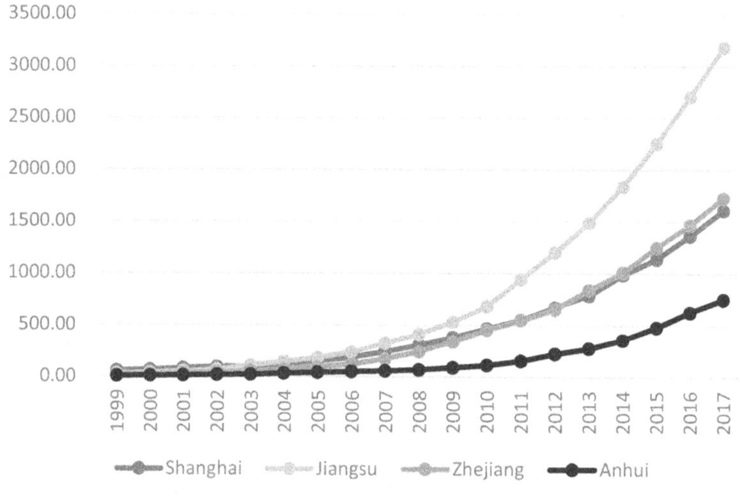

Figure 8.7 The absorption ability effect in the three provinces and one city in YRD

the perspective of scale, Jiangsu was in the leading position, followed by Zhejiang and Shanghai, while Anhui was the lowest. From 1998–2005, the general scale of absorption ability is at a relatively low level with a low growth rate. But since 2005, Jiangsu left the other regions far behind with an explosive increase; Shanghai and Zhejiang grew steadily; and Anhui kept expanding although still at a relatively low level. The staged change of absorption ability was caused by the "15+N" pattern in the YRD at the end of 2004, which verified the success of the YRD expansion and indicated a steady rise and good development trend of the collaborative innovation level in the YRD.

Section 4 Research design

1. Measurement model setup

Based on the endogenous growth theory, industrial cluster theory, and state innovation system theory, Feldman and Florida (1994) first brought up the production function of geographical innovation centers. Later, Furman et al. (2000) and Furman and Hayes (2004) established the production function of state innovation ability. These functions more generally defined the main factors that influence the innovation output and innovation ability in a country or region. Based on the research and hypothesis of the mechanisms of scientific and technological collaborative innovation integration in the YRD, this chapter refers the production function of geographical innovation by Feldman and Florida (1994), Furman et al. (2000), and Furman and Hayes (2004). It takes innovation output as the explained variable, introduces three core explaining variables, i.e., government-industry-academy cooperation, technology spillover, and absorption ability, and takes the possible factors as control variables, such as human capital, knowledge stack, basic research in universities and institutions, FDI, etc. The basic theory is presented in formula (8.5):

$$Innov_{i,t} = \delta_{i,t}\left(X_{i,t}^{GIU}, X_{i,t}^{\text{Spill}}, X_{i,t}^{\text{Assi}}, X_{i,t}^{\text{Univ}}, X_{i,t}^{FDI}\right)H_{i,t}A_{i,t} \tag{8.5}$$

And formula (8.6) is the logarithm of formula (8.5):

$$\begin{aligned} lnInnov_{i,t} &= \alpha_{i,t} + \beta_1 \ln X_{i,t}^{GIU} + \beta_2 \ln X_{i,t}^{\text{Spill}} + \beta_3 \ln X_{i,t}^{Assi} \\ &+\beta_4 \ln X_{i,t}^{Univ} + \beta_5 \ln X_{i,t}^{FDI} + \gamma \ln H_{i,t} + \varphi \ln A_{i,t} \\ &+\varepsilon_{i,t} \end{aligned} \tag{8.6}$$

In the formulas, i represents region; t, a specific time; $Innov_{i,t}$, innovation output; $X_{i,t}^{GIU}$, the vector set of the government-industry-academy connection; $X_{i,t}^{Spill}$ and $X_{i,t}^{Assi}$ are technological spillover and absorption ability respectively; $X_{i,t}^{Univ}$, the basic researches in universities and institution; $X_{i,t}^{FDI}$, FDI; $H_{i,t}$, R&D human capital input in the region; $A_{i,t}$, accessible knowledge stock; $\alpha_{i,t}$ is parameter, while $\varepsilon_{i,t}$ random error term.

2. Variable description

(1) Explained variable

Innovation output is often measured through patents worldwide. However, there are some obvious deficiencies to this: first, not all innovation output is protected in the form of patent, leading to underestimating the value of it. Second, some patents lack commercial value, leading to an overestimated value. This chapter adopts the method of Acs et al. (1992), Feldman and Florida (1994), and Liu and Buck (2007), i.e., using the sales revenue of new products as the innovation output to reflect the innovation performance that has been widely recognized by the market and has proven its commercial value.

(2) Core explaining variables

1. Government-industry-academy cooperation

According to the views of He Xiaozhou and He Youjun (2016), the government-industry-academy cooperation is conducive to the effective combination of production factors for technology innovation and is the significant means of industrialization of scientific and technological achievement. In the meantime, the various cooperation mechanisms between innovative entities is considered as this chapter measures the cooperation through the proportion of university R&D expenditure from government and enterprise, respectively. There has been a common phenomenon in the R&D investment of public finance in Chinese government sectors: the funds for scientific research are mainly the interaction between government and universities without an orientation of commercialization, i.e., the cooperation between government and enterprise is insufficient. Since enterprise R&D expenditures are mainly their own fund, this index will not be considered in this research.

2. Technology spillover

The research methods of Marjolein and Verspagen (2001) and Funke and Niebuhr (2005) are adopted here to measure the inter-dependent relationship between the three provinces and one city in the YRD. For example, a Suzhou pharmaceutical manufacturing enterprise, because of its closeness to Shanghai or Hangzhou, may obtain positive technological externality through leaning or a negative one when being imitated. There has long been a reciprocal effect between provinces in the YRD, which is a significant basis for the formation of collaborative innovation integration. With the expanding scale of cooperation, the effect of technology spillover weakens when geographical distance increases, i.e., the neighboring regions have a stronger technology spillover effect, which means the reciprocal effect between "core cities" is stronger than that between "peripheral cities".

3. Absorption ability

The research method of Watanabe et al. (2001) and Tang Qing and Fu Qiang (2010) is used to measure the absorption ability effect in the YRD. For different recipients of the same source of technology spillover, their different innovation ability, knowledge stock, policy environment, etc. have led to different effects, i.e., the absorption ability of recipient can affect the innovation output.

(3) Control variables

By referring to the existing research achievements, the following possible influence factors are chosen as control variables: (1) Human capital, represented by R&D personnel investment. (2) Knowledge stock in the early stage, represented by the sum of authorized patents in the last three years. According to the endogenous growth theory, the two variables are the original driving power of scientific and technological innovation: the higher R&D expenditure and knowledge stock would lead to higher innovation intensity and thus more output. (3) The basic research in universities and institutions, represented by the sum of R&D expenditure in universities and institutions. Generally speaking, their R&D activities can promote the regional public R&D ability and raise the innovation output. (4) FDI, the international technology spillover channel that greatly influences a country or region, especially those at high degrees of opening. The definition and measurement of the variables are shown in Table 8.2.

Table 8.2 Definition and measurement of variable

Variable type	*Variable name*	*Variable symbol*	*Construction method*
Explained variable	Innovation output	*Innov*	Sales revenue of new products, at constant price in 1998
Explaining variable	Government-industry-academy cooperation	X^{GIU} : Univ-Gover	The proportion of university R&D expenditure from government
		$X^{GIU}: Univ - Indus$	The proportion of university R&D expenditure from enterprise
	Technology spillover	X^{Spill}	Formula (8.1)(8.2)
	Absorption ability	X^{Assi}	Formula (8.3)(8.4)
Control variable	Human capital	*Hum*	R&D staff number
	Knowledge stock	*Patent*	The sum of authorized patent in last three years
	Basic research in universities	X^{Univ}	The sum of R&D expenditure in universities and research institutions, at constant price in 1998, perpetual inventory method
	FDI	X^{FDI}	FDI, at constant price in 1998

Table 8.3 Descriptive statistics of each variable

Variable	*Sample number*	*Average*	*Standard deviation*	*Minimum value*	*Maximum value*
$\ln Innov$	80	6.0623	1.8592	0.7524	9.2664
$X^{GIU}: \ln Univ - Gover$	80	−0.6182	0.2295	−1.4214	−0.2707
$X^{GIU}: \ln Univ - Indus$	80	−1.0518	0.358	−2.0427	−0.2693
$\ln X^{Spill}$	80	1.7548	0.8257	0.1779	3.0958
$\ln X^{Assi}$	76	5.3209	1.5064	1.7798	8.0664
$\ln Hum$	76	9.9405	1.0681	7.7048	11.9019
$\ln Patent$	80	10.7192	1.6232	7.4770	13.4725
$\ln X^{Univ}$	80	3.8483	0.9545	2.0699	5.9293
$\ln X^{FDI}$	80	4.2323	1.2212	1.1569	5.8794

3. Data source and descriptive statistics

All the data is from the *China Statistical Yearbook on Science and Technology, China Statistical Yearbook on High Technology Industry, Jiangsu Statistical Yearbook, Shanghai Statistical Yearbook, Zhejiang Statistical Yearbook, Anhui Statistical Yearbook*, national transport inquiry system, and CEIdata from 1999 to 2018. All the variables in this chapter are measured in logarithmic form, so the regression coefficient can be explained as elasticity of contribution. The sales revenue of new products, university and institution R&D expenditure, and FDI are deflated as a constant price in 1998. R&D expenditure is converted to stock state by perpetual inventory method. The descriptive statistics are shown in Table 8.3.

Section 5 Empirical result and discussion

Based on this analysis, and with the data from 1998–2017, this chapter empirically analyzed the effect of scientific and technological collaborative innovation integration in the YRD by the recursive method of panel data. To avoid spurious regression, we used LLC and IPS for unit root tests and the difference method for unsteady sequences. The result showed that all the variables present a stationary sequence after the first difference. In addition, three situations need to be considered for the regression analysis on panel data model: mixture regression model, fixed effect model, and random effect model. With the results of the F test and Hausman test, this chapter eventually selects a fixed effect model for the regression analysis on panel data.

Geographic innovation production function is a multi-factor system. In order to emphasize government-industry-academy cooperation, technology spillover from neighboring regions, and the absorption ability effect, the regression has three steps: step one, calculate the regression result without considering the government-industry-academy cooperation, technology spillover, or absorption ability, i.e., testing the relation between only the control variables and innovation output;

Table 8.4 The regression result of multi–factor effect on the innovation output in YRD

	lnInnov		
	Model (1)	*Model (2)*	*Model (3)*
X^{GIU} : $\ln Univ - Gover$		-1.879^{***}	-1.490^{**}
		(0.522)	(0.605)
X^{GIU} : $\ln Univ - Indus$		-1.078^{**}	-0.999^{**}
		(0.497)	(0.458)
$\ln X^{Spill}$			0.681^{**}
			(0.327)
$\ln X^{Assi}$			0.475^{**}
			(0.235)
ln*Hum*	0.553^{***}	0.720^{***}	0.398^{*}
	(0.182)	(0.178)	(0.236)
ln*Patent*	0.709^{***}	0.724^{***}	0.486^{***}
	(0.134)	(0.125)	(0.138)
$\ln X^{Univ}$	-0.921^{***}	-0.953^{***}	-0.943^{***}
	(0.266)	(0.247)	(0.266)
$\ln X^{FDI}$	0.526^{***}	0.461^{***}	0.416^{***}
	(0.125)	(0.117)	(0.127)
Cons	-5.758^{***}	-9.484^{***}	−3.496
	(1.075)	(1.411)	(2.306)
Observation	76	76	72
R-sq	0.9081	0.9240	0.940 4
F	167.91^{***}	133.69^{***}	118.27^{***}

Note: the numbers in brackets are standard error; ***, **, and * represent the significance at levels of 1%, 5%, and 10% significance level respectively.

step two, the regression result taking the government-industry-academy cooperation into consideration; step three, the regression result considering technology spillover and absorption ability. The first step is taken as the baseline for comparison in order to identify the influence of government-industry-academy cooperation more clearly, and then technology spillover, absorption ability, and their synergistic effects on innovation output. The regression result is shown in Table 8.4.

The regression result of model (1) indicates that R&D human capital is significantly positively correlated to innovation output at a 1% statistical level with the regression coefficient 0.553. It means that the intense economic and technological competition in the current world is essentially the competition of innovation talents, i.e., the degree of innovation effort is the decisive factor of innovation output. The knowledge stock at the early stage positively improves innovation output significantly at a 1% significance level: every 10% increase of knowledge stock leads to a 7.09% rise in innovation output. The basic research in university and institutions has a negative effect on innovation output. Possible reasons might be:

(1) This chapter measured innovation output through the sales revenue of new products. However, universities and institutions pay more attention to academic values rather than market values and take scientific and technological

theses as their output index. Therefore, the market mechanism cannot play this role in universities or institutions.

(2) The industrialization of scientific and technological achievements in universities and institutions requires support from incubators, technological agencies, and other platforms; the insufficiency of these in the current market in China leads to severely disjointed R&D activities and industrialized applications of technologies. The regression coefficient of FDI is 0.526, significant at a 1% statistical level, indicating that at the advanced position of deepened reform and higher level of opening up in China, YRD is conducive to absorbing international technological spillover and will continue utilizing the external technology resources to raise the level of scientific and technological innovation.

Model (2) tests the relationship between government-industry-academy cooperation and innovation output, presenting significantly negative regression results in proportions of university R&D expenditure from both government and enterprise. It means that the cooperation could not distinctly promote innovation output, which is the opposite of hypothesis 1. The possible reasons are:

(1) From the perspective of universities, the patent for inventions belongs to the organization rather than the individual, so the inventors would not have much enthusiasm for the transformation of scientific and technological achievement, causing problems with insufficient basic research and their transformation.
(2) From the perspective of enterprises, although technology innovation demand is their direct motivation for seeking government-industry-academy cooperation, the pursuit of profit remains their essence: the investment in scientific research requires large amounts with high risk and long periods, while commercial applications have good market prospects and profit margins. Different focuses lead to different inputs and outputs.
(3) From the perspective of governments, there is a lack of systematic legal traction for the transformation from basic research to innovation achievement and then commercial application; there is also a lack of technology agency markets for the transformation from technology and patent to applicable productivity.

Model (3) tests the influence of technology spillover and absorption ability on innovation output. The regression result shows that technology spillover and scaled revenue of new products have a significant positive correlation under a 5% significance level: every 10% increase of technology spillover raises a 6.81% innovation output. Absorption ability significantly promotes innovation output with a regression coefficient of 0.475 under a 5% significance level, i.e., the stronger the absorption ability, the more the innovation output. Therefore, hypothesis 3 is statistically verified. From the perspective of elastic coefficients, a 10% increase of technology spillover leads to a 6.81% increase of innovation output, while that of absorption ability leads to a 4.75% increase of innovation output. Therefore, the innovation output effect of technology spillover is more distinct, which verifies hypothesis 4 statistically.

Section 6 Conclusion and illumination

This chapter, taking the three provinces and one city in the YRD from 1998–2017 as a research sample, studies the innovation integration in the YRD from three aspects: government-industry-academy cooperation, technology spillover, and absorption ability, and their influence on innovation output. The following are the main conclusions:

(1) The measurement of government-industry-academy cooperation indicates that first, the proportion of university R&D expenditure from government support has been above 50% in the whole area, even reaching 80% in Anhui, with a relatively steady increase in general. This means the interaction between government and academia is getting closer, and government is playing an increasingly important role in the innovation system. In comparison, the proportion of university R&D expenditure from enterprises showed a decreasing trend at around 30%, indicating that the cooperation between enterprises and universities was not close enough and was in a bad condition. It caused the insufficient utilization of innovation resources in universities; on the other hand, the innovation achievements cannot be industrialized, leading to the sinking commercial value of some scientific research projects. From the perspective of different regions, the universities in Anhui have the highest proportion of R&D funding from government and the lowest from enterprises, while the universities in Jiangsu have the highest proportion of R&D funding from enterprises and the lowest from government, leaving Shanghai and Zhejiang in between.
(2) The measurement of technology spillover indicates that the diffusion effect of Shanghai is not strong enough for Anhui to completely be integrated into the YRD; Jiangsu receives and exports the most technology spillover on average under the cooperation mode; Zhejiang takes technology inflow from Shanghai and Jiangsu and exports to Anhui; while Anhui benefits the most in obtaining positive technology externality from Shanghai, Jiangsu, and Zhejiang. The measurement of absorption ability indicates that the four places all grew rapidly: Jiangsu exceeded Shanghai in 2003 and remained at the top; from the perspective of absolute scale, Jiangsu was the biggest, followed by Zhejiang and Shanghai, and Anhui is the smallest.
(3) Empirical regression results indicate that government-industry-academy cooperation does not have a distinct promoting effect on innovation output; it has an obstructive effect. It contradicts the theoretical analysis and hypothesis 1. This means that the transfer mechanism between government-industry-academy cooperation and innovation output of new products is imperfect and requires the government's preferential policy, more investment, and guidance on the transformation. In the meantime, in the process of R&D investment of public finances, the government should strengthen direct support for enterprises.
(4) Empirical regression results also show that technology spillover and absorption ability are both significantly promoting innovation output: the innovation effect of technology spillover is more distinct, which matches the theoretical

analysis and is verified by statistics. Therefore, the governments in the YRD should continue focusing on raising their technology spillover and absorption ability in the region, increasing investments in all aspects, in order to promote the innovation integration in the YRD.

To deal with the weak links and problems in the innovation integration mechanism in YRD, this chapter proposes the following policy suggestions:

First, YRD governments should collaborate with each other on the investment in university R&D: they should jointly select a batch of universities with strong innovation ability and high-level industrialization and marketization to avoid "scattered" investment. In addition, regional governments should strengthen their direct investment in enterprise R&D or make R&D a tax offset to encourage enterprises to conduct R&D independently or to cooperate with universities.

Second, YRD governments should stimulate the enthusiasm for innovation by policies and launch a Chinese version of the *Bayh – Dole Act*. They should explore and establish a rational and effective benefit distribution mechanism, taking all the parties (R&D platform, R&D teams, technology agency, transformative enterprises, etc.) into consideration, to boost the initiative of a creation of all the innovation entities.

Third, to enhance the promoting effect of government-industry-academy cooperation on innovation output, it is important to develop a strong market for technology transformation agency to link the technology and market and maximize the value of technologies in the most suitable market. The key is to construct the technology broker system, along with the matching law and financial service to raise the efficiency of the marketization of technology.

Fourth, the government should strengthen their professional abilities and hire specialized talents for specific fields. Their projects should be followed in real time, supervised, evaluated, and inspected in terms of the effect on investment so they can choose the optimal objects and project teams.

References

Z.J. Acs, D.B. Audretsch, M.P. Feldman. Real Effects of Academic Research: Comment. American Economic Review, 1992 (2).

K.J. Arrow. The Economic Implications of Learning by Doing. Review of Economic Studies, 1964, 29 (3).

E. Borensztein, et al. How does Foreign Direct Investment Affect Economic Growth? New York: Social Science Electronic Publishing, 1995.

W.M. Cohen, D.A. Levinthal. Innovation and Learning: The Two Faces of R&D. Economic Journal, 1989, 99 (397).

M.P. Feldman. The New Economics of Innovation, Spillovers and Agglomeration: A Review of Empirical Studies. Economics of Innovation & New Technology, 1999, 8 (1–2).

M.P. Feldman, R. Florida. The Geographic Sources of Innovation: Technological Infrastructure and Product Innovation in the United States. Annals of the Association of American, 1994, 84 (2).

M. Funke, A. Niebuhr. Regional Geographic Research and Development Spillovers and Economic Growth: Evidence from West Germany. Regional Studies, 2005.

J.L. Furman, R. Hayes. Catching up or Standing Still? National Innovative Productivity Among "Follower" Countries, 1978–1999. Research Policy, 2004 (9).

J.L. Furman, M.E. Porter, S. Stern. The Determinants of National Innovative Capacity. Research Policy, 2000, 31 (6).

T.M. Jorde, D.J. Teece. Innovation and Cooperation: Implications for Competition and Antitrust. The Journal of Economic Perspectives, 1990, 4 (3).

B.L. Kedia, R.S. Bhagat. Cultural Constraints on Transfer of Technology Across Nations: Implications for Research in International and Comparative Management. The Academy of Management Review, 1988.

Chen Liu. FDI Technology Spillover, Local Innovation Ability and Economic Growth in the Yangtze River Delta Region. World Economy Studies, 2007 (1).

X.H. Liu, T. Buck. Innovation Performance and Channels for International Technology Spillovers: Evidence from Chinese High-tech Industries. Research Policy, 2007, 72.

C.J. Marjolein, B. Caniels Verspagen. Barriers to Knowledge Spillovers and Regional Convergence in an Evolutionary Model. Journal of Evolutionary Economics, 2001, 11.

Wang Peng, Zhang Jianbo. Foreign Direct Investment, Government-industry-academy Cooperation and Regional Innovation Output: The Empirical Research Based on the Panel Data of 13 Provinces and Cities in China. Economist, 2013 (1).

Tang Qing, Fu Qiang. Measurement and Analysis on the Assimilation Ability of Technology Spillover between High Technology Industries in China. Science & Technology Progress and Policy, 2010 (3).

D. Schartinger, A. Schibany, H. Gassler. Interactive Relations between Universities and Firms: Empirical Evidence for Austria. The Journal of Technology Transfer, 2001, 26.

Wei Shouhua, Jiang Ning, Wu Guisheng. Indigenous and International Technology Spillover: Evidence from the Industrial Innovation in China. Journal of Finance and Economics, 2010 (1).

C. Watanabe, et al. Global Technology Spillover and Its Impact on Industry's R&D Strategies. Technovation, 2001 (5).

He Xiaozhou, He Youjun. Research on Mediating Effect of Government-Industry-Academy Cooperation between Social Capital and Innovation. Science & Technology Progress and Policy, 2016 (9).

Wu Yuming. Government-industry-academy R&D Cooperation, Knowledge Spillover and Regional Patent Innovation Output. Studies in Science of Science, 2009 (10).

S.A. Zahra, G. George. Absorptive Capacity: A Review, Reconceptualization, and Extension. Academy of Management Review, 2002, 27 (2).

9 Listed company reconstruction and Yangtze River Delta integration

Jianzhong Zhang and Zhibiao Liu

Section 1 Introduction

There are four generally accepted methods of reflecting or measuring economic integration (Xu, 2002). The first is through the similarity of output structure: with the deepening of economic integration, the economy in a country shows distinct regional work division or agglomeration for the difference of factor endowment, economies of scale, spillover effect, etc.; thus the regional distribution of different industries presents divergence rather than convergence. The research of Young (2000) discovered that since the tax-sharing reform, the output structure of products in different regions in China has started to converge, leading to the conclusion that China is evolving into a segmented domestic market pattern dominated by regional protectionism and controlled by local governments. Bai Chong'en reached the opposite conclusion by analyzing the similarity of industrial structure (Bai Chong'en et al., 2004). Naughton believed that it lacks theoretical support to measure integration through output structure. The convergence of output structure in China has its internal logic and mechanism: it is probably just one of the staged characteristics of industrialization. The process means the industry is improving, so it is not the sole evidence against integration (Naughton, 2003). The second measurement of economic integration is provincial trade flow. Naughton measured the provincial trade flow in China in 1987 and 1992 through this method and discovered that the inflow and outflow in 1992 was much higher than those in 1987, indicating a raised level of integration. However, he also admitted that this method only indicates the cross-regional trade relations within a country, without leading to a conclusion of what level of trade represents integration (Naughton, 2003). The third is also the most common method: using the degree of price convergence to measure economic integration (Xu, 2002). However, the price is restricted by its availability; and the measurement based on the law of one price can only reflect the distance between current Chinese market to a market of perfect competition. The problem is that price dispersion is caused by multiple factors which may or may not be the evidence of non-integration. The fourth, more macroscopic, is called business cycle method by Xu (2002). It is conducive to research on the effectiveness of macro policies, but its conclusions are ambiguous without a clear reflection on the internal unified mechanism of integration.

DOI: 10.4324/9781003455943-9

The four methods focused on using macro-indexes to measure economic integration. However, the non-integration they explained is not caused by perfect competition, but by the insufficient competition caused by excessive government intervention. If the market is perfect, then the enterprises without enough competitive advantages will automatically exit, rather than continue operating despite their loss. Only a perfect market can lay the micro-foundation for the high-quality development of economic integration in the YRD (Liu Zhibiao, 2019). In this case, what are the corresponding micro measuring criteria? This chapter believes that research at the enterprise behavior level can lead to deeper understanding of the process of economy and regional economic integration in China and provide a more realistic and specific micro basis. In the meantime, the transition from trade liberalization to investment liberalization is also a significant characteristic and future trend of regional economic integration (Jiang Fuxiu, 2015). This chapter studies the integration level in the YRD from the perspective of regional economy through the micro data of mergers and acquisitions in the YRD.

The structure of this chapter is as follows: the first section provides the empirical and theoretical support for measuring the integration by the frequency of cross-regional merger and acquisition; Section Two theoretically explains the reasons and mechanism of the local merger and acquisition of state-owned enterprise object integration; Section Three statistically tests the level of integration in the YRD; and Section Four reaches the conclusion.

Section 2 The frequency of merger and reorganization as a proof of regional economic integration

1. Integration promotes merger and reacquisition: experience from the European Union

There is factual evidence from the EU to improve that integration promotes enterprise merger and reacquisition. The EU legislative practices support the activities of merger and acquisition between member states in some respects and become significant for forming a unified EU market. Since the Treaty of Rome was signed by six Western European countries in 1957, the EU has never launched any policy to specifically control mergers. Although merger itself may cause the high market concentration ratio and weaken the result of competition, the EU did not adopt any controlling policy specifically on mergers until the EU Act in 1985 to form a single market (Lyons, 2008). The Treaty of Rome does not include regulations on mergers similar to those in American's antimonopoly laws. According to Banks, this is not a mistake or neglect, but a decision under thorough consideration to accelerate the integration of the European economy by competition policies. Mergers, especially cross-country ones, are regarded as a part of the economic integration in Europe (Banks, 1998).

As shown in Figure 9.1, the number of cross-country mergers and acquisitions of enterprise in Europe presented a rising trend year by year with the boost of EU integration, especially in 1986–1991. Although it dropped to some extent after

1991, the mergers within Europe were still more than those with enterprises outside the EU before 1995. According to the data released by the European Commission, the number of cross-country mergers and acquisitions between EU members reached 1984 by 2006, more than double of that in 1991.[1]

With the progress and expansion of integration, the cross-regional merger and acquisition has become gradually popularized rather than concentrated in a certain area, which has been proven by the EU experience. Garnier proposed that the EU integration accelerated the merger and acquisition of enterprises spreading among member states, especially the new ones, leading to a more dispersed cross-country merger activity based on how long since they joined the EU, except for the earliest 15 countries (Garnier, 2004). Figure 9.2 showed that the merged and acquired enterprises by the 15 EU countries are increasingly from EU member states; new ones especially, except for Turkey and Hungary. It proves that when more countries and regions are integrated into the unified market, the cross-regional mergers and acquisitions become more pervasive.

2. The theoretical proof for integration promoting merger and reacquisition

The theoretical research on integration promoting merger and acquisition has already started. Bjorvatn believed that a more open and competitive market environment raised the frequency of mergers and acquisitions among enterprises because competition mechanisms caused obsolescence of more enterprises, one

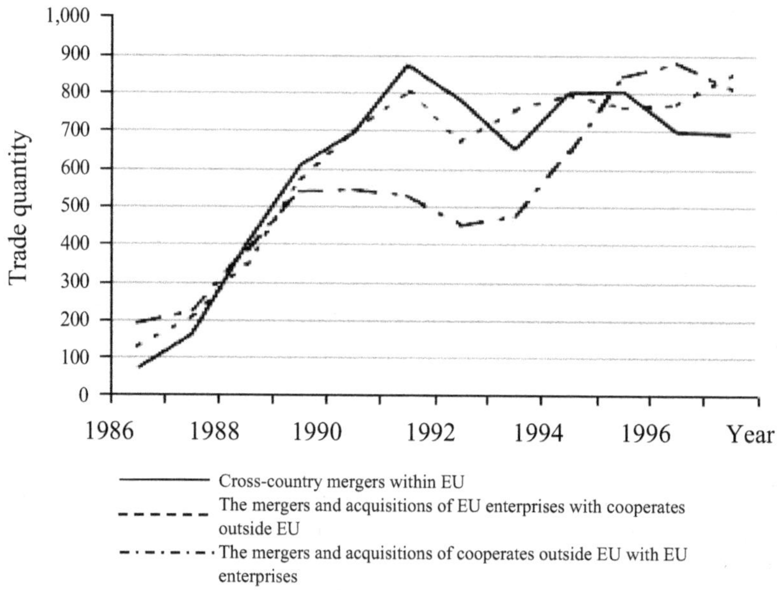

Figure 9.1 The distribution of numbers of EU enterprise mergers[2]

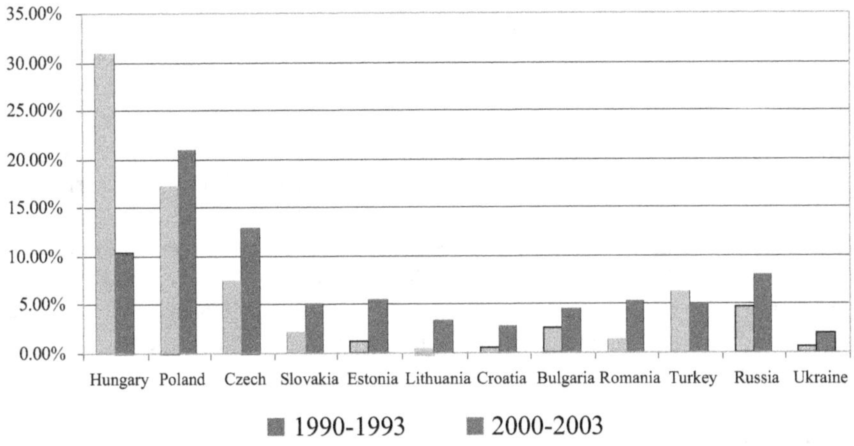

Figure 9.2 The distribution of cross-country merger and acquisition activities of enterprise in 15 EU countries during the process of EU integration

of the results of which is being merged (Bjorvatn, 2004). Neary verified the inevitability of activities and consequent waves of merger and acquisition with the deepening of economic openness and integration by the general equilibrium framework of oligarchy. Such inevitability originated from the differences of technologic capability between enterprises. Through mergers and acquisitions, segmented economic entities have more rapidly formed a pattern of division based on comparative advantages between countries and between regions, consequently promoting the formation of economic integration (Neary, 2007).

Brakman et al., by using the Thomson database, tested and reached one of the conclusions that economic integration stimulates the cross-regional merger and reacquisition (Brakman et al., 2006). Their research noted that the proportion of cross-country mergers and reacquisitions within Europe to the total number in the world rose 15% from 1986–1990 to 2001–2005, making it the most important position among all the countries and regions. Brakman et al. believed that the reason lies in the high level of European economic integration.

Baldwin, in the systematic research on EU integration, pointed out the intrinsic mechanism of integration promoting mergers. In the accelerating process of EU integration characterized by open markets, enterprises have been facing more competitive pressures, so they have to lower the price of products and services. The profit stress and market scale effect drive enterprises to form an internal mechanism of automatic reorganization (Baldwin and Wyplosz, 2015). Therefore, integration has a positive promoting effect on the frequency of cross-regional mergers and acquisitions: the higher the degree of integration, the higher the frequency of merger activities. In a regional economy, less frequent cross-regional mergers and acquisitions usually reflect a low level of integration.

There are two questions that need to be clarified: (1) some research on the cross-regional mergers and acquisitions did not take the ownership of enterprise into consideration. The following analysis indicates that different properties of ownership would lead to various types of mergers and acquisitions. Therefore, a cross-regional merger and acquisition could be evidence of non-integration. (2) The frequency of a merger and acquisition in essence reflects the free mobility of capital between regions indirectly. The more direct method of measuring the integration is the Q value dispersion in different regions by Tobin's Q (Jovanovic, 2002). However, the extreme difficulties of data acquisition forced us to measure the integration indirectly through the mergers and acquisitions of enterprise. Thus, the openness of trade and investment is reflected by the frequency of enterprise merger and acquisition; and the index, with micro basis, reflects the level of integration comprehensively.

Section 3 Local governments push for local merger and acquisition activities taking state-owned enterprises as tools

1. The local protectionism behaviors through solely state-owned or state-holding enterprise by local government

(1) The reasons for market segmentation and the specific forms of local protectionism

Poncet (2002, 2003), based on the decreasing proportion of inter-provincial trade flow in China, proposed that provinces tend to become self-sufficient and the domestic market is going to "non-integration". Bai Chong'en et al. (2004) noticed that the regional specialization in China from 1985–1997 experienced a considerable increase after a slight drop at the beginning, so they believed the Chinese market integration is developing positively. Xu (2002) agreed, although he deemed it difficult to measure the degree of integration. Lu Ming et al. (2004) noticed that both the national and regional market segmentation have experienced the trend of shrinking after expanding. Since the reform and opening up, the Chinese domestic market has been changing toward integration in general. From this research, we can see that scholars have reached different conclusions through various measuring methods. Although there is not an agreed-upon conclusion on the changing trend of Chinese market segmentation, the existence of market segmentation is commonly recognized.

The earliest discussion on the formation of Chinese market segmentation can be found in the discussion on "Federalism, Chinese Style" by Qian Yingyi. Administrative and fiscal decentralization endowed local governments with enormous initiative to develop their local economy (Qian and Roland, 1998). On the one hand, according to Naughton, fiscal decentralization raised the inter-provincial trade flow and productivity; on the other hand, it also triggered the local government's motivation for local protectionism. The local protectionism is the most convenient increase of investment in productive infrastructure by local government with limited financial resource cutting down on other public expenditures, such as education and health care (Wang Yongqin et al., 2007). Local government also raised their economic development rate by lowering the security and environment standards to attract investment, leading to vicious competition between local governments. About thirty years after the decentralization reform, the development of the Chinese market economy still faces multiple serious problems and barriers; for example, the segmentation of regional markets, food and drug safety, administrative monopoly, excessive government regulation and interference in industries and enterprises, etc. (Zhou Li'an, 2004). Under the motivation of developing local economy and the strong incentive for promotion caused by political tournaments (He Zhimei and Wang Jingyun, 2007), local government reduced local competition and raised monopoly profits of local enterprises by administrative interference like raising trade barriers.

(2) Another form of protectionism: mergers and acquisitions by state-owned property

The economic system in China presents a mixed ownership. Therefore, the properties of enterprise and ownership structure inevitably caught the attention of some scholars who study domestic market integration. They may notice some other specific manifestations of local protectionism which would enlighten our research. Bai Chong'en tested the phenomenon that market segmentation and regional non-specialization appear more easily within industries with high after-tax profit and proportions of state-owned shares. This originates from the particularity of state-owned economy, also an undeniable fact: local government benefits more from the state-owned enterprise than from other types. The mechanism of local government controlling the state-owned economy and thus forming regional segmentation works by putting relative staffs in some positions in a state-owned enterprise through political procedures rather than market mechanism. Local government would use the state-owned enterprises' profits for public or private expenditure. These profits provide local governments with strong motivation for protecting state-owned enterprises. Ping Xinqiao's empirical conclusion revealed that there are tremendous material benefits behind the protection and control of state-owned property and industries by local government. The high marginal productivity of production factors (mainly labor force) leads to the motivation of local government to regulate the industry, which is the economic basis for the long-existing local protectionism (Ping Xinqiao, 2004).

Fang Junxiong regarded the nature of enterprise as their motivation for mergers and acquisitions (M&A) and a significant influence for enterprise to select their M&A target. The enterprise under the direct control of local government can more easily conduct local M&A; while the state-owned enterprise under the central government is more capable of cross-regional M&A (Fang Junxiong, 2008). Although the research was focused on the motivation of M&A, it actually provided another indirect evidence for local protectionism hindering the process of integration; i.e., the local government can merge local enterprises through the state-owned enterprises under their control. Jiang Fuxiu et al. believed that with the deepening reform and opening up, local government tends to adopt more indirect intervention means; for example, direct intervention of state-owned enterprise M&A, procedural intervention of M&A within the area, and keeping their advantageous resources (Jiang Fuxiu et al., 2015).

(3) The mechanism and influence of local mergers and acquisitions

It is believed that local governments merging and reorganizing local enterprise through the state-owned ones under its control is currently one of the main forms of local protectionism. This form, compared to direct administrative interference, is more obscure. It makes local government more easily accelerate the expansion of the scale of state-owned enterprises and raise their profits and taxes through national industrial revitalization programs and supporting policies for some industries. It is undeniable that local M&As may absorb some overcapacity and raise the efficiency of resource allocation. Both economies of scale and scope can reduce production costs and raise the enterprise's profit and government's tax income. However, the effect of this kind of integration cannot be measured.

Local government obstructs the cross-regional M&A by means of local protectionism actions. An M&A leads to the transformation of enterprise ownership (Hart, 1998), so on the one hand, it deprives local government of benefiting from the merged enterprise, and on the other hand it reduces the total investment stock of the enterprise and potential possibilities to gain profits and taxes. Local governments would be especially prudent with those M&As involving state-owned enterprises controlled by government of other regions, because they would not want to help their political competitors (Xu Xianxiang, 2007). They would raise the enterprise transaction cost by setting barriers like tax, quality control, security inspection, etc., which reduce the motivation of cross-regional M&As, for enterprises would be reluctant to lose their control power over their affiliates to governments of other regions. Therefore, the market for cooperative control is severely segmented without enough motivation for M&As for state-owned enterprises.

In a local market, compared to private companies, state-owned enterprises have a strong motivation for M&A (Méndez-Naya, 2008),[3] i.e., they have relatively strong profit and tax incentives. If the market structure presents a Cournot competition, then the more market shares of state-owned enterprise, the more beneficial it is for both parties. State-owned shares are usually in the controlling position; their proportion reflects the local government's control over the state-owned listed companies and thus their capacity of promoting an M&A. The more centralized the shareholding is, the easier it is for holders to control the operation by appointing relevant representatives. A high proportion of shares would be a more attractive motivation for a government's M&A, because it represents more future profit. Therefore, the higher the proportion of state-owned shares in local state-owned enterprises, the higher the frequency of a local government's M&A activities. The expanding scale of state-owned enterprise would have two consequences:

(1) The M&A of state-owned enterprise in a local market would have fewer local competitors. The awakened competition allows the enterprise to raise their prices and receive more profit and revenue. The production and

operation activities of other enterprises may encroach the market shares of state-owned enterprises and threaten their profit through fierce competition. Therefore, having control over competitors directly would create a loose competition environment and gain more profit.

(2) Local M&A expands the capital scale of state-owned enterprises, which raises the possibility of political promotion by making the "local champion" bigger. The leaders of local state-owned enterprises are generally nominated by local SASAC (State-owned Assets Supervision and Administration Commission) and answer to local government. It has two motivating aspects: the better the performance of a state-owned enterprise, the higher the possibility of political promotion for its leader and for the local government officials. However, a local M&A would aggravate market segmentation and obstruct the process of economic integration. This happens where local government can control state-owned properties and enterprises. Therefore, although an M&A centralized the local industrial structure, it may cause an anti-integration trend.

First, the more frequent the local M&A activities, the higher the possibility of industrial structure convergence. The segmented takeover market creates a positive condition for local governments to foster the local champion, but causing the consequence that government focuses on M&A with high profit and returns without considering the overall development strategy of the local economy. Such behavior would lead to the convergence of investments between regions and intensify the convergence of industrial structures (Zhang Ye and Liu Zhibiao, 2005).

Second, the weakening of the local competition raises the cost of enterprise of other regions' purchasing local enterprise and thus intensifies regional segmentation. The M&A activities led by the government can target the top enterprises in the market. The left enterprises may be those with poor production capacity and technological synergistic effect, so they are not helpful for nonlocal enterprises in obtaining economies of scale or opening local markets. From a dynamic perspective, the weakened local competition restrains enterprise competitiveness in the wider market. In fact, effective local competition is a significant factor for enterprises keeping their competitiveness when facing external competitors. Because of the tenure of their positions, myopic government officials would not develop the enduring competitiveness of enterprise, but would raise the general revenue of state-owned enterprises by M&A.

Last, local M&As will endow local governments with stronger controlling power over the economy, causing inequality between enterprises in the same industry. In a specific regional market, listed enterprises are generally the top ones in the industry, as the Stackelberg leadership model suggests. The leaders make M&As of small enterprises; if they cannot win them the advantages in terms of economies of scale, they would only reduce market competition. In addition, local government would further strengthen the dominant position of state-owned enterprises through obvious or indirect administrative means and promote their M&A process. The result of an M&A is the increase of profit and tax revenue, a bargaining chip for the intervening economy and further stimulating the local M&A activities by local government. The vicious circle would deteriorate the competition environment for private and middle and small-sized enterprises.

Based on these points, we believe that local M&As, especially by state-owned enterprises, can be regarded as an indirect index for measuring the degree of economic integration.

2. The characteristics of local M&As hindering economic integration

Characteristic one: local state-owned enterprises, compared to those controlled by central government and the private ones, conduct more M&A activities which exert diffusion and a demonstration-imitation effect. Under the promotion tournament system, local governments on the one hand all start to merge and purchase their local enterprises for higher revenue, regarding an M&A as an effective tool for their competition; on the other hand, they launch various barriers to prevent non-local enterprises from merging local ones to defend the revenue of local state-owned enterprises. Such competitions between local governments are further intensified through their mutual imitation, concentrating M&As within an administrative region. It means that local governments tend to conduct M&As within their administrative regions, which has become a popular phenomenon. In the meantime, private and foreign-invested enterprises are less controlled by local government, so they would pursue cross-regional M&As more. They may still be obstructed by non-local governments for the loss of revenue and employment (Fang Junxiong, 2008). Compared to the local state-owned enterprises, a cross-regional M&A in a regional economy is more likely to happen among private enterprises.

Characteristic two: private enterprises conduct more cross-regional M&As than state-owned ones. Private enterprises show more dynamic through less consideration for social welfare or tax revenue but more for their own profits when making market decisions. Therefore, their M&A activities should meet their profit target. In fact, there is a possible competitive relation between private enterprises and local government, since they are both part of the local economy. According to the three aspects of how local a M&A hinders integration, the result of a local M&A by the government is pushing private economy into a disadvantageous competition environment, forcing them to conduct non-local investment activities. A less rigid local competitive environment is conducive to a local M&A by private enterprises for higher profit; otherwise, it may become the proof of an obstructed market integration. Therefore, the local M&A that hinders economic integration would force the private enterprises into a non-local M&A.

Section 4 Statistical inspection of the enterprise merger and reorganization activities and integration in the Yangtze River Delta region

1. Sample description

The conclusions in Section Two need to be tested. We measure the level of YRD integration through statistical inspection of the previous two characteristics by

2328 M&A samples of listed companies in the YRD during 1999–2018 from the China MA of Wind Information Financial Data (see annexed Table 9.1[4] for more information). The first column means that a listed company is the subject of the M&A. If the object company is in the same city as the subject, then the M&A is an "intra-city transaction"; if it is in the same province but different cities, then it is an "intra-provincial cross-city transaction"; if it is in different provinces (including Shanghai) in the YRD from the subject, then it is a "YRD inter-provincial transaction"; if it is outside the YRD, then it is a "non-YRD transaction". Such a division considers both the different administrative levels and the regional factors.

According to the property of the subject enterprise, the M&A activities are divided into mainly four types: central state-owned enterprise, local state-owned enterprise, private enterprise, and foreign-invested enterprise. The local state-owned enterprise can be further divided into provincial and municipal ones based on the administrative level of the actual controller according to Wind Chinese Enterprise List (CEL); for example, the central or local State-owned Assets Supervision and Administration, or a natural person, etc. See annexed Table 9.2 and 9.3 for the statistical samples. In the whole statistics of the three provinces and one city in the YRD, private enterprises conducted far more M&As than all kinds of state-owned enterprises. In the given classification, Shanghai presents the most local M&As by state-owned enterprise than other provinces and regions; Jiangsu and Zhejiang have the most M&As by private enterprise. This data is obtained through manual collection.

2. The influence of potential M&A resources

The cross-regional M&A of enterprises may happen because of the lack of corresponding enterprise resources in local places.[5] Since the data of heterogeneity of resources is extremely difficult to access, we can only conduct limited analyses based on the relevant materials. According to the characteristics of object enterprises of cross-regional M&As, especially inter-provincial ones, the possibility of "lack of relevant resource in local place" can be basically eliminated.

3. The statistical test taking the YRD as a whole

(1) The influence of enterprise property on M&A

First, we target the general M&As of listed enterprises in the YRD. Attached Table 9.2 reflects the enterprise property and the region of the object company of the 2328 M&A activities. In terms of the absolute quantity of the M&A within a city/province, the number of private enterprises is higher than those of state-owned enterprises, reaching a ratio of 3:1, which is reflected in the total of the first and second lines. In terms of the cross-provincial and non-YRD M&A activities, private enterprises also present an absolute predominance. It means that the M&A activity of private enterprise is in general more active than that of state-owned enterprise. A statistical significance test is required to reflect the difference of cross-city/provincial M&A between private and state-owned enterprises.

We use the relative number to represent the frequency of M&A. It can eliminate the interference of the total number of M&As; otherwise, the high absolute number of a certain type of M&As may be caused by the huge total number. Specifically, the number of transactions divided by corresponding cardinal number (for example, the transaction of provincial state-owned enterprise within a city divided by the total transaction of provincial state-owned enterprise) equals a relative number which reflects the frequency of M&As of different types of enterprises. The formula is shown here:

$$\text{The M \& A of type } i \text{ enterprise in region } j = \frac{\text{the number of M \& A whose object belongs to region } j}{\text{the total M \& A number of type } i \text{ enterprise}}$$

Based on the formula, we have the M&A frequency of all types of enterprises; see Table 9.1.

Table 9.1 The M&A frequency of listed companies in YRD

M&A type	*Central state-owned enterprise*	*Local state-owned enterprise*		*Private enterprise*	*Foreign-invested enterprise*
		(Provincial level)	*(City and county level)*		
Within a city	0.333	0.719	0.643	0.358	0.389
Cross-city within a province	0.065	0.054	0.086	0.133	0.056
Cross-provincial within YRD	0.203	0.108	0.070	0.211	0.389
Non-YRD	0.399	0.119	0.200	0.299	0.167

The chi-squared tests of every two groups are shown in Table 9.2.

Table 9.2 The result of the chi-squared tests of listed company M&A in YRD

	Intra-city chi-squared test		*Inter-city chi-squared tests in a province*	
Private enterprise	0.358	–	0.133	–
Central state-owned enterprise	0.065	0.33	0.065	10.40***
Provincial state-owned enterprise	0.719	91.76***	0.054	16.89***
Municipal state-owned enterprise	0.643	57.70***	0.846	8.66***
	Inter-provincial chi-squared tests in YRD		*Non-YRD chi-squared tests*	
Private enterprise	0.211	–	0.167	–
Central state-owned enterprise	0.203	0.04	0.399	6.03**
Provincial state-owned enterprise	0.108	11.02***	0.119	26.75***
Municipal state-owned enterprise	0.070	20.90***	0.200	7.92***

Note: *** represents significance at 1% level; ** represents that at 5% level.

The major test results are all at levels of 1%~5%, indicating a significant difference between groups. Therefore, we have reached the following conclusions:

(1) In terms of intra-city transactions, the frequency of local M&As of provincial and municipal state-owned enterprises are significantly higher than those of central state-owned and private ones: an average of two times according to Table 9.1. It verified the first characteristic of integration: a local state-owned enterprise conducts more local M&As than central state-owned and private enterprises. It indirectly proves that as a whole regional economy, YRD integration is not realized yet.

(2) In terms of inter-city transactions in a province, the M&A frequency of state-owned enterprises distinctly differs from that of private enterprises because of the enterprise resources controlled by all levels of government, so the enterprises in different cities but the same province are more advantageous than the private ones. The disadvantage of private enterprise means that the state-owned enterprise controlled by a provincial-level government has more influence on the intra-provincial M&A. Provincial state-owned enterprises conduct more frequent M&A activities than central and municipal ones, indicating a more significant role in local M&As.

(3) In terms of inter-provincial transactions in the YRD, the variances between different properties of enterprise are huge. On the one hand, the difference between the central state-owned enterprise and private enterprise is not significant; on the other hand, the difference of promoting inter-provincial M&A in the YRD between local state-owned enterprise and private enterprise is significant. It further verifies the second characteristic: a private enterprise conducts more cross-regional M&As than a local state-owned enterprise. The conclusion means that private enterprise plays a more important role in promoting YRD integration through the cross-provincial M&A.

(4) In terms of non-YRD M&A, the M&A activity between state-owned and private enterprise presents a significant difference, which indirectly verifies characteristics one and two. The local state-owned enterprise in the YRD distributes more resources among local enterprises, encroaching on the space for the development of private enterprise, interfering with the competition environment, and therefore forming a pattern that state-owned enterprises tending to M&A within the YRD while private enterprise prefer non-YRD M&A.

(2) The time trend of YRD integration

From the perspective of the ten-year developing trend, the absolute number of M&As of state-owned enterprises is relatively steady, while that of private enterprise showed an overall rising trend (see Figure 9.3). Private enterprises are the main force that promote M&As in the YRD, with an increasing gap in numbers of M&As with state-owned enterprises. This is because of the relatively large number of listed private enterprises in the YRD, as well as the more flexible internal management system and resilience to market of private enterprises.

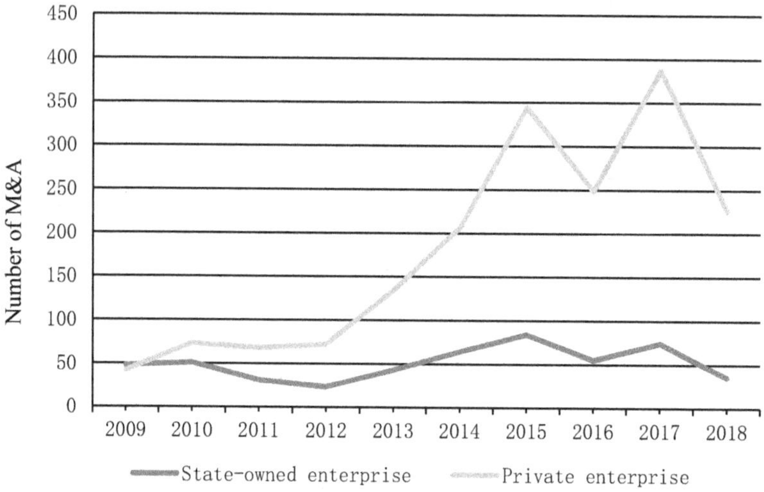

Figure 9.3 The time trend of numbers of M&A of state-owned and private enterprise in YRD

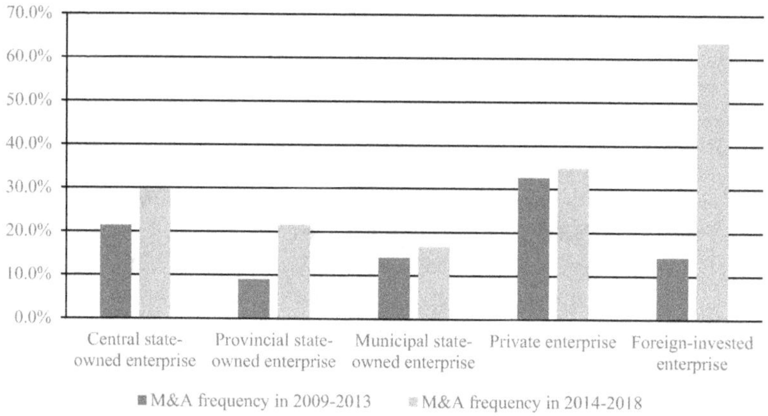

Figure 9.4 The time trend of cross-regional M&A in YRD

In order to see the time trend of YRD integration, the sample is divided into two time periods: 2009–2013 and 2014–2018. Eliminating the influence of the total amount of M&A, the cross-city M&A in a province and the cross-provincial M&A within the YRD of every company average are analyzed to calculate the total M&A frequency. The statistical result is shown in Figure 9.4.

The M&A frequency of central and provincial state-owned enterprise and foreign-invested enterprise in the YRD was distinctly increased. Their M&A activities may contain the factors that promote integration. The frequency of municipal state-owned and private enterprises presented a slight trend of increasing, but also a certain integration trend. From the perspective of the different properties of

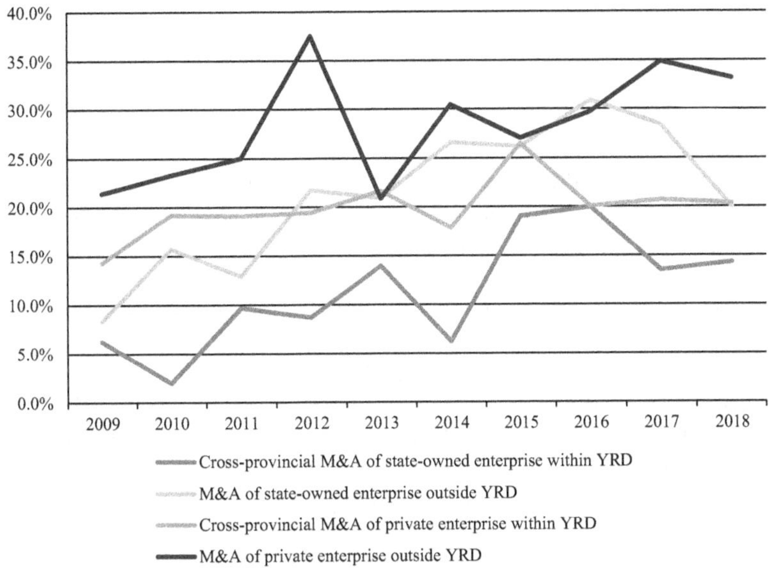

Figure 9.5 The time trend of integration measured through cross-provincial M&A

enterprises, a general integration trend is shown in the YRD. In other words, compared to 1998–2008, there were more signs of integrated economic development in the YRD in recent decades. The research conclusions on the M&A activities altered from the ten years before 2008.

In addition, we compared the intra-regional and inter-regional situation of the inter-provincial M&As. Figure 9.5 shows that both private and state-owned enterprises are more active in terms of M&A activities outside the YRD. Particularly since 2013, the frequency outside the YRD exceeded that within the YRD. The trends indicate that at the inter-provincial level, there is not a more integrated trend of YRD economic integration.

Based on the analysis of local M&A frequency, it is discovered that the participants of the local M&A in YRD are mainly local state-owned enterprises; while the private ones are less interested in M&A. In comparison, the M&A outside is more involved with private enterprise than state-owned ones. It basically verifies the non-integration trend in YRD; i.e., provincial and municipal governments were expanding the scale of local state-owned enterprises through M&A in order to raise their revenues.

By considering the factor of time, it is noticed that private enterprises are the most active entities in the YRD in terms of M&A activities. The data reduction and analysis provides us with results at two opposing aspects. On the one hand, taking five years as a phase, the frequency of cross-regional M&As of both private and state-owned enterprises in the YRD rose in general, indicating an integrated time trend. On the other hand, the frequency of their M&As outside the YRD also rose, higher than that of cross-regional ones since 2013. It might be caused by the deteriorating local competition environment for private enterprise and the high cost of coordination for the inter-provincial cooperation. The gradually increasing frequency of M&As outside the YRD is not sufficient to prove the trend of economic integration in the YRD.

4. The comparison between the three provinces and one city

We further analyze the provincial M&A activities in the YRD. The sample size is shown in Table 9.3, as well as the result of the comparison of M&A frequency between different types of enterprise and the significance of their differences determined through the chi-square test.

The integration level of the three provinces and one city in the YRD are different.

(1) In terms of intra-city and intra-provincial M&A, the differences between local state-owned enterprise and private enterprise in Shanghai are significant at the level of 1% and 10% respectively. In Jiangsu, only the difference between local state-owned and private enterprise in regard to intra-city M&A is significant. In Zhejiang, only the difference between municipal state-owned and private

Table 9.3 The result of the chi-square test of the M&A of listed company in YRD

		Intra-city chi-square test		*Intra-province chi-square test*	
Shanghai	Private enterprise	–	–	0.406	
	Provincial state-owned enterprise	–	–	0.802	57.54^{***}
	Municipal state-owned enterprise	–	–	0.848	23.80^{***}
Jiangsu	Private enterprise	0.320		0.136	
	Provincial state-owned enterprise	0.727	8.17^{***}	0.091	0.18
	Municipal state-owned enterprise	0.628	29.25^{***}	0.115	0.25
Zhejiang	Private enterprise	0.233		0.206	
	Provincial state-owned enterprise	0.333	1.13	0.118	0.79
	Municipal state-owned enterprise	0.455	9.09^{***}	0.077	5.07^{**}
Anhui	Private enterprise	0.219		0.102	
	Provincial state-owned enterprise	0.484	8.89^{***}	0.226	3.50^{*}
	Municipal state-owned enterprise	0.455	5.51^{**}	0.136	0.23
		YRD cross-provincial chi-square test		Non-YRD chi-square test	
Shanghai	Private enterprise	0.205		0.389	
	Provincial state-owned enterprise	0.111	5.47^{**}	0.087	39.31^{***}
	Municipal state-owned enterprise	0.091	2.48	0.061	14.07^{***}
Jiangsu	Private enterprise	0.159		0.385	
	Provincial state-owned enterprise	0.000	2.07	0.182	1.89
	Municipal state-owned enterprise	0.051	6.46^{**}	0.205	9.75^{***}
Zhejiang	Private enterprise	0.267		0.126	
	Provincial state-owned enterprise	0.059	3.70^{*}	0.294	4.10^{**}
	Municipal state-owned enterprise	0.096	7.39^{***}	0.212	3.03^{*}
Anhui	Private enterprise	0.227		0.453	
	Provincial state-owned enterprise	0.161	0.63	0.129	11.01^{***}
	Municipal state-owned enterprise	0.045	3.84^{**}	0.364	0.61

Note: ***, **, * represents the significance at level of 1%, 5%, and 10% respectively.

enterprise in regard to M&A within a city/province is significant. From the perspective of M&A within a city/province, Shanghai and Anhui have a more distinct trend toward non-integration, followed by Jiangsu. Zhejiang has a small gap between private and state-owned enterprises in terms of local M&A, probably because of its special characteristic of being a well-developed private enterprise. It also reflects that the competition environment for private enterprise in Zhejiang is better than in Shanghai and Jiangsu.

(2) In terms of cross-provincial M&A in the YRD, the difference between private and municipal state-owned enterprise in Jiangsu, Zhejiang, and Anhui are statistically significant: private enterprise is more active, while the municipal state-owned enterprise tends to be the "local champion". The difference between provincial state-owned and private enterprises in Shanghai is statistically significant for it is a municipality directly under the central government. In regard to the regional development in the YRD, private enterprise prefers cross-provincial M&As more than local state-owned enterprise does, although its frequency is still lower than that of M&A within a city. It verifies that the level of integration in the YRD is still relatively low.

(3) The frequency of M&A outside the YRD of private enterprise in Shanghai, Jiangsu, and Anhui is significantly higher than that of local state-owned enterprises (municipal state-owned enterprise in Jiangsu and provincial state-owned enterprise in Anhui). The frequency of M&A outside the YRD of private enterprises in Zhejiang is significantly lower than that of local state-owned enterprise (both municipal and provincial). If we use the frequency of M&As outside the YRD of private enterprise to indirectly represent non-integration, then this conclusion indicates that there is a non-integration trend in the YRD to some extent.

Section 5 Conclusion

Measuring economic integration through enterprise M&As provides a more reliable micro basis to the integration process under the background of the special economic system in China. From the perspective of the local government controlling the state-owned economy, we notice that local government conducted more frequent local M&As through local state-owned enterprises than the private enterprises did. The frequent M&As of local state-owned enterprises on the one hand intensified the market segmentation, and on the other hand, they deteriorated the competition environment for the private economy. Therefore, the private enterprises are forced to seek M&A objects outside the local region.

In terms of regional level, the regional economy in the YRD is far from being integrated. Therefore, we propose that: first, promote the cross-city/provincial mergers and reorganizations through the marketization mechanism, referring to the experience of the EU. After gradually eliminating the administrative barriers, the YRD should provide an open environment for market competition and investment. It should be able to absorb overcapacity automatically through the open market; maximize the market scale effect for the Pareto improvement of economic structure; and further perfect the systems of YRD integration. Second, establish a market environment of fair competition through laws and regulations. It is important to form a market system based on the equal competition between private and state-owned enterprise by gradually eliminating the preferential systems for state-owned enterprise and discriminative ones against private enterprise. By setting a modern market competition system, the regional resource distribution should be optimized. Third, with the systematic market tool of asset reorganization, the joint construction of a giant capital holding group led by the government would solve the previous problem of repeated construction of infrastructure and lack of scale effect (Liu Zhibiao, 2019). If the government can integrate the resource and enterprise to build a specialized regional group company, then it will not only counteract the adverse effect of stock, but also raise the integration level of economic development in YRD.

Notes

1 European Commission DG ECFIN, Mergers & Acquisitions Note, No. 4 April 2007, p. 7.
2 Ietto-Gillies, G., and Meschi, M. Cross-border mergers and acquisitions: patterns in the EU and effects. This essay is part of the EU commission's project "Technology, Economic Integration and Social Cohesion". http://meritbbs.unimaas.nl/tser/tser.html.
3 Méndez-Naya (2008) considered the profitability of state-owned enterprise merging private ones in the mixed oligopoly. One major reason for promoting this kind of M&A originates from the target of state-owned enterprise, i.e., the general social welfare.
4 The original data of M&A is processed through these steps: (1) eliminate the M&A whose object enterprise is in the financial industry; (2) eliminate the M&A with zero total value of transaction; (3) select the completed M&A; (4) select the domestic M&A.
5 The factor of the M&A resources existing in local places but not in other places is even harder to inspect. It would make enterprise choose local M&As rather than cross-regional ones. We presume that the possibility of obtaining resources from other regions is higher than that from local.

References

R. Baldwin, H. Wyplosz. The Economics of European Integration, 5th edition. London: McGraw-Hill Higher Education, 2015.

K. Banks. Merges and Partial Mergers under EEC Law. In Annual Proceedings of the Fordham Corporate Law Institute. New York: Matthew Bender, 1998.

K. Bjorvatn. Economic Integration and the Profitability of Cross-border Mergers and Acquisitions. European Economic Review, 2004 (6).

S. Brankman, H. Garretsen, C. van Marrewijk. Cross-border Mergers & Acquisitions: The Facts as a Guide for International Economics. CESifo Working Paper, 2006.

Bai Chong'en, Du Yingjuan, Tao Zhigang, Tong Yueting. Local Protectionism and Industrial Concentration in China: Overall Trend and Important Factors. Economic Research Journal, 2004 (4).

Bai Chong'en et al. Local Protectionism and Regional Specialization: Evidence from China's Industries. Journal of International Economics, 2004 (8).

Jiang Fuxiu, Zhang Min, Liu Zhibiao. Economic Development, Government Intervention and Domestic Economic Integration: A Research Based on the Perspective of the Mergers & Acquisitions of Listed Enterprise in China. Academic Research, 2015 (6).

G. Garnier. International M & A Activity: Impact of Globalization. DG ECFIN European Commission No. 1, 2004, Mergers & Acquisitions Note: 7–14.
O. Hart, translated by Fei Fangyu. Firms, Contracts and Financial Structure. Shanghai: Shanghai Sanlian Bookstore, Shanghai People's Publishing House, 1998.
B. Jovanovic, P.L. Rousseau. The Q-theory of Mergers. The American Economic Review, 2002, 92 (2).
Fang Junxiong. The Government Intervention, the Nature of Ownership and Enterprises' Mergers & Acquisitions. Management World, 2008 (9).
Zhou Li'an. The Incentive and Cooperation of Government Officials in the Political Tournaments: An Interpretation of the Prolonged Local Protectionism and Duplicative Investments in China. Economic Research Journal, 2004 (6).
B. Lyons. An Economic Assessment of EC Merger Control: 1957–2007. Social Science Electronic Publishing, 2008 (3).
J. Méndez-Naya. Merger Profitability in Mixed Oligopoly. Journal of Economics, 2008, 94.
Lu Ming, Chen Zhao, Yan Ji. Increasing Return. Development Strategy and Regional Economic Segmentation, 2004 (1).
B. Naughton. How Much Can Regional Integration do to Unify China's Markets?. In How Far Across the River? Chinese Policy Reform at the Millennium. Stanford: Stanford University Press, 2003.
P.J. Neary. Cross-border Mergers as Instruments of Comparative Advantage. Review of Economic Studies, 2007, 74 (4).
S. Poncet. Measuring Chinese Domestic and International Integration. China Economic Review, 2003.
S. Poncet. The "Non-integration" Trend of Chinese Market? Comparative Analysis on the Market Integration in China and the World. World Economic Papers, 2002 (2).
Y.Y. Qian, G. Roland. Federalism and the Soft Budget Constraint. The American Economic Review, 1998, 88 (5).
Regional Economic Segmentation. Economic Research Journal, 2004, 581 (1).
Ping Xinqiao. Motivation and Effect of Government Protection: An Empirical Analysis. Finance and Trade Economics, 2004 (5).
Xu Xianxiang, Li Xun, Wang Meijin. Regional Integration, Economic Growth and Political Promotion. China Economic Quarterly, 2007 (7).
X.P. Xu. Have the Chinese Provinces Become Integrated under Reform. China Economic Review, 2002, 13 (2–3).
Zhang Ye, Liu Zhibiao. Industrial Convergence: The Economic Analysis on the Behavior of Local Officials. Economist, 2005 (12).
Wang Yongqin et al. On China's Development Model: The Costs and Benefits of China's Decentralization Approach to Transition. Economic Research Journal, 2007 (1).
A. Young. The Razor's Edge: Distortions and Incremental Reform in the People's Republic of China. The Quarterly Journal of Economics, 2000, 115 (4).
Liu Zhibiao. Promoting YRD Integration by Market Mechanism. China Reform, 2004 (5).
Liu Zhibiao. The YRD High-quality Integration Must Rely on Perfect Competition. Economic Information Daily, 2019–04–17. https://idei.nju.edu.cn/05/06/c26391a525574/page.htm
He Zhimei, Wang Jingyun. An Analysis of Local Protectionism – A Game Model of Political Promotion. Journal of Shanxi University of Finance and Economics, 2007 (5).

Appendices

Table 9.4 The statistical sample of cross-regional transaction in YRD (2009–2018)

Type of M&A	*Shanghai*	*Jiangsu*	*Zhejiang*	*Anhui*	*Total*
Transaction within a city	301	293	300	56	950
Cross-city transaction within a province	0	107	142	26	275
Cross-provincial transaction within YRD	109	121	183	35	448
Non-YRD transaction	179	297	103	76	655
Total	589	818	728	193	2328

Table 9.5 The enterprise property in YRD and the M&A types (2009–2018)

Type of M&A	*Central state-owned enterprise*	*Local state-owned enterprise*		*Private enterprise*	*Foreign-invested enterprise*	*Total*
		(Provincial level)	*(Municipal level)*			
Transaction within a city	46	133	119	645	7	950
Cross-city transaction within a province	9	10	16	239	1	275
Cross-provincial transaction within YRD	28	20	13	380	7	448
Non-YRD transaction	55	22	37	538	3	655
Total	138	185	185	1802	18	2328

Table 9.6 The enterprise property in YRD and the location of the subject of M&A (2009–2018)

	Central state-owned enterprise	*Local state-owned enterprise*		*Private enterprise*	*Foreign-invested enterprise*	*Total*
		(Provincial level)	*(Municipal level)*			
Shanghai	75	126	33	342	13	589
Jiangsu	38	11	78	691	0	818
Zhejiang	13	17	52	641	5	728
Anhui	12	31	22	128	0	193
Total	138	185	185	1802	18	2328

Table 9.7 The enterprise property in YRD and the frequency of M&A of each province and city (2009–2018)

	Type of M&A	*Central holding enterprise*	*Provincial state-owned enterprise*	*Municipal state-owned enterprise*	*Private holding enterprise*
Shanghai	Transaction within a city	0.360	0.802	0.848	0.406
	Cross-provincial transaction within YRD	0.240	0.111	0.091	0.205
	Non-YRD transaction	0.400	0.087	0.061	0.389
Jiangsu	Transaction within a city	0.395	0.727	0.628	0.320
	Cross-city transaction within a province	0.079	0.091	0.115	0.136
	Cross-provincial transaction within YRD	0.184	0.000	0.051	0.159
	Non-YRD transaction	0.342	0.182	0.205	0.385
Zhejiang	Transaction within a city	0.077	0.333	0.455	0.233
	Cross-city transaction within a province	0.231	0.118	0.077	0.206
	Cross-provincial transaction within YRD	0.231	0.059	0.096	0.267
	Non-YRD transaction	0.462	0.294	0.212	0.126
Anhui	Transaction within a city	0.250	0.484	0.455	0.219
	Cross-city transaction within a province	0.250	0.226	0.136	0.102
	Cross-provincial transaction within YRD	0.000	0.161	0.045	0.227
	Non-YRD transaction	0.500	0.129	0.364	0.453

10 The construction of China's value chains in the Yangtze River Delta integration

Mingchao Yu

Section 1 Introduction

The Yangtze River Delta region is one of the most economically dynamic, open, and creative areas. The GDP per capita in Shanghai, Suzhou, Nanjing, Wuxi, Hangzhou, etc. in 2018 all surpassed 20 thousand dollars, indicating post-industrialism. Benefiting from the export-oriented globalization strategy and the low factor cost and regional advantages, enterprises in the YRD joined the Global Value Chain (GVC) through OEM and processing trade in the early development phase. They rapidly boosted industrialization by transforming their comparative advantage into competitive advantage in the international market. However, the global financial crisis in 2008 seriously impacted the Chinese economy, especially in coastal areas, and exposed the disadvantages of being at the low end of the GVC. The recent international trade protectionism, especially the intensifying trade friction between America and China since 2018, means that the previous external environment that supported the Chinese export-oriented economy has fundamentally changed. When the economic development reaches a certain level, China can no longer expect Western countries to support its industrial upgrading. Only based on the domestic market can a reliable industrial relationship and system be formed for Chinese enterprises.

The future development strategy for the Chinese economy lies in the development and utilization of the domestic market and the transformation toward a domestic demand-oriented economy. Researchers have pointed out the disadvantage of fragmented participation in the GVC. For example, the disconnection from the domestic market and advanced service industry caused by the segmented production network (Jiang Jing and Liu Zhibiao, 2010), which weakened the inter-regional industrial connections and the motivation for regional integration (Zhang Shaojun and Liu Zhibiao, 2013). Therefore, the transition from GVC to NVC is not only the approach to promote industrial upgrading, but also the objective demand of regional integrated development. NVC is the guidance for the domestic work division system where local enterprises gain brands, channels, and independent R&D abilities through competition in the domestic market based on the enormous domestic market demand (Liu Zhibiao, 2011). It is believed that making YRD integration a national strategy is an opportunity to accelerate the inward opening up

DOI: 10.4324/9781003455943-10

and to lower the cost of constructing NVC by opening market access and creating a neutral business environment. The focus will shift to the redistribution of industries and development of a domestic market in order to build a NVC network and governance structure based on domestic market demand. In the meantime, the method of participation in GVC should be adjusted: the Belt and Road Initiative creates a historical opportunity for expanding multinational corporations, further exploiting "hidden champion enterprises" in the key links of production, and gradually building a China-led GVC when establishing NVC.

Section 2 The weakening effect of captive GVC to regional economic integration

According to the definition by the United Nations Industrial Development Organization, GVC is an international cross-enterprise network organization that connects the process of production, sale, recovery, etc. for the value of products and services around the world. Since the enterprises in developed countries control the marketing and sales, those in developing countries are put into the production links with low added value, forming a relationship of the capturer and the captured (Humphrey and Schmitz, 2004). When taking advantage of scale economies effect of the international market, that of the domestic market is abandoned. It may intensify the market segmentation between regions and obstruct regional integration objectively (Lu Ming and Chen Zhao, 2009). The potential adverse effect may influence the following aspects: industrial structure convergence, weakened industrial connection and income misallocation, weakened spatial technology spillover effect, and the lock-in in the low end.

1. Industrial structure convergence

The participation of the YRD in GVC has promoted the local specialization and formed numerous export-oriented industrial clusters. The open production organization mode and the link of business cycles are controlled by the international big buyers or multinational enterprises. For the domestic business cycle, this kind of link lacks initiative and controllability. The foreign market orientation causes a competition between regions: they produce similar products for the international market without cooperation or work division, leading to the so-called "industrial convergence" which is usually measured through the Krugman index:

$$S_{ij} = \sum_{k=1}^{n} \left| \frac{q_{ik}}{q_i} - \frac{q_{jk}}{q_j} \right|$$

In the formula, q_i represents the gross output in region i; while q_{ik} represents the gross output of industry k in the region. According to the definition, the range of the index is 0–2. If the industrial structure of the two regions is exactly the same,

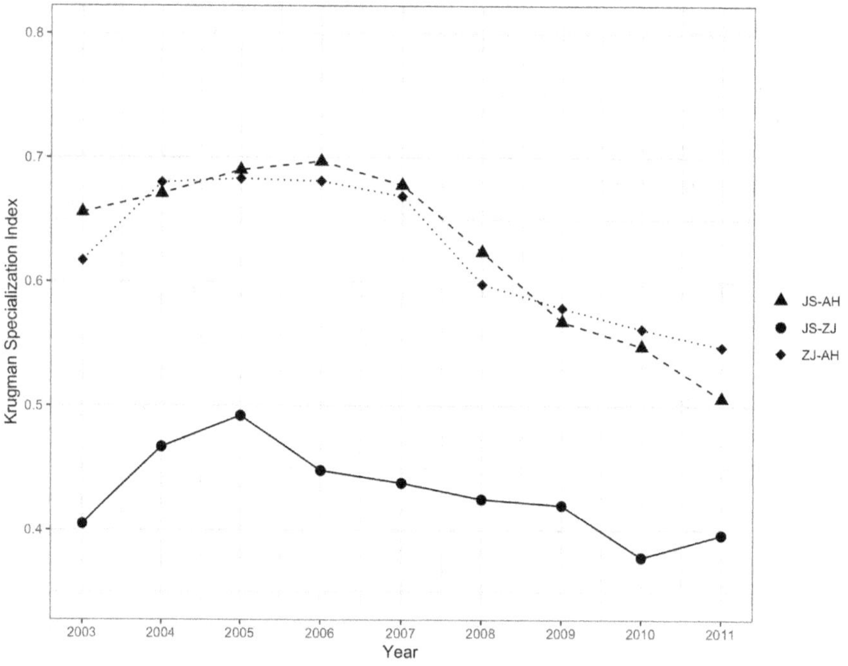

Figure 10.1 Krugman specialization index

Data source: EPS data platform

the value is 0; if it is completely different, it is 2. The smaller value indicates more serious convergence. Shanghai, as a service industry-dominated municipality directly under the central government, is not comparable to the three provinces in the YRD. Therefore, with the data of the total industrial output value of the manufacturing industry in Jiangsu, Zhejiang, and Anhui, we have their Krugman index in 2003–2011 in Figure 10.1. The industrial convergence between Jiangsu and Zhejiang is apparently more serious than that between Jiangsu and Anhui and Zhejiang and Anhui, because the similarity of their development level and their dependence on foreign trade is much higher than Anhui.

In addition, coastal areas, by attracting raw materials and labor forces from the less developed areas, hindered their development of labor-intensive industries that match their comparative advantage, and thus forced them into being simply a source of raw material and labor force, which expands the economic gap between regions. The manufacturing enterprise at the low end of GVC is in a weak position, so their suffocated industrial upgrading could not pass the dynamic regulation to other regions but could cause a severe crowding-out effect on those with insufficient comparative advantages. It is a significant factor that caused the intra-YRD gaps of development, and the obstruction against the establishment of a modern multilevel industrial system.

2. The weakened industrial connection

Multinational enterprises lead the high-end non-substantive activities in the GVC, allocating R&D to the country to which they belong. However, their expanding active scale and deepening connotation would not promote the development of service industries in local countries but instead substitute them. The segmented developing mode makes local enterprise tend to rely on the international enterprises of developed countries and breaks the industrial link and cycle system of domestic industry. Some scholars noticed that the regions with a well-developed manufacturing industry usually have a less-developed service industry (Tan Hongbo and Zheng Jianghuai, 2012). The main reason lies in the relatively low level of income per capita in the current development stage and the deep participation in the global industrial division. The fast-developing international market of the manufacturing industry supports the continuous growth of the secondary industry in China, while the market of the service industry is not globalized. The local market and its scale limit the growth of service industry (Zhang Ping and Yu Yuxin, 2012). As shown in Figure 10.2, although the income per capita of Jiangsu is much higher than the national average, its proportion of the tertiary industry was lower than the average for a long time, at around 40% before 2012.

3. Income misallocation

Being locked in the low end of GVC by the developed countries makes it hard for developing countries to continuously raise their marginal output, which is how

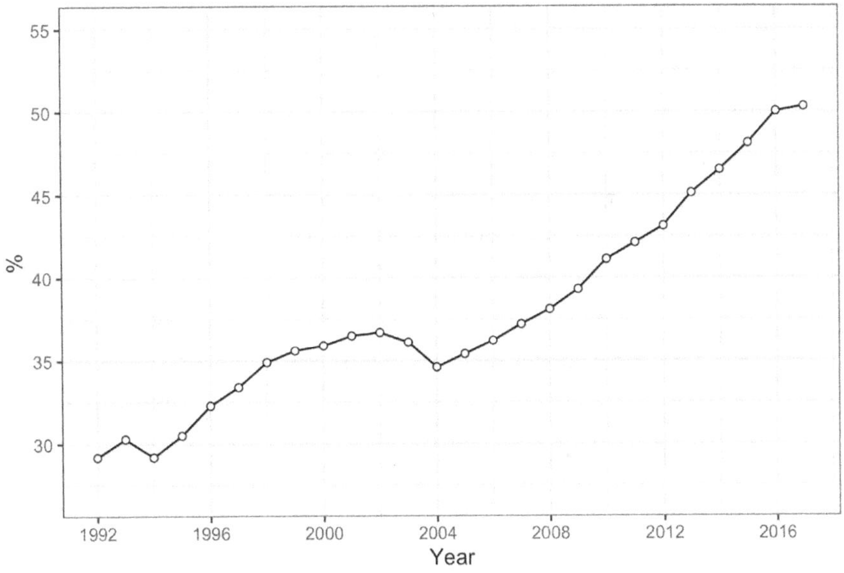

Figure 10.2 The proportion of the tertiary industry in Jiangsu

Data source: The Statistic Yearbook of Jiangsu (2018)

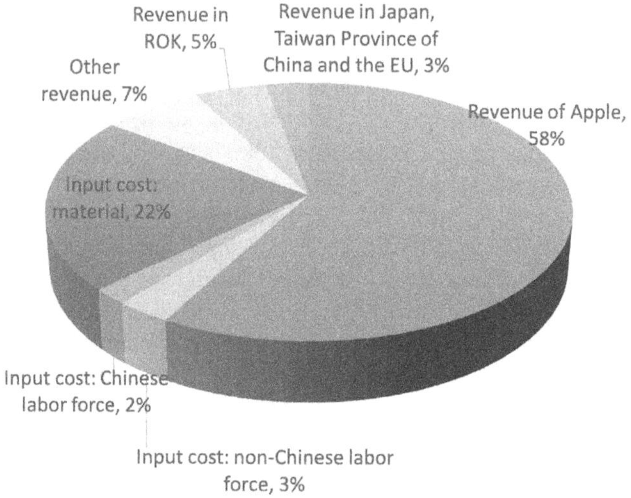

Figure 10.3 The distribution of revenue of iPhone in the value chain

GVC greatly influences national income distribution. In the buyer-driven GVC, there are huge differences between the market powers of each entity. For example, although Apple, Disney, and Wal-Mart are oligopoly enterprises, the numerous domestic industries in the form of industrial clusters are basically in perfect competition. The difference between the market power of buyers and sellers puts the international market in the monopolistic position, which means the foreign enterprises gain the majority of revenue while local enterprises only receive a small part of processing revenue, i.e., the income misallocation. Taking Apple as an example, the iPhone is a typical product of GVC: its design, software development, product management, marketing and other occupations of high salary are based in America, while the production and assembly are completed by Foxconn in China. The biggest beneficiary is still the American economy. The research of Kraemer et al. (2011) on the profit distribution of the iPhone in 2010 indicates that Apple alone occupies about 60% of the revenues along the value chain. Since cost information like the price of raw material and a worker's salary is relatively transparent and the competition between enterprises is fierce, a single enterprise lacks bargaining power. Therefore, the revenue of Chinese participation is mainly the worker's salary, at about 2% of the total revenue, much lower than that of ROK and Japan (see Figure 10.3). It is because Apple controls the whole supply chain that it maximizes its portion of value created by the supplier.

4. Weakened spatial technology spillover effect and the lock in the low end

Participation in the low end of GVC is against the spatial spillover of technology. Generally speaking, technology spillover is influenced by the technology gap, technology absorption ability and spatial distance, etc. For the early participants in GVC, the selective technology transformation leads to a relatively low ability of spatial spillover. Because of the low level of original technologies, the "production capacity" is accumulated in the low end of manufacturing through an intensive labor force without the "knowledge capacity" that leads the industry value chain. The knowledge of raising the production capacity is transferred by the international buyers to meet their demand. In addition, in the industries led by foreign capitals, an enclosed production network excludes local enterprise from the range of technology spillover (Yu Mingchao et al., 2006). In this kind of system, foreign capital participates in the GVC led by international big buyers as the top-level manufacturer, and the second level leads enterprise to form an enclosed production network with the matching enterprises transformed to local places along with it. The technology transfer or spillover happens within the network, so other regions can barely benefit from the technology spillover.

The participation in GVC rapidly brings the domestic enterprises the advanced technologies from the specialized enterprises in the GVC and lowers their access barrier to the international market. Taking smartphones in China as an example, Huawei, Xiaomi, and OPPO have the major market share not only in China, but also in the global market. If the technology transformation and spillover is for the benefit of developed countries in the GVC, then it exerts a significant upgrading effect on the technology and product in developing countries; if it is against the core benefit of developed countries in terms of R&D or brand, then they will obstruct the transformation and spillover. Table 10.1 shows that the huge amount of expense on R&D of the top ten semiconductor enterprises in the world has formed a barrier in the GVC. When Chinese enterprises attempt to upgrade their functions along the GVC, they may substitute the leading enterprises and harm their benefits to some extent, so they would be obstructed by all the tangible and intangible means in the international market.

Table 10.1 The top 10 semiconductor enterprises of R&D investment in 2017

Rank	*Enterprise*	*R&D expense ($M)*	*R&D/Sales (%)*
1	Intel	13,098	21.2%
2	Qualcomm	3,450	20.2%
3	Broadcom	3,423	19.2%
4	Samsung	3,415	5.2%
5	Toshiba	2,670	20.0%
6	TSMC	2,656	8.3%
7	MediaTek	1,881	24.0%
8	Micron	1,802	7.5%
9	Nvidia	1,797	19.1%
10	SKHynix	1,729	6.5%
	Total	35,921	13.0% (average)

Data source: reports from the listed companies

Section 3 Strategic adjustment of development of the Yangtze River Delta: constructing a NVC parallel to GVC

The American offensives on Chinese science and technology enterprises since 2018 have proved that cooperation in the value chain would become a conflict once the technology level of Chinese enterprise reached that of the leading enterprise (Humphrey and Schmitz, 2002). Constructing an NVC parallel to GVC can leverage the accumulated production and design capacities in the domestic market, integrate the industrial connection and business cycle system for enterprises in the YRD based on emphasizing both the international and domestic market, build the administrative structure of domestic value chain, and set a solid development platform for upgrading the manufacturing industry and the high-quality economic integration in the YRD.

1. The influence of NVC on regional integration

Compared to GVC, the function of NVC to regional integration is providing a connection that facilitates the inter-regional mobility of factors, products, and technologies, and the motivation for regional integration across administrative boundaries. The industrial connections completed based on the endogenous industrial demand will form a closed cycle with benign feedback, which is the source of endogenous integration in the process of economic integration. Its functions on regional integration are presented in the following aspects:

(1) Accelerate the mobility of factor, product, and technology

First, production factors, including the free mobility of labor force, capital, and entrepreneur, are the driving force of regional economic integration and the manifestation of regional integration. The quick aggregation of a large amount of capital promotes industrial integration in the whole region with the emerging complementary effect. In the case of the IT industry, it has initially formed a rather complete industrial chain in the YRD: the relatively high-level chip design, production, packaging and test chain in Shanghai (see Figure 10.4); a manufacturing base of IT products in Suzhou-Wuxi-Changzhou region; a Japanese capital agglomeration in Wuxi focusing on communication and production of PC components. Second, the competing infrastructure like the high-speed train ensures the fast development of the logistics industry in the YRD. As the supporting area of E-commerce, the YRD accounts for over 40% of the national production value of the logistics industry, and it has bred a batch of top international logistics enterprises such as SF Express and YTO Express. Third, information and technology have the properties of public products. In Marshall's theory of external economy, the spatial spread of knowledge will raise productivity. In specialized regional production, each cluster requires not only the tangible factors from others, but also professionalized knowledge combined with the advanced service industry or the benefit from knowledge spillover. The mobility of information and technology could be official, i.e., a formal cooperation relationship like technology transfer, consulting, and service; and unofficial, i.e., the technology spillover caused by staff mobility, technology imitation, etc.

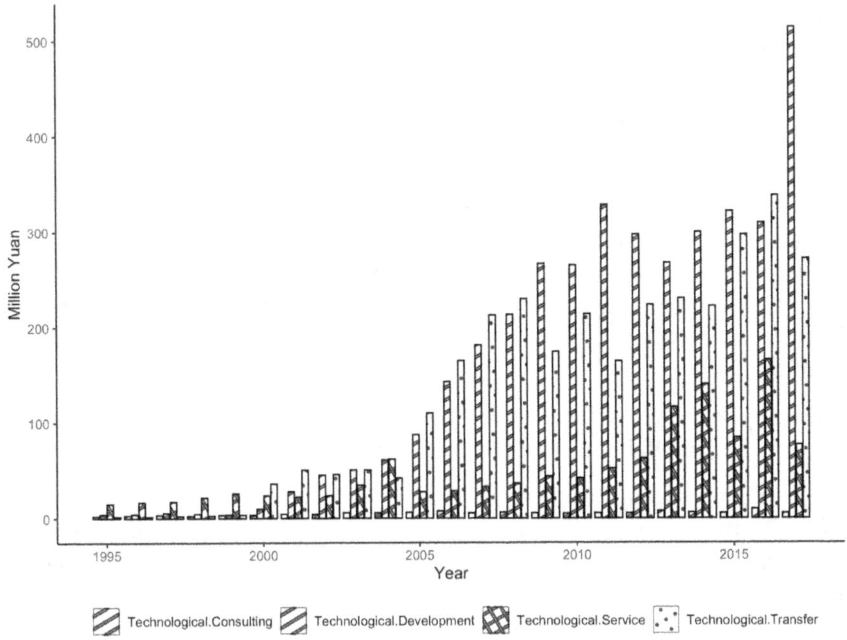

Figure 10.4 The trading volume of all kinds of technology contract in Shanghai (100 million yuan) (1997–2017)

Data source: Statistical Yearbook of Shanghai (2018)

(2) Lower governance cost of complex transaction

Gereffi et al. (2005) generated five types of global value chain governance according to the complexity of transaction, enterprise network, and learning ability: hierarchy, captive, relational, modular, and market. Among them, market and hierarchy are at the top and bottom of the value chain in terms of entities' coordination ability. Domestic enterprises usually participate in the less complex market or modular value chains. However, NVC can not only integrate factor endowment between different regions and coordinate the regional economic development, but can also use foreign endowment advantages by outsourcing the orders. Therefore, the industrial transfer becomes the international resource integration for China.

(3) Maximizing the correlation effect between industries

The correlation effect between industries can drive the development of the upstream and downstream industries and solve the problem of a too-short GVC in China. The extension and completion of the chain prolongs the production line and deepens the professionalization, which not only achieves economies of scale and scope, but also accumulates high-end human and intellectual capital. The NVC is mainly based on local enterprises so its profits remain in China, which therefore promotes economic development from the perspective of investment or consumption. In the meantime, the leading enterprises of GVC could access more resources for R&D, creating a solid material basis and precondition for future investment and the elimination of regional gaps.

2. The strategic focus of constructing an NVC parallel to GVC

Some scholars divide the GVC into two types: "producer-driven" and "buyer-driven" GVC based on their core functions, forming the theory of the binary dynamic mechanism of GVC (Gereffi, 1994).[1] Similarly, the essence of NVC is its leading power. Since the enterprise of platform-type has boomed rapidly in recent years and formed a strong dominant power in the market, we should put the focus of constructing NVC on three types: producer-driven, buyer-driven, and platform-driven.

(1) Support and foster the multinational enterprises with leading power, taking the Belt and Road Initiative as an opportunity

The countries along the Belt and Road Initiative have abundant resources and strong aspirations for development. Their participation in an interconnected network can promote the economic opening and achieve a win-win situation with the strong industrial capacity in the YRD. Whether in the producer-driven or buyer-driven NVC, multinational enterprises are all in the dominant position and receive a major part of the profit created along the chain. The producer-driven NVC is usually the capital- and technology-intense industry; for example, automobile, aircraft, and special equipment manufacturing. The producer's investment and technological progress drive the market demand to form a vertical division system of a production supply chain. In this type of NVC, major domestic manufacturing enterprises play the leading role by controlling the operation of their subsidiaries in different regions and the mobility of capital, technology, and labor force within the company and driving the development of regional integration. "Developing a first-class enterprise with global competitiveness" is actually the strategic demand of the "chain leader" in NVC.

With the increasing economics of scale, there have been more Chinese enterprises in the Fortune Global 500: reaching 120 in 2018, close to 126 in America, 13 of which are in the YRD. Some countries along the Belt and Road have a relatively low development level in the fields of electricity, industrial engineering, transportation, and infrastructure, and urgently require a promotion of production efficiency and energy efficiency in terms of the power grid, mine, steel, non-ferrous metals, oil, gas, and chemical industries, etc., and investment in construction or renovations of airports, ships, ports, highways, and other transportation infrastructure. Their requirements provide significant opportunities for Chinese equipment manufacturing, the development of engineering corporations, and the formation of multinational enterprises. For example, the XuZhou Construction Machinery Group (XCMG) in Jiangsu province has accelerated their internationalization since 2010 and achieved 95.1 billion yuan of operating revenue, 1.05 billion dollars of export value and exporting to 178 countries in 2017. It ranked 7th in the global list of

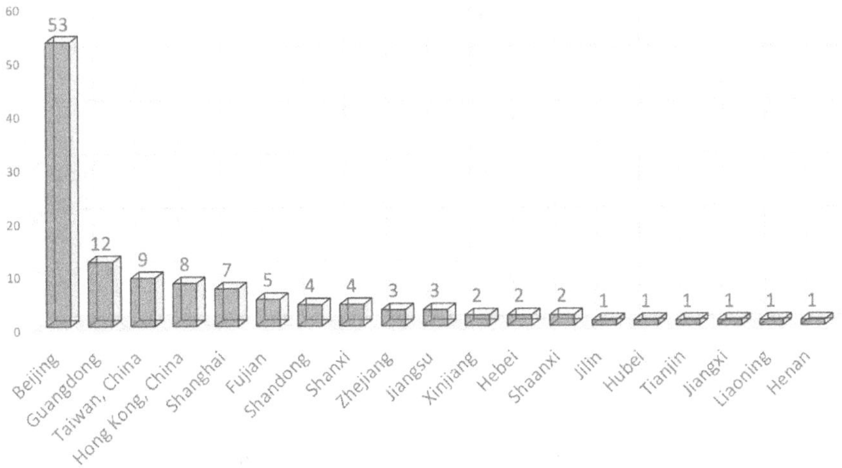

Figure 10.5 The number of Fortune Global 500 in each region

the industry published by China Construction Machinery Industry Association, the only Chinese company in the top ten. The company has three large-scale manufacturing facilities, 10 assembly factories, and over 3 thousand foreign staff members. By building factories overseas, the company has kept opening the international market, learning advanced technologies through international M&As. The German company Schwing, merged with XCMG, has become the top brand in the Western market of concrete machinery. The products of XCMG have been sold to the 57 countries out of 65 along the Belt and Road; the significant construction projects in Uzbekistan use almost all equipment from XCMG.

(2) Deepening the function of transaction platform and building the value chain driven by the market

The domestic market has a strong market scale effect to maximize the advantage of local enterprises. Most places in the YRD have a specialized market to connect buyers and sellers, which is a significant method to construct the NVC. The connections between industrial clusters form a virtual network of the production, sales, and distribution of products as a transaction platform between the supply system of producers and the demand system of consumers. The virtual network mode itself does not possess much technical strength, only providing standard and traditional products. Its core advantage lies in the specialized big market and the economies of scale brought about by the modern logistics system. It forms a strong market cohesion by integrating market transactions, logistics, and delivery, and comprehensive business across the regional boundaries achieve economies of scale and scope and specialized advantage.

With the popularization of E-commerce today, the tangible market is transforming to an intangible one, while E-commerce platforms like Taobao, JD.COM, and

Suning have developed into world-class enterprises. For example, the revenue of Alibaba in 2018 reached 250.3 billion dollars, so it was called "the biggest market in the world".[2] The rapid development of E-commerce relies on mobile communication technology, as well as convenient transportation and a well-developed logistics system that connects all the enterprises to the whole world. The value chain of E-commerce contains the merchants at the top end, E-commerce platform in the middle, and payment, logistics, and consumer at the bottom. E-commerce enterprises have the advantage of a bilateral trade platform, so they are at the leading position of the value chain.

(3) Extending the industrial chain upward: develop the "hidden champion" in the GVC

Participation in the highly collaborative GVC is conducive to overall technological improvement, but it also leads to the mutual dependency of enterprises in the value chain to a high extent. Many enterprises, although their scale is not large, have become the suppliers of the key intermediate input in the GVC for its high professionalization. Therefore, they not only obtain a stable profit, but they also become the key to industry security at crucial times. German researcher Hermann Simon called these middle and small enterprises the "hidden champion". They are not directly connected to the consumers, but are usually the actual controller of the fate of an industry because they grasp the key knowledge and technologies of the industry. Only when we master the core technologies, critical components, and special materials, can we guarantee independent industrial development in our country. As President Xi has emphasized many times, core technologies are important instruments of the state and the biggest risk when they fall into others' hands. "If we build a house on others' foundation, it cannot withstand a single blow no matter how beautiful it looks".

Extending the industrial chain upward and developing the "hidden champion" in the GVC by breaking through the bottleneck sectors can start from the infant industries. According to the experience from Germany, Japan, and ROK, a staged protection period can be set for infant industries to prevent external competition. During the protection period, consumers are encouraged by subsidies, and the advanced enterprises are encouraged to expand rapidly through M&A. Of course, considering the international division of labor, it is not necessary to obtain an absolute advantage and control in all areas and links. Zhejiang and Jiangsu have already been promoting the task. For example, Zhejiang has published a list of 23 "hidden champions" and 260 developing enterprises in 2017,[3] focusing on the development of technologically specialized and advanced micro-, small-, and medium-sized enterprises. The companies are distributed between biotechnology, medical equipment, new material, and other emerging technological industries. In 2018, Jiangsu published a list of 173 technologically specialized and advanced manufacture enterprises, among which there exist 80 "technological little giants", 27 "hidden champions", and 16 "hidden little giants".

Section 4 Conclusion

Although GVC participation has brought the manufacturing industry in the YRD unprecedented opportunities of development, it also sets a perceptible barrier against industrial upgrading and imposes an adverse influence on the regional economic integration by weakening the connection between industries. The construction of NVC is one of the significant measures to get rid of the dependency on GVC and export orientation and to achieve sustainable upgrading and development. It is also a driving force to promote economic integration in the YRD. However, NVC cannot be accomplished overnight; it requires a competitive environment, acceleration of inward opening up parallel to high-quality outward opening up, and the elimination of market segmentation between regions to reduce the institutional cost of constructing NVC.

In the 19th National Congress of the Communist Party of China, it is explicitly required to "introduce a negative list for market access nationwide". In 2018, the National Development and Reform Commission and other departments issued the *Negative List for Market Access*, specifying that all market entities can equally enter the markets outside the list in obedience to the law. The government cast a strict restriction on market access in the era of insufficient production capacity in order to protect the infant industries. With the soaring domestic economic power, most manufacturing industries have been opened already. For example, the restriction on foreign capital in the automobile industry, the financial and telecommunication industries, have all been loosened up. At the same time, the inward opening up of private enterprises is conducive to the competitiveness and operation efficiency of industries. Meanwhile, the government should create a competitive environment and turn preferential policies into inclusive ones. Under the circumstances of an inclusive system, the government would provide some support and protection to certain specific enterprises when the business environment is incomplete in order to make it more attractive. It would help the enterprise to attract more resources, but it only works in a certain space; this leads to regional discrimination, artificially enlarged gaps between regions, and excessive resource mobility. In the new era, the equal rights of development and elimination of preferential policies require an improvement of the investment environment, i.e., enhancing the synchronization with global economic and trade rules, strengthening the transparency of government operations, reinforcing the protection of private enterprises and property of foreign capital, encouraging competition, objecting to monopolies, and creating a more attractive investment environment for enterprises.

Notes

1 Some scholars also added a "hybrid NVC" with the characteristics of both buyer- and producer-driven types. For example, mobile phone industry is a typical mixed type: the manufacturers have great brand advantage in terms of sales, i.e., the tycoons like Apple and Samsung have a complete sales network around the world; while on the R&D end, the enterprises of chip design and manufacturing like Qualcomm grasp multiple patented technologies and form high barriers to entry by making industrial standards.

2 "The world's greatest bazaar", Economist, May 23, 2013.
3 www.zjjxw.gov.cn/art/2017/10/13/art_1097558_5928.html.

References

G. Gereffi. The Organisation of Buyer-Driven Global Commodity Chains: How U.S. Retailers Shape Overseas Production Networks. In G. Gereffi, M. Korzeniewicz (eds), Commodity Clains and Global Capitalism. Westport: Praeger, 1994.

G. Gereffi, J. Humphrey, T. Sturgeon. The Governance of Global Value Chains. Review of International Political Economy, 2005 (1).

Tan Hongbo, Zheng Jianghuai. The Mystery of Coexistence of Rapid Economic Growth and Lag of Service in China: A Research Based on the Perspective of Sector TFP. China Industrial Economics, 2012 (9).

Zhang Hui. The Dynamics Model of Global Value Chain and Industry Development Strategy. China Industrial Economy, 2006 (1).

J. Humphrey, H. Schmitz. Chain Governance and Upgrading: Taking Stock. In Hubert Schmitz (ed), Local Enterprises in the Global Economy. Cheltenham: Edward Elgar Publishing, 2004.

J. Humphrey, H. Schmitz. How Does Insertion in Global Value Chains Affect Upgrading Industrial Clusters?. Regional Studies, 2002, 36 (9).

Jiang Jing, Liu Zhibiao. Can Orientation to Workshop of the World Promote China's Producer Service Development. Economic Theory and Business Management, 2010 (3).

K. Kraemer, G. Linden, J. Dedrick. Capturing Value in Global Networks: Apple's iPad and iPhone. Working Paper, 2011. https://www.investmentoffice.com/Observations/Beyond_Finance/Capturing_Value_in_Global_Networks_Apple_s_iPad_and_iPhone.html

Lu Ming, Chen Zhao. Fragmented Growth: Why Economic Opening May Worsen Domestic Market Segmentation? Economic Research Journal, 2009 (3).

Yu Mingchao, Liu Zhibiao, Jiang Jing. Obstacles and Breakthrough of Chinese Local Firms' Upgrading: A Case Study of Taiwanese Notebook Computer Industry's Close-type Network. China Industrial Economy, 2006 (11).

Zhang Ping, Yu Yuxin. Does Exporting Trade Influence Share of China's Service Sector. The Journal of Quantitative & Technical Economics, 2012 (4).

Zhang Shaojun, Liu Zhibiao. Industrial Upgrading and Balanced Development of Area: From Global Value Chain to National Value Chain. Economic Management Journal, 2013 (8).

Liu Zhibiao. Reconstruction of National Value China: The Reflection on Transforming the Development Pattern of Chinese Manufacturing Industry. Forum of World Economics and Politics, 2011 (7).

Liu Zhibiao, Yu Mingchao. From GVC to NVC: Integrity and Industry Upgrade in the Delta of Yangtze River. Academia Bimestrie, 2009 (9).

11 Industrial coordination in the integration of the Yangtze River Delta integration

Jing Jiang and Jingwei Wu

Section 1 Introduction

It was once believed that the integration of the Yangtze River Delta (YRD) needs to be coordinated at the government level and ultimately require a unified administrative organization, similar to the EU, to overcome local protectionism. The Yangtze River Delta City Economic Coordination Committee, founded in 1997, has held 18 conferences through April 2018, which play a crucial role of accelerating the process of YRD market integration. On the one hand, it solves the problem of local protectionism and achieved free mobility of factors and commodities to some extent; on the other hand, it defines the relationship between regions within the YRD and solves the problem of work division and cooperation between Shanghai and other cities. In 2018, the Yangtze River Delta Regional Cooperation Office was jointly founded in Shanghai by the three provinces and one city in the YRD.

Early in May 2016, the State Council issued the *Yangtze River Delta City Cluster Development Plan*, expanding the YRD region to 26 cities by including Hefei, Wuhu, and Ma'anshan in Anhui province. The *Three-year Action Plan for Yangtze River Delta's Integrated Development*, officially published in July 2018, further illuminated the schedule and path of the integrated development of the YRD, accelerating the process of all the specific tasks. By 2020, a basic framework of a world-class city cluster, an innovative regional industrial system, and a collaborative innovation system should be completed in the YRD. This three-year plan focused on seven key areas, including transportation interconnection, mutual support of energies, industrial collaborative innovation, etc., and covers 12 cooperative subjects, including transportation energy, science and technology innovation, industry, etc., among which the driving forces of innovation and collaborative innovation in the YRD require a joint construction of an open innovation network that unifies the inside and cooperates with the outside, promoting the deeper integration of industrial chains in the YRD and cross-regional integrated development.

In November 2018, the regional integration of the YRD was officially made a national strategy, marking a new phase of its accelerated development. In January 2019, the central government first brought up the concept of "The Yangtze River Delta integration demonstration zone". Currently, the first draft of *The Outline of the Yangtze River Delta Regional Integrated Development Plan*, drawn up

DOI: 10.4324/9781003455943-11

by mainly the National Development and Reform Commission, has been completed and is soliciting for advice before publication. It is certain that the significant content of YRD integration would include the construction of innovation-led regional industrial systems and the strengthening of industrial integration.

The current theoretical research on YRD integration are from two aspects: the first is to analyze the obstruction of integration based on the perspective of "market integration", aiming at eliminating regional market segmentation, establishing a unified open market in the YRD, and promoting the coordinated development of a regional economy; the second is to analyze the construction of regional industrial systems and the thorough integration within an industry from the perspective of "regional integration".

Manufacturing industry and service industry are the two major parts of national economic accounting and the main foothold of analyzing industrial coordination. The industrial coordination in integration is essentially the endogenetic relationship and possible mutual influence between the manufacturing industry and service industry in the YRD. The existing research on their relationship has focused on the analysis of the service industry, especially on producer services that made vital contributions to the increased competitiveness of manufacturing industries, but neglected the effect of the manufacturing industry on the service industry. The conclusion based on such analyses is that the government needs to encourage the development of the service industry by supply-based policies, such as preferential tax, institutional reform, etc. However, those analyses are based on the hypothesis that the service industry is an exogenous variable, so their conclusion may not have practical significance. Therefore, we attempt to analyze the development of the service industry and manufacturing industry by putting them in the same system, which is an important approach to achieve economic integration in the YRD.

The structure of this chapter is as follows: Section Two is the logical analysis, reviewing the existing research and summarizing the mechanism of the connection between the manufacturing industry and service industry; Section Three depicts the fact that manufacturing industry and service industries are intermediate input of each other based on the input-output table of Shanghai, Jiangsu, and Zhejiang in 2002, 2007, and 2012, which brings up a hypothesis; Section Four empirically tested the hypothesis by constructing the simultaneous equations model; and Section Five is the conclusion.

Section 2 Logical analysis

Porter (1990) pointed out that the development of a high-end manufacturing industry requires the input of professionalized and advanced production factors; i.e., the development of high-end service industries needs to meet the demand of high-end manufacturing industries. This is the definition of the relationship between the service industry and manufacturing industry from the perspective of industrial connections and emphasizes the possible mutual influence between them. As we pointed out earlier, most research neglected this endogeneity, so here we will analyze them respectively.

1. The influence of service industry on the rising competitiveness of manufacturing industry

Numerous researchers have proved that, as a high-level production factor, the service industry reduces not only the production cost of the manufacturing industry but also the transaction cost, thereby enhancing the efficiency and competitiveness of the manufacturing industry. Hansen (1990) pointed out that in a flexible production system led by knowledge and technology, the service industry, either as a sector within the manufacturing industry or an independent enterprise, has played an important role in terms of expanding labor divisions, reducing costs, and raising labor productivity, etc. Glasmeier and Howland (1993) also noticed that the development of producer services in a region raised the competitiveness of other local industries. The mechanisms are originated from these three aspects:

First, the separation of the manufacturing link and service link reduces the fixed cost of the manufacturing industry. The specialized work division promotes the development of the service industry, so that the manufacturing industry can focus on their core businesses and outsource the non-core links (for example, legal service and financial service) to the professional services enterprises. This is how service links are gradually separated from the manufacturing enterprises. Because of the relatively high set-up cost of service links, their outsourcing to professional service enterprises can transfer part of the fixed cost to variable cost and thus reduce the overall cost to a large extent. Abraham and Taylor (1996) believed that enterprises are more willing to purchase professional services from external markets than provide it by themselves for the purpose of saving labor costs and gaining specialized production from the service industry.

Second, cutting the knowledge-intensive service factor input can reduce the production costs of manufacturing industry and enhance their control power over the market. The service industry is characterized by incomparable and inimitable high-level factors that may continuously create value, especially producer services that contain a large amount of knowledge, technology, and human capital. The research of Grubel and Walker (1993) indicates that the service industry can introduce gradually specialized knowledge, human, and technology capital into the process of commodity production, deepening the capital while enhancing the roundaboutness of the modern production process. It raised not only the contribution of service input to the efficiency of the manufacturing industry, but also the productivity of other production factors. Markusen (1989) pointed out that the service industry is characterized by knowledge-intensiveness and differentiation. The acquisition of knowledge requires enormous initial investment, but it causes economies of scale when the marginal cost drops later. The enterprises capable of differentiating products have relatively stronger market power and form a market structure of monopoly competition for the service industry. The characteristics of market structure of the service industry, combined with the oligopoly market pattern of the manufacturing industry, lead to an untraditional development pattern in terms of both productivity and technological levels, and the control power over market and the increment of value. This is how the service industry increases the added value and international competition of the manufacturing industry to a large extent.

Third, the development of the service industry lowers the transaction cost of the manufacturing industry and creates a new institutional environment for its competition. Some service industries, such as financial service and logistic service, are part of the transaction cost, so their development can directly reduce the cost of financing and distribution; while the information service industry drops the production cost by providing technological support and further improves the information superiority of enterprises. For example, the development of the internet provides enterprises easier access to all kinds of information and thereby changes their profit model; professionalized business services like financial affairs, tax administration, legislation, and consulting services support the enterprises in regard to the guarantee of contract fulfillment and conflict settlement; and the services of catering, accommodation, post, and communication provide residents with a more convenient living condition while creating a better investment environment for the manufacturing industry, which plays a significant role in attracting FDI in an export-oriented economy.

2. The supporting function of manufacturing industry to service industry

The influence of the manufacturing industry on the service industry is manifested in driving the demand that the development of the manufacturing industry raises the market demand of the service industry and thus drives its growth. It is shown in two aspects: the expanding scale of the service industry and the rising quality and efficiency of service.

First, the increasing demand brought about by the manufacturing industry enlarged the scale of the service industry. In the early stage of industrialization, the relatively small scale of the manufacturing industry did not require a large amount of service; i.e., there is not enough space for the external service provider. Therefore, most enterprises tended to self-service, i.e., the development pattern of "large and complete, or small and complete". Especially in some countries with a less-developed market economy, enterprise groups would be formed so their administrative headquarters can provide their branch enterprises services like financing, management consulting, and law. Therefore, service industries are included within the manufacturing enterprises. In this case, the service industry is apparently underestimated, and the external small-sized service providers cannot form a professionalized service market due to the lack of market or competition. However, with the development of the manufacturing industry, the market space of the service industry is expanding and its specialization is intensifying, leading to its separation from manufacturing enterprises to form an independent industry. Bhagwati (2010) proposed that both domestic and international production process are continuously differentiating. Separating the service industry from the manufacturing industries raised its proportion. A more important reason lies in the structural transformation of the manufacturing industry: it requires more intermediate service input in the productive process. He further pointed out that the development of the ITC industry plays an important role in this differentiation. Later research (Francois, 1990; Rowthorn and Ramaswamy, 1999; Klodt, 2000) has supported this conclusion, believing that as the intermediate demand, the manufacturing industry plays a significant role in the development of the service industry.

Second, the intrinsic requirements of the differentiation and competitiveness of the manufacturing industry are also conducive to the improvement of service quality and efficiency. Guerrieri and Meliciani (2005) pointed out that different characteristics of the manufacturing industry have various requirements of the service industry. Their research proposed that technology and knowledge-intensive manufacturing enterprises, such as computer communications, electronic equipment, chemical industry, and pharmaceutical industry, are more demanding of services industries, especially the finance, insurance, and business services, while the labor-intensive enterprises have relatively fewer requirements. It means that the requirements for high-level service increasingly rise as the technological level of the manufacturing industry continuously improves, providing more markets for the service providers to promote their quality; meanwhile, the labor-intensive enterprises need to enhance their international competitiveness as the market competition intensifies, so they require more high-level factors for raising their productivity, which in turn facilitates the overall level of the service industry. The whole operation of economies also laid a foundation for the increase of quality and efficiency of service products. The development of the manufacturing industry further specified the social work division and made the economies of scale possible. The cost of codified and standardized service activities reduces along with the increasing scale, which greatly raised the efficiency of the service industry itself.

There are also some researchers who proved that the development of the manufacturing industry may compete with the service industry in terms of resources and factors, leading to the crowding-out effect and restrictions on the service industry. However, they have not been empirically tested.

Theoretically speaking, the interaction mechanism of the manufacturing and service industry has been sufficiently illuminated. However, as we pointed out, it has not been analyzed in a unified framework enough to fundamentally solve the endogeneity problem. In addition, whether the mechanism works in the YRD, the most economically developed area in China, has not yet been verified. It is a significant cornerstone of the economic integration in the YRD through coordination. Therefore, this chapter will reveal the endogenous relationship between the manufacturing and service industries in the YRD through the analysis on input-output tables and empirical tests.

Section 3 The statistical description and hypothesis based on input-output tables

This chapter first analyzes the input-output table. It makes up for the defect of national economic statistics based on the added value and reflects the endogenous influences in the development process of the manufacturing and service industry. Based on the input-output table (42 sectors) of the three provinces and one city in the YRD (Zhejiang, Jiangsu, Anhui, and Shanghai) in 2007 and 2012, we calculated two indexes to analyze the interaction of the two industries.

The first index is input ratio of service capital goods for manufacturing sectors, which can reflect the usage of the service industry as a factor input for the manufacturing industry. First, the definition of service capital good and the ratio should be briefly explained. Part of the gross output of the service sector reenters the production process as the intermediate input of other sectors, reflecting the extent to which it is required by other sectors, as a characteristic of means of production in the service factor. The intermediate input is called the service capital good. The proportion of service capital good to the gross output of the service sector is called service capital good rate (Cheng Dazhong, 2006). The analysis based on input-output tables indicate that the changing trend of service capital good rate varies in the three provinces and one city in the YRD. Taking Shanghai as an example, the ratio was 56.3% in 2002, rose to 67% in 2007, and slightly dropped to 59.6% in 2012, 3.3% higher than that in 2002.[1] The industries with a relatively higher service capital good rate in 2012 were "repair and maintenance of metal products, machinery and equipment", "neighborhood service, repair and other services", "rental and business services", "transportation, storage and post services", etc.[2]

Then we inspect the intermediate usage structure of the service capital good and analyze its usage by the manufacturing industry. Table 11.1 shows the input ratio of service capital good for the manufacturing sector.

It is noticed that the input ratio of service capital good rose in four areas during 2002–2012 before dropping. This indicates that the contribution of the service industry as high-level factor to the manufacturing industry in 2005–2007 was increasing. The average input ratios all surpassed 35% in the areas except for Anhui. However, the contribution has decreased in recent years. The indexes of sub-divided industries indicate that the ratios passed 50% in transportation and storage, wholesale and retail (trade), finance and insurance, etc.[3] On the other hand, the input of real estate, tourism, public administration, and social organization to the manufacturing industry is relatively low. The conclusion also provides us with an objective classification method of the service industry, i.e., the productive service industry and consumptive service industry.

The second index is service input ratio. Intermediate input consists of material input and service input. The proportion of service input to the gross input is the service input ratio, indicating the demand of other industries for the service industry. Based on the definition, higher service input ratio means more support from other industries to the market of the service industry, and stronger driving forces in the development of other industries. In order to thoroughly understand the demand of manufacturing industries for the service industry and the influence of the development of the service industry itself, we inspect the service input ratio of both the manufacturing industry and service industry. Table 11.2 presents the service input

Table 11.1 The input ratio of service capital good for manufacturing sector (%)

Subdivided 15 industries	*Shanghai*			*Jiangsu*			*Zhejiang*			*Anhui*		
	2002	*2007*	*2012*	*2002*	*2007*	*2012*	*2002*	*2007*	*2012*	*2002*	*2007*	*2012*
Overall service industry*	34.36	35.84	23.55	33	47.33	34.29	40.95	42.95	35.34	26.52	26.63	25.51
Repair and maintenance of metalware, machinery, and equipment	–	–	69.59	–	–	77.61	–	–	72.56	–	–	66.46
Transportation and storage	33.26	38.21	12.40	51.49	53.77	38.78	59.74	54.20	69.10	35.91	38.41	63.04
Post industry	30.44	24.23		26.21	47.25		36.59	23.24		10.33	15.69	
Information transmission, computer service and software industry	18.12	44.83	16.32	21.44	45.10	42.19	26.58	35.25	36.74	12.99	14.44	37.82
Wholesale and retail (trade)	72.47	62.40	50.41	62.52	74.17	32.39	75.24	78.91	34.96	50.05	57.65	13.28
Accommodation and catering	40.14	19.22	18.04	26.38	37.09	36.00	37.84	18.97	50.06	22.02	16.03	12.28
Finance and insurance	27.68	35.07	18.35	37.22	53.42	43.16	54.14	45.04	36.13	23.95	29.97	25.93
Real estate	7.29	15.60	3.17	8.1	37.85	7.11	10.55	28.15	12.28	8.37	11.21	2.96
Rent and business service	41.01	37.38	15.46	19.93	48.39	44.77	28.79	40.39	31.35	22.90	36.39	24.22
Tourism	8.18	–	–	9.07	–	–	0.48	–	–	3.65	–	–
Research and experiment	81.63	59.63	46.17	15.58	82.20	51.43	45.39	78.96	24.72	54.42	59.94	41.55
Polytechnical services	18.24	48.37		17.94	55.35		18.77	46.80		19.32	41.45	
Other social services	56.07	–	–	16.19	–	–	23.07	–	–	7.71	–	–
Hydraulic engineering, environment, and public facility management	–	20.36	22.97	–	37.14	21.40	–	11.35	27.51	–	18.94	6.16
Neighborhood service and other social service	–	33.83	29.40	–	25.54	38.90	–	18.66	20.87	–	15.37	21.60
Education	42.42	22.12	9.21	23.35	21.16	18.84	27.67	22.73	11.34	15.60	4.40	5.50
Health and social insurance and social welfare	7.92	46.16	0	18.98	74.50	19.16	6.79	79.27	0	6.89	23.83	0
Culture, sports, and entertainment	16.51	5.18	16.53	13.47	36.11	22.03	25.5	31.61	20.37	57.28	12.43	8.62
Public management and social organization	0.01	0	4.97	0	47.89	24.32	0	3.84	6.13	0	0	15.41

Note: * In the overall service industry, the service capital good input ratio of the manufacturing industry is the weighted arithmetic average based on the weight of gross output of each industry. The input-output table changed in 2007: the "trade" in "wholesale and retail (trade)" was excluded; insurance was included in finance; tourism is eliminated; and other social services were further subdivided. New changes in 2012: "Repair and maintenance of metal products, machinery, and equipment" was added; "transportation and storage" and "post industry" were integrated; the "research and career development" and "polytechnic services" were united into "scientific research and technological service industry"; social insurance changed from sector 40 to sector 42.

Table 11.2 The service input ratio of manufacturing sector and service sector (non-material input) (%)

Industry	*Shanghai*			*Jiangsu*			*Zhejiang*			*Anhui*		
	2002	*2007*	*2012*	*2002*	*2007*	*2012*	*2002*	*2007*	*2012*	*2002*	*2007*	*2012*
Overall manufacturing industry*	17.82	29.10	16.14	11.77	14.59	9.23	13.36	16.00	13.02	17.82	23.93	17.67
Food manufacturing and tobacco industry	25.59	26.21	29.47	7.97	11.48	10.41	15.57	13.85	17.86	14.84	21.30	22.75
Textile industry	16.88	20.99	15.00	5.86	7.92	9.43	11.93	10.77	15.77	14.06	19.39	19.87
Leather and down feather products	25.57	30.51	34.76	18.15	12.14	30.61	13.9	12.48	18.32	18.97	22.80	22.46
Timber processing and furniture manufacturing	17.84	35.75	18.45	24.04	11.61	17.58	15.35	12.68	15.91	19.9	20.25	15.31
Paper making, printing, cultural and arts product manufacturing	19.36	28.56	17.63	18.72	11.26	11.33	12.86	11.48	13.37	18.43	22.01	15.74
Petroleum processing, coking, and nuclear fuel processing	19.37	14.90	2.03	24.77	6.98	1.79	4.87	4.73	7.33	10.37	15.76	14.81
Chemical industry	20.62	21.14	16.95	11.68	10.54	9.30	13.56	12.48	12.95	16.29	19.05	18.49
Nonferrous metals products manufacturing	21.1	23.45	21.80	16.52	15.28	9.46	17.01	16.77	21.59	21.92	19.75	16.08
Smelting and pressing of metals	16.3	18.82	7.57	10.23	8.45	5.27	10.09	8.26	7.78	16.78	12.75	13.75
Metal products	16	21.05	17.75	15.09	9.24	13.25	13.34	10.97	12.18	16.55	12.10	12.42
Manufacture of general-purpose Machinery	14.97	19.76	16.30	9.93	11.26	10.25	13.95	13.26	11.53	21.88	15.00	16.84
Manufacture of special-purpose machinery			22.88			10.15			13.22			20.42
Manufacture of transport equipment	16.39	27.87	16.69	9.26	10.37	9.86	11.93	12.36	9.80	19.32	17.92	17.79
Manufacture of electrical machinery and equipment	17.09	25.66	17.44	8.9	9.98	8.65	15.08	12.40	9.82	20.68	13.44	14.56
Manufacture of communication equipment, computers, and other electronic equipment	13.96	14.58	9.69	13.48	11.05	4.81	12.71	13.14	11.38	16.91	17.64	18.29
Manufacture of measuring instruments and machinery for cultural activity and office work	19.69	18.06	–	9.15	10.75	–	14.03	13.51	–	20.67	24.34	–
Manufacture of measuring instruments	–	–	33.95	–	–	10.18	–	–	12.43	–	–	22.67

Other manufacturing	22.3	–	28.99	8.65	–	6.37	12.94	–	16.40	17.11	–	28.53
Manufacture of artwork and other manufacturing	–	35.24	–	–	11.32	–	–	12.96	–	–	22.37	–
Overall service industry*	61.76	66.27	73.88	50.14	49.61	66.17	51.97	52.18	66.16	54.23	47.96	59.18
Repair and maintenance of metal products machinery and equipment	–	–	46.99	–	–	13.93	–	–	17.65	–	–	17.13
Transportation and storage	56.33	62.42	64.43	48.29	34.94	63.40	38.45	35.35	70.92	65.34	45.00	54.65
Post industry	69.54	78.37		85.32	54.26		69.32	64.63		60.15	56.57	
Information transmission, computer service and software industry	63.19	73.65	66.50	38.09	48.30	61.75	48.29	34.23	50.31	53.18	46.12	63.31
Wholesale and retail (trade)	76.78	88.05	94.33	64.16	71.43	85.55	67.97	83.16	90.10	81.27	76.06	84.88
Accommodation and catering	19.53	38.42	39.91	7.95	19.89	30.63	14.06	21.38	43.45	25.37	28.68	33.50
Finance and insurance	81.64	87.03	89.14	63.17	79.12	71.68	64.89	71.31	70.81	68.52	71.93	78.44
Real estate	82.54	68.80	87.03	56.44	53.69	87.74	40.69	39.45	83.71	27.43	39.33	73.18
Rent and business service	64.7	66.32	69.35	74.85	37.35	83.78	89.75	47.04	50.73	55.44	56.32	53.67
Tourism	83.86	–	–	99.66	–	–	96.92	–	–	98.33	–	–
Research and experiment	59.5	65.53	55.20	57.65	26.99	35.74	63.84	23.75	50.01	61.48	18.32	39.10
Polytechnic services	48.41	50.30		68.94	46.02		31.91	32.54		33.81	51.27	
Other social services	38.88	–	–	35.5	–	–	37.29	–	–	29.6	–	–
Hydraulic engineering, environment and public facility management	–	44.48	43.00	–	36.27	33.06	–	51.31	36.11	–	41.28	38.98
Neighborhood service and other social service	–	39.85	57.39	–	33.21	36.11	–	33.14	33.09	–	25.26	35.47
Education	31.75	53.18	66.46	47.17	49.57	59.78	49.48	45.24	69.55	35.14	39.33	54.86
Health and social insurance and social welfare	18.03	13.51	17.18	22.93	17.23	5.91	18.97	15.93	30.87	17.66	17.43	17.30
Culture, sports, and entertainment	51.31	68.99	68.08	34.17	41.28	32.26	52.44	52.09	41.05	43.32	40.48	44.68
Public management and social organization	35.8	48.09	70.98	53.38	53.73	66.37	45.77	78.01	73.02	54.18	71.55	71.87

Note: * The service input ratio of the overall manufacturing industry and service industry are the weighted arithmetic average of each industry.

ratio (non-material input) of manufacturing and service sectors based on the input-output table of 42 sectors in the three provinces and one city in the YRD in 2002, 2007, and 2012.[4]

Although Table 11.1 indicates that there is relatively a large part of service gross input put into manufacturing factors, Table 11.2 shows a not-so-obvious driving force of the manufacturing industry in the YRD for the demand of the service industry. According to the cross-sectional data, the average service input ratio of the manufacturing industry in Shanghai, Jiangsu, Zhejiang, and Anhui in 2002 were 17.82%, 11.77%, 13.36%, and 17.82% respectively, which means the development of their manufacturing industry, driven by material input, did not have a large demand for service input. Although the situation was improved with the rising economic development level, the manufacturing industry's demand for the service industry actually dropped in 2012, especially in Jiangsu. The service input ratio of the manufacturing industry in Jiangsu in 2012 decreased to below 10%: 90.77% of its average input was material and only 9.23% service, which means that the manufacturing industry only has a minor influence on the service industry. From the perspective of subdivided industries, although there are variations between each area, the capital-intensive and technology-intensive industries have a relatively large demand for the service industry generally; for example, the service input ratio of the food manufacturing and tobacco industry, petroleum processing, coking, and nuclear fuel processing, nonferrous metals products manufacturing, etc. are relatively high; while the traditionally labor-intensive industries like textiles have a relatively low demand for the service industry.

In terms of the service input ratio of the service industry, its absolute value is much higher than that of the manufacturing industry: the average number of the four places all surpassed 50%, and Shanghai even reached 61.67%. With the rising economic development level, the service input ratio of the service industry showed an increasing trend, increasing to 73.88% in Shanghai, almost 3 or 4 times that of the manufacturing industry. It means that the development of the service industry is mainly based on the service input rather than material input, which is the opposite of the manufacturing industry. The relatively high ratio of service input of the service industry means its development is restricted by its own development level, which is why the service industry in the YRD and even the whole country has remained steadily at a low level. From the perspective of subdivided industry, tourism, rent and business services, wholesale and retail (trade), etc. have a larger demand for the service industry.

Through the analysis of the two indexes, we discovered that manufacturing and service industries are intermediate factor inputs for each other, so they are endogenous in the economic operation. Based on the conclusion, we brought up the following hypothesis:

Hypothesis 1: the interaction between manufacturing and service industries in theoretical analysis may not exactly exist. As the high-level factor input, the development of the service industry greatly improves the development of the manufacturing industry, while the latter does not have a distinct driving force for the market demand of the former.

Section 4 Empirical test

1. Variables, simultaneous model, and data

Based on the analysis of the input-output table, manufacturing and service industries are the intermediate input for each other and they have mutual bidirectional influence, so the two variables are the potential endogenous variables in the estimation model. To reflect the function of the service industry as an intermediate factor, we use the efficiency index to indicate the development level of the manufacturing industry.

Different researchers have adopted various indexes of the efficiency of the manufacturing industry. Most foreign researchers chose output rate (the proportion of added value to production value), efficiency index (the proportion of the output ratio of a certain industry to its labor input ratio), and labor productivity (the proportion of industrial gross output to employment quantity). As for domestic research, Chen Limin and Tan Liwen (2004) adopted three indexes to measure the competitiveness of the manufacturing industry: industrial profit ratio, market share, and labor productivity. Since the YRD attracts the most labor force in the central and western regions of China, employment factors should be fully considered by taking added value per capita *pro* as the major index for measuring the efficiency of manufacturing industry,[5] i.e., the industrial added value of industrial enterprises above designated size divided by annual average number of employees.

Although the productive service is more directly related to the manufacturing industry and most existing researches are based on it (Gu Naihua et al., 2006; Jiang Jing et al., 2007), the prior analysis based on the input-output table has proved that all kinds of service industries constitute the input for manufacturing industries. On the other hand, some service industries in the economic statistics, for example, transport service and bank service, can be regarded as either the consumptive service for resident and average consumer, or the productive service for enterprises, depending on their different focuses (Cheng Dazhong, 2006). Therefore, our measurement is based on the perspective of the overall service industry. The classification of the services industry in China is not the same as the international standard. The relative statistics of Chinese domestic service industries are based on the Chinese classification, while the Chinese commitments on services are based on the WTO standard. This chapter adopts the tertiary industry in the national economic statistics to represent the service industry, excluding the service industry for agriculture, forestry, animal husbandry, and fishery (primary industry) and the construction industry (secondary industry).[6] Since the population density in the YRD is relatively high, we use the regional per capita output of service industry *ser* to represent the development level of the service industry.[7]

Therefore, we have the following simultaneous equations:

$$\begin{aligned}\mathrm{pro}_{\mathrm{it}} &= \alpha_0 + \alpha_1 \mathrm{ser}_{\mathrm{it}} + \alpha_2 pgdp_{\mathrm{it}} + \alpha_4 \exp_{\mathrm{it}} + \alpha_5 \mathrm{cap}_{\mathrm{it}} \\ &+ \alpha_6 \ \mathrm{firm}_{\mathrm{it}} + \varepsilon_{\mathrm{it}}\end{aligned} \tag{11.1}$$

$$\begin{aligned}ser_{it} &= \beta_0 + \beta_1 \mathrm{pro}_{it} + \beta_2 pgdp_{it} + \beta_4 \exp_{it} + \beta_5 \ \mathrm{urban} \\ &+ \beta_6 \ \mathrm{policy}_{it} + \mu_{it}\end{aligned} \tag{11.2}$$

In the equations, α_0 and β_0 are constant terms; ε and μ are random disturbance terms; subscript *i* represents region and *t* represents time. The control variables in the equations are economic development level *pgdp* and degree of opening *exp*: represented by regional per capita GNP and the ratio of regional gross export value to GDP respectively.

In consideration of the consistency with the input-output table, the relevant data from 2000 to 2012 is adopted for our empirical analysis. Since Anhui was included in the YRD after 2016, we only chose the panel data of 16 cities in Shanghai, Zhejiang, and Jiangsu,[8] the natural logarithm of which is calculated. See Table 11.3 for the specific variable explanation and data source.

2. The selection of instrumental variables

The key to simultaneous equations is to find the instrumental variables for the potential endogenous variable. We take *cap* and *firm* as the instrumental variables

Table 11.3 The explanation of relevant variables and data source

Variable	*Variable explanation*	*Data source*
pro	Efficiency index of manufacturing industry: the natural logarithm of the per-capita added value of industrial enterprises above designated size	Author's calculation based on *China City Statistical Yearbook* and *China Statistical Yearbook for Regional Economy*
ser	Development degree of service industry: the natural logarithm of the regional gross value of tertiary industry per capita	*China City Statistical Yearbook* and *China Statistical Yearbook for Regional Economy*
pgdp	Index of economic development level: regional GDP per capita	*China City Statistical Yearbook* and *China Statistical Yearbook for Regional Economy*
exp	Export ratio: the natural logarithm of the proportion of regional gross export to GDP	*China City Statistical Yearbook* and *Yangtze River Delta & Pearl River Delta and Hong Kong & Macao SAR Statistical Yearbook*
cap	Fixed assets: the natural logarithm of annual average balance of the net value of fixed assets in the industrial enterprises above designated size	*China City Statistical Yearbook* and *Yangtze River Delta & Pearl River Delta and Hong Kong & Macao SAR Statistical Yearbook*
firm	Competition level: the natural logarithm of the number of industrial enterprises above designated size	*China City Statistical Yearbook* and *China Statistical Yearbook for Regional Economy*
urban	Urbanization degree: the natural logarithm of proportion of non-agricultural population to the total population in the region	*China City Statistical Yearbook* and *China Statistical Yearbook for Regional Economy*
policy	Policy dummy variable: development policies of governmental service industry	0 before 2003; 1 after 2003

of the endogenous variable *pro*. There has been a situation of import for export in YRD, i.e., the improvement of the competitiveness of manufacturing industry is highly related to the imported equipment, which is mainly the net value of fixed assets. It is believed that fixed assets affect the development of the service industry by influencing the efficiency of the manufacturing industry, because it is highly dependent on equipment renewal. It may restrict the development of the service industry if there is no higher demand for it. The number of industrial enterprises above designated size measures the degree of competition: the more enterprises, the higher the competition level and more motivation for technological innovation of enterprises. This is how it directly affects manufacturing efficiency.

The first condition instrumental variables need to meet is the high relevancy to the estimated variables, which can be testified easily. The regression of *cap* and *firm* to *pro* shows that their coefficients are significantly positive at the level of 1%,[9] indicating a relatively close correlation with the efficiency of the manufacturing industry. The second condition is the exogeneity of variables, i.e., the irrelevancy to the residual term of the equation of service industry development. Since we adopt two instrumental variables here, the over-identifying test should be conducted on them, i.e., Sargan-Hansen test, the null hypothesis of which is that the selected instrumental variable is valid. The Sargan-Hansen test value is 0.05 in the chi-squared distribution with 1 degree of freedom. Its p value is 0.85; the null hypothesis is true. This test indicates that *cap* and *firm* can be used as the instrumental variable of *pro*.

The instrumental variable of endogenous variable *ser* are the urbanization level *urban* and policy variable *policy*. Urbanization level is represented by the proportion of non-agricultural population to the total population. The research of Riddle (1986) proposed that the development of service industry is restricted by the level of urbanization: a higher level means rapider development of the service industry. Policy variables reflect the influence of government policy on the development of the service industry. China is currently in a transition process where its government plays a leading role in the economic development, so its fluctuations in policy in regard to the service industry would significantly affect it. At the Central Economic Working Conference in 2000, the government first brought up the idea of transformation and improvement of traditional service industries and development of emerging service industries. In December 2001, when China joined the WTO, the service industry became a key area of China's opening up. The rising level of opening up in fields like telecommunication and finance and insurance (Zhang Erzhen and Fang Yong, 2008) has greatly improved the development of the service industry in China. Considering the hysteresis of specific policies for the service industry and the different schedule and opening level of each service industry, we take 2003 as the boundary to measure the policy influence. The two instrumental variables also passed the Sargan-Hansen test.

3. The identification and regression of simultaneous equations

Table 11.4 shows the estimated results of the simultaneous equations model. We clarify whether the simultaneous equations are just identified through the

Table 11.4 Regression result of the simultaneous equations

Equation (1): pro *as the explained variable*				*Equation (2):* ser *as the explained variable*			
Explanatory variable	*Regression coefficient*	*Standard error*	P *value*	*Explanatory variable*	*Regression coefficient*	*Standard error*	P *value*
ser	0.31***	0.15	0.009	*pro*	−0.55	0.41	0.115
pgdp	0.65***	0.10	0.000	*pgdp*	−0.22	0.43	0.653
exp	−0.12***	0.01	0.000	*exp*	0.51***	0.03	0.000
cap	0.41***	0.14	0.005	*urban*	0.35***	0.09	0.000
firm	0.03	0.15	0.852	*policy*	0.24***	0.05	0.000
constant	−1.03***	0.21	0.000	constant	3.11***	1.02	0.000
R^2		0.54		R^2		0.66	
obs		208		obs		208	

Note: calculated by stata13.1, *, ** and *** represent significance at level of 10%, 5%, and 1% respectively.

regression result by checking the rank condition and order condition. First, since the rank of the matrix constituted by exclusive variables in equation (1) (both endogenous and exogenous variables) and the corresponding coefficient in equation (2) is 1, equal to the number of equations in the system excluding equation (1), the structural equation (1) is identifiable and meets the rank condition[10]. Second, based on the regression structure in Table 11.4, the product of regression coefficient of *pro* and *ser* equals -2.3, not 1, so they do not have a linear relation or overidentification. Under the current instrumental variables, the simultaneous equation is just identified. The random simultaneous equations have only one set of estimates of parameters, meaning that the simultaneous equations in this chapter are logical.

4. Brief analysis

First, according to the regression result in Table 11.4, the development of the service industry can distinctly improve the efficiency of the manufacturing industry: the regression coefficient is 0.31 and passes the significance test at a level of 1%. It means that the one percentage point rise in service industry per capita leads to a 0.31 percentage point rise of the value added of the manufacturing industry, sufficiently proving that the service industry, as the high-level factor input for the manufacturing industry, promotes its development to a relatively large extent. The conclusion is consistent with the prior analysis based on the input-output table and existing research (Gu Naihua et al., 2006; Jiang Jing et al., 2007).

Second, the rising efficiency of the manufacturing industry has an indistinct promoting effect on the development of the service industry. The regression coefficient, -0.55, does not pass the significance test, which means that the development of the manufacturing industry in the YRD, the region of rapidest economic growth in China, did not generate more intermediate demand for the service industry or form a market support for it, but possibly crowded it out instead. The reason may lie in the particularity of the development of the manufacturing industry in the YRD. As the foundation of "Made in China", the manufacturing industry in the YRD relied on labor-intensive links to join the international division of labor systems. As the OEM for international big buyers, it was at the lower end of the GVC. Low-end manufacturing industry depends largely on manual labor, with limited demand for high-end service industries. What's worse, the FDI manufacturing industry's demands for productive service industry are generally provided by the headquarters of the multinational corporation, rather than the local service industry. More importantly, multinational enterprises have established R&D centers in the YRD to strengthen their technology monopoly; the FDI of commercial services like consulting, law, and marketing also entered the YRD, squeezing out the local service industry. For example, there have been over 50 R&D institutions founded by foreign investors in Suzhou Industrial Park, including Panasonic Research Development (Suzhou) Limited Company, Emerson Climate Technologies (Suzhou) Co., Ltd, Samsung Semiconductor China R&D Co., Ltd, Andrew Telecom Equipment (China) Limited Company, etc. The FDI in the service industry of these multinational enterprises has restricted the development of a local high-class service industry.

Third, the regression coefficient of the net value of fixed assets in equation (1) can further illustrate that the development of the service industry is constrained by the improved efficiency of the manufacturing industry. According to the regression result, the coefficient of *cap* is 0.41, significant at a level of 1%, meaning that the efficiency of the manufacturing industry increased largely due to the equipment. It verified to some extent the situation of "import for export" in the YRD, i.e., the rising labor productivity of manufacturing industry was achieved through introducing machinery and equipment. However, the equipment-based efficiency improvement leads to a shrinking direct demand for the service industry, because the demand would be based on the home country of the multinational enterprise rather than on the local place.

Fourth, the degree of export-orientation and economic development level are also a vital influence on the efficiency of the manufacturing industry and service industry. The increase of gross exports did not improve the labor efficiency of the manufacturing industry, which further proved that although the YRD fulfilled the noted label of "Made in China", the exports are not technologically advanced, so its manufacturing industry is still at the bottom of the GVC. A vivid description states "800 million shirts for an airplane". However, the rising exports greatly stimulated the development of the service industry. Most YRD exports are products, so its increase means not only the rising degree of export-orientation, but also its competitiveness and development level. Therefore, the positive influence of exports on the service industry also reflects the promoting effect of manufacturing on the service industry. Regional economic development levels greatly improved the efficiency of the manufacturing industry but lowered the output of the service industry to some extent, which means that on the one hand, the mechanism of income elasticity of demand in service industry did not play its role; and on the other hand, the saving ratio in the YRD (or even the whole country) may be relatively high. The residents with relatively high income have relatively low marginal propensity to consume. Therefore, the higher the economic development level, the lower the resident expenditure level, and thus the less incentive for the development of a consumptive service industry. In the empirical result, the two presented a significant negative correlation.

The empirical analysis indicates that this hypothesis has passed the empirical test, which means that there lacks a close interaction between the service industry and manufacturing industry in the YRD. Although the service industry as input improved manufacturing industry to some degree, the latter does not have a distinct demand for the former. The development of the service industry is relatively independent, mainly relying on its own previous development level.

Section 5 Conclusion

From the perspective of industrial collaboration, this chapter analyzed the economic integration in the YRD. Industrial collaboration contains not only the endogenous interaction between the advanced manufacturing industry and modern service industry, but also the influence of the historical development level of the service industry on the current one. Theoretical analysis indicates that the service industry, as high-class factor input, can lower the production and trade cost of the manufacturing industry, and thus promote the efficiency and competitiveness of the manufacturing industry; in return, the development of the manufacturing industry can improve the service industry by expanding its scale and raising its quality. However, the analysis based on the input-output table illustrates that the interaction between the YRD manufacturing industry and service industry may not exist: although the service industry stimulated the increase of competitiveness of the manufacturing industry, the latter failed to provide market support for the former, which develops relatively independently. The manufacturing industry and service industry as intermediate inputs for each other formed their endogeneity, which is tested through simultaneous equations. The empirical analysis based on the 16 cities in the YRD from 2000 to 2012 supported the conclusion. We believe that the characteristics of the export-oriented economy of the YRD are the main reason behind it. The OEM production at the low end of GVC has relatively less demand for high-end service, while the high-end service required by advanced manufacturing FDI is provided by multinational enterprises, which encroaches the space of local service industries. This is the larger reason for the failed mechanism of interaction between the service industry and manufacturing industry in the YRD.

Integration based on industrial collaboration is an important part of the YRD economic integration. The conclusion of this chapter provides a new analysis perspective and policy foundation for achieving the collaboration of the manufacturing industry and service industry and improving economic integration in the YRD.

Notes

1 Based on the data from the input-output table, we can calculate the service capital good ratio of 16 industries and the average ratio based on the weight of their gross output. The ratio of Jiangsu, Zhejiang, and Anhui in 2002 were 58%, 56.9%, and 57.2% respectively, and all dropped to 53.1%, 54.3%, and 51.3% in 2007, and finally reach 52.9%, 58.6%, and 76.8% in 2012. In addition, we can use the intermediate demand ratio to reflect the input of the service sector to other industries as intermediate production factor, which is the proportion of the service industry's intermediate input to the final consumption. The result indicates that the intermediate demand ratio of the service sector in Shanghai rose first and then dropped from 2002 to 2012, while those in other provinces dropped first and then rose. The ratio in Shanghai was much higher than in other places, especially in terms of "rental and business services", "information transmission, computer service, and software industry", "transportation, storage, and post services", etc.

2 The capital good ratio of repair and maintenance of metal products, machinery, and equipment surpassed 500% because the imported output value exceeds the final demand sector. This is why the gross output was smaller than the intermediate usage.

3 The input ratio of finance and insurance industry to manufacturing industry in Shanghai, compared to that in Jiangsu and Zhejiang, is relatively low: it rose from 27.68% in 2002 to only 35.07% in 2007 and then dropped to 18.35% in 2012, not matching the position of the financial center of Shanghai. However, a deeper inspection revealed the opposite. Our statistical index is based on the provincial-level input-output data, so it cannot reflect the influence of the finance and insurance industry in Shanghai on the YRD and the whole country. Therefore, the inspection of the input ratio to Shanghai's local manufacturing industry is not practically significant.

4 Based on the input-output table of 42 sectors, we totaled the 16 subdivided service industries in the intermediate input of each sector, which is the same as the second part of the Table 11.2.

5 We use the industry to represent manufacturing industry approximately due to the lack of the subdivided indexes of manufacturing industry over the years.

6 According to the WTO classification, the service industry for agriculture, forestry, animal husbandry, and fishery and the construction industry also belong to service industry.

7 The service industry here includes these industries: transportation, storage, post and telecommunication, wholesale, retail trade and catering services, finance and insurance industry, real estate, social service, health care, sports and social welfare, education, literature and art, broadcast, film and TV industry, scientific research and comprehensive technology service, government office and social organization, other service industries.

8 The 16 cities are: Shanghai, Nanjing, Suzhou, Wuxi, Changzhou, Zhenjiang, Nantong, Yangzhou, Taizhou, Hangzhou, Ningbo, Jiaxing, Huzhou, Shaoxing, Zhoushan, and Taizhou.

9 The coefficients are 0.61 and 0.03 respectively; both passed the significance level test at 1%.

10 In other words, each equation in the system contains two exogenous variables excluded by another equation, with the ratio of regression coefficient is 0. Therefore, the rank condition for simultaneous equations is met.

References

K.G. Abraham, et al. Firm's Use of Outside Contractors: Theory and Evidence. Journal of Labor Economics, 1996, 14 (3).

J.N. Bhagwati. Splintering and Disembodiment of Services and Developing Nations. World Economy, 2010 (5).

Cheng Dazhong. China's Producer Services: Growth, Structural Changes, and Effects. Finance & Trade Economics, 2006 (10).

Cheng Dazhong. Development Level, Structure, and Impact of Producer Services in China: An International Comparison Based on Input-output Approach. Economic Research Journal, 2008 (1).

Zhang Erzhen, Fang Yong. The Fundamental Experience of Economic Globalization and China's Opening up. Journal of Nanjing University (Philosophy, Humanities and Social Sciences), 2008 (7).

J.F. Francois. Producer Services, Scale and the Division of Labor. Oxford Economic Papers, 1990, 42 (4).

A. Glasmeier, M. Howland. Service-led Rural Development: Definitions Theories and Empirical Evidence. International Regional Science Review, 1993, 16 (1–2).

H.G. Grubel, M.A. Walker. Modern Service Sector Growth: Causes and Effects. Shanghai: Shanghai Sanlian Bookstore, 1993.

P. Guerrieri, V. Meliciani. Technology and International Competitiveness: The Interdependence between Manufacturing and Producer Services. Structural Change and Economic Dynamics, 2005, 16 (4).

N. Hansen. Do Producer Services Induce Regional Economic Development. Journal of Regional Science, 1990, 84 (2).

Jiang Jing, Liu Zhibiao, Yu Mingchao. Development of Producer Service and Manufacturing Efficiency Based on Region and Industry Experience of Panel Data Analysis. Journal of World Economy, 2007 (8).

H. Klodt. Structural Change towards Services: The German Experience. University of Birmingham IGS Discussion Paper, 2000.

Chen Limin, Tan Liwen. Research on Empirical Method of Valuing International Competitiveness of Chinese Manufacturing: Comparing with Porter's Index and Industry Taxonomy. China Industrial Economics, 2004 (5).

J.R. Markusen. Trade in Producer Services and in Other Specialized Intermediate Inputs. American Economic Review, 1989, 79 (1).

Gu Naihua, Bi Doudou, Ren Wangbing. Relationship between Producer Services' Development and Manufacturing's Competence in China During Transition Period: An Empirical Research Based on Panel Data. China Industrial Economics, 2006 (9).

M.E. Porter. The Competitive Advantage of Nations. New York: The Free Press, 1990.

D. Riddle. Service-led Growth: The Role or the Service Sector in World Development. New York: Prager, 1986.

R. Rowthorn, R. Ramaswamy. Growth, Trade and Deindustrialization. IMF Economic Papers, 1999, 46.

12 Research of constructing a generic technology platform for the industry in the Yangtze River Delta

Zhibiao Liu, Shouhua Wei and Jianbing Luo

Section 1 Introduction

The Yangtze River Delta region is at the crucial stage of rapid transition from middle to post-industrialization. The key factor that restricts the YRD's advanced industrialization is the lack of independent innovation ability of enterprises in the region, especially the lack of independent core technology, independent intellectual property rights, and world-famous brands, which could affect the target of building the YRD as an internationally advanced manufacturing base if the situation cannot be changed.

The enterprises in the YRD are currently under pressure to make technological breakthroughs in the upgrading domestic and foreign markets, but they do not have sufficient technological supply. With numerous universities, scientific research institutions, talents and conditions for scientific research in the YRD, it is still difficult to estimate whether a project is actually required in the market. How to transform the demands of market and enterprise into research projects in universities and institutions has become a vital subject to proactively study. The State Council made the YRD's economic integration a national strategy at the end of 2018 and brought up the question of how to establish "a market-oriented technological innovation system in which enterprises play the leading role while enterprises, universities and research institutes cooperate with each other". Practice has proved that under the Chinese national condition, the innovative cooperation mode of government-industry-university-institute collaboration is an effective method and significant task to promote the industrial and scientific development and upgrades in the YRD.

Government-industry-university-institute collaboration is a stable R&D team comprising enterprise, university, research institution, etc., under governmental encouragement, support, service, and guidance. Jointly tackling the significant problems and key technologies that restrict industrial development can drive the development of relevant enterprises and industries and raise the independent innovation ability and international competitiveness of enterprises. Under the previous intense regional competition, although all the administrative regions in the YRD have founded multiple government-industry-university-institute collaborations, their alliance and cooperative mechanisms were restricted by the administrative boundaries, without the overall development goal of "Building the YRD as the region of top comprehensive

DOI: 10.4324/9781003455943-12

strength" in a wider economic range. Therefore, the profit and competitiveness of the collaboration have plenty of room for improvement.

Although the YRD has innate conditions and abundant resource endowments for strong government-industry-university-institute collaboration, it would not be internationally competitive if restricted by administrative boundaries. Facing fierce competition from multinational enterprises, each province or city cannot form a specialized work division, cooperation, or complementary advantages, and lacks the institutional advantage of saving costs and focusing strength for R&D activities that heavily rely on economies of scale. Therefore, with the increasing restriction of markets and resources on the extensive economic development model, it becomes vitally important for the sustainable development and improvement of economic vitality and competitiveness to discuss the government-industry-university-institute collaboration and new cooperative mechanism in the YRD.

This chapter is structured as follows: Section 2 analyzes the motivation and mechanism of the formation of the government-industry-university-institute based on savings cost and raising research input; Section 3 is the international experience of innovative cooperation; Section 4 points out that in the process of YRD integration, the research model should transform from segmented and disordered competition to an integrated system; Section 5 takes the construction of a generic technology platform as an example to conduct detailed research on the innovative formation of a government-industry-university-institute union in the YRD; Section 6 provides policy suggestions.

Section 2 The motivation mechanism formed by the government-industry-university-research collaboration innovation

The drive-mechanism of the government-industry-university-research collaboration innovation can be analyzed by the "cooperative research" and "joint R&D" from the industrial organizational theories. It needs to be pointed out first that the cooperative research in Western theories does not contain government, but it is impossible and unrealistic to exclude government during the economic transformation in China. Moreover, the function of government, especially local government, would not affect the form or conclusion of analyses.

Cooperative research is where the participants sign a contract in a certain form in advance for the R&D investment level, direction, utilization and spread of its achievement, etc. Under the institutional arrangement, the cost and risk of R&D process is shared by the patent manufacturers jointly, i.e., if a new product is developed, then all the participants will hold the patent rights. The effects of cooperative research are as follows:

First, it can bring out the economies of scale of R&D. The cooperation of numerous enterprises can break the restriction of staff, capital, and other resources in single enterprise and carry out the impartible large-scale research projects. The economies of scale of this kind of project vary in different industries and fields of technology. There are sometimes suitable projects for even small enterprises.

Second, the cooperative research of enterprises can prevent overlapping investments. The distribution of tasks among the enterprises could avoid excess investment caused by the spontaneous competition and optimize the R&D in the society. However, it could be difficult to balance their interests when the enterprises are in fierce competition.

Third, cooperative research may be able to internalize the externality of R&D caused by the non-specialized assets. By turning knowledge into a public resource, cooperative research is conducive to information spreading in the whole economic system. It needs to be specifically pointed out that the information exchange between patent manufacturers, though it plays a key role in cooperative research, may lead to a tacit collusion between entities in the market economy and the transition from oligopoly competition to complete monopoly. Cooperative research can punish the partner in excessive competition by threatening to cancel the cooperation (Brodley, 1982). It is the shared asset of all the members who are encouraged to use R&D as a strategic method to raise the entry cost of market, which may benefit all the existing manufacturers in the industry.

These theories can be briefly illustrated by a simple game model. If an industry contains two market entities or enterprises, then the market demand function is: $p=100-Q$, $Q=q_1+q_2$. We use x_i to represent the R&D input level of enterprise i, $i=1$ or2; $c_i=c_i(x_1, x_2)$ represents the unit production cost of the two enterprises, i.e., the production cost is determined by the level of their research input,[1] $c_i=c_i(x_1, x_2) = 50-x_i-\beta x_j$, $i=1,2$; $i\neq j$; $0<\beta<1$.

It indicates that c_i decreases with the increase of research input of the two enterprises; parameter β measures the influence of research input of enterprise j on the unit production cost of enterprise i. Since we assume that $\beta>0$, the research input of enterprise j shows a positive externality. Meanwhile, R&D has its own cost: the cost of enterprise i at research input level x_i is $TC_i(x_i)$. If the R&D cost of unit product increases along with the research input, i.e., R&D follows the rule of decreasing return to scale,[2] then we have the following equation:

$$TC_i(x_i)=\frac{(x_i)^2}{2}$$

Therefore, we have a two-stage game model. The first stage is the enterprise's decision on research input level in terms of saving cost; the second stage is that on the output in market of homogenous product, i.e., Cournot output competition. They are analyzed under non-cooperative and cooperative R&D for comparison.

(1) Case 1: non-cooperative R&D

The backward induction is applied to find the equilibrium solution:

The second stage: since the production decision in the second stage is made after the innovation of cost saving, the c_i in the second stage is already given.

Based on the solution of Cournot model, the corresponding profit level should be:

$$\pi_i\left(c_1,c_2\right)=\frac{\left(100-2c_i+c_j\right)^2}{9}, i=1,2; i\neq j$$

The first stage: with the given research input level of their competitors, each enterprise would choose the research input level with an attitude of non-cooperative game, i.e., with given input level x_j, enterprise i would choose x_i to maximize its own profit:

$$\max_{x_i} \pi_i = \frac{1}{9}\left[100-2\left(50-x_i-\beta x_j\right)+50-x_i-\beta x_j\right]^2 - \frac{\left(x_i\right)^2}{2}$$

The first-order condition is:

$$\frac{\partial \pi_i}{\partial x_i}=\frac{2}{9}\left[50+(2-\beta)x_i+(2\beta-1)x_j\right](2-\beta)-x_i=0$$

If the payoff functions of the two enterprises are symmetrical, then we will have a symmetrical Nash equilibrium in which $x_1=x_2=x^{\text{nc}}$. x^{nc} is the equilibrium research input level of each enterprise when they are not cooperating:

$$x^{\text{nc}}=\frac{50(2-\beta)}{4.5-(2-\beta)(1+\beta)}$$

(2) Case 2: cooperative research

Enterprises know that they will have an output competition in stage two, so they would make the joint decision of x_1 and x_2 to maximize the joint profit, $\max_{x_1,x_2}\left(\pi_1+\pi_2\right)$. The first-order condition is:

$$\frac{\partial\left(\pi_1+\pi_2\right)}{\partial x_i}=\frac{\partial \pi_i}{\partial x_i}+\frac{\partial \pi_j}{\partial x_i}=0$$

The term $\frac{\partial \pi_j}{\partial x_i}$ measures the increment of profit margin of enterprise j, from the spillover effect of the increase of research input in enterprise i.

$$\frac{\partial(\pi_1+\pi_2)}{\partial x_i}=\frac{2}{9}\left[50+(2-\beta)x_i+(2\beta-1)x_j\right](2-\beta)$$

$$-x_i+\frac{2}{9}\left[50+(2-\beta)x_j+(2\beta-1)x_i\right]$$

$$(2\beta-1)=0$$

Therefore, the cooperative research level is: $x_1^c=x_2^c=x^c=\dfrac{50(\beta+1)}{4\cdot 5-(\beta+1)^2}$

By comparing the profit level under non-cooperative and cooperative research, it can be noticed that cooperative research can increase the cooperative profit. Since $0<\beta<1$, we learned that when $\beta>\frac{1}{2}$, i.e., spillover effect of R&D is distinct, the input level of cooperative is higher than the non-cooperative one, i.e. $x^c>x^{nc}$.

Section 3 Competition policies of developed countries on joint studies

The government-industry-university-research collaboration innovation, encouraged, guided, served, and supervised by government, improves the scientific and technological innovation through the cooperation, interaction, and complementarity between enterprises, universities, and research institutions in regard to scientific and technological innovation, new product R&D, talent training, etc. Therefore, all the developed countries have been encouraging innovation through the union. The earliest cooperation model dates back to the 1950s, when the US founded the Stanford Academy. These unions have explored and accumulated valuable experience in the long-term market competition.

The American "basic research based" development path is focused on the technological development of national defense. It was characterized by the government funding at the beginning, and then the NSF connecting the research orientation in universities and industrial demands, and organizing a research center for the two parties. Such measures have combined the basic scientific research and industrial demand in America, so that innovation can be rapidly transformed into product.

In terms of legal support, America passed the *Stevenson – Wydler Technology Innovation Act* and *Federal Technology Transfer Act* in 1980 and 1986, respectively. Since the 1980s, American government has improved the profits of all the participants of innovation by means of "union". There have been all types of cooperation between enterprises, universities, and R&D institutions: the enterprises have been regarded as not only the source of funding, but a significant site to verify the effectiveness of innovation. The jointly established centers by universities and enterprises, along with the open institution, policy system, and innovative culture, have formed the effective American innovation system. Silicon Valley outside of

San Francisco is a typical example of the perfect combination of government, industry, university, and institution.

Japan, relying on the application of research and technology development, focuses on the development of civilian technologies. It conducts a second innovation in introduced foreign technologies on the basis of independency, along the innovation path of "introducing technologies" for the collaboration of "industry, university, institute and government". By introducing a large number of technical patents and manufacturing methods, Japan studies and improves the advanced technologies in the world, and advocates close cooperation between government, universities, and industries. The Japanese government's supporting policies for the key industries have greatly improved the upgrading of the technological structure in their enterprises, as well as the emergence and development of their domestic innovation activities. In addition, the Japanese innovation system also emphasizes the function of non-profit intermediaries for raising independent innovation. For example, the Japan Kyushu Industrial Technology Center has provided a good peripheral environment for the innovation of local enterprises, especially the middle- and small-sized ones.

It needs to be pointed out that the innovation system of cooperative research, although it has caused the integration effect among several enterprises in an industry or among several industries, suppresses competition to some extent and causes the monopoly in some markets. Therefore, in order to push for a competitive market system, Western developed countries use competition policies to regulate the research unions in the competitive research fields, not fundamental ones. On the one hand, they promote cooperative research, and meanwhile they put the utmost restrictions on the possible monopoly in the competitive industries. This is what we have to learn from in the process of YRD integration.

The American antitrust laws, taking the spillover and publicness of fundamental research into consideration, encourage research cooperation rather than regard it as the antitrust target. However, the emphasis of antitrust organizations lies in the cooperative research between leading enterprises in an industry for research applications and those irrelevant to cooperate goals or restrictive on achievement utilization. In other words, American laws attempt to distinguish between research cooperation and joint commercialization of the cooperative enterprises: the former is legal, while the latter is not. However, the distinction is difficult in practice, because the commercialized application and decision of an R&D achievement is the last phase of R&D. In this cooperation, some enterprise may have a competitive advantage in terms of technologies, while some may in market and commercialization. Their complementary advantages are the basis of the R&D cooperation. The cooperation may bring the society some benefit, but it is possible to engender higher price and entry barriers.

The American National Cooperative Research Act of 1984 (NCRA) was aimed at raising the efficiency of R&D activities:

> The framers and supporters of the law hoped that the promotion of cooperation would increase net social benefit of the R&D investment by

improving the specificity of capital, lowering cost and risk and reducing overbidding (too much trial in a sense) and repeated research.

(Scott, 1988)

NCRA mandates that the enterprises registered under NCRA registration procedures would be immune from the compensation of triple actual damage. The maximum compensation the participants of cooperative research need to pay is the actual loss.

The attitude of the European Commission toward cooperative R&D in the early stage is affirmative: it should be encouraged and allowed as long as it does not restrict the market competition. The application of this standard was illustrated in the decision of the Henkel-Colgate case. However, the European Commission noticed in 1971 that if the two leading companies in the global or European market conduct cooperative R&D, then they would make it impossible for competitors to enter their market. Therefore, the *EU Competition Law* Article 81 (1) prohibits it.

However, the EU believes that a joint R&D agreement can promote technology and economy and bring consumers reasonable profit, so it meets the exemption clause of EU competition law. Since the 1980s, the European Commission has developed a series of exemption laws on intellectual property agreement based on the *EU Competition Law* Article 81 (3); for example, Commission Regulation (EC) No 556/84 of July 1984 on the application of Article 81 (3) of patent licensing agreement; Commission Regulation (EC) No 556/89 of November 1988 on the application of Article 81 (3) of know-how licensing agreements; Commission Regulation (EC) No 240/96 of 31 January 1996 on the application of Article 81 (3) of technology transfer agreements. The application of these regulations is rather complicated in terms of their objects and areas.

The EC restrictive exemption regulations in 1984 not only indicated a positive attitude toward cooperative R&D and repeated that the R&D involving cooperative agreements are immune to Article 81 (1), but also partially expanded the clauses approving of cooperative R&D agreement. Meanwhile, it also pointed out that the application of R&D achievement after innovation should be strictly confined (EC Commission, 1985).

Under the new regulations, the cooperative R&D must be conducted within a given frame: only when it objectively benefits the improvement of technologies or economy and becomes the decisive factor of manufacturing or improving products can the form be applied. In addition, the restrictive exemption regulation only applies to the following situations: (1) all the manufacturers are entitled to the R&D achievement; (2) each participant can utilize the research achievement and existing necessary technologies and knowledge freely and independently provided they do not cooperate; (3) each manufacturer has the right to sell the products under the situation of specialization when making new products or improving the current ones.

According to the European Commission, the cooperative R&D is only allowed when the market structure guarantees effective competition. Therefore, there are a series of complex and specific regulations, including white, gray, and black clauses, and the revocation of exemption; see *EU Competition Law* for more information.

Encouraging R&D is one of the distinct characteristics of Japanese industrial policy. Early after the Second World War, Japan often regulated the importing of equipment through exchange, aiming at guiding the R&D projects to the most prospective industries and enterprises. Tax is also a common tool of leading the investment of manufacturers in R&D. First, Japan sets up a research group for a certain field and dissolves it when its goals are achieved (or when the goal's no longer significant). Second, these groups conduct research based on project rather than industry, providing manufacturers with diversified technological bases.

The cooperation between Japanese research groups also plays an important role in terms of promoting R&D. For example, in order to lead the global competition on VLSI, five Japanese computer manufacturers formed the most famous research team in 1976–1979. The team engendered multiple patents and laid the foundation of the semiconductor industry in Japan. Generally speaking, Japanese culture value cooperation more than competition. Although the government has launched antitrust laws and supported research cooperation in many aspects, the competition between enterprises has not been eliminated.

Section 4 Cooperative research and development: from segmented to integrated

Early in 2003, Jiangsu, Zhejiang, and Shanghai founded "the joint conference on the construction of innovation system in YRD", which developed into the "office of the joint conference on the construction of innovation system in YRD" in 2008 with the official document "*The Three-Year Action Plan for Technological Cooperation in the Yangtze River Delta (2008–2010)*". Shanghai, Jiangsu, Zhejiang, and even Anhui have been strengthening the action plan of constructing the YRD innovative community in recent years and have accomplished some achievements. However, the current situation is segmented and the competition is unordered, with the following problems remaining:

(1) Under the segmented administration system, the industries in the three areas are not complementary; the allocative efficiency of research resources is relatively low with the phenomenon of waste and shortage; the frictions over profit in the economic development of the three regions have greatly restricted the range and degree of their technological cooperation.
(2) From the government aspect, the institutional arrangement of technological cooperation, transformation, and sharing is insufficient; there is no link between cooperative policies or a long-term mechanism of cooperation.
(3) The segmentation in market systems hinders the mobility of production factors and weakens the mechanism of technological coordination and development.
(4) The regional resource constraint is distinct. The economic development needs to transform from relying on investment to relying on technique and human capital. The upgrading of industrial structure is desperate for the support of new technology. For example, the agricultural land per capita in the YRD is 500 square meters, half of the national average. Therefore, further development

faces increasing restriction of land and environmental resources and pressure of environmental protection.

In 2008, the "office of the joint conference on the construction of innovation system in YRD" launched *The Three-Year Action Plan for Technological Cooperation in the Yangtze River Delta (2008–2010)*[3], which pointed out the four major tasks: to jointly construct the YRD "scientific and technological innovation center", "scientific and technological resource sharing", "ecologically harmonious and livable area", and "scientific and technological industry innovation center", and one target: to be the most vigorous innovative area with relatively strong international competitiveness in China.

Therefore, the document also contains four action plans: (1) high-tech industrial technology leapfrogging; (2) traditional industry improving; (3) science and technology for people's livelihoods improving; (4) scientific and technological resource sharing, each with their developmental priorities. It is easy to make specific plans but difficult to implement them. The significant tasks and the key to the transformation from segmented to integrated R&D system are:

First, the construction of public service platforms for the development of industrial generic technology and regional technological innovation. Based on the existing platform construction in the three places, we can adopt a mode of "unified standard, independent construction, resource distribution, and system integration" to launch the construction of a "scientific instrument sharing system" and to participate in the regional trial of the national scientific data sharing program for an optimized resource allocation in a wider range. For this purpose, construction planning for basic resources in regional innovation system is required to promote the joint establishment and sharing of R&D bases of major scientific instruments and equipment, laboratory animals, scientific and technological literature, expert database, project database, etc.

Second is the joint declaration and research of significant and crucial industrial generic technology projects. In order to give full play to the national innovation center and scientific research center in the region, we need to orchestrate and jointly declare the important scientific projects of the Ministry of Science and Technology for national support in the process of following the latest development of scientific and technological innovations in the world. Therefore, the focus needs to be concentrated on only key projects to make breakthroughs in a short time and take up the frontier fields of advanced technology.

Third is joint application of constructing a "demonstration zone of comprehensive pilot for national scientific and technological innovation". In order to promote the free mobility of innovation factors and accelerate the major scientific and technological projects, the three regions should jointly apply for the construction of a "demonstration zone of comprehensive pilot for national scientific and technological innovation" from four aspects. First is the exploration of financial, tax, banking, venture capital, and environmental policies for promoting regional independent innovative integration. We need to build a batch of state-level laboratories, key labs, and industrial and engineering research centers in the fields of energy, environmental protection, IT, biological medicine, major equipment manufacturing, textile and clothing, etc., and to construct the "Yangtze River Project Institute" following the principle of national or regional joint construction. Second, we can establish a YRD "guidance fund for independent innovation" for the joint organization and implementation of major scientific and technological projects. Third, we can form a YRD technological trading platform and intermediary under the guidance of government and the participation of agents to promote the technology transfer and spread in the region. Fourth, a scientific and technological talent base should be founded for the interaction and sharing of high-level human resources.

Fourth, the organic integration of a technological innovation chain and industrial chain based on the high-tech development zone and the opportunity of its secondary startups. We need to combine the high-tech industries and the current industries to strengthen the development and integration of key industrial parks; combine the technology introduction and independent development to strengthen the integration of key industrial parks under the unified policies and standards, and to promote the integration of technological innovation chain and industrial chain. The government purchasing policy will support independent innovation and high-tech technology, establish a coordination mechanism of innovation products, and improve the position of the whole area in the GVC.

Fifth, revolving around the development demand of small and middle enterprises, the development planning of cooperation in industrial technology is jointly led by industrial management. The main purpose of the planning is: first, to promote the scientific and technological resource sharing in the industry, and to help the small and middle enterprises with raising their technological innovative ability, products, and marketing brand; second, to accelerate the construction of the YRD's industrial technology transfer network and to promote the inter-regional transfer and trade and commercialization of technological achievement in small and middle enterprises; third, to boost the specialized division of products, improve the service system, and provide better and stronger regional specialized economic service for the unique products and brand of enterprises.

Sixth, the significant support for technological innovation and commercialization based on financial service innovation. Aiming at lowering transaction cost and optimizing the allocation of financial service resources, we need to promote the service measures and concepts for technological innovation in the financial industry, starting from the innovation of financial services. Oriented by enterprise demand, it is essential to develop the new financial products and pay more attention to the financial service and product innovation related to the development of industries and projects in the region; for example, the industrial investment fund, securitization of project assets, innovative floating-rate bonds, etc. It's also necessary to develop financial derivatives and accelerate financial informatization and digitalization for the e-bank industry.

Seventh is the construction of a regional intellectual property management and protection system. The construction of a government-industry-university-research alliance system needs to emphasize the creation, sharing, and utilization of IP and to form an effective risk and interest sharing mechanism, so that the technological achievements can enter the industry chain and raise industrial competitiveness. Therefore, it requires an IP service platform in the region, an IP management and protection system of integrated administration, judiciary, and industrial self-discipline, an enterprise-led, market-oriented, and industry-university-institute-closely-combined IP generating system, and an integrated IP application and public service system guided by the government with the participation of all parts of society. The integration of administrative law enforcement and judicial resources in the YRD needs to be reinforced by constructing an information sharing platform for law enforcement and a coordination mechanism of IP protection in the YRD and forming a developmental environment for protecting established brands.

Section 5 Construction of an industrial generic technology platform in the integrated development

1. The necessity and feasibility of constructing an industrial generic technology platform

Industrial generic technology drives the technological level, industrial quality, and production efficiency of the whole industry, and generates enormous economic and social benefits. Therefore, the construction of a platform is a typical application of the government-industry-university-research alliance system. In the process of regional economic integration, the YRD can better carry out the modern industrial technological system with the support of the government-industry-university-research alliance system based on its industrial characteristics and advantages.

The YRD has the objective conditions and subjective intention of constructing an industrial generic technology platform. In terms of objective conditions: first, the close connection between industries, the relatively high level of market integration, and the good relationship and combined effects of economic technologies. Second, the distinct industrial agglomeration and large-scale industries; for example, the industry of textile and clothing or the IC chip industry. Third, the solid base of the regional economy and technology, the connected areas, and the communication and cooperation with a long history in the region. In terms of the subjective intention: the current regional cooperation in the YRD has developed from driven by market to drive by both market and government; the local governments in the region have reached a win-win consensus. Therefore, raising the industrial technology level in the YRD by constructing an industrial generic technology platform is the internal demand of regional development, and the implementation is the historical task of the national independent innovation strategy.

2. YRD industry and the distribution characteristics of its technologies

Constructing the industrial generic technology platform first requires an analysis of the industrial development level in the YRD and the distribution characteristics of its technologies. We adopted the market share and competitive advantage and compared the data in 2006 and 2016 to observe their changes.

(1) The characteristics of development level of manufacturing industry in the YRD

First, we calculate the market share of Shanghai, Jiangsu, Zhejiang, and the overall YRD manufacturing industry in the whole country and their competitive advantage index in 2006. The result is shown in Table 12.1.

(1) The industries at relatively high development levels in the YRD are manufacture of chemical fibers, manufacture of textile, apparel, footwear, and caps, and textile industry. In general, the YRD has an advantage in textile industry and some capital- and technology-intensive industries. The industries of low development level are processing of food from agricultural products, processing of petroleum, coking, processing of nuclear fuel, and manufacture of foods, beverage, and non-metallic mineral products. Generally speaking, the resource and energy processing industries in the YRD were at a disadvantage. The industries at medium development levels are manufacture of metal products, manufacture of electrical machinery and equipment, manufacture of communication equipment, computers and other electronic equipment, manufacture of chemical raw materials and chemical products, manufacture of special-purpose machinery, manufacture of transport equipment, manufacture of paper and paper products, manufacture of tobacco, manufacture of medicines, smelting and pressing of ferrous metals, smelting and pressing of non-ferrous metals, etc.

(2) In Shanghai, the industries at high development levels are manufacture of general-purpose machinery, manufacture of measuring instruments and machinery for cultural activity and office work, manufacture of communication equipment, computers, and other electronic equipment, and manufacture of transport equipment. To sum up, Shanghai has the advantage in capital-intensive industries and high-tech industries. The industries at low development levels are processing of food from agricultural products, processing of petroleum, coking, processing of nuclear fuel, smelting and processing of non-ferrous metals, and manufacture of chemical fibers. Therefore, Shanghai is at a disadvantage in terms of traditional resource processing industries.

(3) In Jiangsu, the industries at high development levels are manufacture of chemical fibers, textile industry, manufacture of textile, apparel, footwear, and caps, manufacture of communication equipment, computers, and other electronic equipment, most of which are related to the textile industry and its upstream and downstream industries. The industries at low development levels are processing of petroleum, coking, processing of nuclear fuel, food manufacturing, processing of food from agricultural products, beverage manufacturing, i.e., mainly the food and energy processing industries, which is similar to the situation in Shanghai.

Table 12.1 The index of economic level of YRD manufacturing industry (2006)

Industry	*Shanghai*		*Jiangsu*		*Zhejiang*		*YRD*	
	Market share (%)	*Competition advantage index*	*Market share (%)*	*Competition advantage index*	*Market share (%)*	*Competition advantage index*	*Market share (%)*	*Competition advantage index*
Processing of food from agricultural products	1.07	21.8	5.92	57.9	2.07	27.9	9.06	40.2
Manufacture of foods	5.64	115.3	4.30	42.1	3.26	43.9	13.21	58.6
Beverage manufacturing	3.12	63.7	6.04	59.1	5.02	67.5	14.17	62.9
Manufacture of tobacco	8.80	179.8	7.83	76.6	6.15	82.7	22.78	101.0
Textile industry	2.74	56.0	23.33	228.3	17.37	223.6	43.44	192.7
Manufacture of textile, apparel, footwear, and caps	8.81	180.0	21.78	213.1	15.45	207.8	46.03	204.2
Papermaking and paper products	2.98	60.8	11.42	111.7	8.42	113.2	22.81	101.2
Processing of petroleum, coking, processing of nuclear fuel	2.53	51.8	3.34	32.7	3.20	43.0	9.08	40.3
Raw chemical materials and chemical products	6.06	123.8	17.18	168.1	5.91	79.5	29.15	129.3
Manufacture of medical products	4.62	94.4	10.22	100.0	7.25	97.6	22.09	98.0
Manufacture of chemical fibers	2.68	54.8	36.50	357.2	23.57	317.1	62.75	278.3
Manufacture of non-metallic mineral products	3.20	65.4	7.65	74.8	4.80	64.6	15.65	69.4
Smelting and processing of ferrous metals	5.59	114.3	11.81	115.5	2.06	27.8	19.46	86.3
Smelting and processing of non-ferrous metals	2.55	52.2	9.25	90.5	5.52	74.3	17.33	76.8
Manufacture of metal products	8.52	174.1	17.65	172.7	9.97	134.1	36.14	160.3
Manufacture of general-purpose machinery	10.73	219.2	16.78	164.2	12.16	163.6	39.67	176.0
Manufacture of special-purpose machinery	6.78	138.6	12.89	126.1	7.12	95.9	26.79	118.8
Manufacture of transport equipment	10.03	204.9	8.68	85.0	6.70	90.2	25.41	112.7
Manufacture of communication equipment, computers, and other electronic equipment	10.37	211.8	19.66	192.4	3.22	43.3	33.25	147.5
Manufacture of measuring instruments and machinery for cultural activity and office work	10.49	214.4	16.12	157.8	10.82	145.6	37.44	166.1

Data source: author's calculation based on *China Industry Economy Statistical Yearbook*, Beijing, China Statistics Press, 2007.

(4) In Zhejiang, the industries at high development levels are manufacture of chemical fibers, textile industry, manufacture of textile, apparel, footwear, and caps, manufacture of general-purpose machinery, mainly the textile industry and its upstream and downstream industries, which is similar to those in Jiangsu. The industries at low development levels are smelting and processing of ferrous metals, processing of food from agricultural products, processing of petroleum, coking, processing of nuclear fuel, manufacture of communication equipment, computers, and other electronic equipment, mainly the resource and energy processing industries. It is noticeable that although the manufacturing industries in Zhejiang, China's southeast coastal area, are well-developed with relatively high technological levels, the manufacturing of communication equipment, computers, and other electronic equipment does not have the advantage in China.

Similarly, we calculate the market share of Shanghai, Jiangsu, Zhejiang and the overall YRD manufacturing industry in the whole country and their competitive advantage index in 2016. The result is shown in Table 12.2.

(1) The industries at relatively high development levels in the YRD are manufacture of chemical raw materials and chemical products, manufacture of general-purpose machinery, manufacture of transportation equipment, manufacture of computers, communication, and other electronic equipment, and manufacture of electrical machinery and equipment. The industries at low development levels are processing of food from agricultural products, manufacture of foods, manufacture of alcohol, beverages, and refined tea, manufacture of tobacco, manufacture of leather, fur, feather, and related products; footwear industry, processing of timber, manufacture of wood, bamboo, rattan, palm, and straw products, manufacture of furniture, manufacture of paper and paper products, printing and recorded media, manufacture of articles for culture, education, art, sports, and entertainment, processing of petroleum, coking, processing of nuclear fuel, and manufacture of measuring instruments. The industries at medium development levels are manufacture of textiles, manufacture of textiles, clothing, apparel industry, manufacture of medicines, manufacture of rubber and plastics, manufacture of non-metallic mineral products, smelting and processing of ferrous metals, manufacture of metal products, and manufacture of special-purpose machinery.

The similarities of the situation in 2006 and 2016 are that first, the resource-dependent industries are both weak, which is consistent with the resource endowment in the YRD: mainly the processing and manufacturing industry rather than resource-oriented processing industry. Second, capital-intensive industries in both times have medium competitive advantage. The YRD has been working on industrial transformation, so the mainstay industries like smelting and processing of ferrous metals are not the leading industry. The differences between the two times are

Table 12.2 The index of economic level of YRD manufacturing industry (2016)

Industry	*Jiangsu*		*Zhejiang*		*Shanghai*		*YRD*	
	Market share (%)	*Competition advantage index*	*Market share (%)*	*Competition advantage index*	*Market share (%)*	*Competition advantage index*	*Market share (%)*	*Competition advantage index*
Processing of food from agricultural products	7.47	57	1.60	28	0.70	21	9.77	44
Manufacture of foods	4.81	37	2.25	39	3.15	94	10.21	17
Manufacture of alcohol, beverages, and refined tea	7.33	56	2.60	45	0.83	25	10.76	14
Manufacture of tobacco	6.32	48	5.40	93	10.07	301	21.79	15
Manufacture of textiles	17.81	135	13.06	225	0.56	17	31.44	85
Manufacture of textiles, clothing; apparel industry	16.35	124	10.41	179	1.70	51	28.47	45
Manufacture of leather, fur, feather and related products; footwear industry	6.13	47	7.43	128	1.32	39	14.88	16
Processing of timber, manufacture of wood, bamboo, rattan, palm, and straw products	16.07	122	3.28	56	0.45	14	19.81	19
Manufacture of furniture	4.28	33	10.95	189	3.79	113	19.02	13
Manufacture of paper and paper products	10.41	79	9.67	167	1.96	59	22.05	25
Printing and recorded media	10.07	77	5.47	94	2.45	73	17.99	11
Manufacture of articles for culture, education, art, sports, and entertainment	12.90	98	7.54	130	3.35	100	23.78	28
Processing of petroleum, coking, processing of nuclear fuel	5.48	42	4.17	72	3.01	90	12.66	38
Manufacture of chemical raw materials and chemical products	19.10	145	7.24	125	3.89	116	30.23	185
Manufacture of medicines	14.48	110	4.54	78	2.71	81	21.72	44
Manufacture of chemical fibers	35.90	273	28.04	483	0.47	14	64.41	38
Manufacture of rubber and plastics	11.18	85	8.19	141	3.22	96	22.59	52
Manufacture of non-metallic mineral products	8.09	62	3.32	57	1.05	31	12.46	55
Smelting and processing of ferrous metals	14.81	113	2.73	47	2.80	84	20.33	98

(*Continued*)

Table 12.2 (Continued)

Industry	*Jiangsu*		*Zhejiang*		*Shanghai*		*YRD*	
	Market share (%)	*Competition advantage index*	*Market share (%)*	*Competition advantage index*	*Market share (%)*	*Competition advantage index*	*Market share (%)*	*Competition advantage index*
Smelting and processing of non-ferrous metals	7.64	58	4.24	73	0.84	25	12.73	52
Manufacture of metal products	17.15	130	7.18	124	2.64	79	26.96	73
Manufacture of general-purpose machinery	19.15	146	9.59	165	6.05	181	34.79	119
Manufacture of special-purpose machinery	19.31	147	4.63	80	3.78	113	27.71	74
Manufacture of automobiles	8.87	67	5.85	101	9.74	291	24.46	155
Manufacture of railway, ships, aerospace and other transportation equipment	19.37	147	4.43	76	4.03	121	27.84	35
Manufacture of electrical machinery and equipment	22.74	173	8.95	154	3.17	95	34.86	187
Manufacture of computers, communication and other electronic equipment	17.45	133	3.47	60	5.60	167	26.51	211
Manufacture of measuring instruments	36.09	274	7.96	137	4.28	128	48.33	36

Data source: author's calculation based on *China Industry Economy Statistical Yearbook*, Beijing, China Statistics Press, 2017.

that first, the labor-intensive industries have competitive advantages in 2006 while they become weakened in 2016, which is caused by the industrial upgrading in the YRD. Second, the competitive advantages of high-tech industries are distinct, such as manufacture of computers, communication, and other electronic equipment, and manufacture of electrical machinery and equipment, indicating the accomplishment of YRD transformation and upgrading.

(2) In Shanghai, the industries at relatively high development levels are manufacture of measuring instruments and machinery for cultural activity and office work, manufacture of computers, communication, and other electronic equipment, manufacture of transportation equipment, manufacture of tobacco, manufacture of furniture, manufacture of general-purpose machinery, and manufacture of special-purpose machinery. Generally speaking, Shanghai has the advantage in capital-intensive industries and high-tech industries. The industries at low development levels are processing of food from agricultural products, processing of petroleum, coking, processing of nuclear fuel, smelting, and processing of non-ferrous metals, and manufacture of chemical fibers, i.e., the traditional resource processing industries in general.

By comparing the situation in 2006 and 2016, it is clear that Shanghai has a more distinct advantage in high-tech industries and some capital- and technology-intensive industries, such as manufacture of transportation equipment, which is consistent with Shanghai's industrial orientation in actively implementing transformation and upgrading.

(3) In Jiangsu, the industries at relatively high development levels are manufacture of textiles and clothing, apparel industry, manufacture of chemical raw materials and chemical products, manufacture of chemical fibers, smelting and processing of ferrous metals, manufacture of general-purpose machinery, manufacture of special-purpose machinery, manufacture of railway, ships, aerospace, and other transportation equipment, manufacture of measuring instruments, manufacture of computers, communication, and other electronic equipment, and manufacture of electrical machinery and equipment. The industries at low development levels are processing of food from agricultural products, manufacture of foods, manufacture of alcohol, beverages, and refined tea, manufacture of furniture, processing of petroleum, coking, processing of nuclear fuel, which are mainly the industries of foods and energy processing.

By comparing the changes between 2006 and 2016, we notice that the competitiveness of high-tech industries has raised medium to a higher level, which indicates the achievement of the upgrading of manufacturing industry in Jiangsu, especially in the manufacture of railway, ships, aerospace, and other transportation equipment, manufacture of measuring instruments, manufacture of computers, communication, and other electronic equipment, and manufacture of electrical machinery and equipment.

(4) In Zhejiang, the industries at relatively high development levels are manufacture of chemical fibers, manufacture of textiles and clothing, apparel industry, manufacture of leather, fur, feather, and related products; footwear industry, manufacture of furniture, manufacture of paper and paper products, manufacture of articles for culture, education, art, sports, and entertainment, manufacture of chemical raw materials and chemical products, manufacture of rubber and plastics, manufacture of metal products, manufacture of general purpose machinery, manufacture of automobiles, manufacture of electrical machinery and equipment, manufacture of measuring instruments, mainly the textile industry and its upstream and downstream industries, similar to those in Jiangsu. On the other hand, high-tech industries like manufacture of computers, communication, and other electronic equipment are not competitive in Zhejiang.

Thc comparison of 2006 and 2016 shows that the advantageous industries in Zhejiang are mainly labor-intensive and resource processing industries, while the high-tech industries do not have a distinct advantage. It is possibly because of the highly specialized industrial cluster in Zhejiang, which is characterized by "professionalization and specialization" with "sundown industries and sunrise products".

(2) The characteristics of technological level of manufacturing industry in YRD

First, we calculate the market share of Shanghai, Jiangsu, Zhejiang, and the overall YRD technological level of manufacturing industry in the whole country and their competitive advantage index in 2006. The result is shown in Table 12.3.

(1) The five industries at relatively high industrial technological levels in the YRD are manufacture of metal products, manufacture of measuring instruments and machinery for cultural activity and office work, manufacture of textiles, manufacture of general-purpose machinery, and manufacture of chemical fibers, mainly the medium- and high-tech industries and the traditional textile industries in the YRD. The five industries at low industrial technological levels are processing of food from agricultural products, manufacture of foods, manufacture of paper and paper products, smelting and processing of ferrous metals, and manufacture of tobacco, which are mainly the resource-intensive industries.
(2) In Shanghai, the industries at relatively high industrial technological levels are processing of petroleum, coking, processing of nuclear fuel, manufacture of measuring instruments and machinery for cultural activity and office work, and manufacture of transport equipment. The industries at relatively low industrial technological levels are manufacture of beverages, processing of food from agricultural products, manufacture of chemical fibers, manufacture of non-metallic mineral products, which are still mainly the resource-intensive industries.
(3) In Jiangsu, the industries at relatively high industrial technological levels are manufacture of metal products, manufacture of chemical fibers,

Table 12.3 The index of technological level of YRD manufacturing industry (2006)

Industry	*Shanghai*		*Jiangsu*		*Zhejiang*		*YRD*	
	Proportion (%)	*Competition advantage index*	*Proportion (%)*	*Competition advantage index*	*Proportion (%)*	*Competition advantage index*	*Proportion (%)*	*Competition advantage index*
Manufacture of metal products	12.46	134.90	31.45	300.75	1.13	32.49	45.05	194.45
Manufacture of measuring instruments and machinery for cultural activity and office work	21.56	233.35	9.42	90.06	10.48	302.47	41.46	178.99
Manufacture of textiles	3.12	33.74	30.13	288.03	5.58	161.12	38.83	167.61
Manufacture of general-purpose machinery	12.86	139.22	17.73	169.49	7.97	230.08	38.57	166.48
Manufacture of chemical fibers	1.55	16.76	30.64	292.89	6.38	184.00	38.56	166.46
Manufacture of textile, apparel, footwear, and caps	15.08	163.15	12.15	116.16	10.28	296.58	37.50	161.89
Manufacture of chemical raw materials and chemical products	8.78	95.07	21.19	202.56	5.63	162.38	35.60	153.67
Processing of petroleum, coking, processing of nuclear fuel	32.11	347.50	0.92	8.82	0.15	4.21	33.18	143.23
Manufacture of special-purpose machinery	8.89	96.21	14.88	142.25	7.07	204.10	30.84	133.14
Manufacture of medicines	8.98	97.14	11.43	109.31	7.56	218.19	27.97	120.74
Manufacture of transport equipment	18.05	195.32	6.37	60.94	1.79	51.62	26.21	113.15
Manufacture of electrical machinery and Equipment	3.86	41.82	12.94	123.71	3.06	88.18	19.86	85.73
Manufacture of communication equipment, computers, and other electronic equipment	9.38	101.50	6.44	61.61	1.72	49.54	17.54	75.72

(*Continued*)

Table 12.3 (Continued)

Industry	*Shanghai*		*Jiangsu*		*Zhejiang*		*YRD*	
	Proportion (%)	*Competition advantage index*	*Proportion (%)*	*Competition advantage index*	*Proportion (%)*	*Competition advantage index*	*Proportion (%)*	*Competition advantage index*
Manufacture of non-metallic mineral products	2.15	23.29	10.33	98.71	4.85	140.05	17.33	74.81
Manufacture of beverages	0.08	0.92	4.19	40.04	11.18	322.51	15.45	66.69
Smelting and processing of non-ferrous metals	3.23	34.93	8.88	84.94	2.71	78.21	14.82	63.98
Manufacture of tobacco	6.98	75.49	6.15	58.78	1.57	45.18	14.69	63.41
Smelting and processing of ferrous metals	5.29	57.26	8.17	78.11	0.79	22.68	14.25	61.50
Manufacture of paper and paper products	5.42	58.67	3.39	32.43	5.40	155.94	14.22	61.37
Manufacture of foods	6.36	68.82	2.89	27.59	0.58	16.70	9.82	42.41
Processing of food from agricultural products	0.63	6.78	1.41	13.48	4.80	138.38	6.83	29.49

Data source: author's calculation based on *China Industry Economy Statistical Yearbook*, Beijing, China Statistics Press, 2007.

manufacture of textiles, manufacture of chemical raw materials and chemical products, which are mainly the medium and low technological industries and traditional industries. The industries at relatively low industrial technological levels are processing of petroleum, coking, processing of nuclear fuel, processing of food from agricultural products, manufacture of foods, and manufacture of paper and paper products.

(4) In Zhejiang, the industries at relatively high industrial technological levels are manufacture of beverages, manufacture of measuring instruments and machinery for cultural activity and office work, manufacture of textile, apparel, footwear, and caps, and manufacture of general-purpose machinery. The industries at relatively low industrial technological levels are processing of petroleum, coking, processing of nuclear fuel, manufacture of foods, smelting and processing of ferrous metals, and manufacture of metal products.

Similarly, we calculate the market share of Shanghai, Jiangsu, Zhejiang, and the overall YRD technology levels of manufacturing industry in the whole country and their competitive advantage index in 2016. The result is shown in Table 12.4.

(1) The industries at relatively high industrial technological levels in the YRD are manufacture of textiles, manufacture of clothing, apparel industry, manufacture of leather, fur, feather, and related products, footwear industry, processing of timber, manufacture of wood, bamboo, rattan, palm, and straw products, manufacture of furniture, manufacture of paper and paper products, manufacture of articles for culture, education, art, sports, and entertainment, manufacture of chemical raw materials and chemical products, manufacture of chemical fibers, manufacture of rubber and plastics, manufacture of metal products, manufacture of general-purpose machinery, manufacture of special-purpose machinery, manufacture of electrical machinery and equipment, and manufacture of measuring instruments. The industries at relatively low industrial technological levels are processing of food from agricultural products, manufacture of foods, and processing of petroleum, coking, processing of nuclear fuel, while the rest are at medium levels.

The similarities between 2006 and 2016 are: first, the R&D level of resource-dependent and labor-intensive industries remained low, which may be caused by the industrial nature; second, the traditional industries with relatively high levels of R&D have kept a high standard in both time periods. In terms of their differences, there were only 7 or 8 industries of high R&D level in 2006; while in 2016, it rose to 15–16. It means that overall the YRD has been focusing on R&D activities, evolving from a processing and manufacturing center to an industrial innovative center.

(2) In Shanghai, the industries at relatively high industrial technological levels are manufacture of tobacco, manufacture of furniture, printing and recorded media, manufacture of rubber and plastics, manufacture

Table 12.4 The index of development level of YRD manufacturing industry (2016)

Industry	*Jiangsu*		*Zhejiang*		*Shanghai*		*YRD*	
	Proportion (%)	*Competition advantage index*	*Proportion (%)*	*Competition advantage index*	*Proportion (%)*	*Competition advantage index*	*Proportion (%)*	*Competition advantage index*
Processing of food from agricultural products	9.23	63	2.98	36	1.04	24	13.25	48
Manufacture of foods	6.37	38	4.74	69	2.07	72	13.18	54
Manufacture of alcohol, beverages, and refined tea	7.56	91	4.98	56	0.58	5	13.13	65
Manufacture of tobacco	1.21	2	4.44	2	7.54	625	13.20	100
Manufacture of textiles	26.95	92	20.41	241	1.02	9	48.38	130
Manufacture of textiles, clothing; apparel industry	28.75	159	17.69	292	0.52	12	46.96	181
Manufacture of leather, fur, feather and related products; footwear industry	9.71	41	19.36	332	0.72	4	29.79	135
Processing of timber, manufacture of wood, bamboo, rattan, palm, and straw products	38.81	215	10.29	190	0.92	18	50.02	175
Manufacture of furniture	8.05	36	13.65	280	15.63	115	37.33	132
Manufacture of paper and paper products	15.25	113	10.95	140	1.38	10	27.58	106
Printing and recorded media	16.51	80	9.12	101	3.48	139	29.11	97
Manufacture of articles for culture, education, art, sports, and entertainment	23.73	101	17.69	305	2.10	23	43.51	158
Processing of petroleum, coking, processing of nuclear fuel	4.29	10	1.21	14	1.07	18	6.57	13
Manufacture of chemical raw materials and chemical products	20.96	157	8.75	128	3.47	42	33.18	129

Manufacture of medicines	15.58	105	7.25	77	5.00	76	27.83	91
Manufacture of chemical fibers	37.79	195	22.07	443	0.57	4	60.44	250
Manufacture of rubber and plastics	13.72	67	12.41	185	5.49	110	31.63	115
Manufacture of non-metallic mineral products	12.79	88	5.02	98	2.20	47	20.01	85
Smelting and processing of ferrous metals	12.86	99	2.95	71	4.83	52	20.63	82
Smelting and processing of non-ferrous metals	8.66	41	3.99	77	1.09	19	13.74	50
Manufacture of metal products	20.78	133	9.99	148	3.24	48	34.01	125
Manufacture of general-purpose machinery	21.06	134	14.09	162	8.86	162	44.01	148
Manufacture of special-purpose machinery	19.61	113	7.35	89	5.37	84	32.33	100
Manufacture of automobiles	8.14	41	6.39	64	17.17	307	31.70	91
Manufacture of railway, ships, aerospace, and other transportation equipment	11.20	111	4.41	50	7.05	137	22.67	94
Manufacture of electrical machinery and equipment	22.88	143	11.79	120	4.36	69	39.03	123
Manufacture of computers, communication, and other electronic equipment	10.41	107	6.37	43	6.32	40	23.10	74
Manufacture of measuring instruments	30.91	227	15.21	168	5.78	59	51.90	180

Data source: author's calculation based on *China Industry Economy Statistical Yearbook*, Beijing, China Statistics Press, 2017.

of general-purpose machinery, manufacture of automobiles, and manufacture of railway, ships, aerospace, and other transportation equipment. The industries at relatively low industrial technological levels are processing of food from agricultural products, manufacture of alcohol, beverages, and refined tea, manufacture of textiles, manufacture of clothing, apparel, manufacture of paper and paper products, processing of petroleum, coking, processing of nuclear fuel, manufacture of chemical fibers, smelting and processing of non-ferrous metals, and manufacture of computers, communication, and other electronic equipment. Other industries are at medium levels.

The similarities between 2006 and 2016 are: first, the R&D level of the resource-dependent and labor-intensive industries has further dropped, which may be caused by the industrial transformation and relocation; second, the industries with relatively high levels of R&D in 2006, such as manufacture of automobiles, have steadily raised their R&D level. Their differences are first, the high level of R&D in manufacture of tobacco and manufacture of furniture in 2016 was caused by the pursuit of their high added value; second, manufacture of railway, ships, aerospace and other transportation equipment becomes the industry with a relatively high R&D level because of Commercial Aircraft Corporation of China, Ltd (C919 aircraft), indicating Shanghai's effort into strategic industries; third, the R&D level of manufacture of general-purpose machinery was medium in 2016, probably because of the industrial transfer to Kunshan and Taicang.

(3) In Jiangsu, the industries at relatively high industrial technological levels are manufacture of textiles, manufacture of clothing, apparel industry, processing of timber, manufacture of wood, bamboo, rattan, palm, and straw products, manufacture of paper and paper products, manufacture of chemical raw materials and chemical products, manufacture of metal products, manufacture of chemical fibers, manufacture of railway, ships, aerospace, and other transportation equipment, manufacture of electrical machinery and equipment, manufacture of computers, communication, and other electronic equipment, and manufacture of measuring instruments. The industries at relatively low industrial technological levels are manufacture of foods, manufacture of tobacco, manufacture of furniture, processing of petroleum, coking, processing of nuclear fuel, processing of food from agricultural products, smelting and processing of non-ferrous metals, and manufacture of automobiles.

The similarities between 2006 and 2016 are first, the R&D levels of medium and low technological industries are still relatively high, indicating Jiangsu's pursuit of "professionalization and specialization" in some traditional industries, such as Bosideng and other clothing enterprises; second, some resource-intensive processing industries like manufacture of paper and paper products are still not the regional developmental direction because of the regional specialization. Their difference is that there are 13–15 industries with high R&D levels in 2016, much higher than in 2006, indicating an innovation-driven path in Jiangsu. However, the R&D level of manufacture of automobiles has remained relatively low, which is probably a significant defect of Jiangsu industrial development; otherwise, its economic aggregate would reach a higher level.

(4) In Zhejiang, the industries at relatively high industrial technological levels are manufacture of textiles, manufacture of clothing, apparel industry, manufacture of leather, fur, feather, and related products, footwear industry, processing of timber, manufacture of wood, bamboo, rattan, palm, and straw products, manufacture of furniture, manufacture of paper and paper products, manufacture of articles for culture, education, art, sports, and entertainment, manufacture of chemical raw materials and chemical products, manufacture of chemical fibers, manufacture of rubber and plastics, manufacture of metal products, manufacture of general-purpose machinery, manufacture of electrical machinery and equipment, manufacture of measuring instruments. The industries at relatively low industrial technological levels are processing of food from agricultural products, manufacture of tobacco, processing of petroleum, coking, processing of nuclear fuel, manufacture of computers, communication, and other electronic equipment, and manufacture of railway, ships, aerospace, and other transportation equipment.

The similarity between 2006 and 2016 is that the R&D level of medium and low technological industries and traditional industries like textile are stills relatively high, which means that Zhejiang "pursued professionalization and specialization" in some traditional industries; for example, the Shaoxing textile industrial technology has always kept a high level nationwide. Their difference is that there are 13–14 industries with high R&D level in 2016, much higher than in 2006 (5 industries), indicating an innovation-driven path in Zhejiang. However, the R&D level of manufacture of computers, communication, and other electronic equipment, and manufacture of railway, ships, aerospace, and other transportation equipment are relatively low, which might be a deficiency of Zhejiang's industrial development.

(3) The matching characteristics of development level and technological level of the YRD's manufacturing industry

Finally, based on this analysis (Table 12.1 to Table 12.4), we divide the manufacturing industries into four types: "strong economy and technology", "strong economy and weak technology", "weak economy and strong technology", and "weak economy and technology".

(1) In terms of the whole YRD, manufacture of chemical raw materials and chemical products, manufacture of chemical fibers, manufacture of general-purpose machinery, and manufacture of measuring instruments are the "strong economy and technology" type; processing of food from agricultural products, manufacture of foods and manufacture of

beverages are typical "weak economy and technology" type; processing of petroleum, coking, processing of nuclear fuel is the "strong economy and weak technology" type; and smelting and processing of ferrous metals and manufacture of paper and paper products are "weak economy and strong technology" type.

(2) In Shanghai, manufacture of measuring instruments and machinery for office work, manufacture of general-purpose machinery, manufacture of transport equipment, and manufacture of tobacco are the "strong economy and technology" type; manufacture of textiles, manufacture of chemical fibers, manufacture of non-metallic mineral products, processing of food from agricultural products, manufacture of paper and paper products and smelting and processing of non-ferrous metals are "weak economy and technology" type; manufacture of electrical machinery and equipment, manufacture of computers, communication, and other electronic equipment are the "weak economy and strong technology" type.

(3) In Jiangsu, manufacture of textile, apparel, footwear, and caps, manufacture of chemical fibers, manufacture of chemical raw materials and chemical products, manufacture of computers, communication, and other electronic equipment are the "strong economy and technology" type; processing of food from agricultural products, manufacture of foods, manufacture of beverages, manufacture of tobacco, manufacture of furniture, processing of petroleum, coking, processing of nuclear fuel, smelting and processing of non-ferrous metals, and manufacture of transport equipment are the "weak economy and technology" type; manufacture of textiles and manufacture of metal products are the "strong economy and weak technology" type; manufacture of electrical machinery and equipment, manufacture of medicines, and manufacture of paper and paper products are the "weak economy and strong technology" type.

(4) In Zhejiang, manufacture of chemical fibers, manufacture of textile, apparel, footwear, and caps, manufacture of leather, fur, feather, and related products, footwear industry, manufacture of articles for culture, education, art, sports, and entertainment, manufacture of metal products, and manufacture of general-purpose machinery are the "strong economy and technology" type; processing of petroleum, coking, processing of nuclear fuel, manufacture of computers, communication, and other electronic equipment, smelting and processing of ferrous metals, manufacture of railway, ships, aerospace, and other transportation equipment, and manufacture of foods are the "weak economy and technology" type; manufacture of beverages, manufacture of medicines, manufacture of special-purpose machinery are the "strong economy and weak technology" type; and manufacture of chemical fibers is the "weak economy and strong technology" type.

This analysis reveals that the industries of "strong economy and technology" in YRD are mainly medium- and low-technological ones, and some high-technological ones (for example, manufacture of measuring instruments); resource-dependent industries are the "weak economy and technology" type; and the technology-intensive industries and some high-technological industries present the characteristics of the "strong economy and weak technology".

(4) The basic ideas of choosing the YRD industrial generic technology platform

Different technological support and leading methods should be provided for different types of advantageous industries.

The industrial development strategy for the "strong economy and technology" type: double promotion. This type of industry is characterized by the leading level of both scientific and technological strength and economic development in the industrial system and the intensification. Therefore, the corresponding strategy should be focused on the function of technological innovation and systematically integrated innovation, to further expand the market share and scientific innovation at the same time and foster large leading enterprises with international competitiveness.

The industrial development strategy for the "strong economy and weak technology" type: enterprise as driving force. This type of industry is characterized by the leading industrial economic effectiveness in the industrial system and the weak scientific and technological ability. Therefore, the corresponding strategy should integrate innovation resource to raise the technological level, strengthen the "government-industry-university-institute" cooperation, and promote the development of industrial technologies from the perspective of market demand and basic research.

The industrial development strategy for the "weak economy and strong technology" type: lead by science and technology. This type of industry is characterized by the leading industrial science and technology ability in the industrial system and relatively weak economic effectiveness. Therefore, the corresponding strategy should change the mentality of technological innovation and input, focus on the application of scientific and technological achievements, and strengthen the construction of industrialization and the commercialization of scientific and technological outcomes.

The industrial development strategy for the "weak economy and technology" type: industrial integration and transformation. This type of industry is characterized by the weak industrial economic level and scientific and technological ability. Therefore, the corresponding strategy should expand the technological input and activities, focus the limited resources on key fields, and promote industrial development by industrial transition and cooperation with areas of stronger industries.

Section 6 Policy proposals for the construction of an industrial generic technology platform

1. The mechanism of organization and coordination

The YRD's industrial generic technology platform is not only a problem of promoting the industrial technology in an administrative area, but also the joint improvement of the advantageous industries in the two provinces and one city. Therefore, it requires the strengthening of an action plan for technological cooperation in the YRD to coordinate and solve the major problems in constructing the industrial generic technology platform; for example, to conduct research on the promoting mechanism of generic technologies, perfect the management mechanism of joint projects in the YRD, collaborate on research of scientific and technological projects, share scientific and technological resources, and cooperate in capital, etc.

2. The safeguard mechanism of funding

Capital is inevitable for the construction of the industrial generic technology platform in the YRD. Therefore, it is necessary to set up a "joint fund for the construction of YRD industrial generic technology platform" funded by the governments of the two provinces and one city. With the governmental fund as a foundation, enterprises are encouraged to raise extensive social funds with their own money or the enterprise unions.

3. The balance mechanism of regional interests

The construction of YRD industrial generic technology platform needs to reach a relatively balanced interest distribution through the coordination between the two provinces and one city, in terms of the involved industries, cities setting up relevant organizations, etc. It is suggested that the industrial generic technology platforms should be set up for the industries of electronic information, biological medicine, and textile in Suzhou, Shanghai, and Shaoxing respectively, so the cities' industrial foundation can be utilized and the inter-regional profit can be balanced.

4. Mechanism of sharing property rights

The new technologies and intellectual properties developed by the industrial generic technology platform should be spread to similar enterprises in YRD for free or at lower cost, and to enterprises outside YRD for payment. On the one hand, it promotes property sharing in the region; on the other hand, it is conducive to the sustainable development of industrial generic technology outside the region.

5. Optimization mechanism of innovation environment

In order to improve the construction of industrial generic technology platforms, the science-and-technology enterprise, product, and organization accredited by the Science and Technology Section of the two provinces and one city should be granted the same preferential policies; the governments should jointly accredit the YRD's independent innovative products, formulate an innovative product catalog, promote their preference in the YRD's government procurement and major project bidding, and improve the steady development of the YRD's industrial generic technology platform.

6. Implementing principle

In practice, there are three fundamental principles for accelerating the construction of the YRD industrial generic technology platform, especially by the government-industry-university-research alliance system.

Principle one: to guide the implementation of "capital, talent and projects". With the guidance of government, market demand as orientation, enterprises as the subject of technological innovative activities, and universities as the support for the technological exploration, the policies regarding capital, talent, and projects should be implemented to give full play to the national demand and market driving power, the initiative of enterprises, and the advantages of university, i.e., covering extensive fields, active innovative thoughts, advanced research methods, etc.

Principle two: to construct three platforms for technological integration, implementation, and commercialization respectively. Only with the capital, talent, and project in the operating platform between enterprise and university can enterprises give full play to their capabilities and advantages of fundraising, supporting facilities and market driving force, and promote the mobility of high-end research staff between universities and enterprises, so they can achieve a win-win situation, gradually establish a technological innovation system of "production generation, research generation and exploration generation", and fully raise the core competitiveness of enterprises.

Principle three: to guarantee the combination of science and technology and demand, technology and capital, and personnel and project. The purpose of ensuring capital, talent, and projects in the three platforms of enterprise and university is to optimize the allocation of technology, projects, capital, and personnel by the advanced operating mechanism to form an effective technological industrialization chain among the government, enterprise, university, institution, financing organizations, agency, and other entities, and to make sure they all receive their corresponding payback. The close combinations of science and technology and demand, technology, and capital, and personnel and project are the most fundamental environment for the technological innovation and commercialization by government-industry-university-research alliance system.

Notes

1 The examples here are based on the relevant content from *Industrial Organization–Theory and Applications* by Oz Shy. See Shy: Industrial Organization–Theory and Applications. Beijing: Tsinghua University Press, pp. 157–159, 2005.

2 This hypothesis would affect the relevant conclusion of the model because if the research of one manufacturer has the effect of increasing return to scale, then the enterprise will always benefit from operating a laboratory.

3 See www.ahinfo.gov.cn/download/08110809.doc.

References

J.F. Brodley. Joint Ventures and Antitrust Policy. Harvard Law Review, 1982 (5).

European Commission (EC). Fourteenth Report on Competition Policy. Brussels-Luxembourg: EC, 1985.

Liu Zhibiao. Industrial Economics, 2nd edition. Beijing: Higher Education Press, 2009.

13 Analysis of social network in the economic integration in the Yangtze River Delta region

Yunhui Hou, Zhibiao Liu, and Zhonggang Yue

Section 1 Introduction

Regional economic integration is a significant economic condition for the formation of a city cluster (Xu Kangning, 2005). The YRD needs to form an integrated development pattern in order to become an internationally competitive world-class city cluster. Although it is the most economically developed region in China, the YRD still has issues with instability, mismatched administration, overlapping construction, excessive competition, etc. The separated administrative system and friction (Liu Zhibiao, 2004) is detrimental to unified planning and the initiative in the region (Zhang Haohan, 2007), and will decelerate the optimization and upgrading of industrial structures. Therefore, it is vital to promote the research on the YRD regional economic integration immediately.

There have been many scholars who have analyzed the basis, motivation, current situation, problems, influencing factors, and further development measures of the YRD economic integration from the perspective of industry, innovation, institution, education, financing, culture, transportation, commerce, etc. (Zhang Haohan, 2007; Chen Jianjun, 2004; Chen Jianjun et al., 2007; Gu Chaolin et al., 2007). Some research analyzed the basic situation and characteristics of the YRD economic integration based on the data of a survey on 532 enterprises in Ningbo (Zhou Guohong and Lou Xijin, 2007), but without a detailed study of the transition of the YRD economic structure, the economic relations between each city in the region, or their positions in the YRD economy. Answering these questions is significant for the development of YRD economic integration, growth of the Chinese economy, and international competitiveness in the process of globalization. The explicit understanding of the economic relations between each city can provide us with a good grasp of the regional integration, and the accurate judgment and measurement of the relations are the vital basis of formulating the city and regional development strategies (Wang Xin et al., 2006). Therefore, based on the gravity model, this chapter adopts a rectified model to calculate the economic relations between 16 key cities in the YRD city cluster; then, based on the perspective of social network analysis, the economic structure of the 16 cities in seven time points (1998, 2001, 2004, 2007, 2010, 2013, and 2017) are thoroughly analyzed through Ucinet to reach a clear understanding of the developmental process of

DOI: 10.4324/9781003455943-13

YRD economic integration and provide a new analytical perspective and policy basis for the location and construction of a world-class city cluster in the YRD.

Section 2 Building the analytical model of regional economic integration

1. Model description

(1) Gravity model

According to the theory of economic gravity, the economic connections between cities are similar to gravitation: cities in a certain range have mutual effects on each other. Since the 1990s, Chinese scholars have extensively adopted the gravity model of spatial interaction to quantitatively analyze regional economic relations. The typical formula is (Chen Yanguang and Liu Jisheng, 2002):

$$P_{ij} = \frac{\sqrt{P_i \times V_i} \times \sqrt{P_j \times V_j}}{D_{ij}^2} \tag{13.1}$$

In the formula, P_i and P_j are the population indexes of two cities; V_i and V_j are economic indexes, usually GDP (excluding the county-level city under their administration) or total industrial output value; and D_{ij} is the distance between them.

Cities, different from objects in general sense, have their own economic significance and special properties which need to be considered when describing the interactions between them. Since the intercity economic connection can be unidirectional (Wang Xin et al., 2006), the two cities make different contributions to the gravitation between them, which is why the parameter *k* has been introduced into the gravity model. In terms of the calculation of parameter *k*, some researchers used the combined ratio of transportation; some chose the geometric mean of population, GDP, and transportation ratio; and some concluded that *k* should be the characterization of economic structure through an empirical test (Wang Xin et al., 2006). Since the city transportation data in the statistical yearbook is not sorted by cities, the commute data is not enough to accurately estimate the contribution of different cities. Therefore, based on an empirical study by Wang Xin et al. (2006), this chapter regards *k* as a characterization of economic structure. Considering the availability and comparability of data,[1] and the reflection of urban GDP data on the differences of economic structure, we use the proportion of the GDP of one city to the total GDP of two cities to correct the model. In addition, the major transportation in the YRD is the highway, followed by the railway, while aviation and waterways are seldom employed. Therefore, this chapter takes the highways with the heaviest volume of traffic between two cities as their distance in 1998–2007. With the improving highway network, the distance in 2010–2017 can be measured by the time distance to better represent the inter-city accessibility and convenience. The rectified gravity model is:

$$R_{ij} = k_{ij}\frac{\sqrt{P_i \times G_i} \times \sqrt{P_j \times G_j}}{D_{ij}^2}, \left(k_{ij} = \frac{G_i}{G_i + G_j}\right) \tag{13.2}$$

In the formula, R_{ij} is the economic relation of city i to city j; P_i and P_j are population: no-agricultural population in 1998–2017, and permanent urban residents in 2010–2017 since the agricultural residence was canceled in 2016; G_i and G_j are GDP of the two cities; D_{ij} is the distance between them; and k_{ij} is the contribution rate of city i to R_{ij}.

(2) Analysis of social network

Analysis of a social network is a significant research method in new economic sociology. It values the interaction between members, attempts to describe it by graph theory tools and algebraic models, and explores the influence of the relations on each member and the whole. The core of social network analysis lies in the research on social phenomena and structure from the perspective of "relation". The social structure can be behavioral structure, political structure, and economic structure. Any social unit or entity can be regarded as a member in the network.[2] Relations are the basis of the theory of network analysis, the types of which vary among members.[3]

Since French geographer Gottmann first described the series of cities from Boston to Washington in the US as "megalopolis", scholars have formed a unified definition, though different descriptions, of city cluster; i.e., a city cluster is formed by multiple cities whose connections among each other are getting closer and jointly affect the regional development. It is not a simply a geographical gathering: in the whole region, cities of different scales form a value-creating-oriented, vertical and horizontal, formal and informal, open and stable network to obtain capital, technologies, and products with enterprises and organizations in other cities; for example, suppliers, other relevant enterprises, universities, scientific research institutions, governmental financing institutions and intermediaries. By promoting the development of each city, these networked relations drive the overall development of the regional economy. Therefore, to analyze a region requires not only the study of its internal cities, but also the complex connections between them. However, relation data does not meet the "hypothesis of independent variable" in a conventional statistical sense, so it cannot be analyzed through the usual methods of multivariate statistics; but analysis of social networks can make up the deficiency and provide a more accurate judgment and measurement, more intuitive understanding of intercity relations, and a clearer vision of the development process of YRD economic integration. Therefore, based on the perspective of social network analysis, this chapter adopts the Ucinet software and corrected gravity model [Formula (13.2)] to calculate the economic relation value and analyze the density, centrality and centralization, cohesive subgroup, structural similarity, and core-periphery structure of the economic relational network in the YRD in order to reach a comprehensive understanding of the developmental process of economic integration in the YRD.

A. Density

Density, one of the most common measurements in social network analysis, plays a key role. Specifically, it means the closeness between each member in the network; the precise value is the ratio of actual number of relations in the network to the theoretical number (complete graph). The more connections between members, the higher the density of the network.

B. Centrality and centralization

"Centrality" is the key to social network analysis. The member's power in the social network was one of the earliest contents discussed by analysts, which quantitatively defines power from the perspective of relation and measures it through centrality and centralization. Centrality measures the degree of how close a member is to the center of network, in which the degree of centrality is most often used to calculate the directly connected points: a higher value means a more centered position. Centralization measures the degree of centralization of the network, the general integration or consistency of the network. For example, in a star network where all the members center on one member without connection to each other, the centralization is the highest.

C. Cohesive subgroup

Social structure is the existing or potential relational model between social members, which mainly studies the number of cohesive subgroups in a network and their relations. Although there is not yet an explicit definition of a cohesive subgroup, it is generally regarded as the subset of social members with relatively strong, direct, close, frequent, and active relations. If there are multiple cohesive subgroups in the network that are not sufficiently connected, then the development of the whole network would be obstructed.

D. Structural similarity

Structural similarity is the generalized analysis of social behavior and social structure to better grasp the relational mode between members and reach a conclusion that can be widely applied. In a network relation, if the mutual replacement of one member by another does not change the network structure, then the two members are structurally similar. Complete structural similarity is rare, apart from the self-comparison. The analysis of structural similarity is different from in a cohesive subgroup: the former aims at dividing the similar members in mutually exclusive groups so that the members in each group have similar structure, while the latter focuses on finding the subgroups in the whole network.

E. Core-periphery structure

The analysis paradigm of core-periphery structure has become a relatively fixed model in regional economics. With the development of regional economies and increasingly complex inter-city relations, the core, periphery, and semi-periphery keep changing, which affects regional economic development. Therefore, it is necessary to clarify the core-periphery structure in the YRD city cluster and the economic position of core cities in the cluster.

2. Territorial scope of the research and data source

The YRD city cluster in this research includes 16 central cities: Shanghai, Nanjing, Hangzhou, Ningbo, Suzhou, Wuxi, Changzhou, Zhenjiang, Yangzhou, Taizhou, Nantong, Huzhou, Jiaxing, Shaoxing, Zhoushan, and Taizhou. Since the major economic connections between central cities can basically reflect the main economic relations in the region, this chapter studies the economic connections among these 16 cities in the YRD to clarify the spatial pattern of economic connection of YRD cities.

Considering the accessibility and calculation of trends and data of YRD inter-city economic connections, this chapter selects the statistics of 1998, 2001, 2004, 2007, 2010, 2013, and 2017, seven evenly distributed time points in 10 years, from the China Economic Information Statistical Database,[4] to reflect the changes of economic structure of YRD city cluster. Based on Formula (13.2), the economic relation values of the 16 central cities in the YRD are calculated (see Attached Table 13.1, 13.2, 13.3, and 13.4 for more information[5]). The data is analyzed by Ucinet to better describe the economic structure in the YRD and build the basis for the development of YRD economic integration.

Section 3 Social network analysis of the process of economic integration in the Yangtze River Delta region

The density, centrality and centralization, cohesive subgroup, structural similarity, and core-periphery structure of data in Tables 13.1, 13.2, 13.3, and 13.4 are analyzed by the software Ucinet.

1. The analysis of network density

Since the measurement of density is relatively complicated without a consensus among scholars, this chapter supposes that the weighted total number of theoretically possible connections is 15 times of the maximum economic relation,[6] and that the actual weight of connection is the total of all the weighted connections. The result is shown in Table 13.1.

Higher density value means more inter-city channels of economic relation and cooperation. The rising trend of network density among 16 central cities in the

Table 13.1 The density of economic relation network of YRD city cluster

Time	*1998*	*2001*	*2004*	*2007*	*2010*	*2013*	*2017*
Density	0.6048	0.6581	0.7574	0.7717	0.5333	0.6333	0.6958

YRD city cluster indicates an increasingly close and frequent interaction. In the first ten years of the whole time span, the density rose fastest during 2001–2004, while in the second decade, the highest rising speed of density fell in 2010–2013. It means the central cities in the region have a stronger influence on the whole region through the advantages of the city cluster and its scale effect. The intercity economic cooperation enhances the economic strength in the YRD, optimizes the urban functions, and helps promote the development of economic integration.

2. The analysis on network centrality and centralization

Each point in the figure has two centralities: the indegree means the degree of "entering", i.e., how much a city is economically influenced by other cities; outdegree means the degree of "going out", i.e., how much a city influences the economy of other cities. The results are shown in Tables 13.8 and 13.9, the comparison and analysis of which lead to the following conclusions:

(1) Shanghai shows the highest outdegree, indicating its position of the YRD's economic core. The YRD's economic development is driven by central cities. With the growing economy, finance, trade, and other aspects, Shanghai started to gradually spread knowledge and technologies and transfer industries to its peripheries, providing intellectual support for the enterprises in Jiangsu and Zhejiang and a huge market for the large number of intellectual products produced in Shanghai and the whole YRD.

(2) The outdegree of Wuxi, Suzhou, Hangzhou, and Nanjing are after Shanghai. These cities can also exert a distinct influence on the economy of other cities. Nanjing has a relatively slow growth rate and decreasing importance in economic development, probably because of the long distance and weak influence from Shanghai and the vicious competition of attracting foreign investment. The decreasing total industrial output value of foreign invested enterprises and the less attractive development path for investors chosen by the Nanjing government led to a distinctively slower development than south Jiangsu (Zhang Haohan, 2007). The backward economic aggregate and development level would naturally weaken its influence on peripheries. In comparison, Suzhou and Wuxi, although in Jiangsu province, are historically closer to Shanghai with a similar language and lifestyle, so their economies are highly driven by Shanghai, presenting a rapid economic development in recent years.

(3) The indegree of Wuxi, Suzhou, Hangzhou, and Changzhou are relatively high. These cities are quite active in economic development: they actively build relationships with other cities in the YRD region and effectively integrate and utilize the external resources. In addition, except for Hangzhou in 1998–2007 with similar indegree and outdegree, the indegree of Wuxi, Suzhou, Hangzhou, and Changzhou are distinctly higher than their outdegree, meaning that their economies receive more influence from other cities than their influence on peripheral cities.

Table 13.2 The statistic table of the centralization of economic relation network in YRD city cluster

Time	*1998*	*2001*	*2004*	*2007*	*2010*	*2013*	*2017*
Outdegree centralization	31.016%	31.398%	30.506%	29.908%	23.525%	22.582%	23.210%
Indegree centralization	8.159%	7.312%	8.474%	9.266%	8.818%	8.360%	8.737%

The comparison of the standard indegree centralization and outdegree centralization of the whole network[7](see Table 13.2) indicates that outdegree centralization is relatively higher; i.e., the intercity economic relations in YRD city cluster are imbalanced, which is consistent with the conclusion of Wu Zhiqiang et al. (2008) by analyzing the situation of YRD development space with indicator of gravity center. The specific data is shown here:

(1) Outdegree centralization decreased slowly. The potential reasons might be that the economic relations concentrate on a few cities, conducting exchange and cooperation in terms of talent, resource, capital, and information. However, with the deepening interaction activities, and in consideration of polity, trade cost, business cost, reputation, confidence, etc., the scope of intercity economic activity has gradually narrowed.

(2) Indegree centralization increased gradually. A possible reason is that medium and small cities have launched some preferential policies or given full play to their resources to attract external investment and actively develop their local economy. The enterprises in the developed cities in the YRD city cluster are reluctant to invest in less developed cities in consideration of economic efficiency. Therefore, local governments have attempted to change the situation by introducing some preferential policies to compete for projects, resources, and talents, ignoring the risk of pollution, exhaustion, and "impoverished" growth.

The technology, talent, finance, commerce, logistics, etc. in the YRD have different levels objectively, but without a reasonable work division accordingly. In the future development process of economic integration, the first developed central cities should drive the economic development of its peripheral cities, which can help the central city with its industrial upgrading and provide peripheral cities with talent, capital, technology, information, and other high-level production factors through the spillover effect, achieving a win-win situation. If cities only "mind their own business", set up invisible trade barriers and administrative barriers, block information, intensify disordered and vicious competition, and transfer the external diseconomies and negative effects to other regions, then the YRD economic integrated development would be caught in a vicious cycle.

3. The analysis of cohesive subgroup

The cohesive subgroup in the YRD city cluster is not the alliance between cities, but the relatively strong, direct, close, frequent, and active economic relation. This chapter analyzes the cluster through CONCOR (convergent correlations) of Ucinet (see Table 13.3 for the result).

In 1998–2007, with the change in the economic relations among the 16 central cities in the YRD, the members of the cohesive subgroup also varied (except for 2001 and 2004); while since 2010, the members stopped changing due to stabilized economic relations. The analysis result of cohesive subgroups in 2007 is similar to the structural characteristics of the YRD's spatial organization in the research of Wu Zhiqiang et al. (2008). The density of cohesive subgroup increased in 1998–2007 and 2010–2017 (see Table 13.4), indicating the increasingly close and frequent intercity economic relations.

The comparison of the density within and between cohesive subgroups revealed that in 1998, the cohesive subgroup of Shanghai, Nantong, Wuxi, Jiaxing, and Suzhou has a significant economic influence on that of Hangzhou, Zhoushan, Taizhou (Zhejiang), Huzhou, Shaoxing, and Ningbo; while Nanjing has a significant

Table 13.3 The analysis result of cohesive subgroups of economic relation network in YRD city cluster

1998	1	Shanghai, Nantong, Wuxi, Jiaxing, Suzhou	3	Nanjing
	2	Hangzhou, Zhoushan, Taizhou (Zhejiang), Huzhou, Shaoxing, Ningbo	4	Taizhou (Jiangsu), Changzhou, Yangzhou, Zhenjiang
2001	1	Shanghai, Wuxi, Suzhou	3	Zhenjiang, Yangzhou, Nanjing
	2	Hangzhou, Jiaxing, Nantong, Zhoushan, Taizhou (Zhejiang), Huzhou, Shaoxing, Ningbo	4	Taizhou (Jiangsu), Changzhou
2004	1	Shanghai, Wuxi, Suzhou	3	Zhenjiang, Yangzhou, Nanjing
	2	Hangzhou, Jiaxing, Nantong, Zhoushan, Taizhou (Zhejiang), Huzhou, Shaoxing, Ningbo	4	Taizhou (Jiangsu), Changzhou
2007	1	Shanghai, Changzhou, Wuxi, Suzhou	3	Nantong, Hangzhou, Huzhou, Jiaxing, Shaoxing
	2	Nanjing, Zhenjiang, Yangzhou, Taizhou (Jiangsu)	4	Ningbo, Zhoushan, Taizhou (Zhejiang)
2010	1	Shanghai, Wuxi, Suzhou	3	Changzhou, Nanjing
	2	Hangzhou, Jiaxing, Nantong, Zhoushan, Taizhou (Zhejiang), Huzhou, Shaoxing, Ningbo	4	Taizhou (Jiangsu), Yangzhou, Zhenjiang
2013	1	Shanghai, Wuxi, Suzhou	3	Changzhou, Nanjing
	2	Hangzhou, Jiaxing, Nantong, Zhoushan, Taizhou (Zhejiang), Huzhou, Shaoxing, Ningbo	4	Taizhou (Jiangsu), Yangzhou, Zhenjiang
2017	1	Shanghai, Wuxi, Suzhou	3	Changzhou, Nanjing
	2	Hangzhou, Jiaxing, Nantong, Zhoushan, Taizhou (Zhejiang), Huzhou, Shaoxing, Ningbo	4	Taizhou (Jiangsu), Yangzhou, Zhenjiang

Table 13.4 The density of cohesive subgroups in economic relation network of YRD city cluster

1998	1	2	3	4	2001	1	2	3	4
1	2.619	0.937	0.636	0.745	1	15.879	3.305	2.631	3.844
2	0.131	0.339	0.020	0.033	2	0.659	0.540	0.158	0.165
3	1.466	0.387	–	2.596	3	0.874	0.191	3.225	1.230
4	0.237	0.059	0.141	0.458	4	0.651	0.076	0.569	0.268
2004	1	2	3	4	2007	1	2	3	4
1	33.130	6.345	5.541	9.645	1	43.309	8.104	12.838	2.430
2	1.355	1.179	0.351	0.385	2	3.815	8.376	0.899	0.268
3	2.101	0.451	7.975	3.030	3	3.139	0.764	3.741	1.181
4	3.484	0.313	2.219	0.775	4	0.614	0.211	1.022	1.423
2010	1	2	3	4	2013	1	2	3	4
1	18.167	4.75	6.167	2.556	1	28	6.833	9.333	4.111
2	1.167	0.982	0.438	0.208	2	1.625	1.429	0.75	0.417
3	3	0.875	4	4.833	3	5.333	1.25	6.5	7.833
4	0.333	0.083	1	2.167	4	0.778	0.167	1.667	3.333
2017	1	2	3	4					
1	36.333	9.375	12.333	5.667					
2	2.708	2.179	1.125	0.708					
3	8.667	2.125	10	12					
4	1.111	0.417	2.5	5					

economic influence on the cohesive subgroup of Taizhou (Jiangsu), Changzhou, Yangzhou, and Zhenjiang. In 2001, the cohesive subgroup of Shanghai, Wuxi, and Suzhou has a significant economic influence on that of Hangzhou, Jiaxing, Nantong, Zhoushan, Taizhou (Zhejiang), Huzhou, Shaoxing, and Ningbo, and that of Taizhou (Jiangsu) and Changzhou, which became more distinct in 2004. In 2007, the cohesive subgroup of Shanghai, Changzhou, Wuxi, and Suzhou has a significant economic influence on that of Nantong, Hangzhou, Huzhou, Jiaxing, and Shaoxing, and that of Ningbo, Zhoushan, and Taizhou (Zhejiang). In 2010, the cohesive subgroup of Shanghai, Wuxi, and Suzhou has a significant economic influence on that of Changzhou and Nanjing, which became more distinct in 2013 and 2017; in 2013, the cohesive subgroup of Changzhou and Nanjing has a significant economic influence on that of Taizhou (Jiangsu), Yangzhou, and Zhenjiang. In 2017, the cohesive subgroup of Changzhou and Nanjing has a significant economic influence on that of Shanghai, Wuxi, and Suzhou.

The comparison of cohesive subgroups revealed that both Nanjing and Shanghai had a significant economic influence on their peripheral cities in 1998, but Shanghai's influence gets stronger while Nanjing's gets weaker, which is consistent with the analysis of centrality. In addition, some central cities in Jiangsu province broke the administrative barrier and form a cohesive subgroup with Shanghai and some cities in Zhejiang province; while some cities form cohesive subgroups without the provincial capital Nanjing, which indicates a low degree of association and integration and loose intercity relations within Nanjing (Zhao Feng and Jiang Debo, 2008). An image matrix can clearly present the relations between each cohesive subgroup[8] (see Table 13.5).

Table 13.5 The image matrix of cohesive subgroups of economic relation network in YRD city cluster

1998	1	2	3	4	2001	1	2	3	4
1	1	1	1	1	1	1	1	1	1
2	0	0	0	0	2	1	0	0	0
3	1	0	–	1	3	1	0	1	1
4	0	0	0	0	4	0	0	0	0
2004	1	2	3	4	2007	1	2	3	4
1	1	1	1	1	1	1	1	1	1
2	1	1	0	0	2	1	1	1	0
3	1	0	1	1	3	1	0	1	1
4	1	0	1	1	4	0	0	1	1
2010	1	2	3	4	2013	1	2	3	4
1	1	1	1	1	1	1	1	1	1
2	1	1	0	0	2	1	1	1	0
3	1	1	1	1	3	1	1	1	1
4	0	0	1	1	4	1	0	1	1
2017	1	2	3	4					
1	1	1	1	1					
2	1	1	1	1					
3	1	1	1	1					
4	1	0	1	1					

In 1998, the internal economic relations of all the cohesive subgroups, except for the first one, were not close, presenting a lower density than the whole network. The first cohesive subgroup had an economic influence on the other three; so did the third on the fourth, mainly because of Shanghai and Nanjing. In 2001, the internal economic relations of all the cohesive subgroups, except for the first and third one, were not close. The first, second, and third cohesive subgroup had economic influences on each other, so did the third on the fourth. In 2004, the density of all the cohesive subgroups was higher than the overall network density, indicating increasingly close and frequent intercity economic relations. All the cohesive subgroups had economic influences on each other, except for the second on the third and fourth. In 2007, all the cohesive subgroups had economic influence on each other, except for the second and fourth on each other, the third on the second, and the fourth on the first. In 2010, the first and the third cohesive subgroups had economic relations with all the other subgroups. All the cohesive subgroups had economic influences on each other, except for the second and fourth on each other, the second on the third, and the fourth on the first. In 2013, all the cohesive subgroups had economic influences on each other, except for the second and the fourth. In 2017, all the cohesive subgroups had economic influences on each other, except for the fourth on the second.

The gradually enhanced economic relations between each cohesive subgroups are conducive to the resolve of conflicts and to the promotion of YRD economic integration.

(1) The economic influence of Shanghai on Suzhou-Wuxi-Changzhou region is higher than that of Nanjing. The development of the region depends more on

Shanghai, but its development planning belongs to Jiangsu province, which means the neglect of Shanghai's influence on Suzhou-Wuxi-Changzhou region in the future planning would hinder the economic integration of the region and even the whole of south Jiangsu (Zhang Haohan, 2007), and affect Jiangsu's integration with the process of competition and structural integration in the YRD (Chen Jianjun and Yao Xianguo, 2003).

(2) Compared to Shanghai, the economic development of Nanjing is relatively weak, whose economic influence covers Zhenjiang, Yangzhou, and Taizhou (Jiangsu). Although the distance between Nanjing and Shanghai is longer than that between Suzhou-Wuxi-Changzhou region and Shanghai, the development of Nanjing still cannot break away from the influence of Shanghai. Nanjing needs to balance its economic relations with Shanghai, Zhenjiang-Yangzhou-Taizhou (Jiangsu) region, and Suzhou-Wuxi-Changzhou region by actively achieving urban transformation and developing a modern service industry. In the meantime, it should expand the scope and influence of the YRD by giving full play to its advantageous peripheral position in the YRD and help with the YRD's industrial upgrading and relocating in the central and western regions (Zhang Haohan, 2007).

(3) Hangzhou Bay, centered on Hangzhou, adjoins Shanghai with well-developed transportation, so since the complementary effect of service industry supply in Shanghai and Zhejiang is stronger than the substitution effect of demand (Chen Dazhong, 2009), it can keep developing low-tech and labor-intensive industries and following the industrial restructuring in Shanghai in the meantime, and develop the secondary industry of higher levels of technology (Chen Jianjun and Yao Xianguo, 2003) to lay a foundation for the industrial cluster with international competitiveness. In recent years, Shanghai has gradually relocated some less competitive industries to its peripheries, mainly Zhejiang province (Fan Jianyong, 2004).

(4) The region of Ningbo, Zhoushan, and Taizhou (Zhejiang) is mainly centered on Ningbo and focused on traditional competitive industries as the receiver of Shanghai's industrial relocation and the base of industrial collaboration and technology commercialization.

In the process of the YRD's economic integration, the central city of each cohesive subgroup should actively drive the economic integration in the region, break the administrative barrier, market segmentation, and local protectionism (Li Lianshui and Yuan Kezhu, 2007), accelerate the free mobility of economic resources, strengthen the inter-regional economic interaction and cooperation, and effectively promote the overall coordinated development.

4. The analysis of structural similarity

This chapter adopts the percent of exact matches in Ucinet[9] to calculate the percentage of the similarity between the relation of city A and city B with other cities (see Table 13.6[10]) in order to analyze the intercity structural similarity.

Table 13.6 The result of structural similarity of the economic relation network in YRD city cluster

Time	*Similarity*	*City*
1998	82.4%	Wuxi, Changzhou, Yangzhou, Zhenjiang, Ningbo, Jiaxing, Huzhou, Shaoxing, Zhoushan, Nantong, Taizhou (Jiangsu), Taizhou (Zhejiang)
2001	80.0%	Yangzhou, Zhenjiang, Taizhou (Jiangsu), Jiaxing, Huzhou, Shaoxing, Nantong, Zhoushan, Taizhou (Zhejiang)
2004	86.7%	Jiaxing, Huzhou, Zhoushan, Taizhou (Zhejiang)
2007	93.3%	Zhoushan, Taizhou (Zhejiang)
2010	86.7%	Zhoushan, Taizhou (Zhejiang)
2013	80%	Zhoushan, Taizhou (Zhejiang)
2017	76.7%	Zhoushan, Taizhou (Zhejiang)

Taking over 80% as the standard, the number of cities with a similar economic relation structure has dropped from 12 in 1998 to 2 in 2007. The similarity between all the cities was lower than 80% since 2007, except for Zhoushan and Taizhou (Zhejiang); and the similarity of the two cities also dropped below 80% since 2013. The spatial structure connection of each city in the city cluster, mainly economic relations, along with industrial structure, forms the significant structural factors that influence economic development. The two factors have mutual effect: the structure of economic relations indirectly reflects the industrial structure to some extent. If two cities have similar economic relations with other cities, then their industries are possibly convergent. Empirical research has also proved that YRD integration will inevitably enhance the spatial relocation of manufacturing industry and regional structural diversity (Fan Jianyong, 2004). After a decade of adjustment, the intercity structural similarity in the YRD city cluster has distinctly decreased, indicating a lower possibility of industrial convergence, which is conducive to the diversification and complementation of products in each city, and the promotion of regional economic integration along with the optimization of regional product structures. Wu Zhiqiang et al. (2008) analyzed the similarity of the structure of the manufacturing industry in Shanghai, Jiangsu, and Zhejiang and noticed that the homogeneity in the YRD is decreasing. Li Xun and Xianxiang (2006) also noticed the structural difference of the economic level between cities in the YRD through the Chow test. However, the analysis of social networks reveals not only which cities have similar structures of economic relations, but also the specific level of the similarities, which enriches the research results of the spatial structure of city clusters.

5. The analysis of core-periphery structure

Since the original data is scaled, a continuous core-periphery model is needed to analyze the YRD city cluster. In the continuous model after fit test, each point is assigned a measure of core[11] in order to maximize the correlation coefficient between data matrix and pattern matrix which fit well, as the test showed.[12] Table 13.7 presents the results of core-periphery structural analysis.

Table 13.7 The analysis result of core-periphery structural of the economic relation network in YRD city cluster

Time	*Region*	*City*
1998	Core	Shanghai, Hangzhou, Suzhou, Wuxi
	Semi-periphery	Jiaxing, Nantong, Changzhou, Nanjing
	Periphery	Huzhou, Ningbo, Zhenjiang, Shaoxing, Yangzhou, Taizhou (Jiangsu), Taizhou (Zhejiang), Zhoushan
2001	Core	Shanghai, Suzhou, Wuxi, Hangzhou
	Semi-periphery	Jiaxing, Nantong, Nanjing, Changzhou
	Periphery	Huzhou, Ningbo, Shaoxing, Zhenjiang, Yangzhou, Taizhou (Jiangsu), Taizhou (Zhejiang), Zhoushan
2004	Core	Shanghai, Suzhou, Wuxi, Hangzhou
	Semi-periphery	Jiaxing, Nantong, Changzhou, Nanjing
	Periphery	Huzhou, Ningbo, Zhenjiang, Shaoxing, Yangzhou, Taizhou (Jiangsu), Taizhou (Zhejiang), Zhoushan
2007	Core	Shanghai, Suzhou, Wuxi, Hangzhou
	Semi-periphery	Jiaxing, Nantong, Changzhou, Nanjing
	Periphery	Huzhou, Ningbo, Zhenjiang, Shaoxing, Yangzhou, Taizhou (Jiangsu), Taizhou (Zhejiang), Zhoushan
2010	Core	Shanghai, Suzhou, Wuxi, Hangzhou
	Semi-periphery	Nantong, Changzhou, Jiaxing, Ningbo, Nanjing
	Periphery	Shaoxing, Huzhou, Taizhou (Jiangsu), Yangzhou, Zhenjiang, Taizhou (Zhejiang), Zhoushan
2013	Core	Shanghai, Suzhou, Wuxi, Hangzhou
	Semi-periphery	Nantong, Changzhou, Jiaxing, Ningbo, Nanjing
	Periphery	Shaoxing, Huzhou, Taizhou (Jiangsu), Yangzhou, Zhenjiang, Taizhou (Zhejiang), Zhoushan
2017	Core	Shanghai, Suzhou, Wuxi, Hangzhou
	Semi-periphery	Nantong, Changzhou, Jiaxing, Ningbo, Nanjing
	Periphery	Shaoxing, Huzhou, Taizhou (Jiangsu), Yangzhou, Zhenjiang, Taizhou (Zhejiang), Zhoushan

There is a core-periphery structure in the economic relation network of the YRD city cluster. Shanghai, Hangzhou, Suzhou, and Wuxi are the core areas, followed by Hangzhou, which is replaced by Suzhou in 2001; Jiaxing, Nantong, Changzhou, and Nanjing are the semi-peripheries that are influenced by the core cities and influence peripheral cities partially. Huzhou, Ningbo, Zhenjiang, Shaoxing, Yangzhou, Taizhou (Jiangsu), Taizhou (Zhejiang), and Zhoushan are the peripheries whose economic development is mainly affected by the semi-peripheries. Since 2010, Ningbo, with the rising core, has developed from a periphery to a semi-periphery. Based on the developmental situation in recent years, the core-periphery structure in the economic relation network of YRD city cluster has not significantly changed. However, the structure of the economic relation network changes with the drastically changing external environment: the cities in core, semi-peripheral, and peripheral areas are not fixed, which affects the development of the YRD economic integration. The reorganization may lead to a new structure of core, semi-periphery, and periphery, or a reticulate structure.

The sub-center cities, Suzhou, Wuxi, and Hangzhou in the YRD city cluster, are the result of the optimizing functional orientation of cities, and of the economic influence of Shanghai's active development of the service industry. Nanjing, although in the central position of the economic relation network of the city cluster, can control the intercity resource mobility with relatively more competitive advantage in attracting talent, resource, capital, and information than neighboring cities; it did not become a new sub-center in its development, but a semi-periphery and even on the fringes. However, since Nanjing shoulders the responsibility of connecting Shanghai and other middle and small cities, it should still be regarded as a sub-center that influences the north wing of the YRD and the vital base and window of the YRD into the central and western regions (Zhang Haohan et al., 2007). In addition, Hangzhou, with its advantage of a developing service industry, can also play the role of sub-center in the south wing of the YRD. Therefore, in the future developmental process, Nanjing and Hangzhou will be playing a connecting role: on the one hand, introducing the advantageous resource in the service industry from Shanghai; and on the other hand, providing diversified resources like finance, information, technology, and talents to peripheries. More importantly, the development of the two sub-centers should be focused on different areas to avoid vicious competition and perform complementary functions for the rapid development of YRD economic integration.

Section 4 Conclusion

Generally speaking, the current degree of YRD economic integration is not high enough: the overall density of economic relation network of the YRD city cluster is 0.6958 at the medium level; the outdegree centralization is three times the indegree centralization, which means that the economic relation is focused on few cities and the intercity economic relation is imbalanced. There are four cohesive subgroups in the economic relation network showing an integration trend: the overall density is gradually rising, indicating closer intercity economic relations; the densities within and between the four cohesive subgroups are also increasing; the number of cities with structural similarity of economic relation in the YRD city cluster above 80% dropped from 12 in 1998 to 2 in 2007 and 0 in 2013. Each city has gradually developed differentiated and complementary industries. Li Xun and Xianxiang (2006), by means of boundary defining, also concluded that there has been an integration trend between Jiangsu and Zhejiang, Shanghai and Jiangsu, Shanghai and Zhejiang. The YRD integration has risen from low-level to medium-level and is reaching high. Its manufacturing industry is expanding in an orderly manner, enhancing the structural differentiation in each region (Fan Jianyong, 2004).

Because of the particularity of Chinese economic transformation and the segmented administration system, the economic and administrative conflict between regions in the YRD are inevitable and obstructive against the YRD economic integration. In order to achieve our goal of forming an internationally competitive city cluster, we have the following suggestions:

First, each city in YRD should further strengthen its integration and economic relation according to its resource endowment and economic and social development level. Following the principles of "complementation, reciprocity, joint development and common prosperity", and with their resources and peripheral environment, core/periphery cities or different-sized cities should apply a reasonable work division, functional complementation, and development focused on different fields in terms of urban functional orientation, industrial structural optimization, regional joint investment, and construction of major infrastructure, in order to actively promote the development of YRD economic integration.

Second, Shanghai, as the leading city in the YRD, should play its role of a core in multiple aspects. Shanghai's current function of regional service center is increasingly significant; it should continue lowering the trade cost of production activity in both Shanghai and peripheries by the aggregation and development of the service industry (Liu Zhibiao et al., 2008) and actively promote the interactive development and complementarity between cities.

Third, Nanjing, as an important city in the lower reaches of the Yangtze River, plays a unique role of introducing investment from abroad and establishing domestic connections (Luo Shijun et al., 2009). Nanjing should position itself as the service-oriented sub-center of regional economic development. With the advantages of scientific and technological strength and human capital from local universities and research institutions, Nanjing should strive to develop producer services, lower the trade cost of attracting foreign investment and developing manufacturing industry in peripheral regions, provide a good environment, and form a real economic aggregation and proliferation center.

Fourth, within the city cluster, core cities are the center of innovation activities which should perform the function of economic influence and growth point, drive the industrial complementation of peripheral cities, joint construction and sharing of infrastructure, spatial coordination and integration of economic and social development, population resources, and environment, and enhance the competitiveness and influence of industrial development of peripheral economic hinterlands. The central city of semi-periphery on the one hand accepts the industries transferred from the core cities and provides raw materials and markets to them; and on the other hand, it actively adjusts its industries in the whole region by transferring less competitive industries to peripheral regions to drive their economic development. Peripheral cities also accept the transferred industries and provide raw materials and markets to core cities.

Notes

1 Through the surveys on the enterprises in a city, some scholars have calculated the output value of *m* production department or factor of a city (*m* departments in total) relevant to another city, i.e., e_m, and the output value of *m* production department or factor of the city, E_m, then use $(E_m/e_m)/m$ as the correction of economic relation. This method cannot ensure the accuracy, and the geometric mean cannot be applied here for the diversified function and properties of different departments.

2 The member can be an individual, an enterprise, or a collective social unit, or a research office, school, faculty and university, or even a village, organization, community, city and country, etc. (Liu Jun, 2004).
3 The relation between members can be the individual relationship, or inter-city economic relations, or international trade relations.
4 http://db.cei.gov.cn/chengshi.htm
5 The closer the economic relation between two cities, the higher the value. If the number is smaller than 1, then the economic relation is weak and will be recorded as 0 in this chapter. The economic relation of each city itself is not calculated.
6 There are 16 central cities in total, each of which can have maximum 15 connections with other cities.
7 The value getting closer to 1 means a more centralized network.
8 The line and column factors in Table 13.4 are further grouped by building an image of each block. Each term in a block is represented by 1 or 0 depending on their density, bigger or smaller than the overall density of the network. Although it loses some raw information, the matrix is simple and clear.
9 The Pearson correlation coefficient is appropriate to use for analyzing the structural similarity, because it can analyze both the existence of relations and its intensity. However, when the two cities are quite different, the correlation coefficient can be too sensitive to the extremums and errors among the data. Moreover, the Pearson correlation coefficient measures only linear correlation, so it is not suitable for analyzing the data of this research.
10 Table 13.6 lists only cities with a similarity higher than 80%. The similarity of unlisted cities is lower than 80%.
11 The original data, symmetrized before the analysis, can still reflect the original structure of date to some extent.
12 The correlation coefficient between actual data and pattern date is 0.939 in 1998, 0.953 in 2001, 0.935 in 2004, 0.935 in 2007, 0.945 in 2010, 0.930 in 2013, and 0.923 in 2017.

References

Gu Chaolin, Zhang Min, Zhang Xiaoming, Wang Chun, Chen Lu. Prospects of Urban Agglomeration in the Changjiang (Yangtze) River Delta. Scientia Geographica Sinica, 2007 (2).

Cheng Dazhong. The Growth of Service Industry and Urban Transition: Theory and Shanghai's Evidence. China Soft Science, 2009 (1).

Zhao Feng, Jiang Debo. Behavior Choice of Local Government in Yangtze River Delta Integration. Chinese Public Administration, 2008 (11).

S. Goldenberg. Social Structures: A Network Approach. Cambridge, England: Cambridge University Press, 1990.

Zhou Guohong, Lou Xijin. The Basic Situation and Strategic Thinking on Economic Integration in the Yangtze River Delta. Economic Geography, 2007 (1).

Li Guoping, Wang Liming, Yang Kaizhong. The Measurement and Analysis of the Economic Relation between Shenzhen and Pearl River Delta. Economic Geography, 2001 (2).

Zhang Haohan et al. Integration Tenor of Changjiang Delta: Present Development, Obstacles and Tendency. Beijing: Social Sciences Literature Press, 2007.

Niu Hui'en, Meng Qingmin et al. Economic Interaction Analysis Between Regions of Gansu Province and Their Surrounding Areas. Economic Geography, 1998 (9).

Luo Jiade. Social Network Analysis. Beijing: Social Sciences Literature Press, 2005.

Chen Jianjun. Study on Same Structure and Position of Industry in Yangtze River Delta. China Industrial Economy, 2004 (2).

Chen Jianjun, Yao Guoxian. Research on the Shanghai's Construction of International Economic Center and the Industrial Economic Relations in Yangtze River Delta Region: Based on the Economic Relation between Zhejiang and Shanghai. Management World, 2003 (6).

Chen Jianjun, Zhang Xingping, Ding Zhengyuan. The Economic Integration and Innovation Output of Innovation Center in Yangtze River Delta. Shanghai Journal of Economics, 2007 (4).

Fan Jianyong. The Integration, Regional Specialization and Spatial Transition of Manufacturing Industry in Yangtze River Delta. Management World, 2004 (11).

Liu Jun. An Introduction to Social Network Analysis. Beijing: Social Sciences Academic Press, 2004.

Xu Kangning, Zhao Bo, Wang Qi. The City Groups in the Yangtze River Delta: Formation, Competition and Cooperation. Nanjing Journal of Social Sciences, 2005 (5).

Li Lianshui, Yuan Kezhu. Research on the Integration of Manufacturing Industry in Yangtze River Delta: Based on the Comparison with Major Provinces of Manufacturing Industry. Jianghai Academic Journal, 2007 (1).

Xiong Qiong. Reflection on the Process of Economic Integration in Yangtze River Delta. Exploration and Free Views, 2005 (2).

Chi Renyong. The Formation of Innovation Network, Structural Characteristics and Functional Improvement of the Middle and Small-Sized Enterprises in the Region: Based on the Empirical Research on Zhejiang Province. Management World, 2005 (10).

J. Scott. Social Network Analysis: A Handbook. London: Sage Publications, 2000.

Luo Shijun, Jiao Huofu, Wang Bingjian. Urban Agglomeration Spatial Development Trend Based on Growth Capacity in the Yangtze River Delta. Economic Geography, 2009 (3).

Wang Xin, Wu Dianting, Wang Hongqiang. An Attempt to Calculate Economic Links between Cities. Urban Development Studies, 2006 (5).

Li Xun, Xu Xianxiang. On the Temporo-Spatial Variations of the Border Effects: Approach and Empirics. Geographical Research, 2006 (9).

Chen Yanguang, Liu Jisheng. Derivation and Generalization of the Urban Gravitational Model Using Fractal Idea with an Application to the Spatial Cross-Correlation between Beijing and Tianjin. Geographical Research, 2002 (12).

Liu Zhibiao. Promoting the Integrated Development in Yangtze River Delta by Marketization and Globalization. Nanjing Journal of Social Sciences, 2004.

Liu Zhibiao, Zheng Jianghuai et al. The Yangtze River Delta Driven by Service Industry. Beijing: China Renmin University Press, 2008.

Wu Zhiqiang, Wang Wei, Li Weihong, Yu Taofang, Wang Lei. The Process and Trends of Integration in the Yangtze River Delta: Based on Its Change of Boundary, Gravity Centre and Structure in 20 Years. Urban Planning Forum, 2008 (3).

Appendices

Table 13.8 The economic relation values of the 16 central cities in YRD in 1998

Central city	*Shanghai*	*Nanjing*	*Wuxi*	*Changzhou*	*Suzhou*	*Nantong*	*Yangzhou*	*Zhenjiang*	*Taizhou (Jiangsu)*	*Hangzhou*	*Ningbo*	*Jiaxing*	*Huzhou*	*Shaoxing*	*Zhoushan*	*Taizhou (Zhejiang)*
Shanghai	0	3	11	4	12	6	1	2	1	14	2	7	4	1	0	1
Nanjing	4	0	2	2	1	0	2	5	1	1	0	0	0	0	0	0
Wuxi	3	0	0	3	6	0	0	1	0	1	0	0	0	0	0	0
Changzhou	1	0	2	0	1	0	0	1	0	1	0	0	0	0	0	0
Suzhou	1	0	1	0	0	0	0	0	0	1	0	0	0	0	0	0
Nantong	1	0	0	0	0	0	0	0	0	0	0	0	0	0	0	0
Yangzhou	0	0	0	0	0	0	0	1	0	0	0	0	0	0	0	0
Zhenjiang	0	0	0	0	0	0	1	0	0	0	0	0	0	0	0	0
Taizhou (Jiangsu)	0	0	0	0	0	0	0	0	0	0	0	0	0	0	0	0
Hangzhou	1	0	0	0	0	0	0	0	0	0	0	0	1	1	0	0
Ningbo	1	0	0	0	0	0	0	0	0	2	0	0	0	0	1	0
Jiaxing	1	0	0	0	1	0	0	0	0	1	0	0	1	0	0	0
Huzhou	0	0	0	0	0	0	0	0	0	1	0	0	0	0	0	0
Shaoxing	0	0	0	0	0	0	0	0	0	2	0	0	0	0	0	0
Zhoushan	0	0	0	0	0	0	0	0	0	0	0	0	0	0	0	0
Taizhou (Zhejiang)	0	0	0	0	0	0	0	0	0	0	0	0	0	0	0	0

Data source: calculated through the formula (2) based on the data in 1998 from China Economic Information Statistical Database: http://db.cei.gov.cn/chengshi.htm.

Table 13.9 The economic relation values of the 16 central cities in YRD in 2001

Central city	*Shanghai*	*Nanjing*	*Wuxi*	*Changzhou*	*Suzhou*	*Nantong*	*Yangzhou*	*Zhenjiang*	*Taizhou (Jiangsu)*	*Hangzhou*	*Ningbo*	*Jiaxing*	*Huzhou*	*Shaoxing*	*Zhoushan*	*Taizhou (Zhejiang)*
Shanghai	0	10	29	8	31	12	3	3	3	27	5	14	6	3	1	1
Nanjing	2	0	3	3	2	1	4	8	1	1	0	0	1	0	0	0
Wuxi	5	2	0	8	14	1	1	1	1	1	0	1	1	0	0	0
Changzhou	0	1	2	0	1	0	1	1	0	0	0	0	0	0	0	0
Suzhou	4	1	11	3	0	0	1	1	1	2	0	2	1	0	0	0
Nantong	0	0	0	0	0	0	0	0	0	0	0	0	0	0	0	0
Yangzhou	0	1	0	1	0	0	0	3	1	0	0	0	0	0	0	0
Zhenjiang	0	1	0	1	0	0	2	0	0	0	0	0	0	0	0	0
Taizhou (Jiangsu)	0	0	0	0	0	0	1	0	0	0	0	0	0	0	0	0
Hangzhou	7	2	2	1	3	1	0	0	0	0	3	4	5	7	0	1
Ningbo	1	0	0	0	0	0	0	0	0	1	0	0	0	1	1	0
Jiaxing	0	0	0	0	0	0	0	0	0	0	0	0	1	0	0	0
Huzhou	0	0	0	0	0	0	0	0	0	1	0	1	0	0	0	0
Shaoxing	0	0	0	0	0	0	0	0	0	1	0	0	0	0	0	0
Zhoushan	0	0	0	0	0	0	0	0	0	0	0	0	0	0	0	0
Taizhou (Zhejiang)	0	0	0	0	0	0	0	0	0	0	0	0	0	0	0	0

Data source: calculated through the formula (2) based on the data in 2001 from China Economic Information Statistical Database: http://db.cei.gov.cn/chengshi.htm.

Table 13.10 The economic relation values of the 16 central cities in YRD in 2004

Central city	*Shanghai*	*Nanjing*	*Wuxi*	*Changzhou*	*Suzhou*	*Nantong*	*Yangzhou*	*Zhenjiang*	*Taizhou (Jiangsu)*	*Hangzhou*	*Ningbo*	*Jiaxing*	*Huzhou*	*Shaoxing*	*Zhoushan*	*Taizhou (Zhejiang)*
Shanghai	0	21	57	22	61	24	6	6	4	49	10	26	10	6	1	2
Nanjing	5	0	7	9	4	1	10	20	3	3	1	1	1	1	0	0
Wuxi	10	5	0	21	30	2	2	3	2	3	1	2	2	1	0	0
Changzhou	2	4	13	0	5	1	2	4	1	2	0	1	1	0	0	0
Suzhou	11	3	31	7	0	1	1	2	1	4	1	4	3	1	0	0
Nantong	1	0	0	0	0	0	0	0	0	0	0	0	0	0	0	0
Yangzhou	0	2	1	1	0	0	0	6	3	0	0	0	0	0	0	0
Zhenjiang	0	4	1	2	0	0	5	0	1	0	0	0	0	0	0	0
Taizhou (Jiangsu)	0	0	0	0	0	0	1	1	0	0	0	0	0	0	0	0
Hangzhou	13	4	5	4	6	1	1	1	1	0	7	7	9	16	1	1
Ningbo	2	1	1	0	1	0	0	0	0	4	0	1	1	2	3	1
Jiaxing	1	0	0	0	1	0	0	0	0	1	0	0	1	0	0	0
Huzhou	0	0	0	0	1	0	0	0	0	1	0	1	0	0	0	0
Shaoxing	0	0	0	0	0	0	0	0	0	2	0	0	0	0	0	0
Zhoushan	0	0	0	0	0	0	0	0	0	0	0	0	0	0	0	0
Taizhou (Zhejiang)	0	0	0	0	0	0	0	0	0	0	0	0	0	0	0	0

Data source: calculated through the formula (2) based on the data in 2004 from China Economic Information Statistical Database: http://db.cei.gov.cn/chengshi.htm.

Table 13.11 The economic relation values of the 16 central cities in YRD in 2007

Central city	*Shanghai*	*Nanjing*	*Wuxi*	*Changzhou*	*Suzhou*	*Nantong*	*Yangzhou*	*Zhenjiang*	*Taizhou (Jiangsu)*	*Hangzhou*	*Ningbo*	*Jiaxing*	*Huzhou*	*Shaoxing*	*Zhoushan*	*Taizhou (Zhejiang)*
Shanghai	0	38	108	39	113	44	11	11	8	90	18	45	17	10	2	3
Nanjing	10	0	14	17	8	3	20	36	5	7	2	2	2	1	0	0
Wuxi	19	10	0	40	60	4	4	6	4	6	2	4	3	1	0	0
Changzhou	5	8	26	0	9	1	4	8	2	3	1	1	2	1	0	0
Suzhou	22	6	64	14	0	2	3	3	2	8	2	7	5	2	0	0
Nantong	2	0	1	0	1	0	1	0	1	0	0	0	0	0	0	0
Yangzhou	1	4	1	2	1	1	0	10	5	0	0	0	0	0	0	0
Zhenjiang	0	6	2	3	1	0	9	0	1	0	0	0	0	0	0	0
Taizhou (Jiangsu)	0	1	1	1	0	0	2	1	0	0	0	0	0	0	0	0
Hangzhou	24	7	9	7	11	3	1	2	1	0	13	14	17	27	2	2
Ningbo	3	1	1	1	2	1	0	0	0	7	0	1	1	4	5	2
Jiaxing	2	0	1	0	1	0	0	0	0	2	0	0	2	1	0	0
Huzhou	1	0	1	0	1	0	0	0	0	2	0	2	0	0	0	0
Shaoxing	0	0	0	0	0	0	0	0	0	3	1	0	0	0	0	0
Zhoushan	0	0	0	0	0	0	0	0	0	0	1	0	0	0	0	0
Taizhou (Zhejiang)	0	0	0	0	0	0	0	0	0	0	1	0	0	0	0	0

Data source: calculated through the formula (2) based on the data in 2007 from China Economic Information Statistical Database: http://db.cei.gov.cn/chengshi.htm.

Table 13.12 The economic relation values of the 16 central cities in YRD in 2010

Central city	*Shanghai*	*Nanjing*	*Wuxi*	*Changzhou*	*Suzhou*	*Nantong*	*Yangzhou*	*Zhenjiang*	*Taizhou (Jiangsu)*	*Hangzhou*	*Ningbo*	*Jiaxing*	*Huzhou*	*Shaoxing*	*Zhoushan*	*Taizhou (Zhejiang)*
Shanghai	0	8	20	11	44	18	4	3	4	20	12	13	7	8	1	2
Nanjing	2	0	3	5	3	2	6	6	8	2	1	1	1	1	0	0
Wuxi	3	2	0	6	17	3	2	2	2	2	1	2	1	1	0	0
Changzhou	1	3	4	0	5	2	3	3	3	1	1	1	1	0	0	0
Suzhou	8	2	17	8	0	6	2	2	2	4	2	5	3	2	0	1
Nantong	1	0	1	1	2	0	1	0	1	0	0	1	0	0	0	0
Yangzhou	0	2	1	1	1	1	0	4	3	0	0	0	0	0	0	0
Zhenjiang	0	1	0	1	1	0	3	0	1	0	0	0	0	0	0	0
Taizhou (Jiangsu)	0	0	0	1	0	1	1	1	0	0	0	0	0	0	0	0
Hangzhou	5	2	3	2	6	2	1	1	1	0	5	6	5	10	0	1
Ningbo	2	0	1	1	2	1	0	0	0	4	0	2	1	4	1	1
Jiaxing	0	0	0	0	1	0	0	0	0	1	0	0	0	0	0	0
Huzhou	0	0	0	0	1	0	0	0	0	1	0	0	0	0	0	0
Shaoxing	1	1	1	0	1	0	0	0	0	4	2	1	1	0	0	1
Zhoushan	0	0	0	0	0	0	0	0	0	0	0	0	0	0	0	0
Taizhou (Zhejiang)	0	0	0	0	0	0	0	0	0	0	0	0	0	0	0	0

Data source: the economy and population data are from statistical yearbooks of each province or city; the data of intercity time distance is from Google Maps.

Table 13.13 The economic relation values of the 16 central cities in YRD in 2013

Central city	*Shanghai*	*Nanjing*	*Wuxi*	*Changzhou*	*Suzhou*	*Nantong*	*Yangzhou*	*Zhenjiang*	*Taizhou (Jiangsu)*	*Hangzhou*	*Ningbo*	*Jiaxing*	*Huzhou*	*Shaoxing*	*Zhoushan*	*Taizhou (Zhejiang)*
Shanghai	0	11	28	15	63	24	6	5	6	27	16	18	10	11	2	3
Nanjing	4	0	5	9	6	3	10	9	15	3	1	1	2	1	0	0
Wuxi	5	2	0	9	23	5	2	2	3	2	1	3	2	1	0	0
Changzhou	2	4	7	0	8	2	4	5	4	2	1	1	1	1	0	1
Suzhou	18	5	31	14	0	10	4	4	5	7	4	8	6	3	0	1
Nantong	2	1	2	1	3	0	1	1	2	1	0	1	1	0	0	0
Yangzhou	1	2	1	2	1	1	0	6	5	1	0	0	0	0	0	0
Zhenjiang	0	1	1	2	1	1	4	0	1	0	0	0	0	0	0	0
Taizhou (Jiangsu)	0	1	1	2	1	1	3	1	0	0	0	0	0	0	0	0
Hangzhou	8	3	4	3	8	2	2	1	1	0	7	8	7	14	1	1
Ningbo	3	1	1	1	2	1	1	0	1	5	0	2	1	5	1	2
Jiaxing	1	0	0	0	1	0	0	0	0	1	0	0	1	1	0	0
Huzhou	0	0	0	0	1	0	0	0	0	1	0	1	0	0	0	0
Shaoxing	1	1	1	1	1	1	0	0	0	6	3	2	1	0	0	1
Zhoushan	0	0	0	0	0	0	0	0	0	0	0	0	0	0	0	0
Taizhou (Zhejiang)	0	0	0	0	0	0	0	0	0	0	1	0	0	0	0	0

Data source: the economy and population data are from statistical yearbooks of each province or city; the data of intercity time distance is from Google Maps.

Table 13.14 The economic relation values of the 16 central cities in YRD in 2017

Central city	*Shanghai*	*Nanjing*	*Wuxi*	*Changzhou*	*Suzhou*	*Nantong*	*Yangzhou*	*Zhenjiang*	*Taizhou (Jiangsu)*	*Hangzhou*	*Ningbo*	*Jiaxing*	*Huzhou*	*Shaoxing*	*Zhoushan*	*Taizhou (Zhejiang)*
Shanghai	0	15	38	23	85	34	9	7	9	41	23	25	13	14	2	4
Nanjing	6	0	7	13	9	4	14	14	23	5	2	2	3	2	0	1
Wuxi	7	3	0	11	31	6	3	3	4	3	2	4	3	2	0	1
Changzhou	4	7	12	0	14	4	6	8	7	3	1	2	2	1	1	1
Suzhou	20	5	37	17	0	12	5	5	6	9	4	10	7	4	1	1
Nantong	3	1	3	2	4	0	2	1	3	1	1	1	1	1	0	0
Yangzhou	1	4	2	3	2	2	0	9	7	1	0	1	1	0	0	0
Zhenjiang	0	2	1	3	1	1	6	0	2	0	0	0	1	0	0	0
Taizhou (Jiangsu)	1	1	1	2	1	2	4	2	0	0	0	1	0	0	0	0
Hangzhou	15	5	7	5	14	4	3	3	2	0	13	14	11	22	1	2
Ningbo	5	1	2	1	4	2	1	1	1	8	0	3	1	7	2	3
Jiaxing	1	0	1	0	1	1	0	0	0	1	1	0	1	1	0	0
Huzhou	0	0	0	0	1	0	0	0	0	1	0	1	0	0	0	0
Shaoxing	1	2	1	1	2	1	0	0	0	7	4	2	1	0	0	1
Zhoushan	0	0	0	0	0	0	0	0	0	0	0	0	0	0	0	0
Taizhou (Zhejiang)	0	0	0	0	0	0	0	0	0	0	1	0	0	0	0	0

Data source: the economy and population data are from statistical yearbooks of each province or city; the data of intercity time distance is from Google Maps.

Table 13.15 The degree centrality of economic relation network in YRD city cluster in 1998–2007

No.	*Outdegree*								*Indegree*							
	1998		*2001*		*2004*		*2007*		*1998*		*2001*		*2004*		*2007*	
	FREEMAN'S DEGREE CENTRALITY MEASURES															
1	Shanghai	70.601	Shanghai	156.953	Shanghai	303.845	Shanghai	558.432	Hangzhou	24.625	Suzhou	53.428	Wuxi	115.992	Wuxi	229.238
2	Nanjing	20.035	Wuxi	38.149	Wuxi	85.163	Wuxi	165.915	Suzhou	22.382	Wuxi	49.393	Suzhou	109.08	Suzhou	208.272
3	Wuxi	16.582	Hangzhou	36.163	Hangzhou	74.934	Suzhou	140.224	Wuxi	16.775	Hangzhou	35.87	Hangzhou	69.856	Hangzhou	129.09
4	Changzhou	6.268	Nanjing	27.302	Suzhou	69.8	Hangzhou	138.625	Shanghai	12.954	Changzhou	25.265	Changzhou	67.041	Changzhou	125.305
5	Hangzhou	5.213	Suzhou	26.225	Nanjing	67.32	Nanjing	127.967	Changzhou	10.742	Jiaxing	22.082	Shanghai	46.054	Shanghai	88.072
6	Suzhou	5.1	Changzhou	7.114	Changzhou	37.111	Changzhou	70.736	Zhenjiang	10.635	Shanghai	20.05	Nanjing	44.827	Nanjing	83.683
7	Jiaxing	4.577	Yangzhou	6.572	Ningbo	17.544	Ningbo	29.947	Jiaxing	8.713	Nanjing	19.419	Zhenjiang	43.845	Jiaxing	78.218
8	Ningbo	4.494	Ningbo	6.18	Zhenjiang	14.811	Yangzhou	24.571	Huzhou	7.686	Zhenjiang	18.144	Jiaxing	43.2	Zhenjiang	77.845
9	Huzhou	2.436	Zhenjiang	5.298	Yangzhou	13.627	Zhenjiang	23.755	Nantong	7.569	Nantong	15.155	Nantong	31.935	Nantong	59.36
10	Zhenjiang	2.4	Huzhou	3.026	Huzhou	5.401	Jiaxing	9.652	Yangzhou	6.265	Huzhou	15.074	Yangzhou	30.774	Yangzhou	56.569
11	Shaoxing	2.328	Jiaxing	2.553	Jiaxing	5.4	Huzhou	8.409	Taizhou (Jiangsu)	3.933	Yangzhou	12.667	Huzhou	28.751	Huzhou	50.162
12	Yangzhou	2.299	Taizhou (Jiangsu)	1.964	Shaoxing	3.88	Nantong	7.772	Nanjing	3.865	Shaoxing	12.281	Shaoxing	27.941	Shaoxing	48.072
13	Nantong	1.716	Nantong	1.783	Nantong	3.744	Taizhou (Jiangsu)	6.449	Shaoxing	3.419	Ningbo	9.627	Ningbo	21.644	Ningbo	39.416
14	Taizhou (Jiangsu)	1.245	Shaoxing	1.594	Taizhou (Jiangsu)	3.675	Shaoxing	6.117	Ningbo	3.338	Taizhou (Jiangsu)	8.358	Taizhou (Jiangsu)	16.719	Taizhou (Jiangsu)	29.895
15	Taizhou (Zhejiang)	0.287	Taizhou (Zhejiang)	0.834	Taizhou (Zhejiang)	1.524	Taizhou (Zhejiang)	2.259	Taizhou (Zhejiang)	1.532	Zhoushan	2.694	Zhoushan	5.87	Zhoushan	10.958
16	Zhoushan	0.265	Zhoushan	0.345	Zhoushan	0.681	Zhoushan	1.578	Zhoushan	1.412	Taizhou (Zhejiang)	2.549	Taizhou (Zhejiang)	4.929	Taizhou (Zhejiang)	8.252

Table 13.16 The degree centrality of economic relation network in YRD city cluster in 2010–2017

FREEMAN'S DEGREE CENTRALITY MEASURES												
No.	*Outdegree*						*Indegree*					
	2010		*2013*		*2017*		*2010*		*2013*		*2017*	
1	Shanghai	175	Shanghai	245	Shanghai	342	Suzhou	84	Suzhou	119	Suzhou	169
2	Suzhou	64	Suzhou	120	Suzhou	143	Wuxi	51	Wuxi	82	Wuxi	112
3	Hangzhou	50	Hangzhou	70	Hangzhou	121	Hangzhou	39	Changzhou	59	Changzhou	81
4	Wuxi	44	Nanjing	69	Nanjing	105	Changzhou	37	Hangzhou	56	Hangzhou	80
5	Nanjing	41	Wuxi	60	Wuxi	83	Nantong	36	Nantong	51	Nantong	73
6	Changzhou	28	Changzhou	43	Changzhou	73	Jiaxing	32	Shanghai	45	Jiaxing	66
7	Ningbo	20	Ningbo	27	Ningbo	42	Shaoxing	26	Jiaxing	45	Shanghai	64
8	Yangzhou	13	Yangzhou	20	Yangzhou	33	Taizhou (Jiangsu)	25	Taizhou (Jiangsu)	43	Taizhou (Jiangsu)	64
9	Shaoxing	13	Shaoxing	19	Nantong	24	Ningbo	24	Yangzhou	37	Shaoxing	54
10	Nantong	8	Nantong	16	Shaoxing	23	Shanghai	23	Shaoxing	37	Yangzhou	53
11	Zhenjiang	7	Zhenjiang	11	Zhenjiang	17	Yangzhou	23	Zhenjiang	34	Zhenjiang	53
12	Taizhou (Jiangsu)	4	Taizhou (Jiangsu)	10	Taizhou (Jiangsu)	15	Zhenjiang	22	Ningbo	34	Ningbo	52
13	Jiaxing	2	Jiaxing	5	Jiaxing	8	Nanjing	21	Nanjing	32	Nanjing	46
14	Huzhou	2	Huzhou	3	Huzhou	3	Huzhou	20	Huzhou	32	Huzhou	45
15	Zhoushan	0	Taizhou (Zhejiang)	1	Taizhou (Zhejiang)	1	Taizhou (Zhejiang)	6	Taizhou (Zhejiang)	9	Taizhou (Zhejiang)	14
16	Taizhou (Zhejiang)	0	Zhoushan	0	Zhoushan	0	Zhoushan	2	Zhoushan	4	Zhoushan	7

Index